GUATEMALA AND BELIZE

NATASCHA NORTON

Cadogan Books plc
London House, Parkgate Road, London SW11 4NQ

Distributed in North America by The Globe Pequot Press, 6 Business Park Road,
PO Box 833, Old Saybrook, Connecticut 06475–0833

Copyright © Natascha Norton 1993, 1994
Black and white illustrations © Antonia Phillips 1993

Cover design by Animage
Cover illustrations © Sue Dray
Colour illustrations (inside) © Jennifer Robinson
Maps © Cadogan Books plc,
drawn by Thames Cartographic Services Ltd

Series Editors: Rachel Fielding and Vicki Ingle

All rights reserved. No part of this publication may be reproduced, stored in a retrieval system, or transmitted, in any form or by any means, electronic or mechanical, including photocopying and recording, or by any information storage and retrieval system, except as may be expressly permitted by the UK 1988 Copyright Design & Patents Act and the USA 1976 Copyright Act or in writing from the publisher. Requests for permission should be addressed to Cadogan Books plc, London House, Parkgate Road, London SW11 4NQ

Central America first published in 1993. *Guatemala and Belize* extracted, 1994

ISBN 0–947754–92X

A Catalogue record for this book is available from the British Library

US Library of Congress Cataloging-in-Publication Data available

The authors and publishers have made every effort to ensure the accuracy of the information in this book at the time of going to press. However they cannot accept any responsibility for any loss, injury or inconvenience resulting from the use of information contained in this guide.

Photoset in Ehrhardt
Printed and bound in Great Britain by
BPC Wheatons Ltd, Exeter

ABOUT THE AUTHOR

Getting soaked by freezing rain half-way up a volcano, hitching lifts in bullet-riddled buses, or drinking Cuba Libres in gringo bars was all in the line of research for Natascha Norton, who spent over a year based in Central America. A seasoned Latin American traveller, she thought she knew what to expect—everything, that is, except meeting her future husband in Guatemala.

ACKNOWLEDGEMENTS

From Natascha Norton
In England: I would like to thank Rachel Fielding, Vicki Ingle and Chris Schüler of Cadogan Books; the Expedition Advisory Centre of the Royal Geographical Society; my mother for a roof over my head as well as encouragement and advice; Benoît LeBlanc for constructive criticism of first drafts and hours of patient map-making; Tony Davies and Gill Bloyce for their sitting-room floor.
   In Guatemala: thanks to Susan Horn; Tony Evans; the INGUAT staff in Guatemala City; Lisa and Steve Parker; Kevin Savage; Antonio Ramos of Viajes Tivoli; and Claudio and Lies for a beautiful place to live and plenty of excellent meals.
   In Belize: thanks to Alfredo Villoria and Chet Schmidt in Punta Gorda; Rose O'Doherty; Bob Jones in San Ignacio; Josie Pollard in San Pedro; Meb Cutlack; Tom Brown on Caye Caulker; and Joy Vernon of the Belize Tourist Office, Belize City.

CONTENTS

About the Author *Page iii*

Acknowledgements *Page iii*

Introduction *Pages 1–2*
A Guide to the Guide *2*
The Best of Central America *3*
Further Reading *4–5*

Part I: General Information *Pages 7–25*
Before You Go:
   Climate *7*
   When To Go *8*
   Major Events *8*
   Earthquakes and Volcanoes *8*
   Health *9*
   Insurance *9*
   Passports and Visas *9*
   Baggage Checklist *10*
Getting There *10–12*
   By Air *10*
   By Sea *11*
   By Rail *11*
   By Road *11*
   Agents and Specialist Operators *12*
On Arrival:
   Entry Formalities *12*
   Tourist Information *13*
   Maps *13*
Getting Around *13–15*
   By Air *13*
   By Boat *13*
   By Train *14*
   By Bus *14*
   By Car or Motorbike *14*
   By Bicycle *14*
   Disabled Travellers *14*

Money and Official Currencies *15*
Manners and Mores *15–17*
   Crime and Police Business *15*
   Sexual Attitudes *16*
   Tipping *17*
   Beggars *17*
   Drugs *17*
   Photography *17*
Communications and Services *18*
Where To Stay *18–19*
Eating Out *19*
   Drinks *20*
   Restaurants and Comedores *20*
Shopping and Bargaining *20*
Sports and Activities *20*
   Amateur Archaeology *20*
   Diving *21*
   Fishing *21*
   Hiking *21*
   Natural History *21*
   Potholing *21*
   River Rafting *22*
Environmental Issues *22–25*
   Flora and Fauna *23*
   National Parks *24*
   Ecotourism *24*

Part II: History Before Independence *Pages 26–33*

Prehistory *27*
The Maya *29*
European Discovery and the Colonial Era *31*
Independence from Spanish Rule *32*

Part III: Topics *Pages 34–49*

The Maya Universe *34*
Central American Literature *40*
Music *43*
Some Central American Stereotypes *44*
Some Key Players *46*
Melodrama on the Buses *48*

Part IV: Guatemala *Pages 50–173*

Post-Independence History *54–88*
General Information *59–73*
  Best of the Festivals *67–70*
Itineraries *73*
Guatemala City *74–88*
The Western Highlands *89–136*
  Antigua *90–106*
    Semana Santa in Antigua *97*
  Iximché *106*
  Lake Atitlán *107*
  Panajachel *109*
  Around Lake Atitlán *113*
  Chichicastenango and the Ixil
    Triangle *115*
  Nebaj *121*
  Quezaltenango (Xela) *123*
  Huehuetenango and the Cuchumatun
    Mountains *131*
  Todos Santos *134*

The Pacific Coast *136–43*
  Along the Pacific Highway *137*
  Ports and Beaches *139*
The Verapaz Mountains *143–51*
  Baja Verapaz *144*
    The Quezal Reserve *145*
  Alta Verapaz *146*
    Cobán *148*
The Oriente and Caribbean Coast *152–61*
  The Holy City of Esquipulas *153*
  Excursion to Copán in Honduras *155*
  Quiriguá *155*
  Puerto Barrios *156*
  Livingston *158*
The Petén *162–73*
  Flores *164*
  Tikal *167*
  Other Maya Sites *171*
  Onwards to Mexico and Belize *173*

Part V: Belize *Pages 174–233*

Post-Independence History *176–9*
General Information *179–89*
Itineraries *190*
Belize City *191–200*
  Community Baboon Sanctuary *200*
  Altun Ha *200*
The Cayes *201–10*
  Ambergris Caye *202*
  Caye Caulker *206*
The West: Cayo District *210–18*
  Belmopan *211*
  San Ignacio *212*
  Xunantunich *215*
  Caracol *216*
The South: Stann Creek
  and Toledo District *218–30*
  Dangriga *219*
  Placencia *223*
  Cockscomb Basin Jaguar Reserve *225*
  Punta Gorda *226*
Northern Belize *230–33*
  Crooked Tree Wildlife Sanctuary *231*
  Lamanai *231*

CONTENTS

Language *Pages 234–42*

Country Index *Pages 243–7*

General Index *Pages 248–50*

LIST OF MAPS

Central America *Page* 6
Guatemala *Pages* 52–3
Guatemala City *Page* 75
Antigua *Page* 91

Lake Atitlán *Page* 107
Quezaltenango *Page* 124
Belize *Page* 175
Belize City *Page* 192

INTRODUCTION

Huevos y frijoles *(eggs and beans) and* tortillas *are staples of Central American cuisine*

A glance at the world map reveals Central America as one of the most shattered regions on the face of the globe. Here, on the bridge of the Americas, Guatemala, Belize and five other tiny nations are strung out on a slither of land, binding together two vast continents. It's a region in which a fantastic range of political, geographical, ethnic and environmental forces have collided, producing a magical hybrid. In the big cities a version of Coca-Cola culture moves to the rhythm of Colombian *salsa*, while, deep in the forests, species of birds, beasts and plants from north and south live beside local species that are found nowhere else in the world. A complex network of historical and cultural connections cross country borders, but the deepest political and racial divisions slice up nations.

Despite its awesome reputation for death squads and squalor, daily life is astonishingly normal. Most people live close to the land, carving a simple existence from steep hillsides, cutting fields from the forest or working on large coffee, banana or cotton plantations. The great driving forces are not politics and violence, but land, family and religion. Nevertheless a fiery Latin heart beats just below the surface and once a year every village and town explodes into an annual fiesta, with an orgy of drink, dance and wild celebration.

There are still pockets of indigenous culture, united by a rigid adherence to pre-Columbian traditions. These groups of indigenous Indians have managed to preserve their cultural integrity with astonishing tenacity. Virtually untouched by almost five hundred years of white, Catholic rule Guatemala's Quiché Indians still sacrifice animals in honour of ancient gods. These groups, along with many others, are united by ancient traditions which transcend modern borders, while the monumental Maya ruins rising out of the jungles in

INTRODUCTION

Guatemala and Belize are a haunting reminder that the area supported sophisticated cultures long before the arrival of the Spanish, perhaps as early as 1500 BC.

Colonial rule has also firmly stamped its mark, establishing patterns of oligarchic rule, religious hierarchy and exploitative economics which still persist, as well as scattering the region with superb churches and instilling a deep current of racism. Meanwhile, in today's cities a furious swirl of 20th-century chaos mixes all these influences, sweeping up everything in its path and creating a culture that is breathless with energy. Buses growl through the traffic, pot-bellied policemen flirt with young girls, shoeshiners hustle for business, and tower blocks rise above the smog.

Contrary to popular belief Central America is also a land of great subtlety and tremendous beauty. Soft mists rise off the purple peaks of Guatemalan volcanoes, while herds of Panamanian cattle send dust clouds drifting across the rice fields. Large tracts of land remain empty, including great swathes of undisturbed rainforest in Guatemala, Belize, Costa Rica and Panamá; a string of volcanic peaks runs from Guatemala to Costa Rica; massive crater lakes nestle in rugged mountain ranges, all hemmed in by a pair of extremely beautiful coasts. Offshore islands are ringed by spectacular coral reefs, while the entire Belizean coastline is sheltered by a huge barrier reef. Beneath the surface a kaleidoscope of tropical fish are accompanied by sharks, swordfish, marlin and ray.

Visitors should expect the unexpected. While you're sure to stumble across stereotypes, including bizarre religious ceremonies and stone-faced soldiers bristling with firepower, you'll also find that surprises lurk around every corner. Many with a special interest—whether it's ornithology or archaeology, beaches or butterflies, politics or pirates—will find that Central America has a great deal to offer. Those who are open to the experience may find themselves seduced by any of these, or led down new and unexpected paths.

A Guide To The Guide

Part I provides general information about Guatemala and Belize with regard to getting there, getting around and some of the things you might want to consider before you set out.

Next comes a general history of Central America until its independence from Spain in 1821 (after which the individual countries took on more specific identities); and then the Topics, short pieces on some of the main issues and characters of the region's history including the Maya, Central American music and literature, ecotourism and banana republics.

The two subsequent chapters, or 'Parts', cover Guatemala and Belize, opening with an introduction, followed by the post-Independence history of each country; then comes detailed practical information, including how to get there, the various entry requirements, what you might expect to eat and where you might expect to sleep. In the second part of each chapter the countries are laid out geographically, and practical information which is specific to each region given as it is described.

At the back of the guide you'll find a language section and the index.

INTRODUCTION

The Best of Guatemala and Belize

Artesanía; Guatemalan weavings.
Birdwatching: Belizean National Parks.
Books: *Sweet Waist of America* by Anthony Daniels or, for an old-world account, *Incidents of Travel in Central America, Chiapas and Yucatán* by John Lloyd Stephens (see p. 4).
Colonial Architecture: Antigua in Guatemala.
Cup of Coffee: Café Tirol, Cobán, Guatemala.
Diving: Belizean Cayes.
Fiestas: Holy Week in Antigua, Guatemala is the most sombre. November 1st in Todos Santos, Guatemala is among the best Indian fiestas, including drunken horse races, while early December in Chichicastenango is also very good.
Hot Springs: Fuentes Georginas, Guatemala.
Jungles: the Petén in Guatemala.
Lakes: Lake Atitlán in Guatemala is unrivalled for beauty and tourism.
Markets: Chichicastenango in Guatemala.
Month of the Year: the end of rains bringing sunshine and flowers to the entire isthmus; this is November in Guatemala.
Mountain Road: the climb from San Marcos to Tacana, Guatemala.
Museums: the Popol Vuh archaeological museum in Guatemala City.
National Parks: the Cockscomb Jaguar Reserve in Belize.
Pre-Columbian Ruins: Tikal in Guatemala and Caracol in Belize.
Rum: Belize.
Volcanoes: the erupting peak of Pacaya in Guatemala—although this is now dangerous due to armed robberies.

"TAKE CARE OF THE CYCLIST, HE MAY BE YOUR BROTHER"

FURTHER READING

Travel and the Maya
Cockburn, J., *A Journey Overland from the Gulf of Honduras to the Great South Sea*, London, C. Rivington, 1735
Coe, M. D., *The Maya*, London, Thames & Hudson, 1986
Coe, W. R., *Tikal*, University of Pennsylvania, 1967
Dampier, W., *A New Voyage Round the World*, London, A. & C. Black, 1937
Daniels, A., *Sweet Waist of America*, London, Arrow, 1991
Exquemeling, J., *The Buccaneers of America*, London, Routledge & Sons, 1924
Gage, T., *The English American*, London, Routledge, 1928
Hagen, V. (von), *Jungle in the Clouds*, London, Hale, 1945
Huxley, A., *Beyond the Mexique Bay*, London, Chatto & Windus, 1936
Keenagh, P., *Mosquito Coast*, London, Chatto & Windus, 1937
Lester, M., *A Lady's Ride Across Spanish Honduras*, Edinburgh, Blackwood, 1884
Marnham, P., *So Far from God*, London, Penguin, 1986
Maslow, J. E., *Bird of Life, Bird of Death*, London, Penguin, 1987
Morris, M., *Nothing to Declare*, London, Paladin, 1990
Namuth, H., *Los Todos Santeros*, London, Nishen, 1989
O'Rourke, P. J., *Holidays in Hell*, London, Picador, 1989
Squier, E. G., *Adventures on the Mosquito Shore*, New York, Worthington Co., 1891
Stephens, J. L., *Incidents of Travel in Central America, Chiapas and Yucatán*, London, Dover, 1970
Time Life Books, *The Jungles of Central America*
Theroux, P., *The Old Patagonian Express*, London, Penguin, 1979
Thompson, J. E. S., *The Maya of Belize: Historical Chapters Since Columbus*, Belize, Cubola Productions, 1988
Thompson, J. E. S., *The Rise and Fall of Maya Civilization*, University of Oklahoma Press, 1968
Thompson, J. E. S. (ed.), *Thomas Gage's Travels in the New World*, University of Oklahoma Press
Warlords and Maize Men: A Guide to the Maya Sites of Belize, Belize, Cubola Productions, 1989
Wright, R., *Time Among the Maya*, London, Bodley Head, 1989

History and Analysis
Asturias de Barrios, L., Comalapa: *Native Dress and its Significance*, Guatemala, Ixchel, 1985
Belize: A Country Guide, Albuquerque, Resource Center, 1990
Bethell, L. (ed.), *Central America Since Independence*, CUP, 1991
Dobson, N., *A History of Belize*, Longman, 1973
Floyd, T. S., *The Anglo-Spanish Struggle for Mosquitia*, University of New Mexico, 1967

FURTHER READING

Grant, C. H., *The Making of Modern Belize*, Cambridge University Press, 1976
Guatemala: A Country Guide, Albuquerque, Resource Center, 1990
Guatemala: False Hope, False Freedom, London, Latin America Bureau, 1989
Handy, J., *Gift of the Devil*, London, Between the Lines, 1984
Long, T. & Bell, E., *Antigua Guatemala*, Guatemala, 1990
Mayan de Castellanos, G., *Tzute and Hierarchy in Sololá*, Guatemala, Ixchel, 1988
Menchu, R., I ... Rigoberta Menchu. *An Indian Woman in Guatemala*, London, Verso, 1984
Nairn, A., 'The Guns of Guatemala: the merciless mission of Rios Montt's army' in *The New Republic 188.* 14:17–21, 1983
Oakes, M., *Beyond the Windy Place: Life in the Guatemalan Highlands*, New York, Farrar, Straus and Young, 1951
Oakes, M., *The Two Crosses of Todos Santos: Survivals of Maya Religious Rituals*, New York, Pantheon, 1951
Pearce, J., *Under the Eagle: US Intervention in Central America and the Caribbean*, London, Latin America Bureau, 1982
Schlesinger, S. & Kinzer, S., *Bitter Fruit: The Untold Story of the American Coup in Guatemala*, London, Anchor Books, 1983
Sexton, J. D. (trans. and ed.), *Son of Tecún Umán, A Maya Indian Tells His Life Story*, Tucson, University of Arizona Press, 1981
Sexton, J. D. (trans. and ed.), *Campesino, The Diary of a Guatemalan Indian*, Tucson, University of Arizona Press, 1985
Simon, J.-M., *Eternal Spring—Eternal Tyranny*, New York, Norton, 1987
Tedlock, D. (trans.), *Popol Vuh*, New York, Simon & Schuster, 1985
Werne, P., *The Maya of Guatemala*, London, Minority Rights Group, 1989
Woodward Jr, R. L., *Central America: A Nation Divided*, Oxford, OUP, 1985

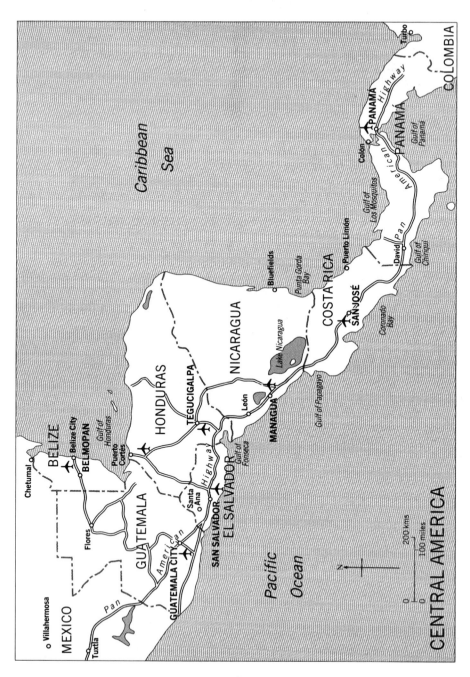

Part I
GENERAL INFORMATION

The Pan-American Highway

Before You Go

The addresses of Tourist Offices and embassies in the UK and US are given in the introduction to the country chapters, although even if you can get hold of one you may find it easier to wait until you get to Guatemala or Belize where they are sure to be better informed.

Climate

Climate in Central America is governed by season and altitude. At any time of year the lowland areas are stiflingly hot; during the rainy season high humidity makes it particularly sticky. Meanwhile up in the highlands it is always pleasantly cool in the shade, although the sun is even sharper. The seasons are very simple indeed: it's either raining or it isn't. The rains start around May and end anywhere between November and December. The rains can be very heavy, particularly towards the end of the rainy season, but they need not stop you travelling; you'll just get less of a tan.

Average Temperature and Rainfall

	Jan	Feb	Mar	Apr	May	June	July	Aug	Sep	Oct	Nov	Dec
Guatemala City	23	25	27	28	29	27	26	26	24	23	23	22
	11	12	14	14	16	16	16	16	15	14	13
	2	2	2	5	8	20	17	16	17	13	6	2
Belize City	27	28	29	30	31	31	31	31	31	30	28	27
	19	21	22	23	24	24	24	24	23	22	20	20
	12	6	4	5	7	13	15	14	15	16	12	14

The first line is the average maximum temperature per month in degrees Celcius, the second the average minimum; and the last line, the average number of rainy days.

When to Go

The year in Central America is dominated by the rains, which start around May and end between November and December. The end of the rains ushers in the finest weather of the year—fresh, clear and warm, and prompts a few weeks, if not months, of indulgence among local people, who like to take it easy towards the end of the year.

Major Events

Local holidays and fiestas are listed in the introductions to each chapter, however, the big events of the Central American year as a whole are as follows:

Easter Week or *Semana Santa*—at its best in Antigua, Guatemala, where the streets are carpeted with coloured sawdust and the Crucifixion is re-enacted.
May 1 (Labour Day)—marching by unions, labour organizations and left-wingers.
September 15 (Independence Day)—marked by military parades throughout the isthmus.
October 12 (*Día de la Raza* or Columbus Day)—big on the Caribbean coast where drunken fiestas last for days.
November 1 (All Saints' Day)—superb in Todos Santos Cuchumatán, Guatemala, where a drunken horse race is the centrepiece in a furious three-day fiesta.
Christmas Day—a fairly subdued, private affair.
New Year—drunken, loud and vaguely international.

Earthquakes and Volcanoes

Earthquakes and volcanoes are a real problem for the residents of Central America, particularly the former which regularly claim lives and from time to time destroy cities and villages. There's absolutely nothing you can do to avoid the danger; your chances of getting caught up in a really dangerous earthquake are extremely scarce and certainly no worse than in Los Angeles. Smaller tremors are very common indeed and you are fairly likely to feel one or two while in Central America, but there is really nothing to worry about and with all that heavy traffic it's easy to get confused. Active volcanoes are dotted throughout Central America, running from Guatemala to Costa Rica, but again the risk of coming to any harm is very remote. However, if you happen to be close to an erupting cone, particularly at night, with sensible precautions it's an exhilarating and relatively harmless experience.

Health

Medical preparation for a trip to Central America should begin with a visit to your doctor at least six weeks before you plan to go as he or she will be able to offer the most up-to-date information. The standard vaccinations for the region are yellow fever, rabies, typhoid, tetanus, polio, hepatitis, and hepatitis B. In spite of the cholera epidemic that began in 1990, even medical experts advise against a vaccination as it is generally agreed that it has little effect and it's simply better to take precautions as you travel—drinking bottled water and avoiding unwashed fruit and vegetables. Malaria pills are only essential for the Guatemalan Petén. Otherwise the risks are minimal and it is not necessary to take malaria pills in cool mountainous regions, but only on the tropical plain and in the jungle.

The most common complaint is 'bad guts', and it's a good idea to bring medicine for this, though it is widely available throughout Central America. Good medical labs operate in all cities and towns, so help is always easy to find. Your embassy can recommend English-speaking doctors in the various capitals. When it comes to theories on avoiding intestinal problems travellers are divided: some insist that you can eat any street vendor's snack and survive, others prefer to avoid street food and fresh salads in all but the best restaurants; however, there are no fixed or guaranteed guidelines.

Sunburn is another problem, and sun screen is not always on sale so do bring your own. Hats are available cheaply anywhere in the region. Contraceptives, tampons and sanitary pads are all available, though again, it is best to bring your own contraceptives or tampons. (Remember that severe diarrhoea can diminish the effectiveness of the contraceptive pill.) Contact lens soaking and cleaning solutions are also best brought with you, as well as insect repellent. If you intend to do a lot of hiking, remember to bring your own padded foot plasters which make open blisters easier to bear. Finally, if you would like a detailed, personalized vaccination assessment and up-to-the-minute advice, contact the excellent Medical Advisory Service for Travellers Abroad (MASTA), at the London School of Tropical Medicine. In the UK British Airways run clinics at 32 locations from Aberdeen to Plymouth; their phone numbers are obtainable from a recorded message on 071–831 5333.

Insurance

Travel insurance, available through any travel agent, is always a good idea. Make sure the policy covers both theft and medical expenses and if you're particularly worried about ending up in a local hospital then make sure that the policy includes a flight home should you get seriously ill. Good insurance policies are available through all the main operators, including Thomas Cook and American Express (for their customers only).

Passports and Visas

The visa requirements for all Central American countries are slightly different and each is listed in the introduction to the individual chapters.

UK citizens do not need visas for any of the countries but Americans, New Zealanders and Australians will not be allowed into parts of the region without one. If you do need visas then try and get hold of them before you go.

Baggage Checklist

Suitable Apparel: The contents of one steamer trunk and one suitcase, and with a handbag for soiled linen, meet the ordinary requirements of one person.

The South American Handbook, 1925

Certain items are vital for Latin American travel; however, before you leave home take another look at your luggage. The chances are you have packed too much; many things such as hats and light clothing can be bought cheaply and easily when and if you need them. If you intend to go walking you should bring sturdy footwear as suitable boots are difficult to find in Central America. You will also need something to ward off the rain, cold and wind, all of which can strike with a vengeance.

Ideally, use a small rucksack or shoulder bag which can be padlocked. This is no guarantee of security but at least it hinders pickpockets. The advantage of small luggage is that you can keep it with you inside buses instead of having it thrown on the roof. In general your things are safe on the roof, but it is better to be safe than sorry.

Always keep with you your passport, vaccination booklet, flight ticket, traveller's cheques, insurance papers, and photocopies of relevant pages in your passport and the counterfoils of your traveller's cheques. Some people find a pocket calculator invaluable for making sense of fluctuating currency values and assessing prices of goods.

Use a money pouch or belt: either a leather belt with a concealed zip, or a wider cotton version that is concealed under your clothing and can fit your money and passport. Pouches can be sewn on to an elasticated armband and worn under clothing.

A basic medical kit should include insect repellent, flea powder, antiseptic, Lomotil for diarrhoea and a rehydration powder like Dioroalyte, antihistamine cream, essential personal medicines, and preferred contraceptive. Foot plasters, sun screen and toilet paper are also very useful. Remember that toilet paper is generally not provided in toilets and should always be carried with you.

Flip-flops are excellent for dubious showers and for general use. Also very useful are a small alarm clock for those 4 am buses, a torch, a camping knife, and sunglasses.

Other things you might want include:
- A universal plug.
- An electrical adaptor.
- Water purification tablets.
- Earplugs.
- Writing materials.
- A simple sewing kit.
- Water bottle.

Getting There

By Air

From Europe

Several major airlines operate a service between Europe and Central America and the price of a return ticket will probably be between £500 and £600. More precise details of flights are given in the introduction to each chapter. Good travel agents will also be able to offer 'open jaw' tickets, taking you into one city and out of another, which shouldn't cost any more than a straightforward return flight, while flights between Central American countries are reasonably priced. Two excellent London travel agents specializing in flights to Latin America are: Journey Latin America, 14–16 Devonshire Road, London W4 (tel 081 747 3108) and Latin American Travel, 28 Conduit Street, London W1 (tel 071 629 1130).

From the US

There are good connections between all Central American capitals and Miami, New York, Los Angeles, Houston, Washington DC as well as several other cities, with daily flights to most of these. Return fares from Miami and Los Angeles are priced at around US$400, but expect to pay twice that if coming from New York. Do shop around as special deals are often available. Among those offering the cheapest fares are Council Travel: in New York at 35 West 8th Street, New York 10011 (tel 212 254 2525); in California at 2846 Channing Way, Berkeley, CA 92093 (tel 510 415 848); and in Washington at 1314 Northeast 43rd Street, Suite 210, Seattle, WA 98105 (tel 206 632 2448).

By Sea

Finding a space on a ship bound for Central America is a time-consuming and uncertain business. Plenty of cruise ships head there and a great many freighters make their way to the Panamá Canal; however, few of these will be enthusiastic about taking on casual passengers. If you do get lucky the journey by sea takes at least two weeks from Europe or a week from the US. If your heart is set on arriving by boat then your best bet is to work as a crew member on a yacht. Boats heading for Central America leave Gibraltar and the Canary Islands in October and November and are often searching for an extra pair of hands, while in the US you'll just have to search around the large marinas and keep an eye on yacht club notice boards.

By Rail

Travellers coming from the US can at least get some of the way to Central America by train, covering the huge expanse between the US border and Mexico City. Reasonably comfortable sleepers operate on this line. However, if you plan to sleep your way out through the boredom then make sure you're absolutely exhausted as the trip takes at least 30 hours, often more!

By Road

Again the overland routes between the US and Central America are relatively direct, with good highways covering the main routes, although they do demand a degree of stamina. From Texas the most direct route cuts down the side of the Gulf of Mexico, bypassing the horrors of Mexico City. From California the drive is almost twice as long. By car you should expect to take at least a week to get through Mexico, even if you do use the most direct route. By bus you'll almost certainly have to travel via Mexico City and change buses. If you're sleeping on the bus it's just possible to make it through Mexico in four or five days, but don't expect to arrive in a fit state to enjoy yourself.

Agents and Specialist Operators

In the UK
Explore Worldwide (small-group exploratory holidays often using local transport, with the emphasis on discovering local cultures and wildlife); 1 Frederick Street, Aldershot, Hants GU11 1LQ, tel (0252) 319448.
Journey Latin America (large range of bespoke and package tours including environmental expeditions and economy journeys); 14-16 Devonshire Road, Chiswick, London W4 2HD, tel 081-747 8315.
Exodus Expeditions (escorted tours to Guatemala, Mexico and Belize); 9 Weir Road, London SW12 0LT, tel 081-675 5550.
Twickers World (tailor-made individual and group itineraries); 22 Church Street, Twickenham, Middlesex TW1 3NW, tel 081-892 8164.
Steamond Latin American Travel (tailor-made special-interest tours and itineraries including bird-watching, scuba-diving, etc); 278 Battersea Park, London SW11 3BS, tel 071-978 5500.
South American Experience (tailor-made packages); 47 Causton Street, London SW1P 4AT, tel 071-976 5511.

In the US
Himalayan Travel (fishing, bird-watching, river-rafting, natural history tours to Costa Rica); P.O. Box 481, Greenwich, CT 06836, tel (800) 225 2380.
Sobek Expeditions (river-rafting, sea-kayaking, and wildlife tours); P.O. Box 1089-60, Angel's Camp, CA 95222, tel (800) 777 7939.
Voyagers (natural history and photography tours to Belize and Costa Rica); Department EC, Box 915, Itaca, NY 14851, tel (607) 257 3091.
Wildland Adventures Inc. (ecotravel specialists); 3516 NE 155th, STE WT, Seattle, WA 98155, tel (800) 345 4453.

On Arrival

Entry Formalities
Formalities must be arranged before you set off but once your plane touches down in Central America you'll face immigration and customs. If you have not got a visa and do not need one then you will be presented with a tourist card. Once you've filled this in it is stamped, along with your passport, and you must keep the two together until you leave the country. All this is usually very straightforward and you're through in a matter of minutes, queues permitting.

The main airports have banks and you should get hold of some local currency if the bank

GENERAL INFORMATION

is open, and track down a taxi to take you into town. If the bank is closed then you should be able to find a taxi driver who will accept US dollars.

Tourist Information

The Guatemalan national tourist board has an office at the main airport in Guatemala City, although it has a strong tendency to remain closed all day. The best tourist information is provided by the main offices, which are all in the centre of the capital cities, and their addresses are listed in the country chapters, so it's best to wait until you have settled into a hotel before you rush off in search of information.

Maps

Local maps are generally available from Tourist Offices in each country while the best overall map of Central America is published by International Travel Map Productions, P.O. Box 2290, Vancouver, BC, V6B 3W5, Canada. Its European distributor is Bradt Publications, 41 Nortoft Road, Chalfont St Peter, Bucks, SL9 0LA, England and it is available from bookshops in Antigua, Guatemala.

Getting Around

This section provides a general guide to the principles of travel within Guatemala and Belize. Information that is particular to each individual country—from car hire to bus timetables—is given at the beginning of the relevant country chapter.

By Air

Flying is easy and always the most convenient option, though certainly not the cheapest or most interesting; however, if time is short you can quickly reach any of the countries' capitals, saving days of bus travel. Prices for return flights tend to be double the single fare, so there is rarely money to be saved on return tickets. You will also find that foreigners often pay a different, more expensive, fare than local nationals. Don't worry, this is standard. Short journeys, such as from Guatemala City to Belize City, cost around US$80 one way. It is always worth comparing prices between airlines offering the same routes.

Aviateca flies between Guatemala City, Managua and San José; **Taca** flies between Guatemala City, San Salvador, San José and Panamá; **Sahsa** flies between Guatemala City, San Salvador, San José and Panamá; **Aeronica** flies between Guatemala City, Managua, San José and Panamá; **Lacsa** flies between Guatemala City, San Pedro Sula, San José and Panamá; **Copa** flies between Guatemala City, San Salvador, Managua and Panamá. There are also connections for Belize City and Tegucigalpa.

By Boat

Except for the ferry route between Puerto Barrios, Guatemala and Punta Gorda, Belize, this is rarely a practical or safe way of getting from one country to another. There is an occasional boat service between Mango Creek, Belize and Puerto Cortés, Honduras, but schedules are haphazard and the danger from bad seas makes it an uncertain option.

By Train

There are no longer any train routes in Central America crossing international borders, although there are domestic services still operating in Guatemala.

By Bus

This is the standard mode of transport for most travellers, and certainly the cheapest, if not the most comfortable. Adequate compensation for the inconveniences and delays, however, is provided by the pleasure of meeting local people and staying close to the region's endlessly varied landscapes.

The international **Tica Bus** route from San José to Guatemala City, via Managua and Tegucigalpa has now reopened, so you should be able to find out about it in any of the capitals it passes through. On the other hand, you can take local buses to the relevant border crossing and change for another bus once through customs. There are usually good connections to and from border posts.

By Car or Motorbike

Driving around by hired car or your own vehicle gives you the advantage of complete freedom of movement. However, when weighing the obvious advantages against possible disadvantages, it is worth remembering that the police earn very little and often supplement their income by corruption. Foreigners are easy prey and it is essential that your papers are in perfect order and available for inspection at all times. It is also much easier to deal with official hazards if you develop an easy-going attitude about checkpoints and border crossings. Usually everything runs smoothly and your way. Repair facilities outside the capital cities are rare, and it is a good idea to have plenty of spare parts with you.

By Bicycle

Cycling is becoming ever more popular. The roads are often rough and unsurfaced, the terrain can be anything from sand to mud to rocks and pebbles, but few other modes of travel allow such close contact with the land and its people. Bicycles are common throughout the region, so basic repairs are no problem, but it is worth carrying essential spares. Insurance against theft is vital. Unfortunately, few places outside the tourist centres of Guatemala hire out bikes. If you are a serious cyclist, take your own (sturdy) machine, and contact the Cyclist's Touring Club, 69 Meadow, Godalming, Surrey, tel (0483) 417217.

Disabled Travellers

Travel in Central America can be quite rough, and no specific concessions or provisions are made to smooth the way for those with a physical handicap. Unfortunately, due to poverty and malnutrition, many more people suffer from disabilities here than in the West. If you or your travelling companion have special needs, you can make life much easier if you can afford to book organized tours and travel, where all aspects of transport are arranged for you, and provided in comfortable vehicles.

There are quite a few organizations which advise and encourage international travel for disabled people. To mention a few: DIVE (Disabled International Visits and Exchanges),

GENERAL INFORMATION

c/o The Central Bureau for Educational Visits and Exchanges, Seymour Mews House, Seymour Mews, London W1H 9PE; SATH (Society for the Advancement of Travel for the Handicapped), International Head Office, Suite 1110, 26 Court Street, Brooklyn, NY 11242, USA.

Specialist guide books or publications include: *Access to the World*, Louise Rice, Facts of File, London (1985); *Disabled Traveller's International Phrasebook*, Ian McNeil, Disability Press, 60 Greenhayes Avenue, Banstead, Surrey; *A List of Guidebooks for Handicapped Travelers*, The President's Committee on Employment of the Handicapped, 1111 20th Street, NW, Washington, DC 20036, USA.

Money and Official Currencies

The best currency to bring with you is the US dollar, since the region is economically dominated by it and always accepts it as payment. For safety's sake, you should bring at least half your money in traveller's cheques, which can be cashed at banks, as well as up-market hotels and even selected shops. It's also a good idea to bring some dollar cash for border crossings and emergencies, or to clinch a bargain, or in case you need to change money outside banking hours. Dollar cash, and sometimes cheques, can also be changed on the black market, which is widely tolerated but illegal. Black-market dealers operate in the streets and usually offer a slightly better rate than the banks, although they often indulge in sharp practices and well rehearsed rip-offs. Up-market hotels usually accept and exchange traveller's cheques, but at a poor rate.

Once in Central America it can be very difficult to buy US dollars, and few banks are willing to break down large bills for you, so avoid US$100 notes, unless you intend to change that much at each transaction. Credit cards are only useful at top hotels and shops, travel agents, and car hire agencies. American Express, Diners, Visa and Access are the most commonly accepted plastic.

A word of advice: do invest in a money pouch that can be discreetly kept under your clothing, and never leave valuables unattended. Most hotels have safes for customers' money and papers, which you should use. The money belt remains the safest place to keep your valuables but is by no means infallible. Everyone knows gringos keep their money around their waist these days, but there is still no need to draw attention to yourself. Purses, wallets and handbags really are a bad idea, since pickpockets are many and expert.

Local Currencies

The relevant local currencies are best bought and sold on arrival in Central America as you'll find that they are hard to get hold of elsewhere, with the notable exception of Miami, where currencies are easily obtained and off-loaded. Avoid bringing local currencies out of their relevant countries, as you will find it very difficult to get rid of them. The Guatemalan currency is the quetzal; in Belize it is the Belize dollar.

Manners and Mores

Crime and Police Business

Perhaps the best way to ensure your safety in Central America is to avoid carrying unnecessary valuables and accept the fact that they may be stolen. Most visitors have no real trouble at all, although petty theft and pickpocketing are widespread and irritating. There's little you can do to prevent this except keep your wits about you and avoid putting your money in easily accessible pockets.

Far more serious and a lot less likely is violent crime. If you are careful to avoid the worst spots—most notably the Pacaya volcano in Guatemala—then you're very unlikely to fall victim to violent crime. Nevertheless women should avoid going out alone at night wherever possible, particularly in the big cities. Here the danger of theft and assault, while small during the day, is very real at night.

One last danger is that of getting caught up in political conflict. Although peace is breaking out all over the isthmus there are still some dangerous areas, particularly some remote sections of the Guatemalan highlands. If you plan to venture into these areas then check with the local tourist office before you do so. More precise information on which areas to avoid and where to take particular care is given in the relevant country chapters.

Sexual Attitudes

> Some travellers don't wear underpants under their shorts with the result that when they sit cross-legged on the floor, anyone sitting opposite is subjected to a view of their genitals; this is usually unpopular.
>
> John Hatt, *The Tropical Traveller* (Pan, 1985)

This being Latin America, *machismo* is alive and well, and the concept of sexual equality is generally not even paid lip service. The traditional roles of women are defined by their place in the family, even though circumstances force the majority of them to work outside the home as well. Men are considered the natural head of the family, though this is often not the case in practice.

However, while sexism has obvious faults, there are also some more positive aspects. Patronage of females means there is always a man around who is willing to help a woman, and even protect her from the advances of other men. Single women travellers often find themselves inundated with advice and help they didn't even ask for, which is often friendly and useful without any expectation of favours in return.

As far as foreign women are concerned, there is a general assumption among Latin Americans that Westerners are sexually easy, a quality which is both admired and despised. Certainly foreigners are popular conquests in certain circles. Male travellers will find themselves untrammelled by local mores, and cheap prostitution appears a real attraction for some. Women, on the other hand, are advised to think carefully about wearing sexy shorts or no bras, since they will undoubtedly attract attention and possibly disgust. Latin American society is astonishingly conservative and the display of naked flesh is regarded as bad manners, with the notable exception of the beach, where anything goes. Men in shorts are often considered to look ridiculous, while walking about bare chested is also inappropriate away from the beach. Topless sunbathing is not a good idea in the local context, though it may be accepted in certain luxury resort hotels, far from the gaze of local people. Among indigenous people you should try particularly hard to keep yourself under wraps. To give you an idea of local custom: women often submerge in the waves fully dressed, trousers and all.

Homosexuality is as much a part of Latin American society as it is of any other, though the demands of *machismo* are strongly repressive and it remains confined to a subculture of known bars in the capital cities and tourist towns like Antigua, Guatemala. Officials, such as the police and military, are well known for their brutality against gays, and foreign travellers should be careful not to draw attention to themselves. Homosexual and lesbian couples will have no trouble with accommodation arrangements since it is very common for travellers of the same sex to share rooms. Double beds are rare anyway. Public opinion on the subject is characterized by a mixture of contempt and amusement.

Tipping

Throughout Central America tips are given in hotels and restaurants and to taxi drivers, porters and chambermaids. However, as in all Central American matters, there are no hard and fast rules and you're free to do as you please, responding to the situation as it arises. Generally speaking the staff in more up-market establishments will expect to be tipped, while those in cafés and cheap restaurants may be pleasantly surprised but will appreciate the gesture. In Guatemala a 10% service charge is sometimes added to restaurant bills, and a 10–15% tourist tax added to hotel bills, although again this by no means rules out an additional tip.

Beggars

Beggars are a depressing reminder of Central America's desperate circumstances and are to be found on the streets of all main cities. They are widely accepted by local people, who are usually willing to give them a coin or two. Beggars are also occasionally allowed to wander into restaurants and bars, becoming very much a part of the everyday chaos, although there is no doubt that their presence takes some getting used to.

Drugs

Drugs of all varieties, quantities and qualities are widely available throughout Central America, washed up on these shores as they travel north to the US. Dance floors in Belize are suffused with the sweet smell of marijuana. The use of soft drugs is widely tolerated in some parts of Central America, particularly Belize, although foreigners must still be discreet to avoid enraging local law enforcement officers. Elsewhere you should be very wary of having anything to do with drugs or those who deal in them, as dealers generally regard tourists as easy money and official penalties are steep, particularly when applied to outsiders.

Photography

With the vivid colours of Guatemalan costumes, the region is a photographers' paradise. Bear in mind that the range of light is enormous; in the clear sunshine of the highlands it can be searing, while little light penetrates beneath the canopy of the forest. So bring a wide range of film, as anything beyond the 100–400 ASA range is not available here. Standard slide and black and white film is available, although only in Guatemala City.

Photographing sensitive subjects, including police and soldiers, can easily land you in deep trouble and you should make a point of asking local people if they mind being photographed. Photographing Indian religious ceremonies is deeply offensive, unless you are invited to do so.

Communications and Services

Throughout Central America all normal services are available to a reasonable standard in the capital cities, although it is worth noting that they deteriorate rapidly as you move out into the smaller towns and villages.

Post Offices and Telephones

These services are provided by state-owned companies which have a main office in the capital and small offices in most towns and villages. The service is usually good and it is well worth making the trip to a large office, where staff are used to establishing long-distance links. It is also possible to make international calls from a private phone or hotel room, although there is a greater degree of uncertainty attached to the process.

Postal services are similarly variable and again it's always a good idea to make a point of using main Post Offices. Letters should take around 10 days to reach the US and 2 weeks to Europe, but it can be a lot longer. Parcels tread a very unpredictable path and are more likely to go missing than letters, particularly if you send them from small, remote post offices.

Details of services available are given at the relevant point in the text.

Newspapers and the Media

English-language newspapers—usually *The Miami Herald* or *International Herald Tribune* or *New York Times*—are sold in Guatemala; elsewhere you'll have to make do with local papers. Otherwise you can keep in touch via CNN which is available in hotel rooms throughout the region.

Electricity

The current runs at 110 volts. This means North Americans can use all their electrical equipment without any problems. Europeans, however, will need adaptors for everything electrical bought in their own countries. Adaptors are not always easy or cheap to find, so do bring your own if you really need one.

Where to Stay

Central America offers the full range of accommodation, from luxury resort hotel to open-air hammock shelter. There are many local variations with a broader range of up-market accommodation in Guatemala, although whatever kind of holiday and expense you have in mind, you will find something suitable in most places. Your choice will be far greater, however, in or near capital cities and if you are not looking exclusively for first-class hotels.

The widest range of accommodation lies in the band from inexpensive to moderate, which broadly speaking encompasses prices as low as US$4 per night to US$30 per night, for a double room. Camp sites are very rare, and guest houses are so cheap that you save no money camping anyway, the only advantage being to get off the beaten track or stay at official sights in distant reserves or up volcanoes.

Prices in the book are grouped under four price bands, which refer to the average price of a double room. (Like everywhere else, single travellers are generally penalized by having to pay almost the same as couples.) To find out what sort of accommodation you might encounter in each bracket look in the general introduction to the country chapters. Guatemala, for instance, is very cheap for the traveller; Belize is more expensive.

To reflect this variety of accommodation, and to avoid a confusion of detail, the price bands used in this guide are quite wide, giving a general indication of what is cheap or expensive.

Remember that local inflation is rampant and prices change constantly in this region. All prices are therefore quoted in US dollars.

Category	Double room
LUXURY:	US$90–US$130
EXPENSIVE:	US$30–US$90
MODERATE:	US$12.50–US$30
INEXPENSIVE:	US$4–US$12.50

If you are travelling on a budget, keep your ear to the travellers' grapevine: the state of places to stay in this bracket changes all the time—and the addition of a (workable) shower, or laundry facilities, can make all the difference. Generally speaking, good value accommodation will be found around bus and train stations, markets, and truckers' stopping places (near gas stations).

Note that room prices will vary according to the season; and wherever you stay, it's worth booking in advance by fax, telex or registered mail.

Eating Out

Local cuisine is commonly characterized by *huevos y frijoles*, eggs and beans, with cheese and meat as optional extras. This is not the most exciting meal in the world, but at least it's filling, and there is always a bottle of hot sauce (*salsa picante*) to liven things up. *Tortillas*, toasted patties of corn, are added to almost any dish, and are usually placed on the table automatically. Regional specialities, such as Belizean seafood or jungle cuisine, are covered in the relevant chapters.

In general, meat-eaters are much better catered for than vegetarians, who get stuck with eggs and beans, pasta, pizza and rice, with few vegetables or salads to choose from safely. Tropical fruit is some compensation for this, and wandering about any local market will show you the amazing variety on offer.

Salads should be avoided except if you are certain they have been cleaned properly, which usually means sticking to expensive hotels for that kind of food. The choice of international cooking is good in the capital cities, with Chinese the most frequent option. Italian, French and Mexican restaurants are also quite common. In provincial areas you will find your choice of foreign meals limited to Chinese, and in villages food is exclusively local fare.

Do try the local *comedores*, where you will find standard Latin meals and a good opportunity to mix with the local people and practise your Spanish. Dishes are simple and cheap and help to make your money go a long way. Another option for enjoying local fare is to head for the market, where boisterous ladies run open-air kitchens; huge pots of soup bubble away next to mountains of fried chicken. The local Chinese restaurants are often very good, but do tend to look rather grubby.

Drinks

Soft drinks (*jugos*)—or *aguas* if they're fizzy, canned or bottled—tea, and coffee are commonly available wherever you go. While travelling by bus, you will also encounter a myriad of homemade drinks, such as *agua de coco* (coconut water), with a lump of cooling ice in it. These are delicious and tempting, but the ice is invariably made from unsafe water. The same goes for any homemade, water-based drink, whether sold on the streets or in local *comedor* eating venues. For your own protection, it is also worth drinking straight from the bottle, rather than using possibly dirty glasses.

Local beers, *cervezas*, are cheap and rather watery, but refreshing in the tropical heat without causing too much drowsiness. Rum, *ron*, is also cheap and often quite good, while regional 'firewaters', *aguardientes*, burn a mean trail down your throat—an effect similar to drinking distilled alcohol. Regional brews are mentioned in the relevant country sections.

Restaurants and Comedores

There is a clear divide between local establishments, where the food is cheap and the atmosphere can be distinctly rough and ready and a rather slicker range of up-market establishment. In the former, it's the setting that provides most of the flavour, while the latter, generally a great deal more expensive, provides your only hope of gastronomic indulgence. These tourist and foreign-run restaurants are bound to be quite expensive by local standards, but the variety of meals is greater and sanitary conditions are usually better. Up-market hotels and restaurants offer an international menu and prices to match.

Shopping and Bargaining

Shopping conditions vary greatly within Central America, ranging from the small village markets of the Guatemalan highlands, where hand-woven cloth is sold alongside a family of pigs, to the swish boutiques of the capital cities.

Generally speaking the best *artesanía* (craft work) and most spontaneous markets are found in Guatemala; among the best locally produced goods are the weavings.

Central Americans have a tremendous capacity for business and take great pleasure in shopping, whether it's toothpaste or tangerines and whether they're buying or selling. Bargaining is always part of the process, particularly in rural markets, and involves an exchange of formalities in which both buyer and seller must preserve their dignity. Bear in mind that the middle ground always exists; it's just a question of reaching it.

Sports and Activities

Sport in Central America is still in the early stages of development. Here is a simple list of the best that's on and an indication of which way to head if you're looking for a particular activity. For more information see the individual country chapters.

Amateur Archaeology

Maya ruins are scattered throughout Belize and Guatemala and offer a fascinating insight into the area's pre-Columbian history. For those in search of ancient history these are the best countries to head for, where the concentration of ancient sites is at its highest.

GENERAL INFORMATION

Brightly coloured friendship bands from Guatemala are popular souvenirs

Diving
Both Central American coasts provide ideal waters for diving and there are many companies offering diving courses and days out. The sport is at its most developed in Belize, which boasts one of the longest barrier reefs in the world. There's no need to bring your own equipment as there are companies catering to tourists in all of these countries.

Fishing
Superb river and sea fishing is available throughout Central America. The sport has been well developed in Belize, where specialist companies offer ever more imaginative types of fishing from big-game blue marlin to rainbow trout in the mountains.

Hiking
There are excellent opportunites for hiking throughout Central America. The range of scenery gives you the option of a short stroll along a sandy beach, the gruelling ascent of a volcanic peak, or wading through jungle mud. In Guatemala it is possible to hire camping equipment and there are well developed trail systems and National Parks.

Natural History
Central America offers superb bird and animal watching, and in Costa Rica alone there are said to be as many species of bird as in the entire United States. There are excellent National Parks in Costa Rica, Guatemala and Belize, which all provide the best opportunities for ornithology.

Potholing
Central America's limestone interior is said to provide some of the finest potholing in the world, although as yet the sport has not been developed in any systematic way. Caves in

Guatemala have been explored, although if you're planning an expedition you'll still need to bring all your own equipment.

River Rafting

Again, this is an up and coming sport in Central America. You'll need no expert training and can simply book a day out once you arrive. For more experienced rafters the rivers of Costa Rica offer some superb challenges, while the sport is slowly being taken up in Belize and Guatemala.

Environmental Issues

The Central American isthmus is riddled with instability. Here the meeting of north and south funnels a range of opposing forces into close contact, generating a tension which manifests itself in volcanic eruptions, earthquakes and political upheaval. However, this uncomfortable relationship has also created a rich and varied environment in which species of animals and plants from both north and south coexist with local species that are found nowhere else in the world.

The region contains an amazing range of environments. The far south, where Panamá merges into Colombia, is one the the most impenetrable jungles in the world, a rugged landscape of low hills, swamps, tortuous rivers and towering rainforest, in which tropical downpours and scorching sunshine conspire to keep the air heavy with humidity. At the other end of the isthmus the Cuchumatanes mountains roll across the border between Guatemala and Mexico, reaching a height of some 3600 metres. Here the jagged granite peaks are regularly bitten by frost and occasionally dusted with snow, while the altitude keeps the air fresh and clear.

Between these extremes a chain of volcanic peaks forms the backbone of the isthmus, including at least seven active volanoes. The best of these are Pacaya in Guatemala and Arenal in Costa Rica, both oozing a steady plume of sulphurous smoke and sporadically spraying fountains of fire into the night sky. A series of broad highland valleys are strung up between the volcanoes, some containing beautiful lakes, others occupied by sprawling moden cities such as San José, San Salvador and Guatemala City. In amongst the volcanoes are several mountain ranges, the largest in Costa Rica and Guatemala, their upper slopes supporting an almost Andean environment of sparse scrub and coarse bushes. The lower slopes, however, are richly fertile, their acid volcanic soils coated in enormous coffee plantations. A few small areas, saved by the difficult terrain and poor infrastructure, are still covered by magical cloud forests, in which the trees are wrapped in moss, their branches dripping with ferns and bromeliads.

Stretching out beneath the highlands a wide coastal plain runs down the Pacific side from Guatemala to Panamá. It's an area of scorching heat and intense fertility now monopolized by commercial agriculture. Huge plantations of cotton and sugar have replaced most of the original vegetation, although in Costa Rica the Santa Rosa National Park preserves the only remaining area of dry tropical forest which once covered the entire coastline. Meanwhile on the other side of the highlands, reaching to the shores of the Caribbean, much of the land remains inaccessible and uninhabited. In Belize and Honduras some regions are now well developed, although in Nicaragua and Panamá the Caribbean coast is a great forested frontier, hundreds of tiny rivers cutting through a tangle of tropical vegetation as they make their way to the sea.

Lying a few miles off the Caribbean coast are several small clusters of islands and coral reefs, the largest running parallel to the coast of Belize and ranking as the world's second longest barrier reef. The seas on both sides of Central America are teeming with a kaleidoscope of tropical fish including rays, sharks, barracuda, swordfish and marlin. If you're snorkelling or diving, the display is incredibly impressive, while the marine life also makes superb eating, served up with spicy creole sauces and sweetened with coconut.

Flora and Fauna

This range of environments in Central America is matched by an equally varied selection of wildlife. In Costa Rica alone there are some 760 species of birds, which is around the same number as are found in the entire United States. In the dense tropical forests **scarlet macaws** waft between the treetops, squawking at uninvited intruders while thumb-size **hummingbirds** buzz among the flowers and flocks of brilliant green **parakeets** chatter as they spin through the trees. Central America is an ornithologist's paradise and even for the uninitiated the variety and beauty of the birds is a real source of fascination. Perhaps the most infamous of all Central America's birds is the **resplendant quetzal**, which was sacred to the Maya and still has a certain magical aura. With its bright green plumage and long, snaking tail the quetzal is an astonishing sight in the wild, its vivid colours providing a sudden flash amidst the soft greys and misty greens of the cloud forest.

Animal life is also profuse, with the remaining swamps, grasslands and forests providing a home to **jaguars, crocodiles, deer**, a weird selection of lizards and **iguanas**, four types of **monkey, coatimundi, armadillos, tapirs, otters, peccary** and more than 15 species of **poisonous snake**, including the deadly fer-de-lance, coral snake and bushmaster. Most of the large animals are extremely elusive, although from time to time they pop up just when you're not expecting them. Nevertheless when wandering through the jungle you get a strong sense of being in somebody else's territory. The rustle of leaves or crack of branches may be all that you hear of a disappearing **deer**, although other species do like to make their presence felt, particularly the monkeys. The acrobatic **spider monkeys** are the most assertive, screeching at you from the treetops and shaking branches to send dead limbs tumbling to the forest floor. Their aim can be extremely accurate and spider monkeys have been known to defecate on intruders, scoring a direct hit from some 30 metres up.

Among the most regular visitors to Central America are the huge sea **turtles**, of which four species come ashore on the Pacific and Caribbean coasts. The females nest during the rainy season, hauling themselves up onto the beach and digging a small hole with their flippers. They then deposit about a hundred eggs as large as a ping-pong balls and cover them in sand before dragging themselves back into the sea. The young turtles emerge a few months later and must make a desperate dash for the surf, many of them being picked off by seabirds before they make it. Turtles' eggs are also sold in the markets and served in bars, where they are eaten raw with a touch of lemon juice and tabasco and are said to have aphrodisiac qualities.

National Parks

The distribution and development of National Parks in Central America mirror the region's political and social problems. The poorer, troubled nations, such as Nicaragua and El Salvador, have done little to protect the environment, attending first to more pressing problems. Meanwhile Belize and Costa Rica have led the way, identifying their most important environmental assets and taking concrete steps to preserve them.

If you're keen to see some of Central America's birds and beasts or visit a wide range of untouched environments then Costa Rica is certainly the most rewarding destination. A little smaller are the National Parks of Belize. Here several specific species are protected, including howler monkeys at the Community Baboon Sanctuary and jaguars at the large Cockscomb reserve to the south of Dangriga. Again every effort has been made to include the full range of environments, from the high mountains to the offshore coral reef, and to provide facilities for visitors, making Belize a close rival to Costa Rica for amateur naturalists and ornithologists.

Across the border in Guatemala the national parks are still in their early days. The country's most important reserve embraces the forest surrounding Tikal in the Petén. The forest here is well preserved and makes a fitting backdrop for the ruins, although sadly much of the surrounding area is now being plundered for oil, while new roads and cattle farms are eating into virgin territory. Guatemala has three other impressive reserves. The first at Monterrico, on the Pacific coast, where a superb black sand beach provides an ideal nesting sight for turtles and a maze of mangroves is alive with fish and birds. Over on the Caribbean coast is the Río Dulce reserve, where the river of the same name cuts through a dramatic steep-sided gorge before spilling into the ocean. Last, but by no means least, is Lake Atitlán, Guatemala's scenic jewel, its turquoise waters ringed by volcanic peaks, although the scale of development is starting to have a damaging impact here.

Ecotourism

Ecotourism has become a catch phrase for a new kind of travel which is committed to minimizing the impact of tourism on sensitive natural environments and their traditional human and animal inhabitants. Belize is at the forefront of this movement in Central America. Government and local agencies have combined to coordinate a programme of development for the country's areas of outstanding natural beauty, both on land and under water. That is the ideal. In practice, 90% of the country's coastal developments are foreign owned, and the risk of unscrupulous exploitation is still high.

Not every package advertised under the 'ecotourism' banner is truly committed to its ideals, and travellers are advised to check carefully what exactly they are being offered. Ecotourism is big business and there is a tendency to overcharge travellers just because a tour is advertised under its label. In particular it should be noted how many people any one group contains, since only small groups can claim to have a low impact on local environments and people. Another good question is to what extent the local people benefit, either financially or in developmental needs for the community.

In Belize itself there are two organizations which offer excellent information, as well as help with organizing visits to areas of interest. The **Belize Audubon Society**, 29 Regent Street, P.O. Box 1001, Belize City, tel (02) 77369 has been given responsibility for the administration of nine of the country's reserves, and can advise on natural resources and conservation in Belize. **Programme for Belize**, 1 King Street, Belize City, tel (02) 75616 is a consortium of British and American organizations concerned with ecological preservation in Belize. In particular they are running a programme of buying Belizean rainforest as a measure to protect it. The Rio Bravo Conservation Area is also one of their projects. Specifically concerned with southern Belize is the **Toledo Eco Tourism Association**, which you can contact via Chet Schmidt, Nature's Way Guest House, 65 Front Street, tel (07) 2119.

Whether you choose to join an ecotour or not, you should note that Belize has certain laws to protect its natural resources, though sadly they are not effectively enforced, so it is up to the visitor to support the country's efforts at preservation. The following are the most important prohibitive laws:

1. Removing and exporting black coral
2. Hunting without a licence
3. Picking orchids in forest reserves
4. Spear-fishing while wearing scuba diving gear
5. Camping overnight in any public place, including reserves

Specialist Operators

Concentrating on adventurous journeys and promoting ecotourism from England are **Wild West Expeditions**, Ashes Farm Cottage, Hayfield, Derbyshire SK12 5LL, tel (0663) 741578; **EcoSafaris**, 146 Gloucester Road, London SW7 4SZ, tel 071–370 1085; and **Twickers World**, 22 Church Street, Twickenham, London TW1 3NW, tel 081–892 8164/7606, fax 081–892 8061.

Part II

CENTRAL AMERICAN HISTORY BEFORE INDEPENDENCE

> Land as slim as a whip,
> Hot as torture,
> Your step in Honduras, your blood
> In Santo Domingo, at night,
> Your eyes in Nicaragua...
>
> Pablo Neruda, *Centro América*

Flying across Central America, the view is astonishing, especially over Panamá. Far below, you see the Atlantic and Pacific oceans at the same time, only a narrow strip of land keeping them apart—a narrow strip which also separates (or connects) the great land masses of North and South America. Central America has somehow always been viewed like that: a ragged bridge connecting two huge continents, or worse still, simply a peninsular extension of North America, giving credence to the modern idea of 'America's Back Yard'—after all, the Darién Gap is a dead end in terms of overland travel. The jungle there is so inaccessible and the land so swampy that no road or rail has yet succeeded in penetrating to the South American mainland. The only way to proceed is on foot or to fly.

Yet there is nothing homogeneous about this region that stretches from the Mexican/Guatemalan border all the way to the swampy jungles of the Panamanian border with Colombia. What looks like a geographical unity is in fact a collection of seven very different countries. There are features which they all have in common, such as the Spanish language, certain tropical export crops, and a subtropical climate. But the human history of the region could hardly be more dissimilar. From prehistoric times quite distinct cultures have emerged, largely defined by the regional differences in geography and vegetation. Even the effect of the Spanish Conquest was regionally disparate.

Prehistory

During the last Ice Age, such vast expanses of ocean were frozen that the earth's general sea level was lowered. One effect of this was that Asia and North America were at times connected by a land bridge, known as the Bering Passage, and it is believed that humans first came into the Americas via this route about 60,000 years ago. Radiocarbon dates from polished bone tools suggest that the entire North and South American continents were populated by 11,000 BC.

The people who lived here in those times were hunter-gatherers, who lived a nomadic existence, following a seasonal cycle after a large variety of animals and easily gathered fruits, nuts and roots. Small family groups would have roamed the landscape, only occasionally coming together into larger camps in order to hunt the giant mammals of the age, such as mammoth, mastodon or bison. But there were many smaller animals they hunted too, such as rabbits, foxes, squirrels, turtles, lizards and quail.

Between 11,000 and 6000 BC the climate gradually became warmer and drier. Huge lakes dried up, grasslands became deserts, and the woodlands shrank, so that slowly the giants of prehistory became extinct. New kinds of food eventually had to be found by humans, and very, very slowly, people evolved new ways of life, where food came from a greater variety of sources.

In the time from 7000 to 1500 BC domesticated plants played an increasingly important role, and larger camps of people developed in response to the greater numbers needed for effective food gathering and hunting. In particular near rivers, lakes and oceans, sedentary groups emerged, who supplemented their fishing culture with gathering a great variety of other food, such as wild cereal plants, fruit, nuts, avocados, squashes, chilli peppers and prickly pears.

The Origin of Agriculture

The evidence for how and when humans first developed agriculture in the Americas is hotly debated. By its nature, plant evidence is hard to come by, and archaeologists have had to make do for their clues with a few cave sites in dry areas, such as in Oaxaca in central Mexico or the Ayacucho basin in the Peruvian Andes. It is at those sites that they have analyzed the ground layers relating to different ages, as well as studying coprolites (fossilized faeces) and human bones. From these combined studies scientists have been able to establish that a major change took place in human diet after 4500 BC and it is only from this time onwards that agriculture can be said to have been important.

To look for an exact point at which hunting and gathering stopped and agriculture began is fruitless. Development is the key word, and the transition from a nomadic hunting way of life to a sedentary agricultural life was gradual. The cultivation of certain plants may not have resulted from the extinction of the larger animals, nor because of the changing climate or population pressure, but for simple practical reasons. For example, one of the earliest domesticates was the bottle gourd for carrying water, and other plants were cultivated for dyes. Some plants, such as the tomato, are believed to have been domesticated incidentally, when genetic changes in the plant, such as increased size, made it a more important and easily gathered food source.

This must particularly apply to the all-important food plant, maize. Whatever the plant ancestor of maize, its cob would not have been larger than a thumbnail, and its use as a food source cannot have been obvious to early man. Instead, the combined effect of incidental domestication and genetic changes in the plant gradually made it more and more useful, and eventually people would have begun to cultivate it in an agricultural way, planting and gathering it specifically for the purpose of food. That these changes must have been slow is underlined by the fact that by 1500 BC maize was still only one-fifth of its present size. What is certain, however, is that man's changed relationship to the environment eventually allowed the first settled cultures to develop.

Early Societies

The earliest evidence for settled communities comes from household tools and crafts, such as simple pottery, and cotton fibre cloth was probably also used, though it has not often survived. From 3000 BC onwards, and certainly from 1500 BC settled communities of between twelve and several hundred people gradually developed a new culture that included ritual and religious belief. Small figurines, believed to relate to ancestor worship or fertility rites have been found from this time. Homes were probably windowless houses made of pole and wattle, with roofs thatched by palm leaf. In the highlands, houses would have been made of mud bricks (adobe), and thatched with straw or coarse grasses. Both these types of housing can still be seen in traditional Indian villages today.

Elite centres appear by around 1000 BC when flat temple platforms indicate ceremonial sites, and unequal burials testify to a stratified society. Some were simply wrapped in a sleeping mat and buried under the family house, while others were buried with great fineries and even human retainers.

One of the earliest Mesoamerican civilizations were the Olmec, who existed between 1200 and 100 BC with their heyday from 900 to 600 BC. However, their territory was almost entirely restricted to the Gulf Coast and the Tuxla Mountains of modern Mexico. The only significant satellite further south was at Izapa, on the Mexican Pacific coast near modern Tapachula. Another Mesoamerican people were the Toltecs, whose capital was the Yucatán ceremonial centre of Tula, and yet another were the Mixtecs, who ruled the area around modern Mexico City after the demise of the nearby city of Teotihuacan. The only Mesoamerican civilization to develop further south was that of the Maya, whose earliest beginnings go back as far as 2000 BC. Their territory is generally divided into three different zones: the Highland Maya of the Guatemalan highlands, the Lowland Maya of the Guatemalan Petén and adjacent Maya Mountains, and the Northern Lowland Maya of the Mexican Yucatán.

The Maya

The history of Maya civilization is divided into three periods: the Pre-Classic (2000 BC to AD 250), the Classic (AD 250 to 900), and the Post-Classic (AD 900 to 1530). They are generally held to represent the development, maturity and decadence of the civilization.

Pre-Classic Maya: 2000 BC to AD 250

From 2000 BC to around AD 150, Maya ancestors lived in the small communities already described. In particular along the Pacific plain of Guatemala, were villages established to harvest both the land and the sea. Their inhabitants lived off shellfish, crab, fish, turtles and iguanas, as well as maize from cultivated fields. The earliest village culture in this region is known as Ocos, and flourished from 1500 BC onwards. Later came the Cuadros village culture, which lasted until around 850 BC. Both evolved fine pottery skills, making a variety of bowls, pots and figurines. A common artefact of the period was the tripod bowl or jar, often decorated with crisscross and zigzag designs, and—uniquely in Central America—patterns made by pressing rope or twine into the wet clay.

Another important centre of early civilization, Kaminal Juyu, lies in the central valley of Guatemala, close to the modern capital. A significant ceremonial centre from earliest Pre-Classic times, it eventually developed into a huge site of at least one hundred buildings, with political and trading links reaching all the way to Mexican Teotihuacán. Even the inhospitable Petén lowlands show evidence of early cultures, and sites such as Altar de Sacrificios, Ceibal, Tikal and Uaxactún were certainly inhabited by 400 BC.

Eventually, some time between 250 BC and AD 300, these simple village cultures scattered across the Maya territory developed the traits of a great civilization. Monumental architecture, sophisticated art forms, timekeeping and elaborate calendars, writing, and the science of astrology were all components of that development. Society became structured by an official religion and a rigid, hereditary class system where even slaves were a hereditary group.

Kaminal Juyu developed into a vast and prestigious city. Temple platforms were raised from the ground, reaching up to 18 metres, and on these stood the simple temples of pole and thatch that so disappointed the Spanish in their search for riches. For those were not to be found in the temples, but in the burial chambers underneath them and around the pyramid platforms.

Classic Maya: AD 250 to 900

The Classic Age was a Golden Age for the Maya civilization, and their sophistication in architecture, art and science can easily match that of the ancient Egyptians or Greeks. Their astronomers could accurately predict lunar and solar eclipses and had recognized many planets, while the Maya calendar reached far beyond the Christian calendar and the complexity of their writing system has yet to be fully understood (see p. 37).

It is during this age that Maya lords built the imposing pyramids of Tikal and Caracol, and sculptural art reached its peak at sites like Copán and Quiriguá. Often these sites are referred to as cities, since as many as 50,000 people once lived in and around them. But that is a misleading term, imposing modern conceptions on the past. It is now generally accepted that it is better to speak of ceremonial centres, since Maya civilization was fundamentally ruled by religious faith and ritual, and all aspects of life, whether the planting season, dates for war, or people's names, were decided by the Maya astronomers and diviners. They

baktun   *katun*   *tun*   *kin*

were at the heart of all decisions, and the position of every person in society was dominated by their interpretation of the celestial and divine cycle.

Only a very small elite of nobles and priests lived at the core of what we see today: the great plazas and pyramids. Nearby there were quarters of artisans, craftsmen and slaves, and spreading out over a much larger area were the dwellings and clustered communities of the peasant majority, who were involved exclusively in food procurement and processing for the central elite, who then redistributed it among the population.

Post-Classic Maya: AD 900 to 1530

Between 790 and 889 AD the Classic Maya civilization abruptly disintegrated. Within a hundred years, the Lowland Maya populations seem to have left, state architecture and monumental building stopped, and even the Maya hieroglyphics appear to have degenerated into simpler forms of pictographic symbolism. Many explanations have been put forward for this collapse: earthquakes or hurricanes, epidemics, ecological disasters, social revolt, foreign invasion or economic decline. Certainly, the warlike Toltecs seem to have moved in from the north around 900, but the evidence from some sources suggests that the decline began before then. Until the Maya script is fully understood, we shall never know more than a fraction of the story.

All we can say for sure is that the Classic Maya civilization did collapse, and from the 10th century onwards, the glorious temples and plazas of most lowland ceremonial centres were left to itinerant squatters, who camped among the abandoned buildings, periodically looting the royal burial chambers or using masonry for their own building needs. Soon the great buildings were reclaimed by surrounding jungle, and by the time the Spanish arrived, the temples and pyramids of the Maya had been derelict for over 500 years, remnants of a 'lost civilization'. The surviving Maya Indians could not shed much light on the magnificent art and architecture of their ancestors, nor adequately explain their culture's historic knowledge of astronomy, science and writing.

But while southern lowland centres of power, such as Tikal, declined, northern lowland centres, such as Chichen Itzá in modern Mexico, expanded. They developed a new style of art and culture, and traded goods along the coast in canoes. Much of this phase of Central American history remains obscure, though Post-Classic culture may have been a fusion of Maya and Toltec. By the time the Spanish arrived, however, Chichen Itzá was also in ruins. In the Western Highlands of Guatemala, though, the Quiché Maya had their powerful kingdom with its capital at Utatlán, the Mam Maya ruled their domains from Zaculeu, and the Cakchiquel Maya governed theirs from Iximché. All these peoples preserved many aspects of Classic Maya culture, and continued to do so after the Conquest.

CENTRAL AMERICAN HISTORY BEFORE INDEPENDENCE

European Discovery and the Colonial Era

Europeans first came to Central America on Columbus' fourth and final voyage in 1502. His ship dropped anchor at Guanaja, one of the Honduran Bay Islands, and much to the excitement of his teenage son, his forces captured a Maya trading canoe, filled with exotic goods such as quetzal plumes, cacao beans, shells and fine pottery. Soon Columbus set sail once more, heading east around the Mosquito Coast, and discovered the Veragua region, which yielded enough gold finds to encourage a steady stream of expeditions to beach on today's Nicaraguan and Panamanian Atlantic coasts.

In 1513, the conquistador Balboa discovered the Pacific Ocean while travelling inland near the Darién forest, and soon Panamá City (1519), León and Granada (1524) were founded. They were some of the earliest colonial settlements in Central America, and flourished as bases from which to explore, as well as exploit local minerals and the Indians. Slavery was good business, and many thousands of Indians were shipped off to South American silver and gold mines. Most died of European diseases and malnutrition before they reached their destination, and once arrived, they were found to be unsuitable for heavy mine work. It was then that the Spanish began importing the stronger African slaves, thus introducing a significant black society to Central America.

Spanish forces were also penetrating south from Mexico City, soon to discover and conquer the Highland Maya of Guatemala and establish the brutal reign of Pedro de Alvarado. It was he who founded the most glamorous colonial city of Central America: Antigua, Guatemala, situated in a beautiful highland valley embraced by three volcanos. Meanwhile Spanish forces also traced the Atlantic coast southwards from the Yucatán, establishing strategic forts near the Honduran ports of Puerto Cortés and Trujillo, as well as inland at San Pedro Sula. These were important in repelling Portuguese and English expeditions, and also as bases from which to exploit the fertile interior for cacao.

After the Conquest, population centres followed the ancient patterns so that the main centre of Spanish rule grew up in the Guatemalan highlands. From there it spread thinly south, neglecting the traditionally 'empty' regions, such as the swampy jungles of the Atlantic littoral, as well as many inland areas, such as the inaccessible Honduran highlands. Much of the interior was left to its own devices by the colonial authorities, with the exception of vital ports along the Pacific, such as Colón in Panamá, and fortifications along the Atlantic, such as Omoa and Trujillo in Honduras.

The Spanish were too preoccupied with extracting the riches of Mexican silver and Peruvian gold to bother much with Central America; its mineral resources were limited, and its largest asset was an enslaved Indian population which did little to increase the wealth of Spain itself. Since the conquistadors had little interest in farming, the great agricultural potential of the region was not exploited intensively until after Independence, although indigo and cacao were relatively lucrative exports from El Salvador and Guatemala. Soon the region became a colonial backwater. Panamá was lumped in under the jurisdiction of New Granada, ruled by the Viceroy of Peru, while the rest became the Captaincy-General of Guatemala in 1543, beholden to the Viceroy of New Spain, the forerunner of modern Mexico. This political division still influences Central American politics today and Panamá retains a unique position, not least because of the US-controlled Panamá Canal.

Unlike the Europeans in North America, the Spanish came as soldiers, not settlers. They did not bring their families, but married and had children by Indian women. The mestizos who resulted from this union soon formed the majority of colonial society. The Spanish crown, however, reserved the positions of highest authority for *peninsulares*—those born in Spain, who brought their families with them—a division that was eventually to spark off the independence movement. Along the Atlantic coast, the presence of African slaves led to a significant society of blacks and mulattos. Added to these peoples were small but coherent groups of Chinese, East Indians and white settlers, usually of religious groups, such as the Mennonites, as well as non-Maya indigenous groups, like the Miskitos or Darién Indians, who survived by nature of their inaccessibility. The Maya themselves succeeded better than any other indigenous people of the Americas in retaining their racial and cultural heritage, and to this day they make up over half the population of modern Guatemala.

Neglect by the Spanish authorities allowed others to make inroads into the territory. English, Dutch and French pirates made their homes along the Bay of Honduras, and by the 17th century, English pirates had even helped their country establish claims to what became known as the Crown Colony of British Honduras. Their legacy still exists in Belize, which has only been independent from Britain since 1981, and the English-speaking inhabitants of the Honduran Bay Islands.

Independence from Spanish Rule

Central America gained independence on the coat-tails of Mexico in 1821. There was no battle for independence in the region, and there were plenty among the economic elite who remained loyal to Spanish authority. They were virtually let go against their will; once the rest of Latin America had gone, the Spanish colonial authorities had no further interest in a region that had always been one of the least profitable possessions.

It was a confusing time, when such disparate groups as the mine owners from Honduras, cacao planters of El Salvador and cattle ranchers of Panamá found themselves in a territory with no political authority and little common ground. As a result the various regions turned inwards, trying to consolidate their own interests, while sporadic battles raged between forces loyal to Spain and those with ambitions for wider political control of the region. A limited consensus was reached in 1823, when all but Chiapas decided not to become part of Mexico, and instead founded the United Provinces of Central America, whose capital was to be Guatemala City. This union was made up of five newly founded provinces: Guatemala, El Salvador, Honduras, Nicaragua and Costa Rica, whose borders were more or less the same as those of the countries of today. British Honduras remained outside the union, while Panamá became a part of Colombia. It was a recipe for political fragmentation, and the union was soon rent by conflicting economic and political interests, falling apart completely in 1839.

Ever since, Central American unity has been a lost cause. Honduras and Guatemala soon emerged as the original 'banana republics', their economic and political destiny closely supervised by US interests such as the United Fruit Company. Panamá declared its independence from Colombia in 1904, supported by the US to facilitate the building of the canal. Central America's role as the 'back yard' of the US has been a constant theme of its history since Independence, and on several occasions economic and political influence has spilled over into direct military intervention: the US occupation of Nicaragua from 1909 to 1933, the CIA-backed coup in Guatemala in 1954, or the invasion of Panamá in 1989.

Admittedly this has produced a level of economic investment which the local governments could never have generated. But the price has been high, and remains the foremost cause of political instability in the region.

Part III
TOPICS

Glyphs for the world directions and associated colours

The Maya Universe

> These are the names of the First People who were made and modelled...
> Thoughts came into existence and they gazed; their vision came all at once.
> Perfectly they saw, perfectly they knew everything under the sky, whenever
> they looked.
>
> The *Popol Vuh* of the Quiché Maya, translated by Dennis Tedlock

Miraculously surviving the ravages of time and the depredations of the conquistadors, the manuscripts, the stone inscriptions, the pottery, the pyramids and temples, and above all, the living tradition itself allow us a glimpse into the extraordinary universe of the Maya.

Maya Gods

The pantheon of the Classic Maya period (AD 250–900) has roots stretching back more than a thousand years earlier to the Olmecs, and continued to be worshipped long after the Spanish Conquest. Because of this long history, and because the Maya were not a centralized empire but a collection of independent peoples, some of the gods have several aliases.

According to some traditions, the original omnipotent spirit was Hunab Ku. He created Itzamná, god of fire, and the inventor of writing; and Ixchel, goddess of medicine and the Old Moon. They created all the other gods, including Chac, the goggle-eyed rain god;

the four Bacabs, who stood at the points of the compass and supported the heavens; the maize god, an ever-present symbol of renewal; and a rather cuddly character known as the Fat God. The monkey-men gods were the special patrons of the scribes.

Of special importance was 'God K'; he was the wind god and the special protector of the Maya rulers, who carried his image on their sceptres. After the arrival of the Toltecs around AD 900, he seems to become identified with Kukulkan. God of the primordial wind, he was known to the Quiché as Gucumatz and worshipped by the Aztecs as Quetzalcoátl—the plumed serpent.

Among the gods of the underworld (Xibalbá), who sent forth owls to summon mortals to their final ball game, were the skeletal Hunahau, the Death God; his assistants Tatan Holon ('Father Skull') and Tatan Bak ('Father Bones'); the Jaguar God; the long-nosed Ek Chuuah, god of merchants; and Ixtab, the goddess of suicides, who is shown hanging from a noose in Maya manuscripts.

Itzamná

Creation Myths

There are many different accounts of the creation from the Maya lands. One version, inscribed on two stones at Quiriguá in Guatemala and Palenque in Mexico, lay unnoticed for millennia until it was deciphered by two US scholars, Linda Schele and David Freidel, in 1992. On 13 August, 3114 BC, the gods lit the flame from which the universe was created, in a hearth of three stones. The fire can still be seen in the sky today—the red Orion nebula, which hangs between the three brightest stars of that constellation. At the moment of creation, though, the sky lay flat upon the surface of the earth in a two-dimensional universe. The gods then used the Milky Way as a great tree to lift the sky up above the earth.

Ixchel, the old Moon Goddess

The creation of human beings is recorded in the Quiché Maya's Book of Creation, the *Popol Vuh*. It took the gods Tepeu and Gucumatz four attempts to accomplish this difficult task. Their first creatures were fashioned out of the earth's mud, but soon disintegrated. The second versions were made of wood, but were stupid and had to be destroyed as unworthy. The third attempt promised well; the creatures were made of living flesh, and had minds too. Disappointingly, they failed to honour their creators (which was supposed to be their main purpose in life) and were punished by being turned into monkeys. The fourth creations, made from maize, at last proved satisfactory, knowing their place and worshipping the gods.

Sun God

Maya Society

At the apex of a Maya city was a ruler who claimed to be descended from the gods. At Copán and Quiriguá, carvings show the new king as the sun rising from the

Chac, the Rain God

jaws of the earth, while his predecessor is swallowed up. To prove that the blood of the gods flowed in their veins, members of the ruling family would shed their blood before their subjects; the men by piercing the penis with a bone spike, the women by dragging a thorn-studded cord through a hole in their tongue. After his death, a ruler would be interred in one of the great pyramids, along with many human sacrifices of men, women and children. Some were undoubtedly captured victims of war, but others would have been kept for sacrifice, especially the children.

An elite caste of scribes descended from the Monkey Man gods recorded every aspect of their society. They kept and consulted the sacred calendars and astronomical tables, which dictated every detail of public and private life. The palace household also included nobles and military officers, who could be sent out to govern conquered cities. Further down the hierarchy were the artisans, artists and traders. Of the ordinary people—builders and farmers, peasants and slaves—we know even less than we do of their ancient Egyptian counterparts.

The Maya cities were extremely militaristic, and in a constant state of conflict with neighbouring centres of power. Their aim was not to expand their territory but to capture high-ranking individuals from rival cities, who would then be sacrificed to the gods. This conflict was also ritualized in the Ball Game. The two rival teams were kitted out in helmets and heavy padding, not unlike modern American footballers. The game was played on stone courts with vertical hoops, such as the one which can still be seen at Copán in Honduras. The stakes were high: the losers often ended up on the sacrificial altar. In the *Popol Vuh*, two young men are challenged to a ball game with the lords of the underworld. After the defeat and death of the two young men, the severed head of one of them impregnates Lady Blood by spitting in her hand. She gives birth to the Hero Twins, who defeat the underworld gods in a return match.

Art and Architecture

For the modern traveller in Central America, the most visible remnants of the Classic Maya civilization are the great temples that rise so dramatically from the forests of Guatemala, Honduras and Belize. The most characteristic structures are nearly always known as 'pyramids'. This is a somewhat misleading term, however, as it conjurs up visions of Egypt, where the pyramids are buildings in their own right. In Central America, they are simply the platform on which a temple was constructed. Sometimes the 'pyramids' are wide and relatively low, as at Copán; sometimes they soar almost vertically, as at Tikal (see p. 168). They are usually surrounded by a complex of smaller temples, plazas, ceremonial avenues, and sometimes a ball court.

Maya architecture never achieved the carefully worked, accurately interlocking masonry so characteristic of the Incas of Peru. Maya buildings usually consist of a core of rubble and cement, faced with a thin cladding of dressed stone, and they stay up by sheer mass rather than geometry. The cladding, however, was covered with intricate relief carving and mosaics, and where the stone was too hard to be easily worked, stucco was moulded into spectacular relief. The principle of the arch was unknown to Maya architects; instead, they constructed their massive vaults by overlapping stone slabs until they met in the centre of the roof. The peak of the vault was often crowned by a highly ornamented 'roof comb'. We are accustomed to the mellow hues of weathered stone, and it takes some effort of imagination to picture the temples in their heyday: painted blood red, with the relief moulding picked out in bright colours.

A prominent feature of Maya monumental art was the stela. These large oblong stones, rising up to 10 metres above the ground, usually stood planted before a circular altar slab in the temple plazas. The stelae were intricately carved with stylized portraits of noble rulers; the sides or back recorded crucial dates in Maya hieroglyphs. Only a fraction of the stelae have been deciphered, but it is generally agreed that they record royal lineages, and the dates of important battles, accessions to the throne, royal birthdays and other significant events.

The Maya 'cities' were home only to the gods, the priests, the ruler, and his dead ancestors. The great mass of the population would have lived nearby, in thatched wooden buildings not unlike the ones their descendants inhabit today. It was for the dead, too, that the Maya reserved their finest pottery and artefacts of jade, obsidian, crystal and other minerals and precious stones. Many surviving vases illustrate scenes of the underworld, and pottery figurines of gods, humans and animals are frequently recovered from graves. The National Museum of Archaeology and Ethnology and the Popol Vuh Museum in Guatemala City (see p. 82) have excellent collections of Maya ceramics, jade and other artefacts.

The Maya Alphabet

Shield Jaguar   *Accession Glyph*   *Birthday Glyph*   *Bird Jaguar*   *Prefix—Female Names and Titles*

Ever since their first discovery by Europeans, the complex inscriptions on Maya architecture and monuments have baffled even the most expert epigraphers. We know far less about the Maya script than we do about Egyptian hieroglyphics, but from what we do know, it is even more complicated than Chinese. Maya scribes made virtuosic use of a complex system. They had a phonetic symbol for every syllable, but also used pictographic images—a flame to signify the word hot, for example. They would also use pictographs to represent the sound or meaning of individual syllables in a word. Furthermore, there are many homonyms in the Maya script, so that the same symbol can have very different meanings depending on the context. For example, the words 'sky', 'four', 'snake' and 'captive' are all pronounced identically and can only be distinguished in the proper context.

Many studies have failed because they have tried to bend this system to the concept behind the Western alphabet. Bishop Landa was one of the first to try this, but never realized that his Maya informant was often giving him the name for a letter, but not the variety of meanings it could carry. Eventually the Maya nobleman's patience wore thin, and he wrote 'I don't want to' in the bishop's book.

Among the small groups of symbols whose meaning the experts agree on are the emblem glyphs for a number of important Classic centres such as Tikal, Yaxchilán, or Quiriguá, and the glyphs relating to noble lineages and important events in their dynastic history. The symbols for birth, death, and accession to power have been recognized, and often their dates have also been found in surrounding glyphs or pictures. Symbols found at Yaxchilán, on the river Usumacinta in the Petén jungle, tell us that the city was ruled by the Jaguar dynasty, fathered by the great lord Shield Jaguar, during the 8th century. The extent of a city's military and political power is often demonstrated by the appearance of its unique emblem glyph at other sites, representing conquest or an advantageous royal marriage.

Maya Arithmetic

The concept of zero, so essential to any advanced mathematics, has been thought of only twice in human history: once in India around 600 BC, and once in Central America. Exactly when it first appeared in Central America is not certain, but it was already in use by the time the Maya came on the scene.

The system of Maya arithmetic was vigesimal, based on factors of 20, but had been adjusted to fit in with the calendar. The numerals were arranged in vertical columns, which increased in value from bottom to top. There were just three symbols: a dot signified 1, a horizontal bar signified 5, and a stylized shell signified zero.

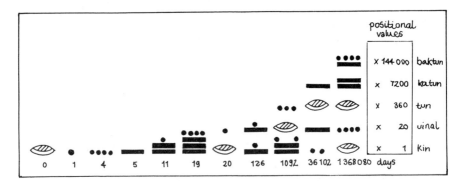

The Maya Calendar

The Maya were obsessed with time, and the keeping of time. The fate of each person was ordained by the date and timing of their birth, and the interpreters of the celestial and divine cycles held immense power over the population, including the nobility. One of the four surviving pre-Conquest books, the Dresden Codex, contains an extraordinarily accurate table of the movements and eclipses of the planet Venus.

From Pre-Classic times, the Maya used two different calendars. Who invented them is uncertain, but most believe that it was probably the Olmecs, and that the Maya simply refined the existing systems handed down to them. The Long Count is a system that hinges on a fixed date in the past, like the Christian calendar, and begins at 4 Ahau 8 Cumku, the equivalent of a day in 3113 BC. According to their belief, this was the beginning of a historic cycle of 13 baktuns (periods of 144,000 days). This cycle is due to be destroyed in the year equivalent to the Christian year of AD 2012, when a new age will begin.

The Maya also used the Calendar Round, which estimated time in cycles of 260 days, each of which held important information for fortunes and ceremonials. This system involved the use of two calendars which ran concurrently. The first consisted of 20 named days with 13 numbers; the second of 365 days, divided into 18 months of 20 days each, with five extra days, called Uayeb, which were considered highly unlucky.

The best way to understand this system in operation is to imagine two interlocking cogwheels of different sizes:

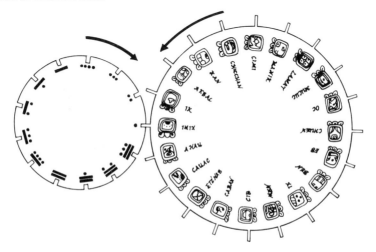

For the two components of this giant cycle to make one completion required 52 solar years, and marked one of the Mayas' most important ceremonial dates.

Use of the Long Count was abandoned towards the end of the Classic Age, and the latest dates known from monumental inscriptions match our year AD 909, taken from a stela at the Mexican site of Tonina. The Calendar Round, however, is still in use today.

The Living Heritage

Although much Maya learning has been lost, centuries of persecution have failed to eradicate it entirely. The Maya Indians survive, and their languages, culture and religion are still a part of their everyday lives. The daykeepers or shamans living in the Western Highlands of Guatemala still keep the sacred knowledge of the Calendar Round. Predominantly Indian towns and villages, such as Chichicastenango, Santiago Atitlán, and Momostenango, are well known for their periodic festivals. But since secrecy has been the key to survival, foreigners are unlikely to witness any ritual ceremonies relating to the Calendar Round. In **San Andrés Itzapa**, however, you can experience the cult of Maximón, a strange hybrid of Maya and Catholic ritual. In a side-street chapel, the cigar-toting effigy of the saint is liberally anointed with rum under the benevolent gaze of the priest. Outside the celebrations continue as fireworks are let off under the auspices of the Maya daykeeper. It is this resilience and power of adaptation that has kept the Maya tradition alive, and makes it one of the most exciting features of Central America today.

Central American Literature: an Introduction

Mis ojos miraban en hora de ensueños
La página blanca.
Y vino el desfile de ensueños y sombras.

It was the hour of dreams. In front of me
A snow-white page outspread I seemed to see.
And a procession came of dreams and shades.

Rubén Darío, *The White Page*

Central American literature has an ancestry at least as old as the Maya civilization itself. The lowland Maya were writing books on deerskin, or paper made from pulverized bark as early as AD 500, and the knowledge they contained stretched back far further. Some, like the *Book of Chilam Balam* and the *Popol Vuh*, recorded creation myths, prophesies and acts of the gods. Others dealt with crop cycles and astronomical calculations. There were histories, biographies, atlases, almanacs and calendars. Written on sheets of paper anything up to 6 m long and folded into pages like a concertina, the manuscripts were elaborately and exuberantly illustrated.

When Franciscan monks arrived bearing the Bible, the Indian priests replied that they preferred to trust their own sacred texts. What followed was a literary holocaust comparable to the destruction of the library at Alexandria. The Spanish burned the 'books of the idolatrous priests' wherever they could find them, often consigning their owners to the flames as well. Only four Quiché Maya manuscripts survive today. The Spanish-Tlaxcalan mestizo Diego Muñoz Camargo recorded the scene in a drawing that accompanies his *History of Tlaxcala*. As two Spanish friars torch a pile of books, gods and animals leap from the flames, as if liberated from the page to inhabit the air.

The Colonial Era
The first colonial writers of Spanish America were the conquistadors themselves and the hard-headed priests who accompanied them. At his house in Antigua, Guatemala, Bernal Díaz del Castillo (1495?–1584), veteran of 119 battles, wrote his argumentative *True History of the Conquest of New Spain* to refute all other accounts. The conquistadors' arch-critic, Father Bartolomé de las Casas (1474–1565), also lived in Antigua for a while. His *Brief Account of the Destruction of the Indies* (1552) described Spanish atrocities in horrific detail, and caused much liberal hand-wringing back in Madrid. To show that the Highland Maya

of Guatemala could be converted to Christianity by peaceable means, he composed hymns in their Quiché language.

Early colonial bards penned ponderous epics extolling the feats of Cortés and Alvarado in the heroic style of ancient Rome and Renaissance Italy, while the church churned out devotional tracts, often in Nahuatl and other indigenous languages. The enterprising priests also wrote and staged sacred dramas (*autos sacramentales*). Like the medieval mystery plays, these were based on Bible stories and performed in the native language with singing, dancing, comic interludes and audience participation.

But New Spain was not a propitious environment for the development of literature. All publications had to be vetted by the censors in Madrid, and Spanish printers held a monopoly which allowed them to flood the provinces with their work. Under these conditions it is hardly surprising that the bulk of Central American literature was provincial and derivative. Little poetry of note was written, and no novels at all.

Meanwhile, the gods and animals that flew from the burning pages of the sacred books still hovered in the air. Storytellers handed down ancestral knowledge from one generation to the next. From sympathy or curiosity, some of the Spanish priests began to write down, from the memories of the Indians, the texts they had themselves destroyed. Even Bishop Diego Landa, the most zealous of the book burners, turned his hand to ethno-history. It is thanks to their activities that the *Popol Vuh* survives today; the earliest copy dates from around 1700.

The *autos sacramentales*, meanwhile, began to assume a life of their own in the hands of their Indian performers. Fables, allegories, parables and satire became important weapons against censorship, and a means of protest against oppression. Brutal landlords could be hidden in animal or mythical characters, ignominiously defeated and held up to ridicule. The comic interludes, often based on Indian folklore, gradually became longer, and in some cases supplanted the Christian element altogether. One such play, the *Baile del Güegüence* from Nicaragua, was written down in the 19th century, although it is probably older. The knockabout plot concerns a Spanish governor who can't afford to stage the customary songs and dances for the Royal Council. He arrests the *güegüence* (village elder) and tries to extort money from him. After much singing, dancing and bawdy farce, the wisecracking elder outwits his blustering overlord.

From Independence to Modernismo

Just as Central America was slow to be drawn into the independence movement of the early 19th century, it was slow to be drawn into the literary tumult that followed. Writers to the north and south, from Mexicali to Tierra del Fuego, produced a torrent of poems, plays and novels celebrating revolution and erotic love, the Aztec warriors of the past and the gauchos of the present. They lurched giddily from the romantic idealism of Byron and Shelley to the gritty realism of Zola. They devoured the latest European authors while proclaiming *americanismo* in literature.

By the time Central America got in on the act, young writers had found a new creed: *modernismo*. The movement began in Cuba and Mexico, but the Nicaraguan Rubén Darío (1867–1916) became its brightest star and acknowledged leader with the publication of his volume of poems *Azul* in 1888.

Modernismo was a far cry from what the name might suggest to a 20th-century reader. A reaction against realism, it was intended to be 'art for art's sake'. Refined, sensual and otherworldly, it owed much to the French symbolists. But Darío, whose ancestry combined Amerindian, Spanish and African, successfully fused the contradictory heritage of the continent into a truly Latin American literature. The beauty of the Nicaraguan landscape suffuses his work, and although Walt Whitman and Edgar Allan Poe were among his literary heroes, this did not prevent him from taking a stab at Yankee imperialism in his poem 'A Roosevelt'.

Darío's fame took him all over Latin America, where his prestige was enormous; to France, where he met Paul Verlaine; and to the United States, where he caught the pneumonia that killed him shortly after his return to Nicaragua. He was Central America's first poet of international stature. 'To enter the city of Nicaraguan poetry,' Steven F. White has written in *Poets of Nicaragua*, 'one must first pass the landmark that guards the gates—Rubén Darío'.

The 20th Century: Magical Realism and Political Commitment

Modern Latin American literature conjures up famous names like the Chilean Isabel Allende, the Argentinean Jorge Luis Borges, the Peruvian Mario Vargas Llosa, the Colombian Gabriel García Márquez, or the Mexican Carlos Fuentes. Yet that peculiarly Latin American form of literature we call magical realism was invented almost singlehanded by the Guatemalan novelist Miguel Angel Asturias (1899–1974). As a young man in Paris, he assisted in the translation of the *Popol Vuh*, which was to influence all his future writing; wrote his first important book, *Leyendas de Guatemala* (Legends of Guatemala, 1930); and completed his novel *El señor Presidente* (The President). He returned to Guatemala in 1933, to spend a miserable decade struggling with political repression, alcoholism and an unhappy marriage. *El señor Presidente* remained unpublished until 1946.

These experiences found an outlet in his best-known book, *Hombres de maíz* (Men of Maize, 1949). This ambitious novel draws on Maya legend, the theories of Marx and Freud, and the literary techniques of Joyce and Eliot, to give a form and a voice to the traumatized subconscious of Guatemala. Like Darío, Asturias conjures up a 'procession of dreams and shades', testifying to the colonization of the spirit as well as of the land; to the loss of identity and masculine pride; and to the powerlessness to keep a woman or refuse a drink. Ariel Dorfman, the Chilean author of *Death and the Maiden*, has described *Hombres de maíz* as 'both the fountainhead and the backbone of all that is being written in our continent today.' Although driven into exile by the 1954 coup, Asturias had recovered his confidence as a writer. Many other novels followed, including his 'Banana Trilogy', which satirizes the activities of the United Fruit Company in Guatemala, and in 1967 he won the Nobel Prize for Literature.

Throughout the 20th century, Central American literature has been closely allied to politics. The Nicaraguan poetic renaissance kindled by Rubén Darío soon turned to political protest in the work of Salomón de la Selva (1893–1958) and the group of poets known as the Vanguard. Inspired by the guerrilla leader Augusto César Sandino, the Vanguard combined poetic avant-gardism with the rhythms of popular songs in a celebration of daily lives and work of the *campesinos* (peasant farmers). One major figure stands outside this mainstream: Alfonso Cortés (1893–1969), affectionately known as *el poeta loco*. After a mental breakdown in 1927, Cortés inscribed his startling, otherworldly poetry on minute pieces of paper while chained to the wall in the house, which had once belonged to Rubén Darío, where he lived with his sisters.

When the Sandinistas came to power in 1979, it seemed as though the poets had actually become the *acknowledged* legislators, if not of the world, at least of Nicaragua. The vice-president was novelist Sergio Ramírez (1942–), whose compelling tales of the influence of North American culture on his country, *Stories* and *To Bury our Fathers*, were published by Readers International in 1976 and 1984 respectively. The internationally respected poet Ernesto Cardenal (1925–), a veteran of the Vanguard movement, was minister of culture; their ambassador to Brazil was the poet Ernesto Gutiérrez (1929–); even the president, Daniel Ortega, was a published poet. Among the fine poets who emerged during these years were Giaconda Belli and Vidaluz Meneses. The daughter of a general in Anastasio Somoza's loathed National Guard, Meneses attempted to come to terms with this painful relationship in her poem 'Last Postcard for my Father'.

Throughout Central America, writers have continued to publish clandestinely in the face of state repression. Quite a few have been the target of assassination or forced into exile. Some, like Salvadoreans Manlio Argueta (1935–)—the author of *One Day of Life* and *Cuzcatlán*—and Jacinta Escudos (1961–) or the Panamanian Bertalicia Peralta (1939–), have been translated into English. Many others have not. *And We Sold the Rain*, edited by Rosario Santos (Ryan Publishing, 1989), provides a good general introduction for English-speaking readers. This collection of short stories offers a glimpse into the lives of the men, women and children of Central America: Maya Indians, Marxist guerrillas and *campesinos*, living, through war and poverty, at the edge of life and death.

Music

Central America's natural history is an interesting blend of the immediate north and south, but its musical roots are far more widespread, combining the rhythms of Africa, native America, the Caribbean, Europe and the US to create a series of unique and energetic hybrids. The entire isthmus is rocked by rhythm, and whether you are in a café, on a bus or walking down the street you'll never be far from the sound of a radio. Central Americans have a passion for music and and a great talent for dance. Their various tastes reflect the region's main historical and cultural divisions. From the steamy, erotic dance-floors of Managua to the misty villages of Guatemala, music is a means of communication and self-expresssion, an essential ingredient in daily life.

Music also played an important role in the region's pre-Columbian cultures, although few details are known. The only surviving instruments are small clay ocarinas which make a high-pitched whistling sound. Nevertheless, archaeologists believe that animal-skin drums, rattles and flutes were all in use and that music enhanced the impact of religious ceremonies, increasing the sense of awe upon which the power of the religious elite depended. It is a theory supported by the murals at the Maya site of Bonampak (on the border between Guatemala and Mexico), which clearly show an assembled orchestra alongside the portrait of a ruler and his assistant.

These ancient traditions doubtless feed the music of today's Indian groups, who still use music in their fiestas and religious ceremonies, although these days they have absorbed a wide range of influences. Most Indian bands still include drums, flutes and whistles, but the principal instrument is now the marimba, a long xylophone-type instrument sometimes played by three or four musicians. The marimba features in most Central American styles, favoured by Indian groups and farmers from Guatemala to Costa Rica and sometimes accompanied by guitars and singers. It's a soft, lilting style of music, appropriate enough to the highlands and to local fiestas, but rarely heard in the cities. Meanwhile, in the wilds of Panamá they have developed a unique and haunting style called *típica*, in which a wailing woman is accompanied by a furious African drum beat. To an outsider the music is disturbing but local people seem to enjoy it, picking out enough rhythm to dance enthusiastically.

The marimba is, in fact, of African origin, having arrived in Central America via Jamaica and the slave trade, although Central America's black communities, based on the Caribbean coast, have now moved on to the more modern sounds of calypso and reggae. The English influence is strong here and many of the local bands sing in English, taking their lead from heroes such as Bob Marley. A local Belizean variation is *Brukdown* which is firmly rooted in creole culture and includes the guitar, banjo, accordion and drums. In Bluefields, Nicaragua, local people still dance the *Palo de Mayo*, replacing its English refrain with a more blatant sexual style. Here the big bands are Dimensión Costeña and Caribe, both churning out a specifically Latin reggae which is big in dance-halls across the isthmus.

Classical music has never really taken off in this part of the world, although the Costa Ricans have struggled to introduce high culture to Central American listeners. Back in the 1940s President Figueres declared 'why have tractors without violins?' and Costa Rica now has the only National Youth Symphony in Latin America. It's not a musical style that has spread to the streets but nevertheless they do stage a series of concerts every year and musicians from around the world perform in San José's Teatro Nacional, undoubtedly the most beautiful theatre on the isthmus.

Back in the world of mestizo popular culture it's *salsa* and *meringue* which are the great Latin sounds, booming out across the dance-floors from Guatemala to Panamá. A lot of the big hits come up from Brazil, Venezuela and Colombia, while other styles, including traditional *mariachi*, which is sometimes played in the streets, come south from Mexico. Meanwhile modern rock and pop music from Europe and the US is also extremely popular with the likes of Madonna and Michael Jackson competing for air-time. Songs come and go here as quickly as anywhere else and the importance of radio ensures that they are widely known. On a typical dance-floor contemporary Latin sounds are mixed evenly with pop and rock, and in this, as in most things, Central America is walking the tightrope, unsure where it belongs.

Some Central American Stereotypes

Banana Republics
Bananas have been one of the great shaping forces in modern Central America. Introduced as a sideline by the company which built Costa Rica's Atlantic railway, banana plantations still dominate much of the Pacific coast from Belize to Panamá, although the political power of the banana companies is not what it once was. The companies grew and developed during the thirties and forties, reaching their zenith in 1955 when the almighty United Fruit Company was able to engineer a coup in Guatemala after the government threatened the compulsory puchase of its unused land. (The coup was backed by the CIA, who have always played a key role in keeping the world safe for banana producers.) Today bananas are still

grown in the steamy lowlands of all Central American republics and in many areas the banana company still dominates the economy. Towns such as Bananera in Guatemala and Almirante in Panamá are almost entirely owned by banana companies and come complete with company housing, shops and transport; in Bananera there is even a small golf course for ex-pat executives.

The Oligarchy
The Generals. Central America's generals have a long history of manipulating the political agenda and it is only in Costa Rica that they remain excluded from power, thanks to the abolition of the armed forces. Elsewhere the men in uniform have always played a major role and at one time or another the army has ruled every one of the republics.

The generals were at their most powerful and eccentric in the early years of this century. Jorge Ubico, who ruled Guatemala from 1930 to 1944 believed that he was a reincarnation of Napoleon, surrounded himself with replica cannons and had the Guatemalan symphony orchestra dressed in military uniform. Meanwhile in El Salvador General Maximiliano Hernández Martínez, a classic Latin American despot who combined extremes of eccentricity and brutality, hung coloured lights in San Salvador in a bid to prevent the spread of smallpox.

In more recent times the generals have shown themselves capable of horrific brutality, killing hundreds of thousands in civil wars in Nicaragua, El Salvador and Guatemala. Thankfully the troops are currently in the process of returning to their barrack. Yet, ousted in Panamá and pushed to one side in Nicaragua, Guatemala and El Salvador, the army still manages to cast a strong shadow over the political agenda and retains a great deal of power. This may not be apparent at first, for techniques have become increasingly sophisticated and the sight of tanks on the streets appears to be a thing of the past. These days the generals flex their muscles through the press, and rumours of a coup serve to keep the government on the straight and narrow.

The last general to be in direct control of his country was the infamous General Manuel Noriega, who used Panamá as a warehouse for the storage and shipment of drugs, guns and money, but was finally deposed by US troops in December 1989.

Coffee Barons. Throughout Central America coffee remains the golden bean and a flicker in the coffee price sends shock waves through the governments of Costa Rica, El Salvador and Guatemala—where the economy is still rooted in coffee production and the coffee producer is a significant man. While light industry is the territory of tomorrow's entrepreneurs, the coffee barons remain a very influential section of the traditional right-wing oligarchy. They are traditional in all they do with a strongly conservative streak and a deep disregard for the workforce (who are mostly press-ganged peasants in El Salvador and Guatemala, while in Costa Rica the relatively high standard of living threatens to undermine the coffee harvest and impoverished labourers now have to be imported from Nicaragua to prevent the beans rotting on the bushes). Ironically it is extremely difficult to get a good cup of coffee in Central America, although the Café Tirol in Cobán, Guatemala is recommended.

Death Squads. Despite the much vaunted sweeping tide of democracy the death squads are still very much in operation, particularly in Guatemala and El Salvador. Responding to international pressure, the armed forces have adopted a new respectable image but old habits die hard and the traditional means of control are still employed on a regular basis. Off-duty policemen and soldiers still act as judge, jury and executioner, when dealing with those they consider their enemies. Their targets have changed little since the early 1960s: the victims are still union leaders, left-wing politicians and human rights workers.

Drugs

Latin America's main producers of marijuana and cocaine remain the giants of Colombia, Peru and Bolivia, with limited production in Central America itself. Nevertheless the isthmus plays a key role as a link with the lucrative northern markets and the shipment of drugs is a growth industry. Cocaine by the ton is regularly intercepted in Central America, with light aircraft, lorries and small boats shuttling merchandise from south to north. Cheap, high-quality drugs are available throughout the isthmus and drug abuse is widespread, taking a heavy toll in certain areas, particularly Colón, Panamá City, Belize City and Puerto Limón, where crack use is now widespread and has spawned an epidemic of violent crime.

Some Key Players

Don Pedro de Alvarado

Handsome, blond, muscular, brave, restless and deeply ruthless, Don Pedro de Alvarado was the archetypal conquistador, tearing through Central America in search of gold and laying waste to all that stood in his way. Alvarado arrived in Guatemala in 1523, sent south by Cortés to claim Central America for the Spanish and instructed to 'preach matters concerning the Holy faith'. Once in Guatemala Alvarado adopted his own approach. Almost immediately his meagre army was confronted by some 30,000 Quichéan warriors. However, he was able to play one faction off against another and used the warring tribes to fight his battles for him. According to Maya accounts the first epic battle ended in a personal duel between Alvarado and the Quichéan king, Tecún Umán, who wore a headdress of Quetzal feathers. Alvarado eventually triumphed. Following their defeat the Quichés invited Alvarado to their capital, Utatlán, but before he entered the city he grew suspicious and had the entire place burnt to the ground.

From 1524 until his death in 1541 Alvarado ruled Guatemala as a personal fiefdom, rewarding his followers with vast tracts of land and the right to use the Indians as they saw fit. He established his headquarters in what is now Antigua, which became the colonial capital for all of Central America. Meanwhile, disappointed by the lack of gold, Alvarado grew increasingly restless and took part in a series of other expeditions, travelling as far as Peru and Mexico. In 1541, on the way to the Spice Islands, he was killed under a rolling horse.

When news of Alvarado's death reached his wife, Beatriz de la Cueva, she plunged Antigua into mourning, had the royal palace painted black, inside and out, and ordered the city authorities to appoint her as the new governor. Then, for several days the entire area was swept by furious storms and, on 10 September 1541, a powerful earthquake shook the valley, releasing a massive volume of water that had built up in the cone of the Agua volcano. A tide of mud and water swept down the mountain and the city was buried beneath it.

Ronald Reagan
Although he rarely visited Central America, Ronald Reagan had the most profound and destabilizing effect on the isthmus and contributed to much of the political turmoil that still persists today. A deep commitment to right-wing politics and fear of communism lead Reagan to take an uncompromising stance on Central America, redirecting US policy from Panamá to Guatemala.

He was dogmatically against the Sandinista regime in Nicaragua, to which he devoted a great deal of energy, eventually bogging himself down in the Irangate scandal. And, although the previous US president, Jimmy Carter, had offered the olive branch to the Sandinistas, Reagan, beginning in 1982, laid siege to the country, providing enormous funds for the rebel Contra army and imposing a trade blockade which crippled Nicaragua's economy. The conflict forced the country into ruin and eventually destroyed the Sandinista government.

In Guatemala he also reversed US policy. In the seventies President Carter cut off US aid in protest against the mounting tide of human rights abuse, but in 1981, with the generals still in power, Reagan lifted the ban on arms sales, ensuring that the army remained a formidable force in Guatemalan politics. Almost a decade later President Bush again suspended arms sales after the army was implicated in the 'death squad' killing of Mike Devine, a US citizen living in Guatemala.

In El Salvador the Reagan administration dropped US support for a seventies programme of limited agrarian reform and put itself behind the army in a commitment to the war of attrition being waged against the FMLN (Farabundo Martí National Liberation Front). The policy increased the intensity of the conflict and deepened the divisions which continued to tear the country apart until long after the end of the Reagan administration.

With regard to Panamá, Reagan was equally determined. Of the canal, he said: 'We bought it, we paid for it, it's ours and we should tell Torrijos and company that we are going to keep it.' It was an attitude which hardened anti-US sentiment in Panamá; thus, when General Torrijos was replaced by his bright young officer, Manuel Noriega, the two countries were locked on collision course. This was the origin of yet another Central American time bomb, which President Reagan eventually handed on to Bush and which has left another corner of Central America in tatters.

Melodrama on the Buses

Of all the Central American melodramas the bus journey is perhaps the most gripping. The show opens with the bus quietly ticking over as the bus-boy hustles business. Rushing around the bus terminal he generates a real sense of urgency, hurrying passengers onto the bus. His priorities are clear: it doesn't matter who you are or where you're going provided you take a seat. Passengers are packed in, waiting in the heat for hours, and the tension steadily mounts. Finally the bus-boy steps into the driver's seat and revs the engine; but this first roar is almost always a false alarm, a little taster to remind the passengers that the bus still works and will eventually leave. More passengers are then packed in, accompanied by chickens, goats and pigs. Here the skills of the bus-boy are stretched to the limit as he attempts to fill the bus to more than double its capacity. Once he is satisfied with his handiwork he again takes the driver's seat, but this time he sounds the horn, summoning the leading man.

Rolling out of a nearby bar, like an overweight prima donna, the bus driver steps onto the stage. He lingers, perhaps airing his belly or picking food from his teeth, and helps a pretty young girl into the seat beside him. As the passengers start to murmur and fidget he pauses to share a joke with another driver, reminding everyone that they're totally dependent on him.

Then, finally in position, the driver is transformed, overcome by a furious sense of urgency. Heading out of town and onto the open road he races through the streets, scattering private cars and pedestrians. On the highway he considers himself the undisputed king of the road, and uses every blind corner to flex his machismo, overtaking with hair-raising confidence. The driver's biggest problem is that both the police and truck drivers also consider themselves the undisputed kings of the road. In most countries truck and bus drivers have formed an alliance and use a complex series of hand signals to warn each other of impending danger, while police are held at bay by healthy backhanders. Meanwhile others, including cyclists and car drivers, soon learn that they are unwelcome intruders. In El Salvador road signs plead with drivers to watch out for cyclists, reminding them that 'he could be your brother'.

Having driven as though every second counted, barely pausing to scoop up waiting passengers, the bus screeches to a halt at a roadside café. Here a special room is often set aside for the driver and he eats an enormous amount of food, whatever the time of day, lingering over a last bowl of soup as the passengers sweat it out in the bus, eager to move on.

Contact between the driver and his passengers is usually quite limited. However, in the event of a breakdown, things often change swiftly as everyone on the bus unites in hardship.

With any luck it won't happen to you, although do bear in mind that these are dangerous roads. High in the Guatemalan highlands many a bus has tumbled over the side, and their rusting carcases are still there to be seen. It's a sight to make you wonder why on earth you embarked on this journey; while to a driver it is a tribute to his immense bravery, and a reminder that they need men like him more than ever.

Part IV

GUATEMALA

Guatemala is a small country, known for volcanoes and cruelty. When I crossed the frontier from Mexico I alternately lifted up my eyes to the hills, and scanned the roadside for corpses. There weren't any, and I felt slightly cheated by the books about Guatemala I had read.

Anthony Daniels, *Sweet Waist of America*

Guatemala is like that. On the one hand you know that terrible things have happened here, still happen here, but on the other hand, you almost never see any evidence of it. Human rights violations usually occur behind closed doors, in remote areas of the country or at night, and are rarely reported in the local press. Instead you see a country whose beauty is unmatched in Central America: a country where smouldering volcanoes rise above green and golden highland valleys, mysterious cloud forests are shrouded in swirling mists, and seemingly endless tropical jungles hide ancient pyramids of the lost Maya civilization. It only takes a few hours to travel from temperate highlands to steamy jungle, another aspect of this tiny country that confuses and delights.

Roughly the size of Ireland or the American state of Connecticut, Guatemala's northern frontier is with Mexico. To the northwest, the Pacific plain soon rises up into the highest mountain range in Central America, the Cuchumatanes, and the border roughly follows this chain northeast until it sinks into the Petén jungle, at which point the official border turns a sharp east before bulging out again to encompass a large area of the Petén lowlands, which make up a third of the entire country. If it wasn't for Belize, most of Guatemala's eastern border would be the Caribbean Sea. Instead an almost vertical borderline divides the two countries, and Guatemala's share of the Caribbean is limited to a tiny bite at the beginning of the Gulf of Honduras. Running diagonally from northeast to southwest, Guatemala's southern border is first with Honduras and then with El Salvador, while the western border is made up by the Pacific coast.

The country divides into distinct geographic regions. The west is characterized by a slim Pacific plain which soon rises into the Western Highlands punctuated by a string of volcanoes towering above a fertile landscape of maize and bean fields, and dotted with countless Indian hamlets and villages. This is the heartland of the modern Maya. Just over half the population are pure descendants of the Maya tribes who have inhabited the region for millennia, speaking their own languages, wearing their finely embroidered weaving, and stubbornly holding on to their traditions. Many of their ancient customs have become mixed with Catholic rituals, and the result is an annual calendar peppered with riotous festivals, where pagan dances accompany huge processions for Christian saints, and acts of worship can include anything from smoking cigars to sacrificing chickens. The weekly markets, which form the cornerstone of Maya social life, are also notable. Every town and village has its own market day, when the Indians come to sell their produce—predominantly maize, beans, cereals and other vegetables, while exchanging the latest gossip or discussing possible marriages.

Eastern Guatemala is clearly divided into two parts: the southeast is cut in two by the desert valley of the Motagua river, which is the main corridor from the Western Highlands to the Atlantic coast, with dry hills leading up towards the borders with Honduras and El Salvador on one side, and the moist Verapaz highlands rising towards the north. In these regions you will find mainly *ladino* culture, which is characterized by a strong Spanish influence. Fiercely Catholic, the people are mestizos, representing all shades of colour from European to Indian, with the occasional black descendant from the West Indies, though most of those live in one single place: the Atlantic settlement of Livingston which can only be reached by boat. *Ladino* is not a racial term, however. Even a pure Indian is a *ladino* if he has abandoned his traditional dress and language in favour of the Spanish inherited culture, and it is a sad fact that many feel pressured to do so to avoid discrimination and abuse.

Beyond the Motagua valley and the Verapaz, the landscape descends onto the Petén plain and the dense jungle that eventually melts into the Mexican Yucatán peninsula. This is the least populated area of Guatemala, though once it was home to the famous civilization that built the giant pyramids of Tikal, now only inhabited by tropical birds, such as toucans and scarlet macaws, and troops of howler monkeys whose loud grunts fill the air at every dusk.

Travelling by bus is the best way to explore this little country. Services are frequent and extremely cheap, making it possible to get from one end of the country to the other in no more than a day, for less than US$5. The distance from the Pacific to the Atlantic coast by road is just 403 km, while from the Mexican to Salvadorean border is no more than 299 km. To reach the Maya pyramids is also easy, since at least three flights daily connect the capital with the jungle town of Flores, near the ruins of Tikal. Because of the country's accessible nature, a short visit of two weeks would still be plenty of time to see a great deal of the country, and if you stayed for six weeks, you would have no trouble seeing the entire country and much of what it has to offer.

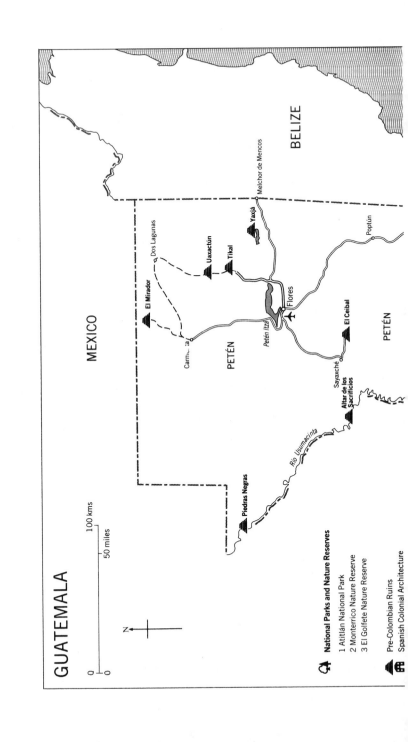

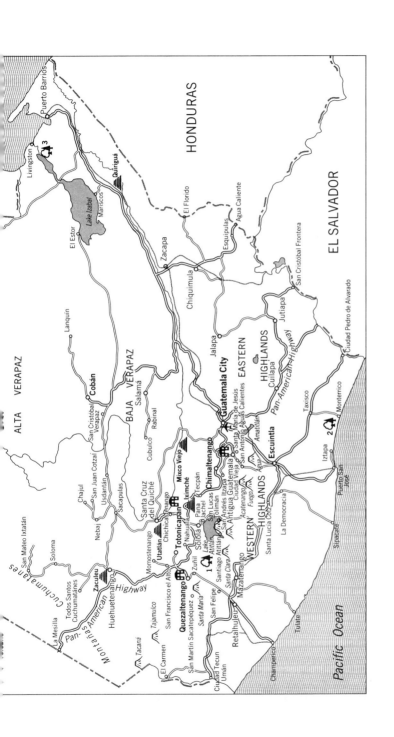

Post-Independence History

A Tragic Heritage

Guatemala's history has always been marred by violence, both natural and human. Earthquakes in the region destroyed the first two colonial capitals, and even Guatemala City has suffered repeated quake damage. Every time buildings and lives were wrecked political change came hot on the heels of physical destruction. The last time was in 1976, when around 25,000 people lost their lives in a huge earthquake that rocked the Western Highlands. In the aftermath of social and economic distress, political unrest grew and the struggling guerrilla groups founded in the 1960s emerged fortified with a new Indian support base. For the first time in centuries, the Indians formed their own armed resistance: the Guerrilla Army of the Poor (EGP) and the Organization of the People in Arms (ORPA). They, and similar organizations, were annihilated by the army in a 10-year counterinsurgency campaign, though the beginning of the 1990s has been marked by a small increase in guerrilla activities, and the armed forces still have a battle on their hands, even if most of the population has been intimidated sufficiently not to support armed opposition.

The country's history is one of the saddest in Central America, beginning with the brutal destruction of Maya tribes in the 16th and 17th centuries, through to the colonial era of institutionalized slavery, and on to the 19th and 20th centuries, which brought more loss of land for the surviving Indians, as well as marginalization and continued abuse.

In the meantime, the new order of creoles and mestizos (called *ladinos* in Guatemala) treated each other only marginally better, and post-Independence society grew accustomed to warring factions fighting for political control, coups and assassinations. The tradition from earliest times was that the strongest man wins political power, by force or fraud, so that democratic processes have never found fertile ground—or rather, they have always been nipped in the bud. This is especially the case in Guatemala, since the majority of the population has long been under the yoke of a small, conservative elite of landowners and the armed forces, traditionally kept in power by US military and economic aid.

The Struggle for Power

The aftermath of Independence, in 1821, brought political fragmentation to Guatemala, which was the traditional seat of colonial power in Central America. On the one side were the Spanish-descended ruling class, who under the colonial administration had always held all important positions of power, as well as having the best pick of the land and its resources, including Indian labour. They were the conservative bastion of a fading empire, determined to hold on to their power and privileges, by force if necessary. Ranged against this formidable group were the mestizos, of Spanish and Indian blood, who had long resented their enforced subservience to the Imperial Spanish Crown and dreamt of complete independence from Spain and her colonial administrators. Deeply influenced by Liberal ideology, they too were prepared to back up their convictions with force, and so it wasn't long before Conservative and Liberal forces were going to battle in various parts of the region. Meanwhile the Maya Indians were at best helpless spectators to the civil war, and at worst forcibly conscripted into armies fighting a cause that had no truck with their concerns.

In 1829, the Liberal forces of Honduran general Francisco Morazán invaded Guatemala, and a year later he became President of the United Provinces of Central America, which had been founded in 1823, though the fighting had never allowed it to develop properly. This marked the temporary end for Guatemalan Conservative forces. The Central American federation, however, did not survive, breaking up into separate republics in 1839, while Francisco Morazán was executed in 1842.

In the new Guatemalan republic the Conservatives once more gained the upper hand, and the country's first *caudillo* (leader), José Rafael Carrera, ruled intermittently from 1844 until his death in 1865. He succeeded in this by playing both factions of Central American politics against each other, and it was not until Justo Rufino Barrios brought down his successor, in 1871, that Liberals regained the political centre stage.

The Age of Liberal Reforms

The Conservative mid-19th-century rulers of Guatemala only succeeded in strengthening their power base to a limited extent. The traditional Spanish-born elite found itself sharing with the *caudillos* and, increasingly, the limited progress of the country's economic expansion meant that the *ladino* population was forever dissatisfied and always ready to mount opposition. Once chemical substitutes had been found for the country's major export crops of indigo and cochineal, a new economic base had to be found and it was the Liberals who seemed to offer the best solutions.

Justo Rufino Barrios (1871–85) instituted a major reform programme that was intended to modernize Guatemala and make it a competitive force on the world market. This development included building a national road and railway network, founding a professional army, and crucially, promoting new export crops, of which coffee was the most important. To do this much Indian land was confiscated, which sowed the seeds for widespread rural poverty and popular discontent for the coming century. Church land was also confiscated, which was a convenient punishment for the Church's traditional support for the Conservatives.

Foreign investment was encouraged by offering huge tracts of land and no export duties, and by 1900, coffee took up 85% of the country's exports, while the new coffee oligarchy came to dominate not just Guatemala's economy, but also her politics. The Indians were brutally forced off their land and pressed into a system of debt-peonage, whereby they had to work as agricultural labourers with no land of their own to sustain them.

The Liberal dictator presidents succeeded in staying in power for many decades, forging a deadly alliance with the military which ensured their survival. Thus two of Guatemala's most dominant traditions were cemented: the landed coffee oligarchy and the military as political power-broker. State terror ensured that any kind of opposition was crushed, and dictators distinguished themselves by their brutality. A prime example was Manuel Estrada Cabrera (1898–1920), who was such a picture-book baddie that Miguel Angel Asturias used him for the basis of his novel on repression called *El Señor Presidente*.

After the world economic collapse in 1929, the Guatemalan leadership sought to broaden its economic base once more, and foreign investment was further encouraged, especially from the United States. One of the American companies that benefited most was the United Fruit Company, who gained outrageously huge land concessions from both Cabrera and the later dictator president Jorge Ubico (1931–1944). The company came to own more land in Guatemala than anyone else, and controlled not only the Pacific railways, but also the ports, the shipping, and all communications and electric power in its territory. Needless to say it also had decisive political influence, which established another Guatemalan tradition: an economy and government closely tied to North American interests. Under Ubico the government stole a great deal more land from the Indians, and further enslaved them to the new system by creating 'vagrancy laws' which made it illegal for Indians not to work on the coffee and banana plantations for a certain period each year. He also repressed any political opposition, as well as labour unions and rural co-operatives. Death or exile were standard punishments for dissenters, another tradition that has survived to this day.

The Spiritual Socialist

Ubico, however, was overthrown by a military coup in 1944, largely because he lost the support of the US, and also because he made the mistake of alienating sectors of the Guatemalan oligarchy and military, frustrated once more by slow economic progress. Worse still, the carve-up of riches and power between United Fruit and the landed oligarchy left little hope for advancement to ambitious young officers, as well as the country's emergent middle class. Thus Ubico was removed and for the first time elections took place, and Juan José Arévalo was elected.

Arévalo was a teacher and writer, who had spent the Ubico years in exile, and returned to his country determined to right the balance of power and welfare. He espoused a doctrine of what he called 'Spiritual Socialism', and under his five-year presidency many reforms were carried out. Social security was established for the first time, as well as a labour code and rural cooperatives, a national educational and health programme was set up, and open elections were encouraged.

His successor, Jacobo Arbenz, continued Arévalo's reforms and even legalized the Communist Party and allowed other political opposition to thrive. This was revolutionary in the Guatemalan context. But like a moth to the flame, Guatemalan democracy was quickly burnt up by traditional power. What finally made the Arbenz administration unacceptable was the 1952 Agrarian Reform Law, which sought to redistribute land to the rural poor. Only uncultivated land was to be taken, but the small group of landowners resented every inch taken from them, most of all the foreign land owner, United Fruit, who found 400,000 acres of its uncultivated land nationalized in 1953.

The company quickly sought to use its contacts in Washington to lobby the US government and put pressure on the Guatemalan administration. There followed a short period of financial sanctions, diplomatic pressure and covert CIA destabilization tactics. But, finally, it was easier to mount a coup and, in 1954, the CIA's 'Operation Success' helped Colonel Castillo Armas take the Presidential Palace. The Guatemalan army refused to defend Arbenz, and thus the humiliated president left for exile and democracy was at an end. Castillo Armas was confirmed as president a year later, and three decades of murderous repression ensued.

The Military Reign of Terror

Armas only lasted a couple of years before he was assassinated, but he had already returned all nationalized land to its former owners, dismantled the labour unions and peasant associations, and mounted anti-communist propaganda backed up by an armed counter-revolution which left thousands dead. US foreign aid flowed freely once more, and the traditional alliance between the agro-export elite and the military was soon re-established.

Armas was followed by the hated General Miguel Ydígoras Fuentes, who had been head of the Secret Police under Ubico. The military put him in power after the 1957 elections had resulted in uncontrollable riots, and from then onwards, the military was firmly in charge of who ran the country. Ydígoras, however, turned out to be too despotic, even for his military supporters, and reformist officers mounted a coup against him in 1960. They were not successful, but those that escaped the firing squad founded the first armed rebel group in Guatemala: the Revolutionary Armed Forces (FAR). Also founded at this time was the 13th November Revolutionary Movement (MR–13), and both groups turned to Marxism-Leninism and Castro's example for their ideology. Ydígoras was finally overthrown in 1963, and while US military aid increased sharply, so did a brutal counterinsurgency programme, which made any kind of open dissent a life-threatening activity.

The 1960s saw the military tighten its grip on the country, and while presidents occasionally denounced the army's violence, the counterinsurgency campaign remained as virulent as ever. The most notorious campaign of the decade was led by Colonel Carlos Arana Osorio, whose 1968 Zacapa campaign was responsible for the deaths of at least 10,000 civilians. Right-wing death squads also emerged in these years, as certain sectors of the Conservative elite became impatient with the army's inability to wipe out armed rebellion completely. Between the years 1966 and 1970, these squads alone are believed to have killed over 30,000 people. Such was the atmosphere of violence and terror that political opposition was all but silenced, and the 1970 'elections' brought the 'Butcher of Zacapa', Carlos Arana Osorio into power.

The 1970s saw a continuation of the previous decade, the Guatemalan military ruling with US support and vital military aid. Only the 1976 earthquake brought disturbance to the army's tight control over the country, and in the wake of high casualties and even higher numbers of homeless and destitute, guerrilla groups re-emerged and found support from the population's Indian majority. Until this time, the revolutionaries had never considered the needs of the rural Indians nor seen them as natural allies, peasants being traditionally conservative rather than leftist revolutionaries. However, they now began to establish themselves in the Western Highlands and remote north, organizing armed resistance and educational propaganda.

The result of the rebels' move into the countryside was tragic for the Indians. The military subjected them to a genocide of such magnitude that it is only now being fully assessed. They devised a scorched earth policy, and entire villages were razed to the ground, their inhabitants tortured and murdered in the most hideous ways imaginable. A common tactic was to herd the women and children into their local church or community hall, and then set the building on fire, leaving their husbands to listen to their death cries before being murdered themselves. The manner of the army's killings were unspeakable, and the files of Amnesty International are full of horrific eyewitness reports from the few survivors that made it to Mexican and Belizean refugee camps.

In the first months of 1981, 1500 Indians were killed in the Chimaltenango Department alone, and the devastation of land and human life continued. In June 1982, one of the country's most notorious generals took power: General Efraín Ríos Montt. He was installed by the military to reduce corruption and lead the country back towards civilian rule. But instead he launched his 'Beans and Guns' counterinsurgency campaign, and the World Council of Churches reported that the government was responsible for the death of 9000 people between the months of March and July that year. He was an extraordinary character who, while the armed forces were murdering in the countryside, harangued Guatemalans with Sunday sermons on television, when he told them not to fornicate or drink, and lead a Christian life. He was deposed by coup in 1983, and has since returned to preaching for the Church of the World in Guatemala City.

Civilian Rule

The army finally handed government back to civilian rule in 1985, and the Christian Democrat Vinicio Cerezo Arévalo became the first civilian president of Guatemala in 31 years. Naturally the democratic process was initiated on the army's terms and the years of Cerezo's government continued to see military offensives mounted in the countryside, and massacres of civilians still occurred, such as the massacre of 22 peasants in the village of Aguacate, near San Andrés Itzapa, in November 1987, and of 14 Indians in Santiago Atitlán in December 1990.

Cerezo's government was followed by the election of Jorge Serrano Elías in January 1991, who is leader of the right-wing Movement of Solidarity Action (MAS) and won a resounding victory with 68% of the vote. This result, however, must be set against a 55% abstention by registered voters, which reflects widespread disillusion with the democratic process in Guatemala and does not bode well for the future. Guatemala is still ranked high by America's Watch for human rights violations, and the UN Human Rights Commission has also condemned the country for the high number of disappearances. Thus the Guatemalan government lives under the pall of human rights violations by the armed forces and also the constant threat of international sanctions because of it, which will severely hamper the country's economic progress.

The Maya Indians, meanwhile, continue to survive in spite of the genocide of the late 1970s and 80s, and their economic, social and political marginalization. Despite continued exploitation and extreme poverty, the Maya culture and traditions are alive in the countryside, especially in the highlands, and a revitalized tourist industry is taking full advantage of the considerable riches they have to offer. To what extent tourism can replace the continuing urgent need for agrarian reform is debatable. But in some regions, at least, controlled tourism can help Indian communities survive where their traditional economic base has been denied them. However, tourism being volatile and dependent on many things, it can never be considered a long-term solution to the needs of Guatemala's rural population, who make up the vast majority of her people.

General Information

Getting to Guatemala

By Air
The main airlines with regular connections to Guatemala City (La Aurora airport) from Europe or North America are British Airways, KLM, Iberia and Eastern. Coming from Europe, there are only two direct flights, KLM from Amsterdam and Iberia from Madrid, otherwise you usually change planes in Miami or Houston. Coming from North America, there are direct flights from Miami, Houston, New Orleans and Los Angeles, with a greater choice of airlines.

Prices are cheaper if you travel on weekdays, between Monday and Thursday, and tickets with fixed dates are always cheaper than open ones. Scheduled return flights from Europe to Guatemala hover around the £600 mark for the cheapest fare, while bucket shops may be able to knock off up to £100. From North America, expect to pay around $350 return from Miami, and double that figure if coming from New York or Canada.

By Boat
The only maritime connection is from the Belizean port of Punta Gorda to the Guatemalan port of Puerto Barrios, on the Atlantic coast. There are two ferries a week, leaving on Tuesdays and Fridays.

By Train
For hardy and patient travellers coming from North America, there is always the train (see Paul Theroux's *The Old Patagonian Express*). The journey from Mexico City onwards becomes extremely slow and hot, with delays a regular occurrence. Once in Guatemala, the trains are even slower than in Mexico, and officially twelve-hour journeys often end up taking twenty-four hours instead, with no food served on the train. There is no longer a public train connection between Guatemala and San Salvador.

By Bus
Bus connections from North America to Guatemala are cheap and regular, but not direct and it will take you a few days to cross Mexico alone, with another day to reach Guatemala City from the Mexican border. Coming from El Salvador, there is a reliable bus route direct from San Salvador to Guatemala City. Coming from Honduras, there are buses to the border posts of either Agua Caliente (best) or El Florido from the Honduran city of San Pedro Sula, and Guatemalan buses will take you to the capital from there. Coming from Belize, there is a very rough dirt road over the Maya Mountains and through the jungle, connecting Belize City and Belmopan to Flores (occasionally impassable during the rainy season). Normally there are no direct buses, so you can expect a change at the border, where you are at the mercy of unscrupulous bus drivers.

By Car

Driving south from North America in your own car is an option you will only want to consider if you like long-haul driving and your nerves can stand the vagaries of Latin American border officials. You will need faultless documents and separate insurance for each country, and if you find yourself leaving Guatemala without your vehicle, you will have a lot of explaining to do and a heavy import duty to pay—even if it was stolen or destroyed in a crash.

Embassies and Consulates

In the UK: 13 Fawcett Street, London SW10 9HN, tel (071) 351 3042.
In the US: Embassy of the Republic of Guatemala, 2220 R Street, NW Washington DC 20008, tel (202) 745 4952.
9700 Richmond Avenue, Suite 218, Houston, TX 77042, tel (713) 953 9531.
584 South Spring Street, Office 1030, Los Angeles, CA 90013, tel (213) 489 1891.
300 Sevilla Avenue, Oficina 210, Coral Gables, Miami, FL 33134, tel (305) 443 4828.
10405 San Diego Mission Road, Suite 205, San Diego, CA 92108, tel (415) 282 8127.
In Canada: The consulate in Montreal is now closed, but there is an embassy in Ottawa at: 294 Albert Street, Suite 500, Ottawa, Ontario K1P 6E6, tel (613) 237 3941.
In Australia: 39 Ocean Street, Woollahra, Sydney NSW 2025, tel (02) 322 965.
In Mexico: Avenida Esplanada 1025, Lomas de Chapultepec 11000, Mexico D.F. 4, tel (05) 520 2794.

Tourist Offices

Guatemala Tourist Commission in the USA: P.O. Box 144351, Coral Gables, FL 33114–4351, tel (305) 854 1544, fax (305) 854 4589, telex 153777 LMART/MIA.
Consulates and embassies in other countries should be able to supply you with at least some brochures, if no maps. In general, however, the best information available is from the national tourist office in Guatemala City itself (see p. 61).

Passports and Visas

Nationals of member countries of the EC (except Greece), Canada, or the United States, have to obtain either a visa, which is valid for one month and can be extended monthly for a total of six months in all, or a tourist card, which airlines or border officals issue for a US$5 fee. The tourist card is preferable because it is possible to request 90 days in one go, thus only requiring one visit to the immigration office for long-term visitors who wish to stay up to six months. Both types of documentation can also be issued by the Guatemalan consulates abroad. It is always advisable to check with them for the latest entry requirements.

Nationals from Australia or the Republic of Ireland must have a visa to enter Guatemala, available from the nearest consulate or embassy. Applications should be handed in at least a week before travelling, along with your passport and one passport photo, plus the relevant fee.

In the USA you also have the option of applying for a one-year visa, where you get three months on entry, renewable every three months, though it is preferable to leave the country for 72 hours since the extension procedure involves filling in many forms, being finger-printed at the police station, and having to leave your passport with the officials for an indeterminate number of days.

The Immigration Office (*Departamento de Migración*) in Guatemala City is at 41 Calle 17–36, Zona 8, tel (71) 7640. Ask at the INGUAT tourist office for the best bus to take from the city centre. The building is not marked, but you can recognize it for its white square shape, about four storeys high.

Customs

Visas or tourist cards can be issued on entry, but it is better to get them before to avoid delay. Leaving by air, there is an exit fee of about US$4, payable in local or US currency. Leaving by land the exit fee is usually about US$1. Officially you must be in possession of a return flight ticket to enter Guatemala by air, and most airlines in the US will not allow you on the plane without a return ticket. On arrival, you may be asked to show you have enough funds for the duration of your intended visit. Normally a credit card or travellers' cheques worth a few hundred US dollars is enough evidence. In practice, arriving passengers are almost never asked about funds.

On Arrival

Tourist Offices

National Tourist Office (INGUAT), Centro Cívico, Avenida 7 y Vía 1, Ciudad de Guatemala, C.A., tel (502) 2 31 1333/47, fax (502) 2 31 8893, telex 5532 INGUAT GU. (Open Mon–Fri, 8.30–4.30 and Sat, 8.30–noon.)

The only other places where you will find INGUAT offices in Guatemala are Antigua, Panajachel, Quezaltenango and Flores.

Orientation

All Guatemalan towns, including the capital, are laid out in a grid system, whereby calles run north to south, and avenidas run east to west. Additionally, the bigger towns are divided into different zones, and the street numbers are repeated in each zone, so it is vital to know which zone you need. Addresses are written so that the street the place is actually on comes first, then comes the number of the nearest crossroad, and then the house number. For example, the El Dorado hotel is at 7 Avenida 15–45. This means the building is located on 7 Avenida, between junctions 15 Calle and 16 Calle, at number 45. It's easy once you get used to it.

Maps

The best and cheapest map available is the one sold by the Guatemalan Tourist Board, though you will undoubtedly be able to find others in map shops before you leave home. This map not only features the country, but also small street maps of the capital and a few major towns and tourist attractions.

Large-scale topographical maps are produced by the Guatemalan Military, which you can inspect, but need special permission from the Ministry of Defence to buy. The address is Instituto Geográfico Militar, Avenida Las Américas 5–76, Zona 13; open weekdays 7–4. Alternatively, the Casa Andinista bookshop in Antigua will sell you photocopies without any problems.

Getting Around Guatemala

By Air
The only internal flight route in operation is the one connecting Guatemala City with the jungle-bound town of Flores. There are three or four flights daily in either direction, and tickets are available at most travel agencies or at the two airports. There are four airlines operating the route: Aviateca, Aerovías, Aeroquetzal, and Tapsa. Prices should be the same whoever you fly with, but always check, because sometimes the agents slap on extras, selling the same ticket at substantially different prices, depending on which airline they use. A return flight costs about $100, and the journey time is about 80 minutes. If possible, you should try to make reservations at least a few days ahead, as flights can be heavily booked, especially during Easter Week or Christmas and New Year.

By Train
As one passenger put it: you'd be faster walking! Nobody uses the Guatemalan trains unless they have no choice or believe it is their kind of adventure. However, they can be a useful option when the country is suffering one of its recurrent national bus strikes.

There is one route running from the Mexican border at Tecún Umán to Guatemala City, via the Pacific towns of Coatepeque, Retalhuleu, Mazatenango and Escuintla. It should take 12 hours, but often takes double that time. The only other remaining passenger service connects the capital with the Atlantic port of Puerto Barrios, a journey that is supposed to take 8 hours, but usually takes nearer 20. (The bus takes 6 hours.)

The train route to the Pacific port of San José no longer takes passengers, nor can you travel to El Salvador by train any more. There is also a strong chance that the two passenger services described above will be discontinued.

By Bus
This is undoubtedly the fastest, cheapest and easiest way to explore most of Guatemala. The country's towns and many villages are linked by good paved or passable dirt roads everywhere except in the Petén, where appalling mud roads regularly disintegrate completely during the rainy season. Bus connections are regular and extremely cheap, though you should always try to travel in the morning, since public transport generally stops by late afternoon. It is also much safer to travel during daylight hours, and less daunting to arrive in a new place before nightfall. Tickets are bought on the bus, and to avoid 'gringo prices', it is always a good idea to ask a local passenger what the fare is, before the ticket man gets to you.

On some routes it is possible to travel by Pullman buses, which are more comfortable than the local 'chicken buses' (old Blue Bird buses or retired US school buses, crammed to bursting point with people and often small livestock too). Pullmans are a bit more expensive, but you get a reserved seat to yourself, and the bus makes fewer stops.

By Car

The roads in Guatemala, excepting the Petén, are generally good, and normal passenger cars have no trouble here. If you intend to go off the beaten track, you will find mostly dirt and gravel roads, where high-clearance vehicles are recommended. Should you want a real adventure and wish to drive to Tikal in the Petén, nothing less than a tough four-wheel-drive vehicle will do, and even then it is not advisable to attempt the journey during the rainy season from May to December.

Be sure to take a spare wheel and any other essential spare parts that may be unavailable here, and a large canister of petrol would be a good idea as well, as petrol stations are few and far between. The Guatemalan Tourist Office (INGUAT) sells a useful road map, which has all petrol stations marked on it, as well as a mileage chart. It is advisable to use secure parking facilities wherever possible, since theft and vandalism is a problem—especially in towns and cities or near tourist attractions.

Traffic outside the cities is very sparse, so driving is relatively relaxed, bar the occasionally hazardous local driving or military checkpoint. These checkpoints are nothing to worry about, however, and normally you will be waved on. Hassle is more likely to come from the police and Guardia de Hacienda (rural police), who like to stop cars with foreign licence plates. There will always be the occasional corrupt officer looking for a bribe, but that is a risk you take driving anywhere in Latin America.

Car Hire

Hire cars are available in the capital and most major towns, though they are expensive at US$55 per day for the smaller cars, and often you have to pay the first $800 of any damage, or there is no insurance at all. Read the small print! This is especially important as foreigners have to pay all damages, whether the accident was their fault or not. To hire any vehicle, you will need a current driving licence and a credit card, regardless of how you intend to pay the final bill. Motorbikes can be hired in Guatemala City, Antigua and Panajachel, for around $20 per day.

Major car hire offices in Guatemala City are the following, and all except Tally have airport representatives: **Avis**, 12 Calle 2–73, Zona 9, tel 316990; **Budget**, Avenida La Reforma 15–00, Zona 9, tel 316546; **Dollar**, 6 Avenida A 10–13, Zona 1, tel 67796; **Hertz**, 7 Avenida 14–76, Zona 9, tel 680107; **National**, 14 Calle 1–42, Zona 10, tel 680175; **Tabarini**, 2 Calle A 7–30, Zona 10, tel 316108; **Tally**, 7 Avenida 14–60, Zona 1, tel 514113.

By Bicycle

Travellers on bicycles are becoming an increasingly common sight in Guatemala, and many locals use them too. There are bike rental shops in most large towns, and there is always someone to be found who can help you fix your bike. The best kind of bike is clearly a mountain bike, with tough wheels and plenty of gears. Should you get tired of cycling, you can always travel on the local buses, which will transport your bike on the roof, normally at no extra charge.

Embassies and Consulates

All embassies and consulates are in Guatemala City, and are normally only open on weekdays, in the mornings. Onward travellers to other Central American countries may need visas, so the relevant offices are listed, where they exist.
UK: Edificio Centro Financiero, 7 Avenida 5–10 (7th floor), Zona 4, tel 321601; (Mon–Thurs, 10–noon and 2–4, Fri, 1–5).
US: Avenida Reforma 7–01, Zona 10, tel 311541/4.
Canada: 7 Avenida 11–59 (6th floor), Zona 9, tel 321411.
Costa Rica: Avenida Reforma 8–60 (third floor), Zona 9, tel 319604.
El Salvador: 12 Calle 5–43 (7th floor), Zona 9, tel 325848.
Honduras: 16 Calle 8–27, Zona 10, tel 373919.
Mexico: 13 Calle 7–30, Zona 9, tel 363573.
Nicaragua: 10 Avenida 14–72, Zona 10, tel 680785.
Panamá: Edificio Maya (7th floor), Via 5 4–50, Zona 4, tel 325001.

Money Matters

Guatemalan currency is the quetzal, and one quetzal is made up of 100 centavos. Notes come in denominations of 100, 50, 20, 10, 5, 1, and 0.50. It is worth trying to avoid notes of 100 and 50 quetzals, since people do not like changing them; and torn or damaged notes should never be accepted because you will get stuck with them.

Exchange rates are volatile in this region of rampant inflation and regular devaluations, but you can be sure that your money will go a long way here. The best currency to have is US dollars, either in cash or travellers' cheques, which you can exchange at most banks and on the black market. You will get a slightly better rate on the black market, though you must be careful: avoid showing your passport, which could be stolen in the process; don't hand over your cash first; and don't go into an unknown house with a supposed money changer. Exclusive hotels and some shops and restaurants also change money.

Guatemalan banks do not charge commission for cashing travellers' cheques, but it can take at least half an hour to get your money because of interminable queues and forms. Make sure you are in the right queue. Every town has at least one bank, and often there are a few to choose from, such as the Banco de Guatemala, Banco del Ejército, Banco del Agro, Banco Industrial, and Lloyds Bank. The daily exchange rate is displayed, and is fixed by the government so it is the same in all banks. Banking hours are normally Mon–Fri, 9–3, though some open as early as 8 am.

Wiring money from abroad should be avoided if possible, since delays and other trouble is virtually guaranteed. If you have no choice, then you will be paid in local currency and can rarely buy back US dollars at the bank. Best use Lloyds Bank International, 8 Avenida 10–67, Zona 1; or Bank of America, 5 Avenida 10–55, Zona 1. Another bank that has been known to pay out in US dollars or travellers' cheques is Banco Internacional, 7a Avenida 11–20, Zona 1; telex 5488 BANCOIGU; tel 518066. Amex card holders can also get dollars at their office, simply by writing a personal cheque.

Credit cards, such as American Express and Visa, are generally accepted. Diners Club and Access/Mastercard can also be used. Of course plastic money will only help in the most expensive hotels, shops and restaurants, for hiring cars or buying flight tickets.

Post Offices

There are post offices (*correos*), open Mon–Fri, 8–6 in the capital, 8–4 everywhere else, in every major town, and often even in the smaller places. When sending letters, it is always best to send them airmail and express—they will still take up to six weeks to reach Europe and a couple less to North America. Generally the postal service is slow but safe, and even parcels arrive back home eventually. To send any parcel which weighs over 2 kg, you will have to take it to the main post office in Guatemala City open for inspection, so take string and sticking materials to finish wrapping at the counter. There are strict regulations about the way parcels should be wrapped. If you can afford it, you may prefer to use DHL or UPS offices for extra safety and speed. Or you could use the services of the **Get Guated Out** agency in Panajachel (see p. 113).

Receiving mail is straightforward via the *lista de correos* at any Guatemalan post office. The central post office in Guatemala City is the safest. Letters from Europe or North America normally arrive in ten days. To avoid mix-ups, make sure letters are addressed to you by your surname only, with no initial or title prefixed. That way there is only one choice of letter under which to sort your mail. To get your post you will need your passport, and will be charged a tiny fee for each piece of mail. The address for the central post office in the capital is: Lista de Correos, Correo Central, 7 Avenida and 12 Calle, Zona 1, Guatemala City, Guatemala, C.A.

Alternatively, members of American Express, or even holders of their travellers' cheques, could have their mail sent to the offices of American Express, Avenida Reforma 9–00, Zona 9, Guatemala City, Guatemala, C.A. They keep mail longer than the post office and are probably a bit safer, though there's not much in it.

Telecommunications

Payphones do exist, for which you will need plenty of 25 and 10 centavo coins, but more numerous are the offices of the national telephone company, GUATEL, open daily 7–10. Often chaotic places, they are nevertheless the best choice for making local and international calls. Be warned that international calls are very expensive, and just three minutes to Europe will cost you over US$20. Reverse charge calls can only be made to the US, Canada, Italy and Spain.

The main GUATEL office in Guatemala City is near the main post office, at 7 Avenida 12–39, Zona 1; there are a number of others, including one on Avenida Reforma 6–29, Zona 9. Your other option is to use the luxury hotels, who will allow you to phone at exorbitant rates.

Police and Military

In spite of Guatemala's appalling human rights record, its waning guerrilla war and other horrors, it is extremely unlikely that you will be affected. As a foreigner you are not a target for terror. It is the Indians and street children who are in danger.

In fact, Guatemala is one of the safest Latin American countries to travel in, as long as you take the normal care and attention necessary anywhere in this part of the world. Watch out for pickpockets at markets and bus terminals. Although you should guard your baggage while travelling, do not worry too much if your pack is on the roof during bus journeys. Unless it falls off, it will most likely still be there when you arrive at your destination (you have to be much more careful in South America).

You will see guards armed with machine guns in all government offices, banks, and many commercial stores, and although intimidating at first, they are quite harmless as far as you are concerned. Most uniformed officials will be very courteous and only too pleased to help you if they can. Should you get stopped, for example at one of the standard military road blocks, or need to report a theft, always remain calm and polite, no matter what. Bribes should never be more than a last resort, and best avoided by unpractised players.

The police wear uniforms of dark blue trousers and light blue shirts. The military are in familiar khaki, with high-ranking members in olive or dark green uniforms. The chaps in grass-green, with the strange hats, like Canadian mounties gone wrong, are members of the Guardia de Hacienda, and responsible for policing the countryside.

Also in the countryside, mainly in the Western Highlands, you will see groups of civilian men armed with rifles, guarding villages, markets or strategic roads. These are not bandits, but civil defence units organized by the military, their job being to defend their village against lurking guerrillas.

Medical Matters

Farmácias, as chemists are known, stock all types of drugs, many without a prescription, and many that are banned in Europe and North America. Clearly, it is best to bring your own medicines with you, but you should be able to buy most things you need here. If you plan on visiting the jungle, don't forget to bring the relevant malaria pills. Contraceptives, such as the pill or condoms, are readily available. Sanitary towels can be bought anywhere in the country, and tampons in the cities. Two items you will have difficulty finding are earplugs and contact lens soaking solutions, and mosquito repellent is also rare. (In the capital you can buy contact lens solution at Optica Moderna, 12 Calle 4–48, zone 1.)

Should you suffer an attack of persistent bad guts, you would be well advised to visit one of the many biological labs, which will analyze your problem and prescribe the appropriate remedy. In most cases these labs will be better qualified to recognize what is wrong than your doctor back home, so do trust them to help you, rather than suffer until returning to your own country. There are good labs in Guatemala City, Antigua and Quezaltenango. Alternatively, go to the nearest private hospital you can find, which will always be better than the state's institution, and not that expensive.

Public Holidays and Opening Hours

Banks and government offices close on official holidays, though public transport can always be found even when officially not running.

GUATEMALA

New Year's Day
6 January—Epiphany
Easter Week (*Semana Santa*)—most important festival
1 May—Labour Day
30 June—Anniversary of 1871 revolution
15 August—Assumption, celebrated only in the capital
15 September—Independence Day
12 October—Discovery of America
20 October—Revolution Day
1 Nov—All Saints' Day
24 Dec—Christmas Eve
25 Dec—Christmas Day
31 Dec—New Year's Eve

Most places are open Mondays to Fridays, 9–4, and slightly shorter hours at the weekend. Many places close over lunchtime, and some are shut on Mondays and weekends. Check opening times before setting out as there is considerable local variation. Archaeological sites are open daily, usually 8–4, though this also varies. Shops tend to open at 8 and close at 5.30; markets normally run from dawn until 4, with most of the action over by lunchtime.

Festivals

Guatemala is rightly famous for its traditional Indian festivals, times when the air is thick with incense and resounds to the constant blast of earpiercing firecrackers. You will see the Maya heritage at its most vibrant, with people decked out in their best native costumes, outrageously drunk, yet with untiring energy for another dance or song or candle-lit procession. These festivals are normally in honour of a Christian saint, but contain elements of earlier Indian celebrations that the colonial church was incapable of supressing. What we see today is a remarkable mixture of two very different heritages.

The festivals of the *ladino* population are no less riotous, with plenty of colour and noise, and a bullfight or two. Both kinds of festival usually have attendant fairs and markets, and normally go on for a week, the last two days being the most important and interesting for visitors.

The most famous Indian festival in the country is the December one in Chichicastenango, while Easter Week in Antigua is celebrated with an extravagance you are unlikely to find anywhere else in Central America. There are many others worth making an effort to see as well, such as the horse races in Todos Santos, or the kite-flying in Santiago Sacatepéquez, both on 1 November. Every town and village has at least one special day for a festival, which will be listed in the text. For the two most famous events, you will need to book accommodation well in advance or get there at least a day early.

BEST OF THE FESTIVALS

January
1–5 Jan **Santa María de Jesús**, a small Indian village near Antigua.

GUATEMALA AND BELIZE

15 Jan Annual pilgrimage to **Esquipulas**, a *ladino* town near the Honduran border and home to the famous Black Christ.
19–25 Jan Traditional dances at **Rabinal**, a small Indian village in the department of Baja Verapaz.
22–26 Jan **San Pablo la Laguna**, a normally quiet Indian village on Lake Atitlán.

February
1st Friday of Lent **Antigua**, former colonial capital near Guatemala City.

March
Easter Week (*Semana Santa*) This is one of the most interesting times to be anywhere in Guatemala, when the whole country is celebrating, and nowhere more so than in **Antigua**.
Easter Saturday Indians from all around Lake Atitlán come to be baptized in its waters at **Panajachel**.

April
Whitsun **Aguacatán**, a small place near the town of Huehuetenango, celebrates Whitsun with a festival and interesting market.

May
2–3 May **Amatitlán**, near the lake of the same name, has its annual pilgrimage across the waters.
8–10 May **Santa Cruz la Laguna**, a small Indian village on Lake Atitlán.

June
12–14 June **San Antonio Palopó**, Indian village on Lake Atitlán.
24–29 June **San Pedro Carchá**, outside Cobán, a mainly *ladino* festival with plenty of traditional dancing.
27–30 June **San Pedro la Laguna**, Indian village on Lake Atitlán.
28–30 June **Almolonga**, a bustling Indian village near Quezaltenango, with nearby hot springs in which to recover if needed.

July
1–4 July **Santa María Visitación**, a village near Sololá, above Lake Atitlán.
16–22 July **Puerto Barrios**, port city on the Atlantic coast, has a *ladino* festival, very loud and with plenty of sleaze.
20–25 July **Cubulco**, a remote *ladino* farming community in the Baja Verapaz, whose festival still includes many traditional Indian dances.
21 July–4 Aug **Momostenango**, a remote Indian town in the mountains near Quezaltenango, holds a traditional festival and has beautiful woven blankets at its market.
23–27 July **Santiago Atitlán**, the country's most visited Indian village, on the shores of Lake Atitlán, with a very popular festival.
31 July–6 Aug **Cobán**, coffee capital of Guatemala, has its annual festival at this time, and also hosts the **National Festival of Folklore**, where representatives come from all over the country to show their native costumes and participate in many traditional dances. An agricultural fair is also held.

GUATEMALA

August
6–15 Aug **Joyabaj**, an out of the way town east of Santa Cruz del Quiché, where you will see traditional dances rarely performed elsewhere.
11–17 Aug **Sololá**, perched above Lake Atitlán, springs to life for its annual festival, with a good market attached.
12–15 Aug **Nebaj**, northeast of Huehuetenango, where the Indians wear one of the most beautiful costumes in the country.
12–18 Aug **Cantel**, an Indian village outside Quezaltenango, located in a gorgeous valley.
22–28 Aug **Lanquín**, a remote town east of Cobán.

September
12–18 Sep **Quezaltenango**, the country's second city.
24–30 Sep **Totonicapán**, near Quezaltenango, a traditional town with one of the largest markets.

October
1–6 Oct **San Francisco el Alto**, a hillside settlement near Quezaltenango, with an interesting animal fair.
2–6 Oct **Panajachel**, favourite gringo spot on Lake Atitlán.
20–26 Oct **Iztapa**, a small town on the Pacific coast, and one of the few places worth visiting there.
21 Oct–1 Nov **Todos Santos**, a remote Indian village northwest of Huehuetenango, with chaotic horse races 29 Oct–1 Nov, worth making an effort to see.

November
1 Nov **Santiago de Sacatepéquez**, near the highway between the capital and Chimaltenango, where giant kites are flown in the cemetery as part of the Day of the Dead celebration.
22–26 Nov **Zunil** is a small village outside Quezaltenango, where the local costume is all shocking pinks and purple.
23–25 Nov **Nahualá**, a rarely visited Indian settlement, halfway between Los Enquentros and Quezaltenango, has a very drunken and colourful festival, where men sport their traditional skirts.
25 Nov **Santa Catarina Palopó**, a small village on Lake Atitlán.
27 Nov–1 Dec **San Andrés Itzapa**, a small town near Antigua, interesting for its shrine to Maximón, the notorious Indian saint.

December
5–8 Dec **Huehuetenango**, the largest town to the northwest of Guatemala City.
7 Dec The Burning of the Devil takes place symbolically, as bonfires of rubbish are lit throughout the country, but mainly around **Quezaltenango** and in **Guatemala City**. (Very smelly.) **Antigua** also has a ceremonial burning, usually attended by a street party and fireworks.
13–21 Dec **Chichicastenango**, a staunch Indian town, where Catholic and Maya traditions have merged into a unique festival of worshipping, dancing, processions, and live music, accompanied by the richest handicraft market you will find in Guatemala. Of

the dances, the most famous is the *Palo Volador*, which is not so much dancing as dicing with death: pairs of men swing from the top of a 60-foot pole on the end of an unravelling rope.

24–31 Dec **Livingston**, the only black community in Guatemala, on the Atlantic coast, celebrates Christmas with occasional live singing of African songs on the streets, and a couple of good reggae discos at night.

31 Dec New Year's Eve resounds to the deafening noise of dynamite firecrackers, with the best parties happening in **Antigua, Panajachel** and **Livingston**.

Markets

If you cannot make it to one of the festivals, then there are always the markets as consolation. Every town and village in Guatemala has a weekly market, and that is always the best time to be there. The most interesting are in the Western Highlands, where the majority of Indians lived, who flock to their nearest market, bent double by the wares carried on their backs. Walking around the stalls and baskets of farm produce and small livestock, you will notice that the atmosphere is refreshingly tranquil. This is because Guatemalan Indians come to market foremost to socialize: to keep up with the latest news from distant hamlets, establish family ties, and set up potential marriages. Buying and selling is just by the by for these people, who live off the land and are almost outside the money economy of the rest of the country.

Of course the *artesanía* or *típica* markets are quite different: here the Indian traders, usually women, drive a tough bargain, and are uncharacteristically pushy in getting you to look at their goods. The best craftware and textile markets are in Guatemala City (daily), Antigua (daily, but weekends best), Panajachel (daily), Chichicastenango (Thursday and Sunday), Momostenango (Wednesday and Sunday), Nebaj (Sunday) and Todos Santos (Wednesday and Sunday). There are many others well worth seeing, and all other market days are listed in the text.

Shopping

The markets are the best places for shopping—if you know how to bargain. The big attraction is the Indian hand-woven textiles, which are made into anything from rugs, blankets, bags, *huipiles* (blouses), skirts and hats, to wall-hangings. These textiles are often also elaborately embroidered, showing the traditional patterns of each region or village, and thus half the pleasure of buying these things is identifying them with a particular place or region, where you have seen them worn or used in their original context.

Hand-made linen tablewear is another good buy, with an almost infinite variety of colours and styles available. There is also delicate hand-made pottery, which is rather brittle, so difficult to transport; also a large array of carved wooden masks used during the Indian festivals; wooden furniture; wickerwork and rush mats and baskets; leather belts, bags and suitcases; plenty of silver-leaf filigree jewellery, as well as coral and glass bead necklaces; and finally, in Antigua, there is a great deal of Guatemalan jade for sale, made into anything from reproduction Maya statues to pendants. Watch out for soapstone fakes in the markets, and only buy jade from reputable shops.

A 7% government tax is added to most commercial transactions in shops, though almost never in the markets, where you do not get a bill anyway.

The Media

The two most widely available national newspapers are *El Gráfico* and *La Prensa Libre*, of which the latter is slightly less populist and celebrity orientated, but both are fundamentally right-wing in their political stance. As papers critical of the usually right-wing governments get closed down, this is no surprise. *La Hora*, published in the afternoons and only available in and near Guatemala City, has the most balanced news analysis; *Siglo XXI* is on a par with La Hora and published in the mornings. The weekly magazine *La Crónica* also aims to present a critical and broad analysis of Guatemalan and Latin American events in general. There are a number of other newspapers as well.

Going to the cinema is a favourite cheap pastime in Guatemala, and most large towns have at least one. The programme is often dominated by porn, violent or horror films, but most places usually run the latest North American film releases as well. Foreign films are run with subtitles, not dubbed, but the sound and film quality can be dreadful; unscheduled breaks in the programme or sound are frequent.

TV and radio stations abound in Guatemala, where over 60% of the population is illiterate, and many restaurants and hotels have radios and TVs permanently switched on, so you will soon get to know them well. Satellite and cable TV are also quite common here, and 'gringo' bars and restaurants in Antigua even show American CNN news.

Where to Stay

There are luxury hotels of international standard in Guatemala City, Antigua, Panajachel, Chichicastenango outside Tikal, and in El Relleno on Lake Izabal; first-class hotels in Quezaltenango and Livingston; and otherwise perfectly good standard hotels and guest houses in most of the places you will want to visit, with a price that suits your pocket easy to find. Should you go off the beaten track to remote Indian towns or villages, you will find very basic guest houses, or sometimes none at all. Where there is no official guest house, your best option is to find the local *alcalde* (mayor), who will either find you a reputable private house to lodge in, or let you sleep on the floor in the local council building or school. If you plan on visiting remoter places in the Highlands, remember your sleeping bag, since it can get very cold at night.

Prices for even the cheapest hovel are fixed by the national tourist board (INGUAT), so you can always see what the correct price is supposed to be. However, many places neglect to get their annual review, so don't be surprised if the price notice is a few years out of date, and expect to be flexible. Officially, there is a 17% tax added to all hotel bills, so always check if a price is inclusive or not. Cheap accommodation normally has taxes already included. Guatemala has the cheapest accommodation in Central America: the most basic double rooms cost around US$2, reasonable guest houses offering rooms for as little as US$7, while slightly up-market hotels charge from US$14 for two.

There are many different names for accommodation, but they basically all mean the same thing and do not necessarily indicate differences in standard. *Hotel, pensión, posada, hospedaje* and *huésped* are standard descriptions of the whole gamut of Guatemalan accommodation. Although phone and fax numbers have been listed in the text where available, most places will not accept verbal reservations, and even written ones are difficult to get with any but the most expensive. All you can do is phone to see if rooms are free and then turn up and try your luck.

There are no youth hostels in Guatemala, and only two places where you can camp with reasonable facilities and safety: Panajachel and Tikal. But accommodation is so cheap that there really is no advantage in camping, and the only time you might need a tent is climbing one of the volcanoes or hiking in remote mountain or jungle areas. If you do not want to bring your own, you can hire most camping equipment in Antigua, either from the *Casa Andinista* or the many tour agencies.

Commercial renting of holiday homes or flats is not an established business here, but you can find long-term lets in the two gringo centres of Antigua and Panajachel, and possibly in Quezaltenango. Again, unless you plan on staying for months on end, you will not save much money by renting, when you can find pleasant, cheap guest houses and meals too.

Eating Out

Food is not Guatemala's strong point. The basic dish is eggs and black beans (*huevos y frijoles*), usually greasy and fried. These mostly come with fried chicken (*pollo frito*) or beef (*lomito*); and then there are the other two standard foods, which are actually Italian: pasta and pizzas. All these dishes are usually served with warm tortillas, which are roasted cornflour patties, or with tasteless white bread. You do, however, have a good choice of international cuisine in most towns, with at least one Italian or Chinese restaurant, and plenty of fast-food burger places.

Having said this, there are a few tasty local snacks to try, such as the *tamale*, which is an envelope of banana-leaf (not edible) with steamed maize paste inside, often mixed with other vegetables or bits of meat. *Tamales negros* are sweet, made with prunes. *Chiles rellenos* are peppers stuffed with bits of meat and vegetables, often served with hot sauce—as is everything here, unless you say otherwise. *Antojito* is a small tortilla 'sandwich', usually filled with a thin piece of fried beef, onion and tomato. *Enchiladas* are another standard, composed of crispy tortillas piled high with chopped vegetables, salad or meat, or a bit of each. And finally, the *fiambre* is not a snack but a giant salad of meats, fish, and cheese with assorted greenery, all piled up together, normally only eaten on 1 November.

All these dishes (except the last) are commonly served by vendors on the streets or at bus stations, but you would be safer eating them in restaurants, where hygiene is marginally better, or in the markets, where food is freshly made on the day. The best places to try them is in the *comedores*, which are typical Guatemalan restaurants that serve a limited range of local food at the cheapest prices you will find in the country.

More up-market restaurants rarely serve traditional food, unless they specialize in 'typical' dishes. One of the best restaurant chains of this type, only in the capital, is **Los Antojitos**, listed in the text. There are also restaurants which serve traditional Maya food, which adds some exotic meats to the standard eggs and beans. For example, you could eat stewed armadillo, turkey (*pavo*) or *tepezcuintle*, which is a jungle animal that looks like a strange mini-deer, but is in fact the largest member of the rodent family: delicious when not overcooked. A good alternative to the eggs and beans are *plátanos fritos*, which are fried savoury bananas.

On either coast, you will also find delicious fresh seafood, usually fish, shrimp or squid, and a special dish you should try here is *ceviche*, which is chopped pieces of fish and onions marinaded in lemon juice, served cold. (Avoid as long as there is a cholera problem.) Tropical fruit of all kinds is sold all over the country, but is best here, and the local coconut bread (*pan de coco*) is very good, though do not eat too much unless constipation is the desired effect. A 10% service tax is added to all restaurant bills.

Drink

The most common drinks available are canned or bottled fruit juices, fizzy drinks or watery local beers. For the climate, the local beer is ideal; served very cold it is refreshing without making you dozy. *Gallo* or *Moza* are the most common, the latter a dark beer. *Cabro* beer is brewed in Quezaltenango and usually only available in and around that town. Avoid the delicious freshly-made shakes made with water (*licuados*), until you feel your stomach can cope with the local microbes. In the better restaurants, fruit juices and shakes are made with sterilized water, but always ask to make sure, since local tap water is generally not safe. Guatemalan wine tastes like a cross between vinegar and petrol, and is best avoided. But the rum is cheap and all right if mixed. Best buy is *Ron Colonial*, while *Ron Botran* and *Venado Especial* will give you a severe hangover (*goma*). Hardened drinkers will appreciate the local firewater called *Quetzalteca*, which blasts a burning trail down your throat.

In spite of the fact that Guatemala is a coffee-growing country, the drink is almost universally weak, normally made of instant powder and tasting like dishwater. This is a pity, because when you get the real thing, it is very good. The most likely places to find real coffee are the gringo joints of Antigua and Panajachel, or exclusive restaurants. Tea is also disappointingly weak, but a good alternative is the locally produced hot chocolate.

Itineraries

The Western Highlands

Most visitors to Guatemala head for the Western Highlands, and rightly so. This is where the scenery of volcanoes, lakes and pine-clad highland scenery is at its most captivating. It is also where you will meet the majority of the country's Indian inhabitants. The standard circuit would first take you west from the capital to the small town of **Antigua**, with a beautiful setting and fine colonial architecture. From here the Pan-American Highway leads you northwards to beautiful **Lake Atitlán**. Next the road continues to **Quezaltenango**, the country's second city and an excellent base for exploring remoter villages and markets and a bit of easy hiking. Beyond here, the northwestern town of **Huehuetenango** has very little to offer, except that the remote and rough terrain around it is spectacular at times, and if you want to visit the Indian village of **Todos Santos**, you will have to pass this way. Heading south again, there are two routes you could take: either you can return via the paved Pan-American Highway, or you can continue on dirt roads via Sacapulas (east of Huehuetenango), and Santa Cruz del Quiché, meeting the paved highway again beyond **Chichicastenango**. The latter choice is slow but scenicly terrific, and either way, you will want to make sure you visit Chichi, as it is known.

Pacific and Atlantic Beaches

Do not bother coming to Guatemala for the beaches. What you will find on the Pacific side is a 60 km belt of flat plantation country, with little access to the sea itself. Where there are roads to the beach you will find a grey strip of sand, often separated from the mainland by mangrove swamps and a water canal. On the Atlantic side, there is only one place worth going to, and that is **Livingston**, a Caribbean community descended from African slaves, Carib Indians, and the odd shipwrecked sailor. The place is located at the mouth of the River Dulce, and while the beach may not be memorable, the river is, with jungle vegetation and plenty of wildlife to see during boat trips, which can take you all the way to **Lake Izabal**, and waterside **El Relleno**, dotted with some of the country's most exclusive hotels and private holiday villas.

The Jungle

The ruined Maya city of **Tikal** is the most awe-inspiring place in the country. From the present-day town of **Flores**, there are also a number of opportunities to go on jungle tours or organize guides for individual itineraries to distant archaeological sites in the jungle, only accessible on foot, horseback or via the rivers.

The Verapaz Mountains

This large region is the least visited area of Guatemala. Roads are good for the most part, yet you are off the beaten track here. The mountains hide two particular spots worth making an effort to see: the **Quetzal Reserve**, where you might see the country's extremely rare national bird; and the gorgeous forest pools of **Semuc Champey**, an arduous place to reach, beyond Cobán, but well worth it.

The back road connecting **Cobán** in the northeast with **Huehuetenango** in the northwest is unrivalled for its spectacular setting, snaking its way along the edges of a terrifyingly steep river valley and into the **Cuchumatán Mountains**. The last time a bus actually fell off the road was in the mid-seventies.

Guatemala City

Try as it might, Guatemala City just cannot muster the atmosphere of a capital city. Its two million inhabitants are spread thinly throughout the seemingly endless grid of avenidas and calles, and except for Zona 1's Avenidas 5 and 6, the city is strangely quiet—more reminiscent of a provincial town.

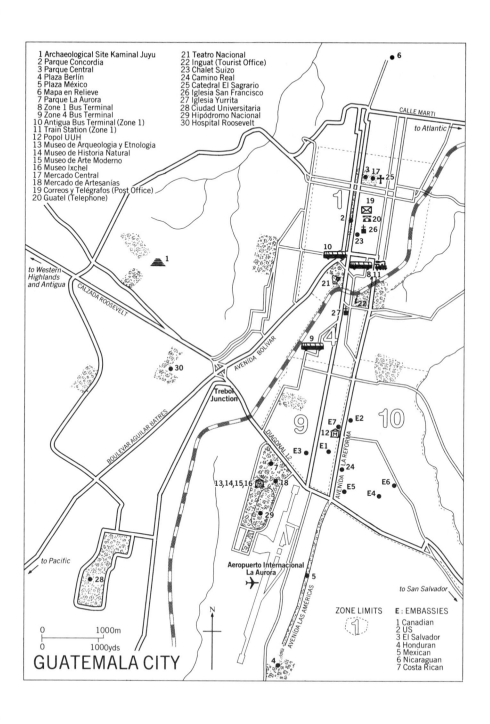

In the expensive southern quarters of Zonas 9 and 10, it is particularly quiet, with only the guards hanging around at the entrances of walled compounds that hide the city's finer residences. As in Latin America generally, exclusive usually means boring and empty, since any existing life is rigorously kept behind high walls and barbed wire. The so-called *zona viva* could hardly be less so, the restaurants, bars and occasional clubs being dull, though always expensive.

In fact, there is really no good reason to stay long in Guatemala City, known as *Guate* locally, though foreigners soon dub it 'Grotty'. Three or four days is plenty of time to see all the museums and churches, and stroll along the hybrid streets of Zona 1, the centre, where you will also find the city's most colourful places: the squares and the central markets. Bar the appalling pollution, this is painlessly done, since the city is 'an extremely horizontal place ... like a city on its back.' (Paul Theroux).

History

Guatemala City was founded in 1774, after the country's previous capital, like the two before it, had been destroyed by an earthquake. It was not an auspicious moment, and in spite of the desolation and disease which racked Antigua, their former capital, many of its survivors had no desire to up and leave. The rich and the ecclesiastical and government bodies were loath to start from scratch, developing a new city from nothing on an open plain near Lake Amatitlán, while the townfolk and Indian peasants had nothing to gain by moving away.

However, the government made it compulsory to move, and thus the country's new capital was reluctantly filled. Slowly, a new city was built, designed on the standard Spanish colonial grid system, which has gradually spread out to cover the entire plateau the city is perched on. Today its edges teeter on the brink of dusty ravines that cut the sandy earth like giant wrinkles. As the shanty towns grow, even these steep gashes are being filled, rubbish and shacks clinging desperately to the sides.

Perhaps not surprisingly, the exuberant glamour of Antigua's architecture could never be re-created on the same scale, and Guatemala City has always been a visually monotonous place. This being earthquake country, most buildings are squat and no higher than a few storeys, though 20th-century technology has allowed some skyscrapers to raise their glassy shoots, and these have become useful landmarks, if nothing else. Most architecture dates from this century, since Guatemala City has not been spared the battering quakes any more than its predecessors, and the massive quakes in 1917 and 1976 have ensured that little remains of the 18th and 19th centuries. What you find is a modern city with the occasional old church or municipal building, the finest of which is the cathedral on the central square.

GETTING TO GUATEMALA CITY

By Air
La Aurora airport is in Zona 13 of Guatemala City itself, just around the corner from all the top hotels in the exclusive Zonas 9 and 10. The city centre (Zona 1) is a 10-minute drive away, and the taxi there should not cost more than US$5. There are no meters so

GUATEMALA

always fix a price before the journey begins. Buses nos. 5 and 6 run from near the airport exit to the city centre every 30 minutes during daylight hours. Note that the airport shuts down at night, so you cannot sleep there.

There are regular flights from the following Central American and Caribbean cities: San Salvador, Tegucigalpa, Mexico City, Belize City, Managua, San José, Panamá and San Andrés. Most flights from South America are via Panamá/San José. There are no direct flights from Peru or Ecuador.

Aeronica, 10 Calle 6–20, Zona 9, tel 325541.
Aeroquetzal, Avenida Hincapie and 18 Calle, Zona 13, tel 365214.
Aerovías, Avenida Hincapié and 18 Calle, Zona 13, tel 347935.
Aviateca, Avenida Hincapié, Zona 13, tel 318227.
British Airways, Avenida Reforma 8–60, Zona 9, tel 312555.
Continental, at airport, tel 312051/5.
Iberia, Avenida Reforma 8–60, Zona 9, tel 373914/5.
Eastern, at airport, tel 321325.
KLM, 6 Avenida 20–25, Zona 10, Edificio Plaza Marítima, tel 370222.
PanAm, 6 Avenida 11–43, Zona 1, tel 532523.
Taca, 7 Avenida 14–35, Zona 9, tel 322360.
Tapsa, Avenida Hincapié, Zona 13, tel 314860.
Virgin Atlantic, Avenida Reforma 9–00, Zona 9, Edificio Plaza Panamericana, tel 312070.

By Train
The train station is on the same square as the Zona 1 bus terminal, though you would never know it. It is the wooden building behind all the buses, away from the main street. You have two choices of destination only: to Puerto Barrios on the Atlantic coast (Tues, Thurs and Sat, at 7.30 am) or Tecún Umán on the border with Mexico (Tues and Sat, at 7 am). The journey to the coast can take up to 20 hours, through hot and arid countryside, with no restaurant carriage. The journey to Tecún Umán can be equally slow, but the countryside is much more interesting, as you pass over the Western Highlands and then along the foothills bordering the tropical Pacific plain. Again, there is no food provision on board, and delays are frequent. Best buy your ticket in advance, and always check days and times of departure, since these can change at any time.

By Bus
The **main bus terminal** is in Zona 4, where you will find 2nd-class buses going to almost all parts of the country, as well as nearby places, such as Lake Amatitlán. These buses are normally in good repair, though they do get very crowded and the seats are tight. It is best to turn up in the mornings for long-distance journeys. **Zona 1 bus terminal** is on a square, on the corner of 18 Calle and 9 Avenida, and here you will find 2nd-class buses and Pullman-style buses leaving for destinations in the Eastern Highlands and the Atlantic coast. All tickets, except those for long-distance Pullman buses, can be bought on the bus. (You *can* travel on the Pullmans without buying a ticket first, but because seats are booked, you will most likely have to stand for the whole journey.)

If you are heading for the former colonial capital of Antigua, one hour from the present capital, you will find buses leaving every half an hour (5 am–8 pm coming from Guatemala City, but 5–5 coming from Antigua), from the junction of 18 Calle and 4 Avenida in Zona 1, and more from the small terminal on 20 Calle, between 2 and 3 Avenue, Zona 1.

The following Pullman companies are recommended for a more comfortable journey, but please note that the journey times are approximate. Buses leave from outside the offices:

To Cobán or the Quetzal Reserve: Escobar/Monja Blanca, 8a Avenida 15–16, Zona 1, tel 511878. Daily 5–4.30; the journey to Cobán takes 4 hrs, to the Reserve 3 hrs.
To Esquipulas: Rutas Orientales, 19 Calle 8–18, Zona 1, tel 537282. Daily every half hour, 4 am–6 pm; the journey takes 3 hrs.
To Flores (for Tikal): Fuente del Norte, 17 Calle 8–46, Zona 1, tel 86094/513817. Daily at 1, 2, 3, 7 am and 11 pm, officially a 14-hr journey, but normally nearer 24. Reservations are essential.
To Huehuetenango: Los Halcones, 15 Calle 7–66, Zona 1. Buses run daily, 7–2; the journey takes 6 hrs.
To Puerto Barrios: Litegua, 15 Calle 10–42, Zona 1, tel 27578. Daily every hour, 6–5; the journey takes 6 hrs. Their best Pullman service leaves for the coast at 10 and 5 daily, which should be non-stop and a bit faster.
To Panajachel: Rebuli, 3a Avenida 7–36, Zona 9. Daily every hour, 6–3; the journey takes 3 hrs.
To Quezaltenango: Transportes Galgos, 7a Avenida 19–44, Zona 1, tel 23661, and **Líneas Américas**, 2a Avenida 18–74, Zona 1. Both companies run daily buses, 5.30–9; the journey takes 4 hrs.
To San Salvador (El Salvador): Quality, 6 Avenida 9–85, Zona 9. 1st-class Pullmans run daily from Guatemala City, departing from Hotel Villa Española 6 am, Hotel Fiesta 6.30 am, arriving in San Salvador at the Hotel Fiesta 10.45 am, Hotel Camino Real 11 am, and at Hotel Presidente 11.15 am. Tickets can be bought at the main office and the hotels where the buses stop. Buses leave San Salvador for Guatemala daily at the same time, 6 am.
Melva Internacional, 4a Avenida 1–20, Zona 9, tel 367248. Daily, 6–11 am, 12 and 1 pm; the journey takes 5 hrs. The Salvadorean borders are open daily, 6–8.
To El Florido (for Honduras): Rutas Orientales, 19 Calle 8–18, Zona 1, tel 537282. Buses run daily, every half hour, 4–6; the journey takes 4 hrs as far as Chiquimula. There you must change buses for El Florido, taking a **Vilma** bus, which leaves from the back of the market. Last bus from either Chiquimula or the border leaves at 4.30 pm and takes around 2 hrs. From the border, a Honduran minibus will take you to the town of Copán Ruinas in 40 min. The Honduran borders are open daily, 6–6.
To La Mesilla (for Mexico): El Condor, 19 Calle 2–01, Zona 1, tel 28504. Daily buses 4, 8, 10 am, 1 and 5 pm; the journey takes at least 7 hrs. You travel faster by taking a **Los Halcones** bus to Huehuetenango, and changing there for a bus to the Mexican border. **Cristóbal Colón** buses connect with Mexico City and all cities along the way on the Mexican side, the first one leaving around 8 am.

There are also bus routes to the Mexican border towns of Talismán run by **Transportes Galgos** (see Quezaltenango route) and to Tecún Umán, run by **Fortaleza**, 19 Calle 8–70, Zona 1, tel 517994. The Mexican borders open daily from 6–6.

GETTING AROUND GUATEMALA CITY

By Bus

There are **municipal buses** (*buses urbanos*) running to all parts of the city from around 6 am until 8 pm. Fares are ridiculously cheap, so it is always worth having small change in your pocket rather than having to bring out high denomination notes in public. Unfortunately, there is no such thing as a bus timetable or even a brochure outlining which bus goes where. The whole system changes constantly, and nobody can claim to know its logic or routes. The good news is that there are probably only three buses you will want to use, remembering always to confirm with the driver that he is going where you want to go.

Bus no. 5 not only connects the airport to Zona 1, but also connects the centre with the city's most important complex of state-run museums. If you are coming from the airport, you want to make sure the bus says *Parque Central* in the window. Another bus connecting Zona 1 with the airport is **no. 100**, which is usually an orange colour.

If coming from Zona 1, the best place to catch this and the other buses, is beneath the hilltop Teatro Nacional, which is on the continuation of 6 Avenida, beyond 18 Calle. The no. 5 is normally a dark-green colour, and if it is going to the airport, it should say *aeropuerto* in the window. It will also take you to the cluster of the **Museo Nacional de Arqueología y Etnología**, the **Museo Nacional de Arte Moderno** and the **Museo de Historia Natural**, all next door to each other. Best ask to be dropped off here, otherwise you are likely to miss it first time.

Bus no. 2 is also normally a green colour, and stops at the same place underneath the Teatro Nacional. This one will take you from Zona 1 to Zonas 9 and 10, travelling along the Avenida Reforma, which is the main dual carriageway through the southern quarters of the city. Returning from Zonas 9 and 10, the bus drops you off just past the city's tourist office INGUAT, one street east of the Teatro Nacional. If you are heading further into the centre of Zona 1, stay on the bus and it will most likely take you all the way to the Parque Central. Any bus stopping at the Teatro Nacional which says *terminal* in the front window, will take you to the city's main bus terminal in Zona 4. Ask to be dropped off at the appropriate place, and you will find yourself right in front of the terminal.

By Taxi

Taxis can be flagged down anywhere, but there are two regular stands worth knowing about, both in Zona 1: on the **Parque Concordia** and the **Parque Central**. There are also always taxis at the airport and around the bus terminals. Always agree a price before getting into the car, as there are no meters. If you cannot face the buses, and do not wish to hire a car, you can use taxis for journeys as far as Antigua. You should not pay more than $25 one-way for the journey to Antigua, while inner-city journeys should never come to more than $4 for a long run.

TOURIST INFORMATION
Instituto Guatemalteco de Turismo (INGUAT), Centro Cívico, 7 Avenida 1–17, Zona 4, tel (502–2) 31 1333/47, (Mon–Fri, 8–4.30 and Sat 8–1).

The office has very helpful staff, who speak English as well, and can offer a limited range of brochures and listings, make hotel bookings, and assist in route planning around Guatemala.

ORIENTATION
Guatemala City is not that large, but because it is on a grid of numbered streets, it can be a confusing place at first. The city is divided into zones, and the system for numbering avenidas and calles is repeated in each zone so that the same number of avenida can be in very different parts of the city, and very different kinds of neighbourhood. Consequently you must first find the right zone before you look for the right street. Occasionally street signs are missing, which does not help, but if you always keep counting as you walk, you will have a rough idea where you are. See p. 61 for an explanation of Guatemalan addresses.

WHAT TO SEE
Zona 1: the City Centre
Zona 1 is the city centre, which is basically an oblong box of streets defined by the Parque Central to the north, and 18 Calle to the south, Avenida Elena to the west, and the railway track to the east. It takes about half an hour to walk its length, so even if you do get lost, it will not take long to find a familiar spot. The main arteries of commerce are Avenidas 5, 6 and 7, as well as 18 Calle.

Around here you will see the hub of the city's life, from seedy bars and strip joints near 18 Calle and 9 Avenida, to shops and stalls, cinemas and hotels, to street performers and shoeshine boys around the Parque Concordia on 6 Avenida and 15 Calle; and finally there is some interesting architecture, not only the Palacio Nacional and cathedral, but also the churches of San Francisco and Santa Clara on 6 Avenida.

Heading up 6 Avenida, you come to the courtyard of **San Francisco** church on the junction with 13 Calle. It is not a large building, yet the chunky colonial Baroque columns of the entrance are attractive, and as you pass the wrought-iron gates, you find yourself in a peaceful gloom. The most famous sculpture here is the 'Sacred Heart', which was brought from Antigua. Across 13 Calle, the church of **Santa Clara** is even smaller and more unassuming, a quiet haven for tired beggars, not often visited by anyone else. Other churches in Zona 1 worth visiting include **La Merced** (11 Avenida and 5 Calle), which has a very fine interior brought from ruined Antigua churches—note especially the organ, pulpit and altars—and the **Santuario Expiatorio** (26 Calle and 2 Avenida), which is extraordinary for its exterior, shaped like a fish, as well as the modern mural on the inside.

Reaching the **Parque Central**, you get a refreshing sense of space after the claustrophobic streets behind you. It is not particularly attractive: a large expanse of concrete surrounded by the washed-out colours of modern buildings to the west and older architecture to the east. The most important modern building is the **Biblioteca Nacional**, which is situated behind the bandstand and shrub terraces, known as the

Parque del Centenario, though there is little to separate it from the rest of the main square except a road. Directly opposite is the **cathedral**, its brown façade valiantly standing despite the cracks. Inside, the interior is all whitewashed pillars and dour Passion paintings, though there is a certain Baroque elegance about the place, and hundreds of flickering candles before the altars create a festive atmosphere.

At a right angle to the cathedral stands the **Palacio Nacional**, which suffers from being the pale green of mouldy bread, but is otherwise inoffensive neo-colonial. It was begun by President Ubico in 1939, and completed just in time for his enforced removal from office, in 1944. If you bring your passport, you can enter the palace up the left-hand flight of steps, to find two elegant fountained courtyards, lined by three storeys of balconies. Surprisingly, you can wander about freely, and may just bump into a cavalcade of important generals or ministers, in starched uniforms and dark glasses. On the first floor, facing the street, you may be allowed to take a peep into the reception rooms, with their chandeliers and parquet floors. The stained-glass windows remain shattered from the last bomb attack a few years ago.

Worth visiting while you are up this end of town is the **Mercado Central**, in a concrete bunker immediately behind the cathedral. The lowest levels, which are underground, hold the food market and many *comedores*, where you can eat local food freshly cooked. The higher level holds the craft market, where you will find excellent examples of Guatemala's Indian costumes from every corner of the country. There are textiles, basketry, leatherware, jewellery, clothes, shoes, trinkets and tat—almost anything you can get in Guatemala's markets can be bought here. Naturally prices are slightly higher than elsewhere, but they are still very reasonable. It would be a shame to buy here when you first arrive, since you would get no sense of the places and people that make these lovely things. But it will whet your appetite for things to come, and if there is anything you wish you had bought before you leave, you can pop back here and buy it then. On Sundays there is also an open market on the Parque Central itself.

Heading south along 6 or 5 Avenida, you will eventually come to Zona 1's best square: the **Parque Concordia**. Slightly elevated above the black air of the streets, a tree-lined promenade surrounds a small patch of greenery and a central fountain, where instant-photo men, shoeshine boys, preachers, hustlers and street performers vie for your attention. The best time to be here is at the weekends, when you can do some good people-watching or check out the market stalls that cluster alongside. Just a block away, on the corner of 7 Avenida and 12 Calle, the grand, pink, Moorish building is the **Central Post Office**; the **GUATEL office** is next door.

Finally, there are two undistinguished museums you can visit in Zona 1: the **Museo de Arte e Industria**, 10 Avenida 10–72 (Tues–Fri, 9–4; Sat–Sun, 9–noon and 2–4; nominal fee) and the **Museo Nacional de Historia**, 9 Calle and 10 Avenida (Tues–Fri, 8.30–4; Sat–Sun, 9–noon and 2–4; free).

Zona 4

18 Calle marks the border of Zonas 1 and 4, where the scene is immediately a mess of dual carriageways, flyovers, and lung-choking traffic easing its way around the elevated fortress of the **Teatro Nacional** on one side, the large indoor food market in the middle, and the highrise buildings of the **Centro Cívico**, which holds the tourist office and various government offices.

There are three places you will want to locate here: firstly, the extension of 4 Avenida past 18 Calle, where the Antigua buses leave; secondly the urban bus stop at the foot of the National Theatre; and thirdly, the **Tourist Office**, whose entrance is just past the elevated walkway crossing the continuation of 7 Avenida, on the left-hand side. Otherwise you may enjoy exploring the **food market** and hardening your sensibilities with the sights and smells of rotting vegetables and unprettified animal anatomy. Be warned that pickpockets are a danger here, so take nothing with you. Further into the depths of Zona 4, the main bus terminal is best reached by bus or taxi, there being no particular pleasure to exploring this part of town.

Lastly, and probably least, if you continue past the tourist office on 7 Avenida and turn left on Ruta 6, you will find the **Iglesia Yurrita**. Unfortunately it is closed most days, but the exterior is memorable enough, and surely deserves a prize for bad taste. It was built in 1928, with private funds, to look like a Russian Orthodox church, and is a higgledy-piggledy of mosaics and onion-domed towers, with a bit of Gothic pointiness added for good measure.

Zonas 9 and 10

This is one indistinguishable large area cut down the middle by the spacious **Avenida La Reforma**, with Zona 9 to the west and Zona 10 to the east. It is a relatively new part of the city and is the favoured home of the capital's wealthier residents, as well as their concomitant trappings, such as exclusive shops, restaurants, clubs and hotels. Most of the city's embassies are located around here too, as are some fine private museums.

Coming from Zona 4, the first point of interest on the Avenida Reforma is the **Jardín Botánico y Museo de Historia Natural** (8–noon and 2–6, closed Sat & Sun and National Holidays, free). The best part of this place is the botanical garden, which is small but attractive, while the museum is small and bedraggled; neglected stuffed animals contrast sadly with the living garden outside. Across the road is a slate-grey turreted wall, which encloses a whole block and hides a military training school.

The Avenida Reforma is a couple of kilometres long, so hopping on and off the frequent buses may be a good idea to explore its environs along the whole length. A few blocks on from the military academy, a museum you will want to see if you are interested in Maya sculpture and pottery is the **Museo Popol Vuh** (Mon–Sat, 9–5.30, $1 fee). It is located on the sixth floor of a black office block, at Avenida Reforma 8–60. Consisting of one large room, the museum does not take long to explore.

The main exhibit centres on a collection of Maya funerary vases, ranging from enormous urns the size of beer barrels, to miniature household ones. The museum has few explanatory notices, making it hard for the layman to appreciate the significance of what is on view. Still, the delicate craftsmanship is obvious, and as beautiful now as it was two thousand or so years ago. Additionally, there is a small collection of colonial religious art and icons, as well as many stone carvings from Maya sites in the Petén jungle and the Pacific lowlands. A tiny, well-stocked bookshop is attached, where you will find excellent publications on many Guatemalan subjects. Access to the bookstore only is free.

Travelling southwards on Avenida Reforma, the most exclusive quarter of Guatemala City—called the **zona viva**—begins east of the Reforma, between Calles 10 and 14, and up to 4 Avenida. There is really nothing much to set it apart from the other streets, except that there are a high number of luxury boutiques, hotels and restaurants bunched together. An excellent place for cheap snacks is the **Miga** delicatessen shop (7 Avenida 14–44), which is set back from the road, on the parking lot of a shopping mall and does great bagels.

One of the city's best museums is the **Museo Ixchel** at 4 Avenida 16–27 (Mon–Fri, 8.30–5.30, Sat, 9–5.30, $1 fee). Just like the Popol Vuh, this is a small private museum. Here you will find superb changing exhibitions on Guatemalan Indian costumes, with pieces collected from often remote regions, and presented in an imaginative and informative way. Maya textiles, their method of production and the significance of design and colour are presented here, and make the museum a valuable introduction to the country's rich living heritage. A large shop is attached, where many of the finest textiles can be bought, as well as plenty of trinkets too.

The end of Avenida Reforma, and Zonas 9 and 10, is marked by the large busy roundabout called **Parque Independencia**, beyond which the road becomes the Avenida Las Américas, heading into Zonas 13 and 14, ever more exclusive and residential, until it ends up at the **Plaza Berlín**. This is more or less where the city comes to an end, and if it wasn't for recent building and the smog, you could see Lake Amatitlán directly south, and the rumbling Pacaya volcano beyond.

State Museums in Aurora Park

On the western edge of **Aurora Park**, which is a vast expanse accommodating the airport, a military base, the national hippodrome, a zoological park (depressing and filthy), and an artisan market (tourist trap), there is also a cluster of three state-run museums. The whole complex of Aurora Park is located just southwest of Zona 9, and is best reached on bus no. 5 from the city centre.

The **Museo Nacional de Arqueología y Etnología** (Tues–Fri, 9–4; Sat–Sun, 9–noon and 2–4; nominal fee) is without doubt the best state museum in the country. For a newcomer to Maya history and art, this is the place to be introduced to the subject. Rooms are laid out in chronological order, starting with an assortment of theories on the original population of the Americas, moving swiftly on to the emergence of Maya culture, displayed by a mixture of model scenes from daily life, to pottery, tools, and decorative art from each era.

Archaeologists have established three phases for Maya cultural history, and as we encounter each one, we see the increased sophistication in art, pottery and sculpture. Major sites, such as the jungle city of Tikal, coastal Quiriguá and highland Utatlán, are rebuilt in miniature, giving the visitor a helpful idea of what these places once looked like. One whole room (closed at weekends) is wholly dedicated to Maya jade artefacts and jewellery, including the famous mosaic mask from Tikal. Also on view is a collection of Indian costumes, craftwork and utensils from various parts of the country. As you head for the exit, you pass a pleasant circular patio with a fountain in the middle, where ancient stelae stand tall and enigmatic. They are large stones and sculptured slabs, covered in Maya hieroglyphs, still only partly deciphered.

The **Museo de Arte Moderno** (same times, free) is opposite, and well worth a quick visit. The earliest paintings are from the 19th century, and begin with a rather distasteful anonymous picture of Mary, her heart stuck full of daggers. The exhibition quickly moves on into the 20th century, and although the museum is small, it has a good variety of Guatemalan painters and styles. A couple of artists are particularly memorable. Roberto Ossaye died very young and painted most of his pictures in his twenties, which makes his breadth of technique and use of materials all the more impressive. Rolando Ixquiac Xicara has only three of his works on show, but they are enough to show off his haunting talent. Finally there are about twenty sculptures in metal, stone and wood. One of the best is by Roberto Cabrera, which is an odd assemblage of female torsos and other anatomy, boxed in compartments.

The **Museo Nacional de Historia Natural** (same times, free) is just around the corner from the other two, and not worth visiting. Almost none of its glass boxes of flora, fauna and palaeolithic collections originate in Guatemala, or even Central America.

Parque Minerva and Kaminal Juyu

If you would like a graphic idea of Guatemala's geography, then why not head out to the Parque Minerva, where you will find a giant relief map of the country. It must be said, however, that this is no beauty spot, and the horizontal and vertical scales differ considerably. To get there, take bus no. 1, which runs along 5 Avenida in Zona 1.

Kaminal Juyu, today engulfed by one of the capital's western suburbs, was formerly an important Maya city. In fact, it was once the largest city in the country's highlands, with a sophisticated level of art and writing as early as 400 BC. In later centuries, the city is believed to have had close links with the great city state of Teotihuacan, and declined around the same period that city did, soon after AD 600. The archaeological remains of Kaminal Juyu have only been partly excavated, and the present-day visitor unfortunately gets little sense of the site's scale or importance because what you see is mainly mounds of overgrown earth. The site is open daily (8–6), and can be reached by taking bus no. 17, which runs along 4 Avenida in Zona 1.

WHERE TO STAY
The full range, from sleazy to first class, can be found in Zona 1, the best of which are listed here. There are many more, so you will always find something. If you prefer to stay away from the city centre, or require a luxury hotel, then your choice will most likely be in Zonas 9 and 10. The telephone and fax code for Guatemala is 502; for the capital it is 2.

In Zona 1

EXPENSIVE
Please note that the top range hotels usually add tax to your bill. **Pan American**, 9 Calle 5–63, tel 26807–9, fax 26402, is the best hotel in the city centre. Run by friendly staff, the decor is traditional Guatemalan, the standard of the rooms and restaurant very good. **Ritz**, 6 Avenida A 10–13, tel 81871–5, fax 24659, is a modern hotel of international standard, conveniently located, but nothing special. **Posada Belén**, 13 Calle A 10–30, tel 29226, 513478, is overpriced, but nevertheless the most beautiful and secure guest house in this price range. (Look for the street number as there is no sign.) **Colonial**, 7 Avenida 14–19, tel 26722, 22955, has a guard at the entrance, and clean rooms ranged around a pleasant courtyard. **Hogar del Turista**, 11 Calle 10–43, tel 25522, is quiet,

clean and secure, though it offers less than the Colonial for the same price. No breakfast or other meals.

MODERATE
Hotel Excel, 9 Avenida 15–12, tel 532709, is a clean, modern place with secure parking, and all rooms have private bathrooms and TV.

INEXPENSIVE
Hotel San Francisco, 6 Avenida 12–62, tel 25125–28, is central and good, but noisy because of its location. Best of the cheapies is **Chalet Suizo**, 14 Calle 6–82, tel 513786. Spotless and safe, this place is always oversubscribed. **Hernani**, 15 Calle 6–56, tel 22839, is well-kept and close to Parque Concordia. **Fénix**, 7 Avenida 15–81, tel 516625, is clean and very reasonably priced. **Pensión Mesa**, 10 Calle 10–17, tel 23177, lives on the old rumour that Che Guevara stayed here once. Basic but relaxed and friendly, with a sunny courtyard. **Centroamericana**, 9 Avenida 16–38, tel 26917, is close to the Zona 1 bus station. Dingy rooms and sagging beds around a light, covered patio. It is safe and convenient, though the surrounding area is the red-light quarter.

In Zona 4
EXPENSIVE
Hotel Plaza, Vía 7, 6–16, tel 363173, 316337, fax 22705, is a medium-range hotel, with secure parking and restaurant; clean but close to noisy roads. **Sheraton**, Vía 5, 4–68, tel 341212, fax 347245, is conveniently located, but surrounded by noisy roads.

In Zonas 9 and 10
LUXURY
This region of the city is much quieter, less polluted and also safer. **Camino Real**, 14 Calle and Avenida Reforma, tel 334633, fax 374313, is the capital's most exclusive hotel, matching top international standards. Singles from $110, doubles from $140, plus tax. **Hotel El Dorado**, 7 Avenida 15–45, tel 317777, fax 321877, rivals the Camino Real in every way, and charges the same prices. **Cortijo Reforma**, Avenida Reforma, 2–18, tel 366712, fax 366876, is near the border with Zona 4, better quality and location than the nearby Sheraton, and cheaper. **Fiesta**, 1 Avenida 13–22, tel 322572, fax 682366, is near the *zona viva* and is a top hotel. Singles from $80, doubles from $90, plus tax.

EXPENSIVE
La Casa Grande, Avenida Reforma 7–67, tel and fax 310907, is not as grand as it appears. A beautiful villa set back from the road, this is a small hotel with personal service and a good restaurant.

EATING OUT
As mentioned in the introduction, Guatemala is no place for great food. Having said that, it is possible to find perfectly good international cooking. Vegetarians are not generally catered for, and will most likely find themselves restricted to eggs and beans, or pasta. The cheapest restaurants and *comedores* are in Zona 1, with literally hundreds to choose

from. Fast food joints are everywhere; hamburgers and hotdogs are always to be found. **McDonald's** (10 Calle 5–56, Zona 1; 7 Avenida and Vía 3, zone 4; and elsewhere) and **Pizza Hut** (6 Avenida and 12 Calle, Zona 1) are represented here, as well as many local chains, such as **Pollo Campero**.

In Zona 1

The best restaurant for trying Guatemalan cuisine is **Los Antojitos**, 15 Calle 6–28 (closed Sunday), which does delicious steaks and plenty of traditional dishes, at reasonable prices. Try also **Arrin Cuan**, 5a Avenida 3–66, and **Ranchón Antigueño**, 13 Calle 3–50, for typical meals.

A good Italian restaurant in the centre is the **Picadilly**, 6 Avenida and 11 Calle. Three more worth trying are **Bologna**, 10 Calle 6–20; **Giovanni Canessa**, 12 Calle 6–23; and **A Guy from Italy**, 12 Calle 6–33, and also 5 Avenida 5–70. A popular Mexican restaurant is the **El Gran Pavo**, 13 Calle 4–41. Two Spanish restaurants to try are **Altuna**, 5 Avenida 12–31, and **Isaisas**, 9 Calle 3–59. Chinese food is widely available in Zona 1, usually good and cheap. **Fu Lu Sho**, 6 Avenida 12–09, is recommended. For North-American-style food, try **Danny's Pancakes**, 6 Avenida 9–45, or the **Europa** bar and restaurant, 11 Calle 5–16, which is a reasonably popular gringo bar.

The best place for breakfast is **Delicadezas Hamburgo**, 15 Calle 5–28, which faces onto the Parque Concordia, popular with gringos and locals alike. Others recommended for breakfast or afternoon breaks are: **American Doughnuts**, 5 Avenida 11–47; **Pastelería Austria**, 12 Calle 6–58; **Pastelería Jensen**, 14 Calle 0–53; **Pastelería Bohemia**, 11 Calle 8–48; **Pastelería Lins**, 11 Calle 6–12; and **Pastelería Los Tilos**, 11 Calle 6–54.

In Zonas 9 and 10

Some of the best restaurants in Guatemala City are steakhouses, and a well-priced one is **El Rodeo**, 7 Avenida 14–84, Zona 9. If you want something special, try **Hacienda de los Sanchez**, 12 Calle 2–25, Zona 10. There are plenty of others, such as: **Gauchos**, 13 Calle 1–20, Zona 10; **Nim-Guaa**, Avenida Reforma 8–01, Zona 10, and **Tambasco 2**, 7a Avenida 9–15, Zona 9.

For typical Guatemalan dishes, there is **El Parador**, Avenida Reforma 6–70, Zona 9. Two very good Italians are **Ciao Italia**, 15 Calle 3–48, and **La Trattoria**, 13 Calle 1–55. Fancy French food at fancy prices can be had at **Estro Armónico**, 15 Calle 1–11, Zona 10, and **La Boheme**, 3a Avenida 10–41, Zona 10. Vaguely French and easily affordable is **La Crepe**, 14 Calle 7–49, Zona 9, which does a huge variety of crêpes, both sweet and savoury. Fish and seafood specialities are served at two recommended restaurants: **La Mariscada**, 6a Avenida 9–64, Zona 9; and **Marina del Rey**, 16 Calle 0–61, Zona 10. If you do not want to travel to Nicaragua, but would still like to taste its national dishes, why not visit **Caprichos**, 1a Avenida 13–74, Zona 10. You have a wide choice of Chinese restaurants in this part of town. Some of the favourites are: **China Queen**, 6a Avenida 14–04, Zona 9; **Palacio de Oro**, 8a Calle 6–01, Zona 9; **Palacio Royal**, 7a Avenida 11–00, Zona 9; and **Real Capitol**, 6a Avenida 9–11, Zona 9. Last, but not least, there is **Arbol de la Vida**, Avenida Reforma 12–01, Zona 10, which is your only choice for a vegetarian restaurant.

Cafés and cake shops are in good supply, and if you cannot find one, you can always try the luxury hotels. A personal favourite for chocolate cookies is **Q Kiss**, Avenida Reforma 3–80, Zona 9. Just as delicious are the sweets at **Pastelería Zurich**, inside the shopping centre at 4 Avenida 12–09, Zona 10. Other good places to try are: **Café Milot**, Avenida Reforma 13–70, Zona 9; **Pastelería Los Alpes**, 10 Calle 1–09, Zona 10; and **Pastelería Jensen**, 7 Avenida 12–13, Zona 9.

ENTERTAINMENT AND NIGHTLIFE
Guatemala City at night can be a dangerous place, especially in Zona 1, and it is not a good idea to walk the streets alone whether you are male or female. Zonas 9 and 10 are quieter, but even there it would be best to take a taxi to your destination, unless it is just around the corner from your hotel. Having said this, the capital is strangely quiet very early on. Public transport becomes rare after 8pm, and there is a distinct lack of obvious nightlife other than the girlie bars around the Zona 1 bus station.

Your choices for nightclubs are almost entirely restricted to the ones attached to the exclusive hotels of Zonas 9 and 10, which are predictably middle-aged in atmosphere, and have nothing Guatemalan about them. The best music bar is **El Establo**, Avenida Reforma 11–83, Zona 10. Favourite discos in town are **Kahlua**, 1 Avenida 13–29, Zona 10; **Le Pont**, 13 Calle 0–48, Zona 10; **Dash Disco**, 12 Calle 1–25, Zona 10; **Basco's Disco**, 16 Calle 0-55, Zona 10; and the city's newest hotspot is **Sherlock's Home**, Avenida Las Américas 2–14, Zona 13.

There are numerous cinemas throughout the city, including four on 6 Avenida in the centre. Films are usually in English with Spanish subtitles.

SHOPPING
The **Central Market** behind the cathedral has an entire floor of native textiles and crafts. **La Placita** by Guadalupe Church at 5 Avenida and 18 Calle is recommended. **4 Ahau**, 11 Calle 4–53, Zona 1, is good for textiles and crafts, and **Pasaje Rubio**, 9 Calle, near 6 Avenida, Zona 1 has antique silver trinkets and coins.

USEFUL INFORMATION
Emergencies
Police: large building on 6 Avenida and 14 Calle, Zona 1; emergency tel 120.
Medical: see your embassy for a list of English-speaking doctors and best hospitals.

Archaeological Tour Agencies
Turismo Kim'Arrin, Edificio Maya, Office 103, Vía 5 4–50, Zona 4.
Panamundo, Guatemala Travel Service, 3 Avenida 16–52, Zona 10.
Clark Tours, 7 Avenida 6–53, Zona 4; also has representatives in the Camino Real and Sheraton Hotels.

Further addresses (including tour agencies) can be found in the *Tourist Directory*, supplied free by INGUAT.

Money Matters
Apart from the banks and exchange offices, there is a daily exchange service at the airport (weekdays 7.30–6.30; weekends 8–11 and 3–6). The black market exchange is on the

streets around the central post office, in Zona 1. Best to use cash only, and get them to hand over the money before you give them yours. Remember that the exchange rate here is always negotiable and should at least match the bank's. Another place to change dollars is at the reception of large hotels.

The **American Express** office is at Banco del Café, Avenida Reforma 9–00, Zona 9, tel 311311 or 347463.

Books
English literature can be bought at Arnel, in the Edificio El Centro, 9 Calle and 8 Avenida, Zona 1. International newspapers and magazines (American usually) are best found at the exclusive hotels.

Post Office
The main post office is on 7 Avenida and 12 Calle, Zona 1.

Telecommunications
International telegrams are sent from the GUATEL office at 8 Avenida and 12 Calle, Zona 1, or any other GUATEL office.

Day Trips from Guatemala City

Guatemala City is not a place you will want to spend much time in, and it is highly unlikely that you will use it as a base. However, **Lake Amatitlán** is just half an hour away, by bus or car, and certainly deserves a visit—not least for the surrounding views of the Pacaya and Agua volcanoes, or a relaxed boat trip across the waters. If you turn up during a weekend, you also have the opportunity to take the **bubble-lift** up to the **Parque de las Naciones Unidas** (if it's working), where you definitely get the best views of all.

The lake is just west of the main highway connecting the capital with the Pacific lowlands, and there are frequent daily buses that leave either from the Zona 4 bus terminal, or you can flag down the appropriate bus on the corner of 20 Calle and 3 Avenida, in Zona 1. You could also go on an organized tour to the lake, and the *Tourist Directory*, supplied by INGUAT, lists recommended agencies.

On the southern shores of Lake Amatitlán rises the small but active cone of Pacaya, which still erupts regularly, occasionally hitting careless tourists over the head with bits of flying debris. At night, the orange haze from its bubbling mouth is particularly mesmerizing, most dramatically visible if you camp out near the summit. Organized trips are the easiest and safest way to explore Pacaya, and there are plenty of agencies which do both day trips and overnight tours (camping equipment can be hired). The Agua volcano is best climbed while based in Antigua, an hour's journey into the highlands from Guatemala City.

Mixco Viejo

A Maya fortress town, **Mixco Viejo** lies 58 km north of Guatemala City, and was once the capital of the Pokomam nation. Of the highland sites, it is one of the best preserved, and is located on a high ledge, surrounded by steep ravines on all sides, making it one of the most impregnable Maya capitals. In fact, Alvarado was only able to conquer this city with the help of an Indian traitor. Squat temple pyramids of stone make for excellent vantage points, and it is the views across the highland countryside that really impress today.

To reach the site is still difficult, and the only way on public transport is to take the Pachalum bus from the Zona 4 bus terminal, leaving around 10 am daily. Ask the driver to drop you at the entrance of the site, where you will have to camp for the night, since the return bus passes the entrance at around 3 am in the morning. A much better option is to hire a car or arrange for a travel agent to take you on a day trip.

THE WESTERN HIGHLANDS

The Western Highlands are the most populated region of Guatemala, home to the Maya Indians, as well as a wonderful landscape of mountains punctuated by volcanic peaks and expansive lakes. Towns and villages cluster among rolling fields of corn and vegetables, bursting into life on market days and during their annual festivals. The tiny cities of Antigua and Quezaltenango make ideal bases from which to explore the area and get to know the indigenous culture. Geographically, the Highlands form a ridge along Western Guatemala from Mexico to El Salvador, with the Pacific Lowlands to the southwest, and the Eastern Highlands and dry valleys heading towards the Caribbean coastal plain. The road network reaches almost everywhere you will want to visit, and whatever transport you choose to use, journey times will never be very long.

The majority of people in the Western Highlands are descendants of the Maya tribes that have always lived here: the Quiché, Mam, and Pocomam. These three indigenous groups are made up of many small related tribes, such as the Cakchiqueles and Tzutujiles of the Quiché group; the Ixil and Aguacateca of the Mam group; and the Kekchi and Pocomam, of the Pocomam group. There are many other tribes too, such as the Jacalteca, Chuj and Kanjobal. But they are much less in evidence, and you will probably not meet any of their members.

Each tribe has its own language and dialects, which can vary even from one village to the next. However, the most common Indian languages to be heard in the markets are those of the Cakchiquel, Tzutujil, Kekchi, Ixil and Quiché. Undoubtedly, the untrained ear will be unable to distiguish one Indian language from another, let alone one tribe from another. What you will learn to distinguish, as you travel the Highlands, is which costume comes from where, fitting together the pieces of a rich puzzle that maps out Indian culture in this part of the country.

Virtually all Indians can speak some Spanish in Guatemala, so they can communicate not only with you, but also with their 'foreign' neighbours. Bear in mind, however, that in a few cases it may be just as difficult for the Indian from a remote village to speak Spanish, as it may be for you. (Although the English word is not loaded, the Spanish equivalent, *indio*, is considered a term of abuse by most Indians in Latin America, who prefer the word *indígena*.)

Antigua

Antigua (altitude 1530 m) nestles in a fecund valley close to the volcanoes Agua, Fuego and Acatenango, with stunning views beyond the tiled roofs. At street level too, the views are picturesque, with cobbled streets lined by chunky colonial houses, ornate wooden window grilles and inviting entrances to green-clad courtyards. Although the town is laid out on the standard colonial grid, finding your way around can be a bit of a torment at times, since there are very few street signs. But Antigua is small enough to comfortably walk from one end to the other in twenty minutes, so wandering about is no hardship. The majority of 'sights' are ruined churches, of which there is an abundance. But even if you are not interested in ruins, the very special atmosphere of Antigua will undoubtedly make it one of your favourite places. After the frenzy of Guatemala City's traffic, Antigua will seem a real haven: the air is clean, the town peaceful, and full of pleasant places to stay, eat and drink.

Inevitably, Antigua is a powerful magnet for gringos, not least because of the twenty or so language schools here. If you do want to learn Spanish, or refresh your existing knowledge, you are spoilt for choice; and in some ways, the preponderance of gringos is very comforting. Antigua is an excellent place to recover from rigorous travel or ease yourself gently into the Guatemalan environment. But after a while, the place can seem a little artificial, so overtaken by gringo needs and tastes that one is undeniably remote from Guatemalan culture and life.

History

The conquistador Pedro de Alvarado founded Guatemala's first capital, Santiago de los Caballeros, in 1524, near the former Cakchiquel capital of Iximché east of Lake Atitlán. In 1527, his brother Jorge de Alvarado decided to move the capital in his absence, mainly due to the difficulties he was having keeping the Cakchiqueles servile. Thus the first permanent colonial capital was founded in the valley of Almolonga, close to the Agua and Fuego volcanoes. The city, now called Ciudad Vieja, took the name of its predecessor, and flourished for almost twenty years before disaster struck.

The pathologically avaricious Alvarado, bent on conquering new lands in Indonesia, began having a new fleet of ships built in 1538. By the time the ships and crew were ready, Alvarado changed his plans. In June 1541 he joined in a battle in Mexico, where he was squashed by a falling horse. His grieving wife, Doña Beatriz, quickly cheered herself up by proclaiming herself 'Governess of the Americas'. She was only 22, and her reign was to last just one day. On 10 September 1541, two earthquakes, accompanied by torrential rains, triggered off a massive landslide which smothered the capital and killed Doña Beatriz along with many of her subjects. *La sin ventura* (the unlucky one)—as she had called herself—was the first and last female ruler of the colonial Americas.

This was the end of the administrative body's second capital. Two years later, in 1543, Antigua was finally inaugurated when the city council held its first meeting in the uncompleted Palace of the Captains General. Antigua was to become one of the most glamorous and sophisticated cities of Spanish America—a place where both clergy and nobility vied for positions, and the most ostentatious convents, churches and palaces

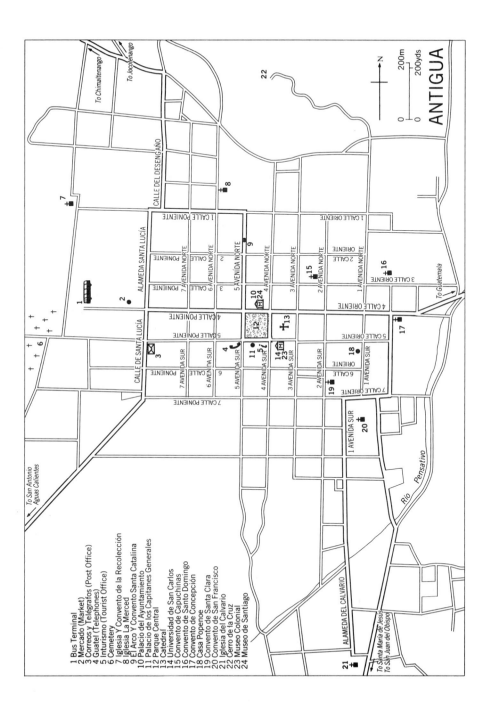

were built; where schools, hospitals, and government buildings provided excellent services for the colonial residents, and life was eased with cheap Indian labour. Violent earthquakes continued throughout the 17th century, but this only increased the building boom. The great Baroque churches and palaces were built with ever thicker walls and better reinforcements. By the end of the century, there were no less than ten convents, three parish churches, five hermitages and four churches, a university, as well as the cathedral, which was the grandest in Central America. All this for a city that was designed for 5000 inhabitants.

By the mid-18th century, there were nearer 50,000 inhabitants, and after just two centuries of existence, Antigua was experiencing its Golden Age: its inhabitants lived in the greatest comfort imaginable at the time. But it all came to an abrupt end with the terrifying destruction caused by the 1773 earthquake, which left Antigua in rubble, many dead buried underneath, and epidemics soon claiming those who survived. The dust had settled on a scene of such death and destruction that the authorities decided the city must be abandoned and the capital moved to a safer location. The subsequent dismantling of Antigua may have caused even more destruction than the earthquake itself. Everything that could be transported away for building the new capital was removed, and Antigua was left defiled and gutted. It is therefore almost miraculous how much of colonial Antigua is left today, and in spite of continued seismic batterings and 20th-century architectural sins, it is a place where the opulent atmosphere of the 18th century remains intact.

GETTING TO ANTIGUA

By Bus

Antigua is easily reached from Guatemala City by bus, which takes about one and a half hours. You will be dropped off at the main bus terminal on the edge of town, which is within easy walking distance of most hotels and guest houses. Usually, there are plenty of 'guides' hovering about, who will direct you to your chosen accommodation, or straight to one of the language schools, who pay them a small fee for this service.

There are frequent daily buses from the local bus terminal to the capital, surrounding villages and nearby towns from dawn until about 3. By late afternoon, you have little chance of catching a bus to anywhere except the capital. When planning any journey, even to nearby villages, it is always a good idea to ask about times the day before, and especially to find out when the last bus returns to Antigua.

There are buses to **Guatemala City** every 20 minutes from dawn until about 5. There are buses every hour to **Chimaltenango** and all destinations along the Pan-American Highway and the rest of the Highlands. The journey takes about 40 minutes, and you must ask to be dropped off at the junction with the main Highway, in order to catch the appropriate bus onwards into the Highlands. Buses coming from the capital are frequent, and you should not have to wait more than half an hour for a connection to such destinations as Panajachel, Chichicastenango, Quezaltenango or Huehuetenango. There are two daily buses to **Esquintla** on the Pacific Highway, leaving at 6 and 7 am. The route is a rough dirt road, skirting the Agua volcano, and the journey takes around 2 hours.

There are regular buses to surrounding villages such as San Andrés Itzapa, San Lucas

Sacatepéquez, Alotenango (for Ciudad Vieja), Duenas (nearest village to starting point for climbing Acatenango and Fuego), Jocotenango, Santa Lucía Milpas Altas, San Antonio Aguas Calientes, Sumpango, San Juan del Obispo, Pastores, Santa María de Jesús (for climbing Agua), San Pedro las Huertas, and San Luis de las Carretas.
Buses Inter-Hotel and Tourism (B.I.T.) run a private shuttle service operating daily between Antigua and the airport in Guatemala City. On Tuesdays, Thursdays and Sundays there is also a shuttle between Antigua and Panajachel. For prices and timetables, see notice boards at the tourist office, Casa Andinista, and at many hotel reception desks and restaurant notice boards.

GETTING AROUND ANTIGUA
Antigua is too small to have its own municipal transport, and most people get around on foot. Bicycles, motorbikes and cars can be hired for excursions, as can horses. (See Useful Information below.) There is a taxi stand by the bus terminal and on the main square, in front of the cathedral.

TOURIST INFORMATION
The local **INGUAT** office is located in the former Palace of the Captains General, across the street from the cathedral. Its opening hours are daily, 8–noon and 2–6. The office not only provides brochures and general help but can also advise on which language schools are currently the best value.
An excellent source of information on anything from accommodation to tours and travellers' messages is the notice board in the courtyard of **Doña Luisa's**, 4 Calle Oriente 12.

WHAT TO SEE
The Plaza Mayor
As with all Spanish colonial towns, the heart of Antigua is its main square, from which calles and avenidas spread out in straight lines. In former times it was an open expanse where festivals and market days were held. These days you find a landscaped park, centred around a fountain. Visitors relaxing on the park benches and cathedral steps are frequently accosted by the charming but relentless Indian hawkers. *Compra algo* (buy something) will soon become a familiar refrain, or even *toma una foto* (take a picture). But be warned, they expect to be paid—an unfortunate practice that should not be encouraged.
Around the square are ranged the grandiose buildings of the cathedral on the east side, the City Hall (Ayuntamiento) on the north side, the Palace of the Captains General on the south side, with Agua's cone towering behind, and an arcade hiding a bank, shops and cafés along the west side. The square is quite small, and the whole effect is almost cosy.
The whitewashed façade of the **cathedral** sadly shows the scars of many tremors and quakes, and the interior is mostly ruined. Completed in 1680, what we see today is just a small reflection of what was once not only the grandest cathedral in Central America but also a magnificent Archbishop's Palace. Originally there were twelve naves, and the present church is made up of just two chapels of the original cathedral, while the palace is

no more than fallen masonry and broken columns, some of which still retain their intricate stucco. Wandering among the debris, you might even find the odd human bone, excavated from the many crypts underfoot, where Alvarado and his wife lie buried, as well as the famous chronicler of the conquest, Díaz del Castillo. Entrance (small fee) to the ruined palace is via the gate on 5 Calle Oriente.

The **Palace of the Captains General** stands at right angles to the cathedral. It is now home to the local police headquarters, municipal offices, and the tourist office. The covered arches provide welcome shade as you walk around to the commercial west side of the square, where street vendors and shoeshine boys sit in wait of custom.

Completing the square is the elevated walkway that fronts the **Ayuntamiento**, again shaded by covered arches, which date from the 18th century. The two-storeyed Tuscan columns neatly mirror those of the Palace opposite. In fact, they are the only part of the square's buildings that survived the earthquake of 1773 relatively intact. Originally, this building not only housed the City Hall, but also offices of the police, and the 'Jail for the Poor', which had a chapel attached where death row prisoners were given their last rites before being publicly hanged on the square.

Today the building houses two museums: in the former prison is the **Museo de Santiago** (daily, 9–4, small fee); and part of the former City Hall now houses the **Museo del Libro Antiguo** (same times, no fee), with a replica of Central America's first printing press and a selection of early religious and scientific books. The Museo de Santiago is ranged around the old prison courtyard which has impressive four-foot-thick walls and heavy iron-grilled doors. There is a small collection of colonial uniforms, and the walls are hung with various portraits, rusty spikes and war regalia, including Alvarado's sword.

East of the Plaza

Heading past the right-hand side of the cathedral, along 5 Calle Oriente, the first building across the street is one of Antigua's finest examples of colonial Baroque, best viewed from the elevated entrance to the Archbishop's Palace opposite. The most ornate stucco is around the entrance of what was once the University of San Carlos de Borromeo. Today it houses the **Museo de Arte Colonial** (Mon–Fri, 9–4; Sat and Sun, 9–noon and 2–4, free), which you should see just for the beautiful inner courtyard. The nine rooms inside contain a range of 17th- and 18th-century colonial art and statuary, as well as an example of the dyed sawdust carpets Antigua is decked out with during Easter Week.

Turning right, down 3 Avenida Sur, you soon come to Antigua's most picturesque square, where two columns of palm trees lead the way to a chunky fountain and arcaded wash basins, where Indian women come to do their laundry. As you reach the square, the San Pedro church immediately in front of you gleams in freshly restored splendour. Next door is the **San Pedro Hospital**. Founded for members of the clergy in 1663, it has long since been open to the general public, not least because of the recurrent need to tend earthquake casualties, most recently in 1976. At the other end of the square, behind the washing arcade, is the church of **Santa Clara** and the ruins of the attached convent. Founded in 1699 by nuns from Puebla, Mexico, the convent was built up to its present proportions after the 1717 earthquake, only to be destroyed in 1773. What remains are the cloisters ranged around a spacious plaza and elegant fountain, which is still beautiful.

Past Santa Clara, heading east on 7 Calle Oriente, you come to the high walls hiding the **San Francisco Church**, by far the most impressive of the town's churches—no plain wooden altars here, but richly gold-leafed and intricately carved ones. Founded by the Franciscans in the late 16th century, the attached monastery was once an important centre of religious teaching, and also included a printing press, hospital, and music and art rooms.

Along the left aisle, plaque upon plaque testifies, in good Catholic manner, to the intervention of Antigua's favourite saint, **Pedro de Betancourt**: 'Thank you for releasing me from a vicious woman'. His tomb is newly restored, placed on shiny terracotta-coloured marble. St Pedro, originally from the Canaries, lived in Antigua during the mid 17th century, devoting himself to the poor and sick with such zeal that he is said to have miraculously cured septic wounds by licking them clean with his tongue. Not one to make life easy, he flagellated himself daily, and during Easter Week, he would crawl past the twelve altars of the Stations of the Cross (see below) on his knees. He died in 1667. A small museum (small fee) adjoins the church, dedicated to St Pedro, where you can see a few old books and some of the man's garments, including his ancient underpants.

Continuing on 7 Calle Oriente and turning left on Calle del Hermano Pedro, you come to the ruins of the **Concepción Convent**, which was the first and grandest nunnery in Antigua. Sadly, the ruins offer little idea of its former splendour, but there are some attractive colonial tiles near its main entrance. Founded in 1578 by a Mexican abbess, it attracted large numbers of nuns from the wealthiest families, and the convent expanded rapidly, thus becoming the richest and largest of its kind. Over a thousand women lived here at one time, including the numerous slaves that tended the religious ladies' every need. The most notorious inmate was Doña Juana de Maldonado, who brought the convent into disrepute by regularly entertaining a bishop in her quarters. Thomas Gage, writing in the early 17th century, commented that 'here is not only idolatry, but fornication and uncleanness as public as in any place of the Indies.' However, this statement has to be set against the fact that Gage was an English lapsed Catholic turned fanatic Protestant. Moreover, he wasn't a very savoury character himself: in 1640s England it was illegal to preach a Catholic mass, and Gage testified so effectively against former Catholic friends that three were hung, drawn and quartered.

Finally, a short walk away, at the corner of 1 Avenida Sur and 5 Calle Oriente, the Casa Popenoe (Mon–Fri, 2–4) offers an immaculate colonial house, complete with original furnishings, domestic tools and a lovely garden.

North of the Plaza

5 Avenida Norte, easily recognizable by the clock-tower arch that spans the street, takes you north of the Plaza, past a number of Antigua's favourite cafés and restaurants. The arch, a few blocks away from the main square, is part of the **Santa Catalina Convent**, now a hotel and restaurant. It was founded in 1609 by four nuns from the crowded Concepción convent, and the arch was built in 1693, so that nuns could pass unseen to the connected property across the street, acquired to house the ever-increasing numbers of nuns and novices. Now a private residence, it is perhaps one of the most famous landmarks of Antigua, framing the cobbled street and views beyond.

At the end of 5 Avenida Norte is the **Church of La Merced**. It has the most ornate stucco of all the churches in Antigua, with twirls of vines, leaves and flower patterns delicately sculpted onto its columns and walls, their creamy colour perfectly highlighted against an ochre backround. On the small square in front of the church, a few Indian women normally sell their textiles under the shade of pine and palm trees. The beautiful fountain nearby dates from the late 17th century, and originally stood in the cloister of San Francisco.

Heading one block east, along 1 Calle Poniente, you reach the remains of **Santa Teresa Convent**, originally home to Carmelite nuns from Peru, but now a gloomy prison for local criminals. Passing swiftly by, the street opens up into a tree-lined avenue, a peaceful corner of Antigua, where some of the town's most desirable residences hide behind thick wooden doors. To the right, down one block of 2 Avenida Norte, a deceptively nondescript entrance leads into **Las Capuchinas**. The spacious ruins, in rather better repair than most, now house the National Council for the Protection of Antigua, which also organizes regular exhibitions of local artists' paintings and sculptures.

The convent was founded in the early 18th century, with only a short life, brought to ruin by the 1773 earthquake. Today the convent is the subject of a tantalizing mystery. What was the circular structure just north of the cloister for? Centered around a supporting tower, a second-floor patio is ringed by eighteen nuns' cells, while underneat, there is a large open room which is bare on the inside, but whose wall contains unexplained niches all around the outside, some containing stone rings on their sides. Was this building for torture, a bath house or a store room? The experts continue to argue.

After a while, ruin-fatigue may set in, and a refreshing antidote is a stroll up to the **Cerro de la Cruz**. This is a hill-top cross, perched directly north of town, a short half-hour walk away, and with a great view of all Antigua and the surrounding countryside. To get there, follow 4 or 3 Avenida Norte to its northern conclusion, turn right, and then left, up the hill and beyond the last houses. It is probably a good idea to ask directions along the way, but you should come to some paved steps and a path winding through some pine trees to your left, which eventually comes out onto an open clearing overlooking Antigua. Although so close to town, this path is regularly dogged by thieves and muggers. It is therefore advisable not to go alone, and not in the late afternoon or after dark.

West of the Plaza

Leaving the Plaza along 4 Calle Poniente, three blocks ahead leads you to Antigua's lively bus terminal and permanent market, located beyond the tree-lined road of Alameda Santa Lucía. '*Guate! Guate!*' shout the bus conductors, as you approach, and black clouds blast from revving engines. Market stalls spill out from the purpose-built wooden shacks: cigarettes, fruit and vegetables, hardware, Indian *artesanía*—almost anything can be bought here. It is one of the country's best markets for buying Indian craftwork at reasonable prices, so it is worth taking the time to shop around here.

One block south of the bus terminal, the extension of 5 Calle Poniente crosses the Alameda Santa Lucía, and ends at the entrance to Antigua's **cemetery**, which is a good place for a quiet walk among gaudy shrines to the dead, complete with plastic flowers and glittering streamers. You will notice a lot of blue and green paint here, as in every other cemetery. These are the traditional colours of mourning for the Indians. For a slightly less morbid pastime, the **Casa Kojom** (Mon–Fri, 9–5, US$1) is not far away, and an excellent museum dedicated to Guatemala's indigenous musical heritage. It is reached by turning right, into Calle de los Recoletos, just before the cemetery. The museum is a small bungalow, set back from the dirt road, in a well-kept garden. It displays many of the Maya Indians' musical instruments, and shows how these were either given up or adapted to colonial tastes after the Spanish arrived. Some instruments, such as the marimba, are still in common use today. The museum has an audiovisual show, demonstrating music from many of the instruments displayed. There are also useful books on traditional Maya festivals and religious ritual.

Continuing past the museum on the dirt road, you soon reach yet another of Antigua's abundant ruins. This one is known as **La Recolección**, after the Recolect friars who came to found a mission here in the late 16th century. Until the 1976 earthquake, its ruins and one remaining arch were considered some of the most evocative by romantics. Now the crumbling walls and weathered boulders tend to get used as a convenient toilet facility or shelter for the destitute.

South of the Plaza

The southern quarter of Antigua has the least to offer in the way of monuments and ruins, and so gets fewer visitors, which is a relief after the crowds around the main square. As you walk its peaceful streets you will see the wonderfully photogenic ruined church of **San José el Viejo**, framed in greenery by nearby trees. It is located at the junction of 5 Avenida Sur and 8 Calle Oriente.

Following 8 Calle Oriente east, past four blocks, will bring you out on the Alameda del Calvario, that runs directly south from the gates of San Francisco. Probably one of Antigua's most unattractive streets, with regular traffic throwing up swirls of dust, it becomes a focal point during the famous Easter Week processions, when ceremonial floats are carried past the twelve altars built along the road representing the Stations of the Cross, and ending up at the church of **El Calvario**, which is still in use today. By the entrance you will see a gnarled old tree, planted by Pedro de Betancourt on 19 March 1657—another place where the Indians come to pay their respects to him. The altars are neglected, and there is really little reason to come out this far, apart from the beautiful stone fountain, which is set into the road in front of El Calvario. It too is neglected, but some of the delicate carving remains.

One of the best detailed introductions to Antigua's historical buildings and monuments is *Antigua Guatemala*, by Elizabeth Bell and Trevor Long, originally written in 1978, and revised in 1990.

SEMANA SANTA IN ANTIGUA
Easter Week in Antigua is one of the most dramatic and colourful festivals in Latin America, and the largest in Central America. Thousands of Guatemalans and foreigners gather to fill the cobbled streets and cram the hotels. Almost all of Antigua's inhabitants

are involved in some aspect of the huge processions, biblical re-enactments and religious services that take place throughout the week, and many more come from far and wide to participate as musicians and singers at the numerous concerts and parties. It's a time of wild celebration and joy—deeply religious fervour mixes easily with drunkenness and dancing. Firecrackers blast in the streets day and night, and the squares are decorated with beautiful flowers, and crammed with people.

The tourist office annually publishes a detailed programme of events. However, a few things are worth knowing in advance: events often happen hours later than stated; banks operate a half-day on Wednesday, and close from Thursday to the following Monday; the food market closes down after Wednesday; from Thursday to Sunday, restaurants and bars often reduce their menus to a few items, usually the most expensive ones, and prices can double; and all accommodation prices double and even triple, and booking in advance or arriving a few days early is essential.

Palm Sunday: Begins early, with 7, 8 and 9 am processions setting off from the major churches after Mass. The main procession of the day starts at 2 (approx.), from outside La Merced church. Jesus' entry into Jerusalem is re-created for the **Jesús Nazareno de la Merced** procession, and his effigy is carried on a huge float (*anda*), which weighs many thousands of pounds. The men shuffle in slow unison, gently swaying as they take turns in shouldering the impossible weight. Eventually, at around 10, the procession of many hundreds of participants wends its way around the main square and returns to La Merced. This final stage is the most dramatic, as the many faces are lit by flaming torches, purple-robed Israelites swing great copal burners, spreading thick clouds of incense and firecrackers explode all around.

Monday: See the freshly decked out altars at La Merced church.

Tuesday: Festivities, mass and worship centre around San Francisco church from 6 am to 11 pm, honouring the city's patron saint.

Wednesday: Main action centres around Escuela de Cristo church, from 6 am to 11 pm.

Thursday: This is one of Easter Week's highlights, and you certainly will not want to miss the night, during which the famous dyed sawdust, pine needle, seed, and flower carpets are delicately sprinkled onto the streets, only to be destroyed by the most dramatic procession of them all: the 3 am **Procession of the Roman Soldiers**. They run around the city's streets, announcing the *sentencia*, the death sentence for Jesus. Others gallop on horseback, and behind them come the modern-day Guatemalan military, giving the spectator an almost too realistic sense of the fearful drama. Meanwhile marimba bands play all over town. It really is worth staying up—or rising early—to see this memorable performance of religious theatre. Some restaurants and bars stay open 24 hours to help you get through the night.

Good Friday: The Procession of the Roman Soldiers comes to a bleary-eyed end around 6 am, only for yet another procession to set off from La Merced church an hour later, passing through town, and eventually returning to its starting point sometime around 3. As a mark of devotion, many of Antigua's inhabitants lay yet more perishable carpets before their front doors.

At midday, the re-enactment of the Crucifixion takes place at the Escuela de Cristo church, while at 2 pm, the Song of Pardon is sung in front of the City Hall, as part of the La Merced procession that began in the morning. After the singing, a lucky prisoner from the local jail is released. Meanwhile, there are many other ceremonies taking place all over town.

Easter Eve: The streets are quiet, but more carpets are laid out, and the procession of mourning, **la procesión de la Virgin de la Soledad**, in the evening, is one of the most moving you will see. Women dressed in black carry enormous floats of the virgin, draped in black and bedecked in long-stemmed red roses.

Easter Sunday: A 'morning after the night before' atmosphere pervades the town, as the festival comes to an end and the majority of visitors quickly depart.

WHERE TO STAY

There are almost as many hotels and guest houses as there are private homes in Antigua, so your range of choices is excellent. No place listed is more than a short walk away from the main square; they are given in order of price in each category, and all prices are inclusive of tax. Remember that Antigua is always popular, so you may have to hunt around, and that during Christmas and Easter Week it can be very hard to find anywhere at all. It is best to get there a few days early, or book in advance where possible. The telephone code for Antigua is 0320.

LUXURY

The **Ramada Hotel**, 9 Calle Poniente and Carretera Ciudad Vieja, tel 011–015, fax 287, has standard North-American hotel facilities in a predictably neutral atmosphere; pleasant garden with pool (open to non-residents for US$3); also sauna, jacuzzi and vapour room. **Panza Verde**, 5 Avenida Sur, is a colonial house with a good and expensive restaurant; there are only four rooms. **Hotel Antigua**, 5 Avenida Sur and 8 Calle Oriente, tel 331/288, fax 807, is the best large hotel in town. Housed in a colonial-type building, the hotel has a beautiful garden and swimming pool. By the time you read this the **Hotel Casa Santo Domingo**, 3 Calle Oriente, tel 102, should also have opened. Located in one of the oldest convents, this will be a very glamorous place to stay, with stunning gardens containing ruined arches and beautiful fountains. Unfortunately, at the time of writing, the restaurant cannot be recommended for anything other than salads and cocktails.

EXPENSIVE

Posada de Don Rodrigo, 5 Avenida Norte 17, tel 291/387, is without doubt one of the most beautiful colonial residences in Antigua, and all rooms and furnishings are period, often even originals. The cobbled main courtyard has two resident macaws who give a tropical flavour, and the restaurant in another courtyard is excellent, though expensive. **Hotel Santa Catalina**, 5 Avenida Norte 28, is housed in an immaculately restored convent, bright rooms and restaurant ranged around a spacious courtyard. Excellent value. Very peaceful, **Aurora**, 4 Calle Oriente 16, tel 217, is housed in a large colonial residence, spacious rooms opening onto a private courtyard.

MODERATE

Posada San Sebastián, 7 Avenida Norte 67, tel 465, is in a newly restored colonial house, a very peaceful place with a wonderful orchard attached. The same owners also run the **Posada San Sebastian**, centrally located at 3 Avenida Norte 4. Rooms are immaculate, but there is no garden. **Posada Asjemenou**, 5 Avenida Norte 31, tel 865, is the best value guest house in this range. A lovingly restored colonial house, with clean and attractive rooms around a spacious courtyard. Delicious breakfast available. **Hotel El Descanso**, 5 Avenida Norte, tel 142, is a delightful small hotel, with rooftop terrace and clean rooms. **Hotel Santa Clara**, 2 Avenida Sur, tel 342, is an immaculate little place, not far from the San Francisco church.

INEXPENSIVE
La Casa de Santa Lucía, Alameda de Santa Lucía 5, is one of the most popular in this category. Clean rooms around a cool courtyard. **Posada Landivar**, 5 Calle Poniente, has modern rooms, immaculately kept, and a rooftop terrace. **Posada de Doña Angelina**, 4 Calle Poniente 33, has rooms around a verdant courtyard. Standards vary, depending on what you wish to pay. **El Placido**, Calle del Desengaño 25, is unfortunately located on the thundering road all buses use coming from Guatemala City. However, rooms are around a lovely courtyard, and you have use of the kitchen. **El Pasaje**, Alameda Santa Lucía 3, is basic but friendly, with great views from the rooftop terrace. **Posada El Refugio**, 4 Calle Poniente 28, has no frills, but serves cheap breakfasts.

EATING OUT
Antigua has some of the best cafés and restaurants in the country, with a wide choice of local and international cuisine, many run by resident foreigners. New places are opening all the time, and the following is just a selection from many more. For example, all the top hotels and guest houses have restaurants, and are not mentioned here.

For cheap snacks and simple *comedor*-style food, try the market and nearby spots on the Alameda Santa Lucía, past the new shopping arcade, but on the same side. **Peroleto** does good snacks and lots of fruit juices. Along 4 Calle Poniente, places like **Panificadora Colombia** and **Antigua Capri** can be recommended for simple fare, as well as **San Carlos**, which is on the main square. For quick take-away snacks of filled bagels and the like, try the American-run **Deliciosa**, 4 Avenida Norte 100.

Some of the best foreign food in Antigua is Italian. **Queso y Vino**, 5 Avenida Norte (closed Tuesdays), has pasta made fresh on the premises, as well as excellent pizzas. **Asjemenou**, 5 Calle Poniente (closed Mondays), has good pizzas, as well as delicious breakfasts and the best cappuccinos and coffee in town. **Martedino**, 4 Calle Poniente, is consistently excellent value for all types of Italian food—in spite of the neon light and bathroom tiles on the wall. **El Capuchino**, 6 Avenida Norte, is expensive but good.

Delicious German food, such as *schnitzel*, can be enjoyed to the sounds of classical music at the **Oasis del Peregrino**, 7 Avenida Norte. Good, but more expensive and thin on atmosphere is **Welten**, 4 Calle Oriente. The hotels **Santa Catalina**, 5 Avenida Norte, and **Panza Verde**, 5 Avenida Sur, both have expensive but highly recommended restaurants serving German and international dishes. For something really special, international cuisine is served at **El Sereno**, 6 Calle Poniente, in the refined ambience of a colonial house. Newly opened, and competing against the latter, is the **Fonda del Pinzón**, just past the cinema on 5 Avenida Sur.

Mistral, 4 Calle Oriente, serves bland French and international meals in a pleasant covered courtyard, and also has a comfortable bar with cable TV. **Doña Luisa**, 4 Calle

Oriente, is in a restored colonial house with a beautiful courtyard, and is a long-standing favourite in Antigua. It is one of the best places for breakfast, but also serves a few meals, such as chilli con carne or soup. Added features include American cable television, a small library, *Time* and *Newsweek* on sale from the cashier, and the travellers' noticeboard. A strong contender for Doña Luisa's business is **Sueños del Quetzal**, 5 Avenida Norte, which has a sunny balcony instead of a courtyard. Good but over-priced, meals are vegetarian, and snacks include fresh bagels, with a choice of fillings. An extra attraction (or deterrent!) is the American cable TV. Next door is **La Fonda de la Calle Real**, which does good meals, including Guatemalan fare, but has excruciatingly slow service. For excellent service and meals try **Coma y Punto**, on the corner of 6 Avenida Norte and 2 Calle Poniente, which also has a small bar and good music. On 6 Avenida Norte, near La Merced, you will find the **Tecún** restaurant, which regularly presents Maya art and culture with exhibitions and live performances of dance and music.

El Churrasco on 4a Calle Poniente has good cheap steaks. **Los Gauchitos**, on the same street, is good for the money, in spite of the fast-food atmosphere. **Las Antorchas**, on 3a Avenida Sur, is expensive and excellent. Finally, there is the Japanese restaurant **Zen**, on 3 Avenida Norte, which gets very mixed reports for its food, but is located in a pleasant colonial courtyard; it is worth trying at least once, but especially on New Year's Eve, when the best party is traditionally held here.

There are a few excellent cafés (excellent for cakes and pastries—not coffee). The best is **La Cenicienta**, 5 Avenida Norte, closely followed by **Las Américas**, on the corner of 6 Avenida and 5 Calle. Also worth trying is **Café Jardín**, on the west side of the main square. Just for cookies, see **Cookies etc**, on 3 Avenida Norte, which is the only place that serves good coffee as well.

ENTERTAINMENT AND NIGHTLIFE

With so many resident and visiting foreigners, Antigua's nightlife is rapidly expanding. Apart from restaurants that double up as drinking spots, there are eight music bars, most conveniently in the same street, and open until one in the morning, while the law remains forbidding the sale of alcohol after 1 am.

La Chimenea, on the corner of 4 Calle Poniente and 7 Avenida Norte, has comfortable sofas and chairs and an atmosphere reminiscent of an English pub. The music is standard American pop. Heading north, up 7 Avenida Norte, **Café Latino** hosts regular live bands, including reggae from Belize. On the same side of the street, **La Boheme** is now a restaurant/bar, and only has music in the early evening. A few stumbles further, **Picasso's** is the best bar in town, and certainly has the best range of taped Western music. Virtually across the street is **Bota Tejana**, which is a no-frills bar and the only one where you can mix more with local people than foreigners. Out of favour these days, and too expensive, is **Moscas y Miel**, on 5 Calle Poniente, which also has a tiny dance-floor. Equally ignored is the **El Cabildo**, on 7 Avenida Sur, though it certainly deserves more foreign custom than it gets. The newest bar is **Macondo**, in the Santa Catalina convent on 5 Avenida Norte, catering to a middle-aged crowd who can afford the expensive drinks. Finally, the Ramada Hotel has a small disco.

The cinema is on 5 Avenida Sur, near the main square and usually shows English-language films with subtitles. **Cinemala**, at 3 Avenida Norte 9, shows three videos a day on a large TV screen, though often the tape quality is appalling and Q5 seems too much for what you get. The programme is widely advertised around Antigua. **Cinecafé Oscar**, on the same street, but behind the cathedral, offers a similar service for the same price. Its programmes are also widely advertised. A third option is **Cine Elektra**, 7 Avenida Sur, next to Govinda's. New places open all the time.

SHOPPING
Antigua's market, near the bus terminal, is one of the best for Indian handicrafts. People come from all over the country to sell here, especially at weekends, when most of the action transfers to the corner of 4 Calle and 6 Avenida. Prices at weekends will be slightly higher, but a practised haggler can still get a good bargain.

USEFUL INFORMATION

Travel Agents:
Viajes Tivoli, above Un Poco de Todo, is the best agent in town, and can book any type of international flight for you, as well as book tours (including to Tikal); and you will find very friendly service at **Centro de Viajes**, on 5 Avenida Norte.

Emergencies
The tourist office can help with recommending English-speaking medics, or anyone local will be able to direct you to the private hospital.

Money Matters
Banco de Guatemala and Banco del Agro on the main square are the best places to change money during the week. The Banco del Agro branch on Alameda Santa Lucía is open Mon–Sat, until 6 pm. For exchange outside banking hours, try the door to the right of Roly Hairdressers, 4 Avenida Sur. The address is well known and the rates for cash or cheques are good. Lloyds Bank International have an office on the main square at 4 Calle Oriente.

Books
A wide selection of books on many Guatemalan subjects, both in English and Spanish, is available at **Casa Andinista**, 4 Calle Oriente; another good place is the **Librería Pensativo**, on 5 Avenida Norte, though most of their books are in Spanish; last choice because of bad prices and abrasive staff is **Un Poco de Todo** in the shopping arcade on the main square.

CIRMA: The Centro de Investigaciones Regionales de Mesoamerica, 5 Calle 5, (Mon–Fri, 8–6, Sat 9–1) is an excellent research library open to the public, where you can find all types of publications in both English and Spanish.

Post Office
This is located on the Alameda Santa Lucía, virtually opposite the bus terminal.

Telecommunications

The GUATEL telephone office is on 5 Avenida Sur, just off the main square. There are many places offering a **fax service** but the cheapest is the J.C. Librería, 6 Calle Poniente 21.

Car and Bike Rental

Avis have an office at 5 Avenida Norte 22, tel (0320) 291387. Mountain **bikes** as well as ordinary bikes can be hired from apt no. 9, Rosario Lodge, 5 Avenida Sur. Prices are steep, with mountain bikes going for $8 per day. Accompanied tours around Antigua and environs have been highly recommended and cost $3.50 per hour. Long-distance cycling tours are also available. **Motorbikes** can be hired from 6 Avenida Sur, 8.

Laundry

There are two places on 5 Calle Poniente, near the main square.

Language schools

The most prestigious and expensive of the lot has long been the **Proyecto Lingüístico Francisco Marroquín**, 4 Avenida Sur 4, whose clientele is overwhelmingly North American. **Maya**, 5 Calle Poniente 20, is equally good, and for some reason favoured mostly by a European clientele. Other establishments that are repeatedly recommended are the **Professional Spanish Language School**, 7 Avenida Norte 82, and **Tecún Umán**, 6 Calle Poniente 34. There are many more schools to choose from, offering every kind of teaching option you might want, as well as accommodation with a local family, if required. Prices range around $60–120 per week for one-to-one teaching, and full-board accommodation with a family usually costs $30 per week extra. If you hire a private teacher, you should expect to pay around $2 per hour.

Volcanoes

Information, maps, hiking equipment and guides are best found by either going to the **Casa Andinista**, 4 Calle Oriente, which also sells photocopies of topographic military maps to the northern Ixil region otherwise unavailable and can give you the latest news on safety (this is also a good place to enquire about travel) or **Club Chigag**, 6 Avenida Norte 34, though the latter gets very mixed reports.

Excursions from Antigua: Villages and Volcanoes

Once you get to know Antigua you will find it hard to tear yourself away; however, there are plenty of excursions worth taking, ranging from energetic volcano climbing to gentler pastimes like soaking in hot springs. The highland valley surrounding Antigua is strewn with Indian hamlets and sleepy villages, while in between, rich farming country is covered with crops such as coffee, maize, cereals, vegetables and fruit trees. Towering above are the three volcanoes of Agua, Acatenango and Fuego, the last of which is still active. Nearer Guatemala City, but usually visited on a tour from Antigua, the active Pacaya volcano is the most dramatic, since for years it has not just been fuming, but actually erupting at regular intervals.

It is a beautiful area, and the inhabitants are friendly too. Armed robbery and rape do occur sporadically, however, particularly on the volcanoes, where it is always best to take a local guide with you or go in a group. Most times everything goes well, so do not let yourself be put off, but it is very worthwhile finding out the latest news on security, either from the tourist office or the local hiking organizations. All villages mentioned can be reached by public transport from Antigua bus terminal, or by taxi; you should always remember to agree on a price first.

Villages

One of the nearest villages is **San Juan del Obispo**, just a couple of kilometres southeast of Antigua. It is chiefly interesting for the restored palace of Francisco Marroquín, who was the first bishop of Guatemala, in the days of Alvarado. The nuns who now occupy the palace do not mind showing visitors around. The church contains some very fine colonial religious artwork from the 16th century. You could walk to the village in an hour, or any bus going to or from Santa María de Jesús can drop you off. Heading onwards to **Santa María de Jesús**, a journey that will take just under an hour from Antigua, you reach one of the best vantage points from which to survey the whole valley that has Antigua at its heart. The views of the twin peaks of Fuego and Acatenango are terrific. The village itself is mainly inhabited by Indians, who sell high-quality *huipiles*, with the best choice on market days: Mondays, Thursdays and Saturdays.

Southwest of Antigua, less than six kilometres away, is the village of **Ciudad Vieja**, which is not really interesting for what it is today, but rather for being near the spot where Guatemala's second capital perished. It was here that the ill-fated town of **Santiago de los Caballeros** was swept away in 1541, when a huge mudslide, caused by an earthquake, came off the slopes of Agua. There are no remains. Also out this way, but clinging to the lower slopes of Acatenango, is **San Antonio Aguas Calientes**, where the Indians have turned their superb weaving into a commercial cottage industry, selling their wares all along the village street. If you are interested, there are plenty of women here who will give you weaving lessons on their backstrap looms—just ask around if no one approaches you first. Trying it yourself, you quickly appreciate the immense amount of time and effort that goes into Guatemalan weaving.

For a change from the swimming pools of Antigua's posh hotels, you could luxuriate in the hot springs of **San Lorenzo el Tejar**, about five kilometres from Antigua. The springs are open daily, 6–5, except Tuesday and Friday afternoons; small fee. To reach them, take any bus heading for Chimaltenango, and ask to be dropped off nearest the village of **San Luis Carretas**, from where it is a short walk. You will find a communal pool, but also private tubs, which you can have all to yourself for as long as you wish. A few kilometres further on by bus, you pass a tiny lake, popularly known as **Los Aposentos**, set amongst a grove of pine trees, and a good place for a leisurely turn in a rowing boat.

Finally, if you only have time to make one day trip, **San Andrés Itzapa** on a Sunday is well worth staying on for. The reason for this lies not in the village itself, which is a dust-blown sort of place that suffered terrible damage during the 1976 earthquake; rather, it is interesting for the local cult of **Maximón**, one of the Maya Indians' most notorious saints, also known as St Simón. A controversial saint, not least because he is supposed to be evil, New World colonists have always tried to suppress the Indians' attachment to him.

In most cases, Maximón is dressed up in Western clothing, often with a fat cigar in his mouth, and Mafia-type sunglasses. The origin of his evil reputation is uncertain, but it may have been propaganda spread by the earliest conquistadors. One theory is that Maximón (pronounced 'Mashimon') was an Indian holy man at the time of the conquest, who was murdered by the Spanish because they feared his influence over the Indians. As a result of his martyrdom, however, he became one of the Indians' most revered saints—a symbol of their oppression as well as of the power they implored against it. Today, there are only a handful of villages left where he is worshipped, and the chapel in San Andrés Itzapa is one of the least visited by outsiders.

Every Sunday, Indian worshippers flock from as far away as Guatemala City, to pay tribute to Maximón. This elaborate ritual necessitates liberal splashings of rum, as well as the smoking of fat cigars (women only), candle-lighting, praying, and even fireworks. People queue to take their turn in front of Maximón's altar, where they will pray to him, all the while splashing him with rum and throwing money into his lap. Occasionally a daykeeper (a traditional shaman) will accompany someone, rubbing their head and neck with rum, and stroking their bodies with special laurels from head to toe.

Afterwards the worshipper will normally choose one of the many stone tables in the chapel on which to light candles. The candles are all different colours, and signify different prayers: red is for matters of love, faith or desire; green is for business or wealth; pink is for health and hope; black is for warding off enemies and jealousy; purple is against vicious or bad thoughts; blue is both for luck in matters of money, journeys or learning, and for anything to do with work; yellow is for the protection of adults; and white is for the protection of children. Once outside again, the burning of fireworks and rum is used to divine fortune, and this part is normally performed with the help of a daykeeper, who is paid for his service.

You will find the chapel easily by turning up an unpaved street, that leads off to the right, just past the main square. Anyone can tell you where if you get lost. Do not take your camera in case it causes offence.

Volcanoes

Two of the volcanoes, Agua and Pacaya, can be climbed on organized day trips, which cost anything from $15 upwards. To find out about the range currently available take a look at the notice board at Doña Luisa's. For official information on the latest security situation, reputable guides, and equipment, compare what is offered at Casa Andinista and Club Chigag, before coming to any decisions. Most people prefer the services of Casa Andinista. If not planning to stay overnight, strong walking shoes, food and water, toilet paper, sun cream and sun glasses are all you need. Remember also, that the temperature at high altitudes is very cold, more so because of the wind chill.

The easiest volcano to climb nearby is **Agua** (3760 m), immediately south of Antigua, which has a clear path leading up it, beginning outside the village of Santa María de Jesús. The slopes of this perfectly symmetrical cone are steep, and the ascent takes a good four to five hours. The high altitude makes it even harder, but once at the crater, you will be rewarded with the extraordinary sight of a football pitch inside the mountain, and views to take away what little breath you have left. The descent is obviously much quicker, and if you set off at 6 am, you can do Agua as a tough but rewarding day trip. If you plan to stay the night near the summit, there is a shelter, but you will certainly need a warm sleeping-bag, and preferably a tent. The dawn viewed from up here is magical, and on a clear day you can see all the way to the Pacific, as well as the surrounding valleys and neighbouring volcanoes of Pacaya, Fuego and Acatenango.

Acatenango (3960 m) and **Fuego** (3835 m), to the southwest of Antigua, are twin volcanoes that only the toughest attempt to climb. The ascent of Acatenango can take anything up to nine hours. You have a choice of two craters to view, as well as a superb panorama stretching from Agua across the valley, to the distant cones surrounding Lake Atitlán. If you have the energy left to climb Fuego as well, you will have to stay the night beneath Acatenango's craters, and continue for another foot-crunching day the next morning. Unfortunately, you have to descend quite a way before you can start climbing Fuego, so you are in for a long day. Near the summit, the crater is continuously spouting sulphurous fumes, so do not be tempted to get too close. You must go back via Acatenango, so the return journey is no easier.

Pacaya (2544 m), rising above Lake Amatitlán near Guatemala City, is a popular day trip—not least because you can drive a good long way before walking, and then the volcano is pretty small. Up top, you will enter a blackened world of burning earth and witches' fumes, petrified lava and strange shapes, the mountain reminding you of its vitality by spouting clouds of smoke and occasional rocks. At night, the volcano's display is the most dramatic, as its cone is wrapped in a haze of orange light. Clearly you need to be careful on Pacaya, never getting too close if the eruptions are fierce. It is also an unfortunate fact that the volcano's popularity makes it most prone to bandit activity, and in 1991 all tours were suspended after a particularly brutal attack. With any luck, things will have improved by the time you arrive, but even an armed guard is unlikely to help, should you meet with robbers prepared to use their guns.

Iximché

Capital of the Cakchiqueles, Iximché was once a city of 10,000 people, founded by proud noble families who had seceded from the greater Quiché empire only 50 years before the Spanish arrived. As happened elsewhere in Latin America, the internal divisions between the Indian nations helped the Spanish in their conquest. In Guatemala, it was the Cakchiqueles who sided with Alvarado and his troops. He arrived in Iximché in 1524, and declared it the first Spanish capital of Guatemala.

It did not take long before the Spanish alienated their Indian allies by demanding ever more labour, riches and women, and by 1526 Alvarado had burnt this Indian city, and its inhabitants were forced to flee. It's a depressingly familiar story, and today the site gives little away of what it once looked like. It may have little to offer as a ruin, but it is a tranquil place and surrounded by beautiful countryside. Its location, about halfway between Chimaltenango and Los Encuentros, make it an easy day-trip away from Antigua, or a short detour from the Pan-American Highway.

It is quite easy to get to the site, though it does involve a good hour's walk if you don't have private transport. Catch any bus to Chimaltenango (40 mins), and wait there for a Tecpán bus (1hr). From Tecpán, it is then a few kilometres' pleasant walk to the site of Iximché (small fee).

Lake Atitlán

> The Indians consider the Atitlán basin the navel of the earth and sky, for as one enters it the sky becomes defined by its rim of smoking cones.
>
> Ronald Wright, *Time Among the Maya*

Lake Atitlán is most extraordinary at sunset. As the cool mountain air turns all the shades from blue to dusty pink to grey, so the waters of the lake change their hues of greenish blue. Every time you watch it happen, the scene will be different. Add to this spectacle the setting of the lake: 18 km long and about 10 km wide, at the feet of three volcanoes piercing white clouds, and you can understand why some people get carried away and insist this is the most beautiful lake in the world. It lies at an altitude of 1562 m, and is ringed by mountains on all sides, often with steep rock faces falling straight into the water, and only a few stretches where the ground is level for any distance. Although dramatic storms occasionally whip up on the lake, the weather here is generally temperate.

The former Indian village of **Panajachel** has long been a popular resort for retired and visiting foreigners. Dotted around the lake are a number of traditional Indian villages, of which Santiago Atitlán is the most famous. But there are plenty of others, less enslaved to tourism, and there are also long distances of the shoreline that are not inhabited at all, perfect for tranquil hiking or boating.

During the sixties, Panajachel was 'discovered' by hippies, who have left an indelible mark on the place. The Indians still sell custom-made waist jackets and skull caps none of them would be seen dead in, and have even mastered the art of tie-dying. All this has

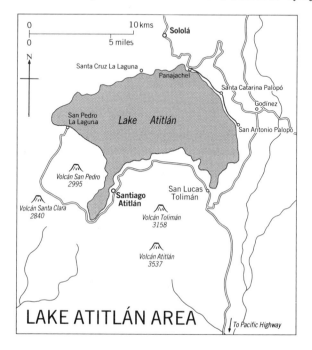

meant that Panajachel has long since stopped being a quiet village and is now a buzzing resort with every kind of accommodation, and a lively nightlife second only to Antigua. Restaurants and lakeside stalls cater to a wide range of tastes, ranging from local fish to Swiss delicacies or health food.

You may find all this commercialism a touch depressing. However, Panajachel is still a very small place, and in spite of Lake Atitlán being one of Guatemala's foremost tourist attractions, you will find yourself in another world almost as soon as you leave the settlement. With luck, the fact that the entire basin is a national park will help to keep it that way.

GETTING TO LAKE ATITLÁN

By Bus

Coming from the capital, the **Rebuli** company runs daily buses, 6–3, from its offices at 3 Avenida 2–36, Zona 9, and the journey takes about 3 hrs. Coming from Antigua, catch a local bus to Chimaltenango, and get off at the junction with the main Highway. From there, flag down any bus with either Panajachel or Sololá painted on the front window. This journey should not take more than 3 hrs either. Bus tickets are very cheap, but always compare with your fellow passengers to make sure you are not paying an inflated 'gringo price'.

GETTING AROUND LAKE ATITLÁN

The road is paved as far as Panajachel, but after that it becomes a very rough dirt road, extremely steep in places, as it follows ridges above the shoreline. Panajachel is located on the northeast shore of Lake Atitlán, and the dirt road curves around the eastern side of the lake, to San Lucas Tolimán, in the southeastern corner, all the way to Santiago Atitlán and San Pedro La Laguna on the southwestern shore. The road is so bad that if you tried to drive the 55 km from Panajachel to San Pedro La Laguna, it could easily take you half a day. There is a new paved road to San Lucas Tolimán, but it leaves the lake, going via San Andrés Semetabaj and Godinez. For an easy day's hike, take an early morning bus from Panajachel to Godinez, and then walk down the mountainside to San Antonio (takes about one hour), and follow the dirt road along the lake for another 11 km, back to Panajachel.

The best way of reaching the lake's southern villages is by taking one of the morning ferries or launches, which leave from the beach in front of Panajachel every day. There are ferries between 8 and 5. To Santiago Atitlán, the crossing takes 45 minutes, and the price is usually around $3 for a return ticket. Do not be conned into buying a return ticket, however, since they are only valid on the boat you bought it on, which may not travel back when it suits you. There are plenty of boats and you can always buy a single if you ask for it. For morning ferries (same times, but check at the tourist office) direct to San Pedro or Santa Cruz La Laguna, head for the jetty just before the **Hotel Tzanjuyu**. A road leads off the main street, taking you straight down to the water. The returning ferry drops in at all the villages along the inaccessible western shore, and the two-hour journey is a lovely way to see this quiet part of the lake. You can, of course, hire the services of a boatman. Agree on a price before setting off and, if possible, go with someone who has been recommended by the tourist office. It is not unknown for the occasional tourist to end up swimming home because of mid-lake renegotiations.

Lake Atitlán

It is possible to travel all the way around the lake by a combination of bus rides, boat trips and walking (not a good idea to go alone). This would take you about four days, and you would need to take your own provisions and tent, though there are simple guest houses in some villages, namely San Lucas Tolimán, Santiago Atitlán, San Pedro La Laguna, and Santa Cruz. To cut this journey by half, you could take a bumpy bus ride from Panajachel to Santiago Atitlán one day (check time with the tourist office, but it is very early), catch a boat to San Pedro La Laguna the next morning, and from there spend two days walking back to Panajachel via Santa Cruz.

Panajachel

The road that turns off the Pan-American Highway for Panajachel and Lake Atitlán is a dramatic short drive. One of the first things you see is the bizarre sight of a giant soldier's helmet set on a pair of boots, which marks the entrance to a large military base. Before you have time to wonder whether you imagined it, you find yourself transported to Sololá, a small town perched high above the lake's basin. Up to here the road is relatively level. But from now on, you are in for a rollercoaster ride, plunging 500 metres in 8 km, on hairpin bends and along steep ridges, with short flashes of the lake below and superb views of the surrounding mountains and volcanoes. A number of *miradores* (viewpoints) have been set up along the road, which are good places to take panoramic photographs.

Panajachel itself is flat and strung out along a dusty main road, lined with hotels, gas stations and restaurants. There are almost no traces of the original Indian village. The 'village' spreads from the main road down to the lake shore, its two main thoroughfares lined with more restaurants and guest houses, and a bustling street market on Avenida Santander, where you will find an excellent range of Guatemalan **artesanía** and textiles.

Prices are not bad either. The waterside is newly landscaped, with a tiny stretch of sand, and a number of wooden shack restaurants, where you can eat delicious food right by the lake. The best beach for relaxed sunbathing is beyond the River Panajachel, just east of the main waterfront, and easily reached by crossing the pebbly estuary of the shallow river.

Avenida Santander branches off the main road by the **bank**, which is also where all buses stop. If you continue straight on, you soon come to the edge of Panajachel and the local market, where the region's indigenous inhabitants retain a vital part of their way of life, with no concessions to tourism. This is the place to buy fresh fruit and vegetables. Apart from this area, Panajachel is dominated by the floating population of foreigners, and the place is often referred to as 'Gringotenango'. However, as a base for exploring the lake it is ideal, and if you prefer to be away from the crowds, you have a number of choices in villages such as Santa Catarina, San Pedro La Laguna, Santiago Atitlán and Santa Cruz.

TOURIST INFORMATION
The **INGUAT** office (Mon, 8–noon; Wed–Sun, 8–noon and 2–6) is located near the bank. They can do little more than tell you departure times for boats and buses, and any other information you require is best picked up from other travellers.

GETTING TO AND FROM PANAJACHEL
There are daily direct buses to Chichicastenango (2 hrs) and Quezaltenango ($2\frac{1}{2}$ hrs) in the early mornings (see the timetable in the tourist office). Otherwise, there is a constant flow of minibuses between Sololá and Panajachel, or to the Los Encuentros junction, where you can easily get an onward connection, either back towards Guatemala City, or heading west. If you are waiting for one of the early morning buses, and the waiting crowd worries you, you have a better chance of getting onto the bus if you wait for it by the old market, where all the early buses stop first. For local buses around the eastern shore of the lake, check with the tourist office for the latest schedule. Normally there is just one bus heading towards San Lucas Tolimán, and the return leaves about the same time from the other end, making it virtually impossible to return the same day.

WHERE TO STAY
You have plenty of choices here, and the only times you might have a problem are over Christmas and Easter, when the place is not only full, but prices can double. Equally, prices can sink very low at quiet times—they are always negotiable, even in the top hotels. The telephone code for Panajachel is 0621.

Directly on the Lakeshore
EXPENSIVE
Hotel del Lago (tel 555/60), at the end of Avenida Rancho Grande, is a largish hotel, with all modern conveniences, including a pool. **Hotel Playa Linda** (tel 159), on the public beach, has a lovely garden and verandah, with most rooms facing the lake. The best private beach belongs to **Hotel Monterrey** (tel 126), off a side road of Avenida Santander. Quite a way from the hub of things, one of the oldest hotels here is the **Hotel**

Tzanjuyu (tel 318), with two storeys facing the water, and an atmosphere and decor that recall 1940s Hollywood movies.

On a small bay at the beginning of Panajachel, there are a couple of good hotels, one dusty kilometre from the centre of Panajachel. **Hotel Atitlán** (tel 441) is the most luxurious hotel on the lake itself, with all the services you would expect, such as private beach, swimming pool and restaurant, as well as plenty of water-sport options laid on. **Hotel Visión Azul** (tel 419/374) is nearest the main road on the bay, a pretty little hotel with private beach and pool and much cheaper than Hotel Atitlán.

The lakeside hotel in Santa Catarina, **Villa Santa Catarina** (tel 291) has an excellent location, though the hotel does clash somewhat with the village, arrogantly spreading itself out on the shore, its back to the Indian inhabitants who used to wash their clothes there.

INEXPENSIVE

The **Arca de Noé**, below Santa Cruz, is a lovely place with excellent meals for guests only, at $3 for five courses. Bungalows with private bathroom (two to three people) go for $10, and simple rooms, sharing shower and toilets, are $5 for two. Get there early in the morning if you want any chance of getting a room or bungalow. Up in the village there's the basic but clean **Hospedaje Hernández**, which charges less than $2 for a room.

In Panajachel

EXPENSIVE

Hotel Regis, Avenida Santander, tel 149/152, is a friendly, well-kept hotel with private garden, right in the middle of Panajachel. **Hotel Primavera**, on Avenida Santander, is clean and has an excellent Swiss restaurant. **Cacique Inn**, Calle Real, tel 205, is expensive for what it offers, but does have a small pool.

MODERATE

Hotel Paradise Inn (tel 021) on Calle del Río offers motel-style accommodation, as near to the lake as possible, without being on it. **Hotel Galindo**, on the main road towards the local market, has a lovely garden and a good restaurant. New bungalows in their own grounds are offered at **Rancho Grande**, Avenida Rancho Grande, tel 554.

INEXPENSIVE

Hotel Fonda del Sol (tel 162), right next to the tourist office, is basic but clean, and excellent value for the price. Of the other cheapies, the favourite is **Las Casitas**, opposite the market on the main road, which has clean rooms around a private garden, breakfast restaurant and very friendly management. **Hotel Naya Kanek**, also on the main road near the market, is less friendly but all right. Finally, anywhere saying 'Rooms' will offer basic accommodation, sharing cold showers at rock bottom prices.

In San Lucas Tolimán

There are a few basic but clean guest houses here—ask for directions: **Pension Central**; **Hospedaje El Exito**; **Pensión Las Conchitas**; and **Cafetería Santa Ana**.

In Santiago Atitlán
First choice has got to be the moderately priced **Posada de Santiago**, just one kilometre outside the village, near the Texaco station. Described by one traveller as 'a little piece of heaven', rooms include private bathrooms and beautiful fireplaces. Meals are excellent if not cheap.
   In the village itself there is the **Hospedaje Chi-Nim-Ya**, and also the **Pensión Rosita**, which is a bit cheaper and much grubbier.

In San Pedro La Laguna
Chuasinahi is a basic guest house near the waterfront, offering rooms for $2. Next door are the wooden shacks that make up **Ti-Kaaj**, favoured by the young hippie set. Also popular with them is the **Pensión Johanna**, located on an inlet beneath the village, where there is another landing stage (ask for directions).

EATING OUT
Most of the top hotels have restaurants, where you can enjoy expensive meals. Apart from them, the choice is good, and one of the best is **Al Chisme** on Calle de los Arboles, which also does good pastries. For excellent vegetarian meals, try **La Unica Deli**, on the main road, up towards the market. A bit further on this way, **Ranch Market** is best for breakfast and pastries, serving good coffee. It also has the added attraction of an English lending library, and American magazines to read.
   For delicious steaks and the like, try **El Patio**, on Avenida Santander, where, as the name suggests, you can sit outdoors on balmy nights. Also on Avenida Santander is the Swiss restaurant of **Hotel Primavera**, which offers immaculate over-priced meals. **The Last Resort** (left after the GUATEL office, if you are coming from the main road, down 14 Calle de Febrero), on the other hand, serves a wide range of filling meals, including breakfast, at rock bottom prices. The atmosphere is relaxed here, as customers listen to the steady beat of reggae or play ping-pong in the back. There are plenty more places to try, and new establishments are opening up all the time.

ENTERTAINMENT AND NIGHTLIFE
For an evening of drinking, the most popular bar these days is **La Casa del Pintor**, Calle los Arboles. Good pizzas are also served here. **Circus Bar**, under the same management, across the street, functions more like a disco, and has live music at weekends. There are also two video bars: **Café Xocomil**, on the main road, near the market; and **Video Bar**, on Avenida Santander, near the GUATEL office; more places open up all the time. Finally there is the disco **Past Ten**, opposite the Hotel del Lago on Avenida Rancho Grande, which is having trouble competing with the Circus Bar.

SPORTS AND ACTIVITIES
There are opportunities for water sports on the lake. Boats, canoes and windsurfers can be hired via the top hotels or direct on the Panajachel waterfront. At weekends the water is invaded by speedboats and water-skiers as many wealthy Guatemalans have lakeside retreats.

USEFUL INFORMATION

Money Matters
The only bank is the Banco Agrícola Mercantil, but there are always moneychangers hanging around outside. Remember that Panajachel is the only place around the lake where you can change money.

Post Office
This is on a small turning off the main road, just after the village church. No parcels can be sent from here, and your best bet is to use **Get Guated Out**, which is next to Al Chisme restaurant on Calle de los Arboles (the office is upstairs). They will charge you around $25 for a 2kg parcel, postage extra. They use the national postal service, so there is nothing safer about their service; it is just a matter of expensive convenience.

Telecommunications
The **GUATEL** office is located halfway down Avenida Santander.

Bike and Motorbike Hire
Bikes can be hired opposite the tourist office, on the main road. They cost about $3 per day, but are available by the hour as well. For **motorbikes**, ask at the tourist office; prices will be around $25 per day.

Art Gallery
La Galería is an interesting art gallery, where Guatemalan painter Nan Cruz has a permanent exhibition, and other artists from all over the world show their locally inspired work.

Volcanoes
There are three volcanoes around Lake Atitlán, and all of them can be climbed. The easiest is San Pedro (3000 m), which can be ascended by a steep trail in about three or four hours; begin from the village of the same name. Tolimán (3120 m), above Santiago Atitlán, takes a few hours longer to climb, while the Atitlán volcano (3535 m) is a tough one that will take all day. It is advisable to take a guide, since trails are not clear, and there are said to be occasional groups of guerrillas camping out up there. Either go via the tourist office in Panajachel, or ask for the *alcalde* (mayor) in the relevant village, and he will recommend someone. Always fix the price first, and remember that you are expected to feed your guide.

Some Indian Villages Around Lake Atitlán

Two Indians tribes lived here before the Spanish Conquest. The western shore, from Santiago Atitlán to San Pedro La Laguna, was inhabited by the Tzutujil, whose capital was on the slopes of San Pedro volcano, but has long since disappeared, destroyed by Alvarado as early as 1524. The rest of the shoreline was the domain of Cakchiquel Indians, who helped Alvarado, only to be subjected themselves. The descendants of these two tribes still speak their different languages, and also wear extremely beautiful clothes, each village distinct from the next. There are about twelve villages around the lake, and only the most interesting and accessible are mentioned here.

Santiago Atitlán

Diagonally across the lake from Panajachel, Santiago Atitlán hides in a protected inlet of the lake, the village and surrounding fields sandwiched in between the volcanoes of Tolimán, Atitlán and San Pedro. Arriving by boat, you pass small reedy islands and fishermen in their dugout canoes, called *cayucos*. By the water's edge, women stoop, washing clothes, while men and boys work in the neatly kept gardens beyond. It is a tranquil and idyllic scene. If you venture up into the village, however, you will be surrounded by women and children trying to sell you their wares, their fierce selling technique only outdone by their aggressive competitiveness towards each other.

The reason for the hard sell is obvious. The villagers of Santiago Atitlán wear the most famous 'costume' of Guatemala's Indians. It is very glamorous as well as superbly made, and tourists often pay a lot of money for the weavings and embroidery. (The average wage for agricultural labourers can be less than US$2 a day, yet selling a small piece of embroidered weaving can net US$10.) All males, young and old, traditionally wear white, knee-length trousers, with dark blue stripes, intricately embroidered with colourful flowers and birds around the knee. A dark red waistband, and white shirt complete the outfit. Today, many men wear jeans and modern shirts, which is a shame. The women are better at keeping to their customary dress, the most famous detail being the headdress—a red ribbon wound round and round the head, eventually sticking out so far that it looks just like a halo. It is called a *tocayal* and is depicted on the 25-centavo coin.

As well as the daily market, another attraction here is the chapel to Maximón, for this is one of the few places in the country where he is worshipped. Unlike in San Andrés Itzapa, Maximón does not have a fixed home here. Instead, a different member of the *cofradía* (religious brotherhood) has the honour of keeping him in his house each year. If you would like to visit him, just ask for the *Casa de Maximón*, and make sure you bring an offering of some rum and a few cigarettes, which will be shared by Maximón and his keeper. Maximón looks quite different here, made of wood and clad in delicate scarves, but still with the dark glasses and cigar. Some have suggested that Maximón is, in fact, a reincarnation of the Maya God, Mam, who also used to be represented as a human, wooden figure.

The local church on the main square has a simple interior of whitewashed walls and wooden benches. It has always been the focus of local rallying against army oppression on this side of the lake, and just by the entrance you can see a stark reminder of it: a small paper cross is fixed on the wall for every member of the community murdered in recent years.

If you can time your visit to be here on Good Friday, you will witness an extraordinary ritual of a both pagan and Catholic nature, when Maximón and Christ are paraded together, though never facing each other. Both are also ritually taken down from their respective crucifixes, testifying to the equal importance the Indians attach to both Christian and pagan saints, and the Catholic Church's inability to eradicate traditional religion in spite of centuries of indoctrination.

Just northeast of the village, there is also a small nature reserve (**Parque Nacional Atitlán**), designated to protect the *poc*, a kind of grebe. Lake Atitlán was the only place in the world where it existed, and strictly speaking it is now extinct, because the bird you see today is a hybrid of the original grebe with the pied-billed grebe. Visiting the reserve by hired canoe from Santiago Atitlán is a very pleasant way to spend a quiet hour or so, though there really isn't anything much to see.

San Pedro La Laguna

Of the many other villages dotted around the lake, San Pedro La Laguna, at the foot of the San Pedro volcano, is a refreshingly quiet place, with none of the frenzied tourism of its neighbour. The main reason for this is no doubt the lack of traditional costume, as most villagers seem to have *ladinized*. However, the reedy shoreline, dotted with gigantic boulders lapped by gentle waves from the lake, make for relaxed days and peaceful nights. No wonder some people head straight for San Pedro, preferring the simple life here to the bustle and noise of Panajachel. There is nothing to do except sunbathe, swing in a hammock or paddle in the water. In between these pastimes, you can eat and drink simple fare at one of the three waterfront restaurants.

Santa Catarina and San Antonio

Following the old dirt road east of Panajachel takes you through a beautiful grove of trees and then out into the sun and along the contours of the lake. If you do not wish to walk, the best way to cope with the steep mud road, slippery pebbles and large potholes is to hire a motorbike, though it is possible to take cars along this route. The first village is 4 km away, the second 11 km.

The first village you reach is **Santa Catarina** (officially Santa Catarina Palopó), nestling in a tight dip between dusty mountain folds. Nothing much goes on here, but the views of the lake in its mountainous frame are terrific. The women wear intricately embroidered *huipiles*, coloured green and blue, with blue skirts. You may have seen them selling their clothes at the Panajachel market on Avenida Santander.

Further on, the road twists and turns, up and around the craggy shoreline, until it reaches **San Antonio** (officially San Antonio Palopó), its mud houses stacked on the hillside above the lake. A lovely crumbling church perches in the middle of the village, and in front of its steps, women and children sell mainly fruit and vegetables. Passing the open doors of some of the homes, you might see one of the giant foot-looms, used exclusively by the men to weave large blankets. The women wear a simple but elegant costume here: red *huipiles* and dark blue skirts, with plenty of silver-leaf necklaces and coloured beads.

Chichicastenango and the Ixil Triangle

The junction of Los Encuentros, on the Pan-American Highway, marks an important turning point for the traveller: the main Highway turns west, passing Lake Atitlán on its way to the city of Quezaltenango, and northwards from there. The equally large branch road heads directly north, taking you to the unique Indian town of Chichicastenango, and the nearby departmental capital of the Quiché region, Santa Cruz del Quiché. Here the paved road comes to an end, continued by a rugged dirt road, which takes the hardy traveller on a five-hour bus journey to a remote region known as the Ixil Triangle.

This distant area in the northern reaches of the Western Highlands is a wild place, where the landscape has something almost alpine about it, beautiful farming valleys nestling in wide bowls between forested mountains. The Indians here favour geometric designs on their clothes, and the *huipiles* of Nebaj rank among the country's most stunning.

Chichicastenango

Famous for its fabulous market on Thursdays and Sundays, and the spectacular festival of St Thomas, *Chichi*, as it is known, has an atmosphere all of its own. This is because most of the inhabitants are pure Maya, and their traditional culture and way of life permeate every aspect of the place.

Set on top of a hill, cobbled streets meander steeply up and around the main square. Adobe houses huddle together and their red-tiled roofs contrast beautifully with the whitewashed walls and rich green pastures all around.

The Church of Santo Tomás

On the main plaza, the church of **Santo Tomás** was brutally plonked on top of an existing Maya temple by the Spanish in 1540. It is one of the best places to observe how the Indians adapted to enforced Christianity by worshipping the Christian god alongside their traditional gods and saints in an unorthodox mixture of Catholic and pagan rites.

The steep flight of steps that leads up to the main church entrance is almost always enshrouded by wisps of incense and smoke, as people burn offerings to the gods or to Saint Thomas, the local patron saint, before entering the church. Foreign visitors should never enter by the main entrance, but by the side, since they have made no offering. The perfumed air is even heavier inside the church, where *brujos* (shamans, also known as daykeepers) swing incense burners up and down the aisles. Low altars, raised slightly off the ground, line the centre aisle all the way to the front. Each one is used for invoking a different blessing: there is the one for the well-being of pregnant women, the one for not feeling sad after the death of a relative, another to remember the victims of the 1976 earthquake, one for weddings, one for Maya priests, one for Catholic priests, and there are quite a few more. Flower petals are offered and candles lit—a set number for each altar. The coloured candles are often lit in pairs. This is a way of communicating with the spirits of the dead: one candle for the living, one for the deceased.

The church is divided along the central aisle. When you are facing the main altar, the left-hand side is dedicated to Maya gods and spirits, while the right-hand side of the nave is for Christian saints. Both groups are given equal reverence, with offerings of candles, flowers, incense and alcohol. On first impression, the altars on either side may look the same, but closer inspection will show otherwise. For example, note the first altar on the left, near the main entrance: the figures are an extraordinary mixture of Christian images and Maya gods. The nubile ladies on the far side are, in fact, the saints of pregnant women, while the angel-type figures in front, each with an arm missing, represent the god Hunahpu, who had his arm ripped off by Seven Macaw, when he was fighting Hunahpu for his sin of self-glorification:

Suddenly Hunahpu appeared, running. He set out to grab him, but actually it was the arm of Hunahpu that was seized by Seven Macaw. He yanked it straight back, he bent it back at the shoulder. Then Seven Macaw tore it right out of Hunahpu. Even so, the boys did well: the first round was not their defeat by Seven Macaw.

The Quiché bible, *Popol Vuh*, translated by Dennis Tedlock

When visiting the church, always keep your distance from any rites in progress inside. Bus loads of tourists come here every week, and the Indians have become very sensitive to disrespectful behaviour by visitors. Photography is obviously out of the question. If you would like to know more about the interior of the church or the rituals performed, you will always be able to find someone near the side entrance, who will oblige for a small fee. Each person will give you a very personal explanation that is true for them.

El Calvario and the Museum

While both Indians and *ladinos* worship in the main church, the smaller church, directly opposite, is just for Indian worshippers. Called **El Calvario**, it is a whitewashed church with a very plain interior. The most important feature is the glass coffin holding the black Christ, who is paraded about the streets during Easter Week. To one side, you will also find a small shrine to the God of Chickens, where the faithful often leave an egg or other offerings, when their chickens are not laying well.

The small museum, on the south side of the main square (8–noon and 2–5; may be closed on Mon and Tues), has an interesting collection of Maya jade artefacts, as well as pottery. The collection belonged to Father Rossbach, who was so popular and trusted by the local people that they made him presents of their precious pieces, kept by their home altars and passed on from one generation to the next. They were collected over a period of 50 years, and left to the town on the priest's death.

The Shrine of Pascual Abaj

Traditionally, the Quiché Indians worship their gods and spirits in many places. Often these are open-air shrines, set on sacred hilltops, in forests, or by streams. Nature is an integral part of Maya religion, with its own spirit and power that must be respected. The hills around Chichi are full of such shrines, most of them secret to outsiders. However, the shrine of Pascual Abaj is well known and regularly visited by foreigners. Just a short walk out of town, you will find it by walking down the hill from the main square, taking the street leading away from Santo Tomás church. Then follow the first right turn, where you will come to an open field, and the path leads off to the left, through someone's yard, and up onto a pine-clad hill.

Most times there is nothing much to see, other than patches of burnt earth around a collection of stones, where fires are lit and chickens ritually sacrificed. Tufts of feathers blow around in the breeze, and most likely children will come scurrying up to sell you some trinkets. But the view of town and the surrounding hills is worth the walk in itself.

THE FESTIVAL OF SANTO TOMAS

Probably the most famous festival in Central America, next to the Easter Week celebrations, the *fiesta de Santo Tomás* takes up a whole week, 13–21 December. It is accompanied by a large market on the main square and endless processions and firework displays. The last three days are the best time to be here, with the town really packed out on 20 and 21 December.

The first processions get under way as early as 6—some are just continuations of ones from the night before—with the participants, both men and women, distinctly the worse for alcohol.

All through the day the sudden crack of fireworks will blast your eardrums, and the town is a constant hum of music and voices. Traditional dances are performed on the main square, the participants dressed in their finest regional costume. At these times you can see virtually all the costumes of the Quiché region in one place, the Chichi dress being one of the most elaborate: the men wear knee-length trousers and jackets made of bark-brown wool and embroidered with red, pink and green silk around the edges. Their shirts are white, but on their heads they wear a triangle of cloth, of the same material as that of their suits, and tied behind the head. The women wear a brown-based costume too, their *huipiles* distinguished by the heavy embroidery of large-petalled flowers of mainly orange, yellow and green.

On the second to last day of the festival all the official dancers assemble on the square to be introduced to the spectators: each couple from each region will perform a short twirl, and then take off their masks to reveal that both of them are, in fact, men. It is an extraordinary transvestite show for deeply Catholic and conservative Guatemala. On the last day the Indians form a large procession of their holy shrines and altars, candle-holding women and children behind each one.

A rare spectacle you will see throughout the festivities is the pole dancers, jumping off a 20-metre pole, tied to a long rope. This dance with death is known as *Palo Volador*, and sounds rather more dramatic than it actually is, since the men's rope is wrapped tightly around the top of the pole, and their body weight slowly unwinds it, allowing them to circle gracefully to the ground. Only occasionally is there some real drama, when one of the participants is so drunk that he falls off his perch before tying the rope on.

GETTING TO AND FROM CHICHI

By Bus
From **Guatemala City** (3 hrs), there are regular daily buses leaving from the Zona 4 bus terminal, from dawn until around 5 pm. Most of them will be heading for the town of **Santa Cruz del Quiché**, *Quiché* for short, and all go via Chichicastenango, as do the buses to **Joyabaj**. Destinations, written in their shortened version, are marked above the front window of all buses.

From **Antigua** (3 hrs), there are no direct buses, but the connection is easily made by flagging down passing buses at the Chimaltenango junction. From **Panajachel** (2 hrs), there are daily direct buses to Chichi at 7, 8, 9 am and 4 pm. At other times, you can easily travel by getting any bus to the Los Encuentros junction, from where you can catch passing buses coming from the capital.

If you are heading for the **Ixil** region, you will need an early start to catch the Nebaj buses leaving Quiché between 8 and 10 am. Buses leave roughly every half an hour for Quiché, and the journey takes around thirty minutes. Wait for them passing just past the Pensión Chuguila, at the top of the steep downhill road leading out of town.

There is a direct bus leaving for the town of Quezaltenango (it will say Xela on the bus), in the northwestern highlands, between 9 and 10 am every morning, journey time 3 hrs; wait for it opposite the Pensión Chuguila. Do make enquiries to check that this bus is still running when you are here. If it is not, you can quickly connect with regular buses for Quezaltenango, Panajachel, or Guatemala City, by taking any bus heading for the Los Encuentros junction.

WHERE TO STAY

The choices for accommodation and eating out are rather limited, considering this is one of the country's most famous tourist attractions. On the other hand, there is something to be said for the fact that Chichi is not enslaved to tourism. Except during the festival, accommodation is easily found. The telephone code for Chichi is 0561.

EXPENSIVE

The **Hotel Santo Tomás**, tel 061/316, fax 306, is the newest hotel in town. Housed in a restored colonial mansion with a courtyard, rooms have modern facilities and open fireplaces, and there is also a good restaurant. Prices are wildly flexible so do negotiate. The **Maya Inn**, tel 176, is near the main square, on the street leading out past the museum. It is the longest established quality hotel, with a lovely atmosphere of colonial splendour frayed at the edges. Spacious rooms are ranged around a variety of courtyards, complete with macaws and tropical foliage.

MODERATE

Maya Lodge, tel 167, is right on the main square, housed in a colonial building, clean but basic. It is not really worth the price it asks. Much better value is **Pensión Chuguila**, tel 134, which has pleasant rooms around its own courtyard and patio restaurant. Secure parking available. Bar those of the top two hotels, the restaurant here is the best in town, which is still only acceptable rather than good. Officially singles are $35, doubles $40. Out of season they are as little as $8 and $9 respectively. **Pensión Girón** is friendly but the rooms, set around a large car park, are bare concrete with ancient beds.

INEXPENSIVE

Most popular of the cheapies is **El Salvador**, conspicuously painted blue and white and overlooking the main square from a nearby rise (down the hill, on the street leading away from the church, and then second right turn). Rooms are grubby, bathrooms dirty, but the place is convenient and friendly. Ask around for other cheap hostels.

EATING OUT

Restaurants are overpriced and low in quality, and you are almost better off eating the freshly cooked meals made in the market. Otherwise try **Txiquan Tinamil**, on the corner of 5 Avenida and 6 Calle; **El Torito**, in the same building as Pensión Girón; or **Tapena**, 5 Avenida, near Pensión Chuguila.

Around Chichicastenango

Just half an hour's bus journey away is the town of Santa Cruz del Quiché, which is the departmental capital of the Quiché region. If you want to head on towards the Ixil region, you will have to come here for the morning buses. The town itself has little to offer the visitor, except a stroll around the large covered market. However, it is near the pre-Columbian capital of the Quiché tribe, **Utatlán**, which certainly merits a visit.

The site can be reached by following 10 Calle west out of town, where a dirt road makes for an enjoyable short walk past corn fields, and on to a small hilltop covered in pine trees. The atmosphere is wonderfully tranquil, and it can be hard to imagine the scene when this was a great city. Before the Spanish arrived, **K'umarcaah**, as the Quiché called it, was a relatively new capital, built for the elite, and incorporating many fine palaces and elaborate fortifications built of stone and covered in white plaster. Twenty-four noble families lived here, with a great many servants, craftsmen and other employees, as well as a large number of warriors who patrolled the city.

Yet Alvarado's forces still managed to burn the city to the ground. He came here in 1524, invited by the Quiché king, who planned to ambush the Spaniards. But Alvarado suspected foul play when he saw only men and soldiers in the city, so attacked immediately. The king's sons, Oxib Queh and Beleheb Tz'i were then publicly burned in the main plaza. There is not much left to see today, though the main plaza is obvious enough. For a clearer idea of what the city looked like, it's worth visiting the small museum on site, where there is a large model, as well as a helpful guardian to answer questions.

The most intriguing aspect of Utatlán is the couple of tunnels below the site. Perhaps they were a secret hideout for the Quiché? Or perhaps they were symbolic entrances to the Underworld, and places of worship? Bring a torch and ask for directions at the museum, since the path is steep and rather obscure. The first tunnel you reach is very narrow, its walls blackened by the Indian shamans, who regularly come here to worship, burning candles and incense. The lower tunnel is more spacious, but the hint of chants and ritual sacrifice teases the imagination, as the smell of burnt copal fills your nostrils.

The Ixil Triangle

Beauty cloaks Guatemala the way music hides screams.

R. Wright, *Time among the Maya*

This area, in the northern region of the department of Quiché, is wild in more than landscape. The entire northwest of Guatemala was and is the main battlefield on which the guerrilla and state forces have been locked in a deadly struggle since the seventies. Although the violence has waned since 1985, sporadic armed conflict does still occur. Some of the most horrific massacres the country has seen have taken place in the Ixil Triangle, defined by the area between the Indian villages of Nebaj, Chajul and San Juan Cotzal, in the northern region of the department of Quiché.

The perpetrators of these crimes come from both sides of the conflict; their victims are almost always the innocent Indian farmers, caught between two forces who alternately try to use them for their own ends, or justify their violence in the name of the indians. Many villages were razed to the ground, only to be rebuilt by the government as 'model villages'. Those inhabitants who survived the nightmare of the eighties are deeply scarred by it.

At the time of writing, the area around the Ixil Triangle is peaceful enough, and for those wishing to learn something of Guatemala's recent history, as well as hike in some of its most gorgeous countryside, there are few better places to visit. Remember, however, that peace in this particular region is deceptive, and violence could erupt again at any time. Understandably, amenities for visitors are very simple indeed. Before visiting the area, it would be a good idea to get advice from the **Casa Andinista** in Antigua. Mike Shawcross, the owner, runs an aid programme in the Ixil region, and he or his staff are well-placed to advise you.

Nebaj

The approaching dirt road takes you over a cold and windy pass, before twisting and turning down towards Nebaj, spread out on the floor of a wide highland valley ringed by steep mountains. It is the largest of the three villages of the Ixil Triangle, and the only one that can offer commercial accommodation for the steady trickle of anthropologists, aid workers and tourists. If you arrive on any day other than Thursday's or Sunday's market, you will find a very quiet sort of place, where the only noise is likely to come from a chicken scratching in the dirt road, or children chasing home-made hoops.

It is a beautiful, crumbling village, where most of the inhabitants still cook on log fires, the smoke rising picturesquely through red-tiled roofs. Nearby, the market is housed in an area of purpose-built wooden shacks, which fill to bursting on Sundays, with more vendors lining up their goods in the surrounding streets. The inhabitants of the surrounding mountainsides and valleys come to sell their vegetables, and small livestock, such as chickens, turkeys and the odd goat. It is then that you get the best chance to see the full glory of local dress, particularly the women's headdress, which is a wide band, folded into knots and bows as it is wrapped around the head, and ending in bushy pompoms, piled on top of their turbans, or hung loosely by the side of the head.

Apart from market day, the other attraction is the beautiful countryside, which offers many walking and hiking opportunities (always given that you have checked the area is safe at your time of travelling). A two-hour walk to the 'model village' of **Acul**, in a neighbouring valley, is highly recommended. The original village was razed to the ground by the army, and then rebuilt, gathering survivors in one easily-supervised location. The neat and orderly rows of houses belie the fact that they are difficult to live in, and the allocated kitchen gardens too small and too close together. People and animals live in unhealthy proximity, making diseases and infection a recurrent problem.

The track is wide and clear, the views reminiscent of the Swiss Alps, and when you get there, you can even purchase home-made cheese at the farm of an ancient Italian, nearing the 100 mark. His homestead is just outside the village; ask anyone for directions.

Another pleasant, less strenuous walk is to a nearby waterfall (*las cascadas*). Follow the road heading to Chajul, and turn left before crossing the bridge where a well-worn dirt track will take you to the falls. You know when you are close when the track takes a sharp bend left and goes steeply downhill before levelling out in front of the waterfall, which dramatically shoots off a ledge to pound the rocks about 15m below. If you are tempted to picnic in the field near the base of the falls, be warned that the mosquitoes will drive you crazy. If staying longer, you could also visit the markets of **San Juan Cotzal** (Saturdays) and **Chajul** (Fridays).

GETTING TO AND FROM NEBAJ

Two or three direct buses for Nebaj (5 hrs) leave daily from **Santa Cruz del Quiché**, between 8 and 10 am. The journey will be long, the ride bumpy, the seating space minimal, but the scenery will be superb.

Buses returning to Quiché leave daily at 1, 3, and 4 am, all of which pass through the town of **Sacapulas**, where you will have to change if you want to take back roads northeast (for **Cobán**) or northwest (for **Huehuetenango**). If you are heading for Cobán, you can catch a noon bus to Uspantán, where you will probably have to stay the night. (For more on this route see p. 132.) If you are heading for Huehuetenango, you will most likely have to wait until the next morning, for the 5 am bus, though you might make it in one go if you catch the 1 am bus from Nebaj.

WHERE TO STAY AND EAT

Undoubtedly the best and friendliest place to stay is **Las Tres Hermanas**, near the main square. (The three ancient sisters who run this place have recently become only two.) A handful of damp, windowless rooms line a pleasantly chaotic courtyard, where a central wash basin stands amongst rose bushes, fluttering washing lines and chicken droppings. Prices are just over US$1 each, and excellent cheap meals are provided on request. Another option is **Hotel Ixil**, on the main road coming into Nebaj, where the standard of rooms is just slightly better, but which does not have the same charm; singles from $4, doubles from $6.

Other than eating at Las Tres Hermanas, you have a choice of two *comedor*-style shacks on the main square, and during market day there are always snacks to be had there.

From Chichi to Quezaltenango

The drive west, from Chichi to Quezaltenango—or *Xela* (pronounced 'shella'), as it's commonly known—must rank as one of the most lovely in Guatemala. Returning to the Pan-American Highway at Los Encuentros, the road sweeps up and around forests and fields, giving you a brief glimpse of Lake Atitlán, lying deep in its rocky cushion of volcanoes and hillsides. An hour passes, while the landscape unfolds into cornfields and thatched hamlets, the occasional cluster of pines or eucalyptus trees swaying in the ever-present breeze.

A small Indian town along here is **Nahualá**, easily missed from the main road, and rarely visited by tourists, other than on 25 Nov, when the place turns into a terrific chaos of drunkenness and revelry for its annual fiesta. The men here wear distinctive thick, knee-length woollen skirts of brown and white checks, together with pink or red shirts. During the festival you will see them in their very best outfits, but another good time to visit is for the Sunday market. This is a staunchly traditional place, and one where the Indian cult of Maximón is alive and well. Sculpted out of one piece of wood, two feet high, the figure here is the least well known in Guatemala. Dressed in a white tunic he has the unusual feature of an open mouth with his tongue sticking out, and is kept in his own permanent chapel.

Beyond Nahualá, the road loops up and onto a sparse and windswept highland plateau, where the cold thin air allows only hardy grasses to grow, but the earth is a rich and fertile black. It's a refreshing contrast to the vibrant colours and sunbaked scene so far, providing a short spell of misty clouds and boggy fields before you descend back into the open sunshine of the Quezaltenango valley. It seems almost to be completely flat—a great open plain, ideal for agriculture, and therefore a region busy with towns and villages. At its heart lies Quezaltenango, Guatemala's second city and an excellent base for excursions to Indian markets and beautiful countryside.

It was here that Alvarado fought one of his most decisive battles against the Indians, and personally slew the great warrior king, Tecún Umán, in 1524. His headdress was made up of splendid quetzal feathers, and the conquistador was so impressed by its beauty, that he declared the present city must be named Quezaltenango—Quetzal Citadel.

Quezaltenango (Xela)

Xela is a rather extraordinary place, giving itself the airs of a city, when it is, in fact, undeniably provincial. Regardless of this inconvenient detail, the burghers have always considered themselves guardians of a notable cultural and economic centre and duly built themselves a Grecian temple (sadly derelict now), and a grand main square, surrounded by columns and steps, and a large cathedral. There is a large theatre as well, fronted by columns and its own small square. All the ingredients of a proper city are there, but somehow they look out of place, and most of the buildings are neglected, lending an air of pleasant melancholy. The weather can often add to this feeling, since Xela's altitude of 2335 m ensures a noticeable chill, and it frequently rains. In fact, the town really is an imitation of its former glory, since it was destroyed by an earthquake in 1902. Wandering along the streets around the main square, you have a chance to see great colonial mansions, unrestored or partially rebuilt, and imagine how they might once have looked.

The actual sights of Xela can easily be seen in one day, and consist of the cathedral and municipal museum on the main square, the outrageously tasteless San Nicolás Church, and the local zoo. Of these, the church is the most diverting: it is a Gothic-style building reminiscent of an overdressed Christmas cake, all pinks, blues, silver and white. The zoo is decidedly unpleasant, as you look at desperately bored felines pacing around in their own droppings. To get to either, take a bus heading for the terminal via San Nicolás, the zoo being just beyond the dilapidated temple that stands by the edge of the market.

One advantage of the pretension to grandeur here is that there are a number of good restaurants, most notably Chinese, and the hotels are some of the best value for money in the country. Local entertainment is thin on the ground, though there are three cinemas and the theatre. The most popular films are either violent or pornographic, but you do stand a good chance of seeing an American movie with Spanish subtitles at the cinema next to the theatre. These last two venues are worth a look in themselves; the buildings are slightly bedraggled but still splendid. In all, Xela is a good place to use as a base for exploring the surrounding region, which has a great deal to offer, and you can easily spend a whole week here, taking a different trip each day. It is also an excellent place to learn Spanish, since there are few tourists and thus plenty of opportunities to use your new language.

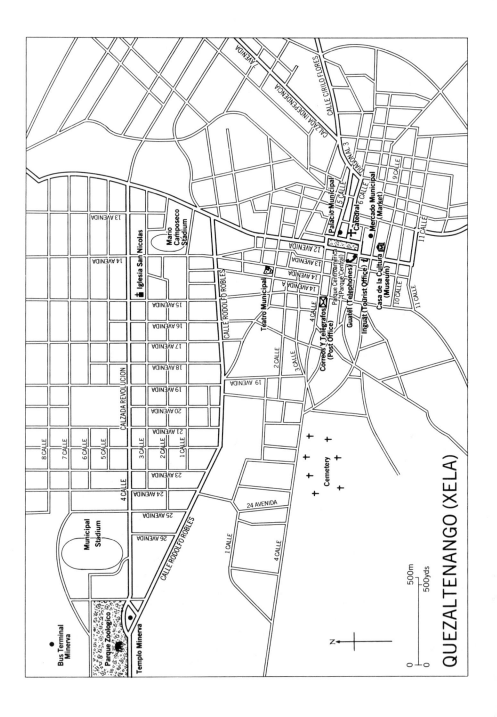

GETTING TO AND FROM XELA

By Bus
From Guatemala City, there are fast and regular Pullmans, the best of which are from the **Galgos** company (see p. 78), and the journey takes around 4 hours. The sign in the bus window will always use the abbreviation Xela. Coming from Antigua, Panajachel or Chichi, all you need to do is get to the nearest junction with the Pan-American Highway, and wait for the relevant bus to pass by. As always, your best chance of catching a bus like this is in the morning and early afternoon.

Arriving at the bus terminal on the edge of town, you can find regular municipal buses heading for the centre if you walk through the market next to the terminal, and cross the main road for the bus stop. The buses are an easily recognizable yellow, and you should ask for one going to the Parque Central.

As the capital of the Western Highlands, Xela is a major transport centre, with buses arriving and leaving for almost all corners of the Highlands, as well as for the Mexican border and down to the Pacific Coast.

The local **Galgos** office (for Guatemala City, and any of the main junctions along the way) is at Calle Rodolfo Robles 17–43, which is also where their buses arrive and leave town. This is within easy walking distance of the main square. **Líneas Américas** have their office on Calzada Independencia, between 5 and 6 Calle, which is the main road coming into town from the Cuatro Caminos junction. **Rutas Lima** are on the same road, near 4 Calle.

If all buses are full or you don't mind the chicken buses, then just head for the main bus terminal, on the edge of town, where regular buses leave from dawn until late afternoon. On the rare occasion when no bus is heading direct to Guatemala City (or Huehuetenango, if you're heading north), take any bus to the Cuatro Caminos junction, outside town, and wait there.

The main **Minerva bus terminal** is the place to wait for regular buses to Huehuetenango (Huehue 2½ hrs) and San Marcos (2 hrs), where you can also change buses for the Mexican border posts of La Mesilla and Talismán respectively. There are frequent buses to regional destinations such as San Francisco el Alto (El Alto, 1 hr), Momostenango (Momo, 2 hrs), and Totonicapán (Toto, 30 min); and also to the Pacific towns of Mazatenango (Masate, 1½ hrs), Retalhuleu (Reu, 1½ hrs), and Coatepeque (Coa, 1½ hrs). If you are heading for the Mexican border town of Talismán, it is quickest to take a bus to Retalhuleu, or any of the large towns on the Pacific Highway, and change there.

Apart from the main bus terminal, there is also a small one, round the back of the cathedral, where you can catch buses to Totonicapán and San Francisco el Alto. Just beyond, by the Shell station, buses leave for Zunil and Almolonga.

GETTING AROUND XELA

In spite of being the country's second largest city, Xela has the proportions of a small and compact town, and walking from the bus terminal to the central park only takes half an hour, though the dusty main road is hardly inviting. Everything you will need or want to see is closely ranged around the main square, so the only time you will need the bus is to travel between the centre and the bus terminal.

TOURIST INFORMATION

The **INGUAT** tourist office is on the south side of the main square in Xela (Mon–Fri, 9–noon and 2.30–5). The helpful and friendly staff can offer information on buses and excursions to the surrounding area, in particular hiking on the nearby Santa María volcano.

WHERE TO STAY

EXPENSIVE

Pensión Bonifaz, 4 Calle 10–50, tel (061) 4241 and 2959. Opened in the 1930s, its refined atmosphere dates from that time also, the furnishings unchanged. It is very quiet, with a good restaurant and café.

MODERATE

Los Alpes, on the road past the Minerva bus terminal, towards San Martín Sacatepéquez (tel 6327) is only worth staying at if you have your own transport. **Modelo**, 14 Avenida A 2–31, tel 2529, is the best medium-priced hotel, with a very good restaurant, centrally located. **Hotel Centro Americana**, on the corner of 14 Avenida and Minerva Boulevard, tel 4901, looks a bit grubby on the outside, but rooms are of a good standard. Secure parking is available.

INEXPENSIVE

Hotel Río Azul, 2 Calle 12–15, located near the main square, is a new hotel with clean, bright rooms and parking facilities. The same prices are to be found at **Pensión Andina**, 8 Avenida 6–7, tel 4012.

Best of the budget places is **Casa Kaehler**, 13 Avenida 3–33, tel 2091, which is very close to the main square and most of the best restaurants. It also really does have hot water—important in this cold town. The only drawback is the paper-thin walls. **Radar 99**, next door, is dirty and very basic. **Posada Belén**, 15 Avenida, is a new guest house on the top floor of a shopping centre, right by the city centre market. There are many more cheap places to stay, so just ask around if the above are full.

EATING AND DRINKING OUT

There are some good places to eat and reasonable spots to drink, though they generally close down by 10.

A favourite Chinese restaurant is the **Shanghai**, just off the main square, on 4 Calle, where you can also eat international and the odd Guatemalan dishes—excellent value. Pizzas are another specialty in Xela, and the best two places to eat them are: **Pizza Ricca**, 14 Avenida, and **Don Benito's**, on the corner of Calzada de la Revolución and 15 Avenida. For steaks try **La Rueda**, next to the market near the Minerva temple. The restaurant of the **Modelo** hotel serves good meals in a quietly refined atmosphere, though not cheap. The same can be said for the **Hotel Bonifaz** restaurant. Finally, if you prefer vegetarian food, try the **El Señor Sol**, 9 Avenida 6–12.

For breakfast, your best bet is one of the café-restaurants along 14 Avenida, one of the most popular being in the **Gran Hotel Americano** (accommodation not recommended, however). Another good place is the **Deli Crepe**, further up the road. If you feel like being civilized and taking afternoon tea, there's hardly a better place than the **Hotel Bonifaz**, which serves great cakes and reasonable coffee too. Rather a long way out, but very good, is the Swiss **Café Berna**, on Calle Rodolfo Robles 23, next to the private hospital.

ENTERTAINMENT AND NIGHTLIFE

Don Rodrigo's Taberna, on 14 Avenida, is the best bar in town, which isn't saying much, but it is a friendly little place. Other than that, you have a choice of small drinking holes near the main square and around the central market at the far end of 15 Avenida.

The best central **cinema** is on 14 Avenida A, next to the municipal theatre. There is also a modern cinema, in the shopping mall on the corner of Calzada Revolución and 24 Avenida, leading out to the Minerva bus terminal.

USEFUL INFORMATION

Money Matters
There are four banks to choose from on the main square.

Post Office and Telecommunications
The post office is on the corner of 15 Avenida and 4 Calle, Zona 1. The GUATEL office is on 15 Avenida A and 4 Calle (opposite the post office).

Language Schools
One of the best schools anywhere in Guatemala is the **Proyecto Lingüístico Quezalteco de Español**, 5 Calle 2–40, Zona 1, tel (061) 8792. One-to-one teaching as well as films and discussions on anything from local politics to Guatemalan culture costs about $100 per week, living with a family (full board).

Laundry
Minimax laundry is on 14 Avenida, Zona 1.

Mexican Consulate
This is in the Hotel Bonifaz, just off the main square, 4 Calle 10–50 (weekdays, 8–noon).

Volcanoes
The beautiful **Volcán Santa María** is visible from most parts of town. It can be climbed in about five very tough hours. If you are already fit, then this is a rewarding expedition, with terrific views of the Guatemalan string of volcanoes (the active Santiaguito just next to you), as well as the surrounding valleys and lush Pacific foothills. Topographic maps for the climb are best bought in the **Casa Andinista**, Antigua. Check with the local tourist office for the latest security report and how to hire a guide, if you would prefer one; the ascent is marked, but the path isn't always easy to follow. To reach the beginning of the trail, catch a bus from 17 Avenida and 1 Calle, to **Llanos del Pinal**, and ask the

driver to drop you at the relevant crossroads. Follow the dirt road until you see painted signs leading to a trail off to the left.

Excursions from Xela

Zunil and Fuentes Georginas

One of the friendliest markets you will encounter is in the village of **Zunil**, just 20 minutes from the city. This is a small Indian settlement spread around a disproportionately large white church, situated in a lovely valley. The market sells mainly vegetables, though there is a cooperative behind the church which sells the unique Zunil textiles. These do not seem to be sold in any of the country's other markets. In fact, the main pleasure of visiting the Monday market is in seeing the local women in their brilliantly pink, purple and puce clothing sitting behind their freshly harvested goods, quietly chatting to one another.

While you are here, you should also have a look in the great Spanish church, its dark interior hiding an unusually precious **silver altar**. The annual fiesta is on 25 November, which is certainly worth visiting if you are in the area; and another special occasion is Palm Sunday. To reach Zunil, catch a bus from the Shell station, beyond the cathedral bus terminal. The last bus back to Xela leaves between 5 and 6 pm.

On the hillside, 8 km above Zunil, are the **Fuentes Georginas** (closed Mondays)—undoubtedly the best hot spring and pool in the country. To get there, you can either walk uphill for two or three hours, or hire a pick-up in the village, which will take you for $4. The mountain is covered in thick tropical foliage, an indication that you are not far from the steamy Pacific. In a fern-clad niche in the mountain a few small bungalows are perched on a ridge with two steaming pools, and a bar-restaurant.

There is a small entrance fee if you do not plan to stay the night, but you'll certainly be tempted by one of the bungalow rooms, each with their own fireplace, bathtub, and barbecue outside. Plenty of firewood is provided to keep you warm all night, as there is a problem with the damp up here. It is a good idea to bring firelighters, sold in any of the markets and, just in case, extra blankets. The price is $10 per night, singles pay $7.

If you don't wish to go all the way to the Fuentes Georginas, you could visit the hot baths in the village of **Almolonga**, on the way to Zunil. These are, however, very much public bathhouses and only worth visiting if you are yearning for a hot soak, rather than a romantic swim.

Lake Chicabal

This small lake, tucked inside the cone of an extinct volcano, is an ideal place for a picnic. The nearest village to the lake is San Martín Sacatepéquez, also known as San Martín Chile Verde, on one of the roads leading to the Pacific. You can reach it by taking any bus from the Minerva bus terminal heading for Coatepeque via this route (check this, as there are others), and the journey takes about 45 minutes. The last returning bus passes by at around 5.15 pm, though if you're lucky there may be one at around 7 pm.

The village of San Martín is an unusual place, since the inhabitants speak a rare Mam dialect that isolates them from the rest of the Indians in this region. Traditional life is strong in this closed community, and the men wear a distinctive white, knee-length tunic, held by a red sash. The nearby lake is considered a holy place, and on 2 and 3 May, shamans gather to perform sacred ceremonies by the water's edge. It is advisable to keep a low profile, particularly at this time, and best not to offend by swimming in the lake if any local people are present.

The walk begins via a small path (ask directions), a little way to the right of the church, and leads gently up and past the last homesteads of the village. Do not turn off until you reach a small concrete bridge, where you take a right, following the track uphill for some time. Your path will take you through the forest and across a small savannah, and then up through forest again, until it ends on a wide dirt track. Take a left and follow the large trail, ignoring smaller ones leaving it, and after a couple of kilometres, you will head over the last hill and into the cone itself, a steep and sandy path leading through dense vegetation to the lakeshore. Often a milky cloud sits low on the crater and you do not see the water until you are virtually in it.

It should only take you about one and a half hours to reach the lake, but it can feel a lot longer as it's mostly uphill. There are not many people up this way, but if you do meet someone, it is worth checking that you are on the right path. Sitting in this cool and beautiful place, the soothing silence all around, it is easy to understand why the Indians chose it as a place of worship.

Some Local Markets
The short drive to the highland town of **Totonicapán** takes you swiftly up to Cuatro Caminos, and the edge of the great plateau. Leaving the dust and commercial struggle behind, the bus enters a beautiful avenue of pines and conifers, the road rising gradually to the town itself, tucked at the far end of a dead-end valley, at a cool 2500m, surrounded by tree-covered hills and craggy, mountainous outcrops on all sides.

The town is an important centre of weaving and pottery, and the large market held on Tuesday and Saturday is filled to bursting with all shapes and sizes of the distinctive orange-glazed pottery. Unfortunately, it is very brittle, so it is unlikely that you will want to carry it home. However, you may be tempted by some of the weaving (though much of it is machine-made) to be found on the second floor of the main market building. There is also fine woodwork, basketry and ropes. The annual fiesta is held 26–30 September.

About an hour's drive from Xela, **San Francisco el Alto** (2640 m) is a small market town, perched on a ledge overlooking the Quezaltenango valley. On the way, the bus crosses a river at the village of San Cristóbal de Totonicapán, remarkable for the huge colonial church, which is famed for its precious altars and fine silver. Market day here is Sunday, and since this is not an obvious place to visit, you may find a good bargain. Continuing on, the road climbs steeply to the windswept San Francisco el Alto, and on Fridays the place is jammed with traders from all over the Highlands, come to sell anything from textiles, crafts, food produce, or animals. One of the largest live-animal markets in Guatemala, the chaotic scenes of pigs being wrestled by men checking their teeth are quite something, though the way the animals are treated is enough to turn you into a vegetarian, if you are not one already.

There is a new guest house here, the **Los Altos** (at the top end of the town), which is clean and friendly, and a good place to stop over if you will be visiting Momostenango market, two days later. The price is just over US$1 per person, and secure parking is available.

The **Momostenango** market is held on Wednesdays and Sundays (main day), so it is not possible to combine it with the one just described. However, it is certainly worth your time to make the two-hour journey to this special Indian village.

After San Francisco el Alto, the road becomes a wide dirt track, bumping the bus slowly up through a pine forest, and down into a remote highland valley that must have taken many days to reach before the road was made. The scenery along the way is beautiful, and it is not surprising to discover that this region is full of sacred hilltops and altars. Momostenango means just that: the place of many altars, and it was here that the American translator of the Maya bible, Dennis Tedlock, spent time as an apprentice daykeeper. Traditions of Maya faith are practised here, more than in many other parts, as it is an important centre for daykeepers, who still keep time by the Maya calendar. They ensure adherence to its annual festivals, in particular the Maya New Year, celebrated every 260 days. To discover when these festivals might be is very difficult, and even if you turned up by chance, you would probably not be welcome—these are secret celebrations, jealously guarded against outsiders, who have so often sought to destroy them. (To learn more about the Maya Calender, see Tedlock's *Popol Vuh*, and Michael Coe's *The Maya*.) The church here is similar in atmosphere to the one in Chichi, mixing pagan and Catholic images and worship, and is the best place to take in the religious significance of this town.

In the market you will see some of the best and cheapest examples of the distinctive woollen blankets that are sold all over the country. Made only here, the blankets come in all shapes and sizes, some natural creams and browns, some interwoven with rich dyes of red, blue and green, with traditional Maya images on them. There are two varieties: thick, woven rugs, most suitable as wall hangings; and the long-haired, soft blankets, which make beautiful bedspreads.

There are plenty of beautiful walks you can take in the surrounding area, and there is very simple accommodation available if you wish to stay. Try either **Hospedaje Paclom** or **Hospedaje Roxane**, but neither has much to recommend it.

Towards the Pacific

Even if you have no intention of going to the Pacific Lowlands, you should consider taking any Mazatenango bus as far as **San Felipe**. The reason is not so much this dilapidated roadside town, but the journey getting there. The drive is spectacular, and you get a real sense of climate being tied to altitude as you travel from Xela's early morning chill down to the hot and humid Pacific coast. As the road plunges ever downwards, the vegetation becomes thicker and greener, and the heat and humidity increase. Every now and then, the view stretches out towards the Pacific, but all you will see is a hazy horizon, the quivering air obscuring the ocean. Behind you tower the Guatemalan Highlands, and looking north and south, you may still see the volcanic cones, rising above all.

San Felipe is the first tropically hot settlement you come to, and although still high up, the atmosphere already belongs to the Pacific. Peeling wooden shutters protect its inhabitants from the worst of the heat, and the place has a dusty, neglected character. There's not really any reason to continue to the Pacific Highway, unless you want to sweat it out in the commercial hubbub of **Mazatenango**, or any of the other dusty towns along there. Plenty of buses pass for Quezaltenango, so you should have no trouble returning.

Huehuetenango and the Cuchumatanes Mountains

Huehuetenango is the last major town before you reach the Mexican border post of La Mesilla, and the focal point for the northern Highlands. There is little to detain you for more than a day, but it is a stepping stone for connections into the remote Cuchumatanes Mountains, the highest range in Central America, offering superb scenery and remote Indian and *ladino* villages. The most famous Indian village is Todos Santos, whose inhabitants have been beautifully portrayed in a black and white photographic book called *Los Todos Santeros* by Hans Namuth. For hiking and walking, there are few places to rival this region, and if you have the time and energy to come here, you will encounter a world quite different from the Western Highlands—wilder and more dramatic.

Huehuetenango

Huehuetenango, or Huehue, as most refer to it, is a small but bustling provincial town with an economy centred on agriculture and some mining. The main square, just five minutes from the busy local market around 1 Avenida, is the most attractive part of town. A colonnaded walkway offers a short stroll in front of the municipal building, while almost opposite, a grand church promises more than its interior rewards. In the middle of the square a neglected relief map of the Cuchumatanes gives you a vague idea of the rugged mountains though most of the flags marking settlements have disappeared.

The town is close to one of the Highlands' more important archaeological sites: **Zaculeu**, ancient capital of the Mam people, located 5 km away—take a minibus from outside the **Hotel Maya** (3 Avenida). For some reason all the surfaces were smoothed over with white plaster in the late 1940s, leaving you with a sense of climbing over giant building blocks rather than the remains of Maya temples. The view of the Cuchumatanes and surrounding countryside is some consolation for this crass restoration.

Pedro de Alvarado's brother, Gonzalo, came here to wreak horrible revenge for the plot to ambush the Spanish in Utatlán, said to have been suggested by the Mam leader, Kaibil Balam. Warned of the approach of over two thousand Spanish troops, the Indians barricaded themselves inside Zaculeu. Two inconclusive battles were fought and, in the end, the Mam were beaten by a bitter six-week siege that almost brought both sides to starvation. (It is an outrageous irony that the infamous counterinsurgency troops—well documented as the perpetrators of the country's worst horrors—are named Kaibiles, after the Indian leader.)

USEFUL INFORMATION
There is no tourist office here, but hotel staff are sometimes a good source of information. The **post office** and **GUATEL** office are next to each other on 2 Calle, opposite the Hotel Mary. **Banks** can be found by the main square. **Mexican visas** or **tourist cards** can be bought from the Honorary Consul at the **Farmacia del Cid**, on 5 Avenida and 4 Calle. If you are continuing north, this is the last **laundry** (8 Avenida 2–39). The telephone code for Huehue is 0641.

GETTING TO AND FROM HUEHUE
From Guatemala City, you face a long, 6-hr bus drive that takes you the length of the Western Highlands, so it is worth booking a seat on a Pullman bus (see p. 78 for the

address in the capital). Returning in this direction, you will find the **Los Halcones** office at 7 Avenida 3–62 (buses at 7 am and 2 pm); alternatively try **Rápidos Zaculeu**, on 3 Avenida 5–25 (buses at 6 am and 3 pm).

From Xela, there are frequent direct buses from the Minerva terminal; or head to the Cuatro Caminos junction and connect there. Coming from anywhere else in the Highlands, you will easily connect from any main junction along the Pan-American Highway.

Leaving Huehuetenango, you will find most buses on 1 Avenida by the market: for example to Sacapulas (2 hrs) heading east; Soloma (4 hrs), high in the Cuchumatanes; and La Mesilla (2 hrs) on the Mexican border, for which there are hourly buses departing until 4 pm. For Sacapulas and Soloma there are only one or two buses, late in the morning, so best check the day before, and preferably buy your ticket then as well. Unlike elsewhere, seat tickets are sold in advance for the local buses, and you may have trouble getting on unless you buy your ticket a few hours before departure.

For the spectacular back road that connects the Western Highlands with the eastern Verapaz range, either catch a direct bus to Sacapulas, or a minibus to Aguacatán, and change there. You will need an early start to make the noon bus from Sacapulas to Uspantán, which is the furthest you are likely to get in one day, and the only place which offers basic accommodation. The bus for Cobán leaves at the antisocial hour of 2.30 am, so take your alarm clock. Alternatively, try hitchhiking on one of the trucks that regularly use the route. The whole point of this adventurous journey is enjoying the scenery and the gut-wrenching road, so avoid travelling at night.

Sacapulas is also where you can pick up buses for Nebaj, coming from Quiché. If you reach Sacapulas by noon, you should have a good chance of catching one of the Nebaj buses. Equally, you can head down south from here, the buses for Quiché passing at dawn.

WHERE TO STAY

INEXPENSIVE

The best hotel in town is the **Hotel Zaculeu**, on 5 Avenida 1–14, tel 068, which is a colonial house with a pleasantly overgrown courtyard. **Hotel Mary**, 2 Calle 3–52, tel 569, is a concrete three-storey building, noisy, but rooms are clean and the water hot. **Gran Hotel Shinula**, on the busy 4 Calle, has the same prices as Hotel Mary, but is worse value for money.

Pensión Astoria, 4 Avenida 1–45, tel 197, is the best guest house, with clean rooms and restaurant attached. **Hotel Central**, 5 Avenida 1–33, is the favourite cheapie, with double rooms only. There is also a restaurant attached. Other, horrible, accommodation is available, but since tourist numbers are low, you should have no trouble finding a place to stay among the above.

EATING OUT

Other than in the hotel restaurants, your choices are limited here. A number of restaurants are along 2 Calle, off the main square: **Ebony**, right by the square, and **Mini Ebony** further on, sell cheap snacks and good fruit juices. A popular pizzeria is **Pizza Hogareña** on 6 Avenida, between 4 and 5 Calle; under the same management is **Rincón Hogareño**, a block further down the street, a *comedor*-style restaurant, good but no pizzas (closed on Mondays). Another place worth trying is the **Café Jardín**, on the corner of 6 Avenida and 4 Calle.

The Cuchumatanes Mountains

Like the remote Ixil Triangle, this distant region of high mountains and desolate plateaus was the stage for unspeakable atrocities during the eighties. Many people, both guerrilla and Indian peasant, fled to its furthest reaches and on into Mexico to live in miserable refugee camps. The remaining Indian men were press-ganged into civil defence patrols by the army. Often armed only with machetes or ancient rifles with hardly any bullets, they were supposed to guard their villages and the roads against insurgents. You will still see members of these patrols now, though local people will tell you that all is *tranquilo*, and the bad times over.

In the early mornings, the earth is white with frost. The altitude hovers around 3000 m, and in many ways the landscape recalls the Andes: trees are short and wind-bent, the sparse grassland strewn with crusty boulders and rocks, and many dwellings are no more than wooden huts thatched with rough grasses. Yet it is still beautiful, and it is hard to reconcile knowledge of the recent nightmarish past with the magnificent landscape all around.

There is only one major dirt road that threads its way past Indian and *ladino* towns and villages to Barillas, a frontier town to Mexico and the mainly uninhabited jungle. There is no road to the border or onwards, so there is little reason to travel this far. The furthest Indian village, of interest only during its market days on Thursdays and Sundays, is **San Mateo Ixtatán**. It takes at least six, very rough, hours by bus, and once there you will find accommodation with straw matresses and very simple food. In your own four-wheel drive, with provisions and camping equipment, you could have a very adventurous time getting here, and plenty of chances to explore far from the beaten track. Without your own transport, the journey as far as **Soloma** will be plenty adventurous, and the scenery is spectacular.

The Journey to Soloma
Leaving Huehuetenango, the bus takes you past the small town of Chiantla, in colonial times a rich silver-mining town, whose church holds one of the country's most precious altars to the Virgin. Protected in glass casing, she is dressed in priceless silver and adornments, which pilgrims come to visit from all over the country.

Once past the last checkpoint, you could ask to continue the journey perched on the roof with the luggage, the most exciting place from which to enjoy the scenery to come. (The driver will think you are mad, but it is definitely worth it.) The dusty road turns back and forth, winding up into the mountains, eventually coming out onto a highland plateau, where the distinctive landscape of the Cuchumatanes first comes into its own. The houses are raggedy wooden or adobe, with a variety of roofs made either of tiles, grass, or wood shingles. Sheep graze in the rocky fields, and if it wasn't for the bus thundering by, all you would hear is the occasional bird, hovering over the stunted trees.

A knobbly pass leads to a steep track descending around mountainous creases and down into a valley containing several small villages, until you eventually reach Soloma, after four hours of having your bones crunched by the bumpy ride. The town is populated mostly by *ladinos*, but you will see a few Indian women, who wear long, white *huipiles* that look rather like nighties. There really isn't anything to do here, except spend half the night in the basic **Hospedaje Central**, by the market square (US$1 each), and get the 4 or 5 am bus back towards Huehuetenango. The adventure is undoubtedly exhausting, but the scenery is worth the aching bones and little sleep. On the return, you can get off at the Paquix junction (referred to as *cruce*), and wait for transport heading to the famous Indian village of **Todos Santos**. On any day other than Sunday, you should have a good chance of flagging down a vehicle. If not, you can always catch something heading back to Huehuetenango until around 3 pm.

Todos Santos

The steep helter-skelter ride down into the valley of Todos Santos is only suitable for tough four-wheel-drive vehicles and very difficult for motorbikes. The sheer mountainsides are terraced with agricultural fields, in between what is left of the pine forest, and deep gashes of eroded ground bear witness to a serious problem. But the people here need the land for food and the wood for cooking and house-building, and it is the government who should be helping with reafforestation programmes.

Todos Santos is a large Indian village, the heartland of the Mam people. The villagers wear one of the most distinctive traditional costumes to be seen. The men are as glamorous as the women, wearing jolly red and white striped trousers held up by a handwoven belt, ending in bobbles. Their shirts of thin white and blue stripes are embroidered around the neck and cuffs with intricate designs in pink, red, purple and blue. They also wear a kind of mini straw bowler, perched above the ears.

The women wear gorgeous *huipiles* made of red or purple cloth, embroidered with complicated designs in the same fashion as the men's shirts. Visitors come from all over to buy them in the local co-op shop, which helps the community in the face of increased land shortage. Prices are rightly high, but still cheaper than in any of the more accessible markets. The crochet bags, used mainly by the men, are also made by them. You see them standing in doorways, chatting, while their hands move with expert speed without so much as a glance at what they're doing. Actual market days are on Wednesday and Saturday.

The location of the village is on a small promontory, overlooking the continuing valley below, so the shingled houses are tightly packed and the narrow streets curl steeply up and around the main square, hemmed in by steep hillsides. The atmosphere is peaceful and friendly, and while there is nothing much to do here, the surrounding countryside offers some beautiful walks.

The only times the village bursts into action are during Easter Week, and the more famous All Saints' festival on 1 November, when the men stage death-defying horse races. Bravado dictates that a rider must not just race his horse but drink great swigs of alcohol as well, with often painful results. During Easter, the most interesting day to be here is Easter Friday, when Romans, dressed in what look like pink and yellow bin liners, and cardboard helmets, run about the streets searching for Jesus. There is much shouting and laughing as the soldiers are pursued by hordes of excited children, until eventually Christ is led away to the Calvario church—fake beard, rosy cheeks and long white gown. One of the strangest sights of all is a resident family of American missionaries, who seem to think they blend in by wearing Indian costume.

GETTING TO TODOS SANTOS

Buses from Huehuetenango leave from 1 Avenida, by the former Pensión San Jorge, at around 11 am. Get there early if you want to be sure of getting on. Alternatively, take any bus heading into the Cuchumatanes, and get off at the Paquix junction, where you might be lucky enough to hitch a lift. Be warned, however, that this is the 'middle of nowhere', and many hours can pass without a vehicle in sight. You could always walk—but from the junction it would be a tough full-day's hike, though mostly downhill.

Buses leave Todos Santos at the painful hours of 3 and 5 am, and failing that, you just have to try your luck with the occasional private vehicle that may be leaving for Huehuetenango. During Easter Week, there are officially no buses at all from Thursday to Sunday.

WHERE TO STAY AND EAT

The better of two very simple places is **La Paz** on the main street. About US$1 per person, the *pensión* (guest house) is basic but friendly, and the best rooms have a balcony looking out over the street. Second choice is **Las Olguitas** (same price), which is also a *comedor*, but the rooms are in a wooden contraption above the kitchen, and the place is not only loud, but very dirty too.

First choice for meals of beans, eggs and tortillas is the *comedor* **Katy** (7 am–8 pm), on the hill above the main square, beyond the small park. You might get bored with the same food three times a day, but it is certainly preferable to the filthy tables at Las Olguitas, and the meals there are made up of the same ingredients anyway. Your best chance of alternative meals is on market days, when a few kitchens operate inside the market building.

Walks Around Todos Santos

Towards San Juan Atitán (2 hrs)

The path leading up the hill past the *comedor* **Katy** will take you up a steep trail, by an open-air shrine hiding among a small outcrop of conifers. There are a couple of crosses here, one of which is of ancient wood and not a Christian cross at all, but a Mam cross signifying Holy Earth. Like Momostenango and Chichicastenango, this is a place where the Maya daykeepers still practise their rites, and in spite of everything in the recent past, tradition is as strong as ever. Some grassy mounds nearby testify to the remains of the small Maya site, **Tojcunanchén**.

From here the dirt track widens and takes you to a pass, where the view across two valleys invites you to take a rest and enjoy the beauty all around. Larks and other birds buzz by, and the fecund fields are riddled with little paths where women patter swiftly past on tough bare feet, usually followed by a gaggle of children and the odd duck. You can either turn back here or continue for another two hours of exhausting walking to the village of San Juan Atitán (Thursday market). Here the men wear a quite different dress from their neighbours: white linen trousers, covered by a brown, woollen tunic, and a red belt around the waist. There is nowhere to stay in San Juan so you need your own camping equipment and provisions. This makes a very rewarding short hike, returning the next day.

Down the Todos Santos Valley (3 hrs)
Following the dirt road out of the village, past the dentist's, you come to a large path leading off to the right, once you have passed the last straggle of houses. Follow this downhill for a while, and you will find yourself walking parallel to the deep ravine that hides a busy river at its base. Past cactuses and the occasional shepherd with his flock, this is a great way to see the nearby countryside and meet the local farmers too. Eventually, you descend to cross the river, and over three more bridges before a dirt track takes you up to the other side of the valley, and a road leading back to Todos Santos. On this side you will pass small homesteads, some of which have roadside stands selling warm sodas, which are very welcome.

THE PACIFIC COAST

Our driver slowed down at last. We were in a street of decrepit shanties; there were children in the dust and wandering pigs. Then, suddenly, vast and blank under a glaring white sky, the Pacific.

Aldous Huxley, *Beyond the Mexique Bay*

From Mexico to El Salvador some 250 km of the Pacific coastal plain lies leadenly flat; with endless dreary plantations cut by potholed excuses for roads, which finally end on grey banks of sand that sink into the sea. You will not find the white beaches of tropical brochures—the sand here is black and volcanic. Nor are there picturesque towns and exotic palm-fringed villages. The towns along the Pacific Highway are intolerably sweaty and choking with pollution and commerce. The villages are some of the most depressing anywhere, populated by underpaid plantation workers. This is a region entirely given over to the country's rich tropical farming, which accounts for the most part of Guatemala's wealth, but especially for that of the landowners, who buzz down from the capital in their private planes, rarely staying overnight to brave the heat and bugs.

Having said this, the Pacific coast does hide some surprises, and although the area is in no way developed for tourism, lacking all facilities in most places, the adventurous traveller will think this an advantage. What the beaches lack in tropical glamour they make up for with their sheer size: one giant sand dune stretching endless and empty into the horizon. The bedraggled fishing villages, with their forlorn streets and neglected huts have a melancholy attraction, and the people are more open, curious to discover what on earth you're doing here. Most are *ladino*, with some migrant Indian labourers, and the markets and festivals are characterized by Spanish heritage rather than Indian.

After the touristic bustle of the Western Highlands, you might find silent days swinging in a hammock just what you want: by day you can watch lizards and iguanas basking in the sun; by night, you will see an explosion of insects around any light and crowds of toads flashing their tongues to catch them. If you would like to see what the coast looked like before it was drained and deforested for agriculture, the **Monterrico Nature Reserve** is the only place where you will find the original mangrove swamps and some of the attendant wildlife. You can see the unique archaeological remains of the coastal civilizations near Santa Lucía Cotzumalguapa. Or you might prefer the energetic sleaze of Guatemala's second port, Puerto San José, where weekend crowds from the capital regularly cause a riot of music and streetlife.

The Pacific Highway actually runs parallel to the coast, 50 km inland, along the foothills of the Highlands; and although you cannot see the sea, it is the country's best and fastest road, and travel is easy as long as you stay on it. Off the Highway, the roads are abysmal, the buses excruciatingly slow and hot. The only exceptions to this rule are the main roads leading to Quezaltenango (from Retalhuleu, Coatepeque or Mazatenango), and to the ports of Champerico and Puerto San José.

The best time to visit the Pacific is during the dry season, normally from October to April. April to July are the hottest months, and at this time the heat and humidity can reduce even the most energetic to brain-dead panting. At any time of year, mosquito repellent is essential, and during the rainy season you should consider taking malaria pills. Protection from the sun is always vital.

Along the Pacific Highway

Connecting with Guatemala City, the Pacific Highway is a major commercial artery. Vast plantations truck out their produce, such as coffee (from the foothills rising off the plain), sugar cane, cotton, rubber, and much more. The towns along here exist almost exclusively on the commerce connected with these primary products, and their markets are sweet with pineapples, papayas, bananas in all shapes and sizes, coconuts, oranges, and plenty besides. The bus terminals are hectic with traders from all over the country, and the black exhaust fumes sit chokingly low in the heat. None of the towns have anything to detain the visitor, and most likely you will see them from a bus window, on your way to somewhere else. You may even pass by in the rattling train, with stations in Escuintla, Santa Lucía Cotzumalguapa, Cocales, Mazatenango, Cuyotenango, Retalhuleu, and Coatepeque before reaching the Mexican border.

Towards Mexico

Coming from Guatemala City, the first major town on the Pacific plain is **Escuintla** (1 hr journey from Zona 4 bus terminal), which is a busy place with a huge market and crowded streets lined with crumbling old buildings. Next to Retalhuleu, it is the best of a ragged bunch—not for its beauty but for sheer chaotic energy. It is also an important junction for many other destinations, such as a back-road connection to Antigua (7 am and 1 pm from the main bus terminal; 2 hrs). Regular buses leave or pass through for Taxisco (2 hrs) and the Salvadorean border (4 hrs), and also for Puerto San José (2 hrs). If you should find yourself having to stay the night, try **Hotel Izcuintla**, 4 Avenida 6–7; or **Campo Real**, on 10 Calle. There is a **Lloyds Bank** on 7 Calle 3–9, and a **Banco de Guatemala** on the corner of 7 Calle and 4 Avenida.

Continuing northwest, you pass dusty Siquinalá (change for Sipacate beach), and then **Santa Lucía Cotzumalguapa**, referred to as *Cotz* and only worth stopping in if you plan to visit the archaeological collection nearby (see p. 142). From here the buses thunder along the Highway, past dusty palms and rows of banana trees, and endless roadside shacks.

The next large town is **Mazatenango** (*Masate* in conversation and on the bus windows), which is unbearably hot and sticky, and the only possible reason to get off the bus is to change for one heading to the remote fishing village of Tulate, two to three hours away through the plantations; or for one of the regular buses to cool Quezaltenango (regular buses, 8–5, 2 hrs). Cuyotenango quickly follows, but the Highway cuts brutally through its middle and leaves it behind, taking you to **Retalhuleu** (*Reu*, pronounced 'ray-oo', for short), a small distance off the main road, and the richest and grandest of the Pacific towns.

Here old colonial splendour mixes with the exclusive new villas of wealthy plantation owners, and the road into town is lined with fortified entrances leading to immaculate lawns and tropical gardens. By no means a beautiful town, the crumbling buildings around the main square are pleasant enough, and the streets around the market are alive with commerce. Unlike the Indian markets, *ladino* ones are definitely there to buy and sell, to spend and make hard cash. Pushing and shoving, shouting and haggling are the norm around here, and it is fun to walk among the overflowing stalls.

Should you wish to stay the night, there are three central hotels to recommend, all around US$5 per person and near the main square: **Posada de Don José**, **Hotel Astor**, and the **Modelo**. If you have your own transport, there are a few motels along the entrance road to town. Change buses here either for regular connections to Quezaltenango (2 hrs) or the small port of Champerico (1 hr). Banks, a post office and GUATEL office are all on or near the main square. A **Mexican consulate** (Mon–Fri, 4–6) selling visas and tourist cards can be found at 5 Calle and 3 Avenida. This is your last chance to purchase these before you reach the border.

Finally, almost an hour later, the last town before the Mexican border is **Coatepeque** (*Coa* for short), a seething place that you will want to leave as soon as possible. However, coming from the Mexican border posts of Tecún Umán (34 km) or Talismán (60 km), this is the first town with hotels, a bank, post office and GUATEL office. You can also change here for frequent buses to Quezaltenango, if you are heading straight for the Highlands.

The Mexican border post by **Tecún Umán**, being the nearest, is the busiest crossing, and most of the heavy trucks and private vehicles take this route. The train also crosses here. Unless you need a visa, you can buy tourist cards for Mexico from immigration officials, and the post is operational 24 hrs a day. Buses leave regularly for the six-hour journey to Guatemala City, and on the Mexican side the town of Tapachula is half an hour away by bus. If not in your own transport, you need to arrive during daylight hours to connect onwards. The border by the **Talismán** bridge (long walk across the bridge) is also open 24 hrs a day, and buses on the Mexican side quickly connect with Tapachula. If arriving from Mexico and heading straight for the Highlands, it is quickest to get any bus to Retalhuleu, and connect there for Quezaltenango.

Towards El Salvador

From Guatemala City, the Highway branches southeast by Escuintla, taking you past the familiar lowland scenery of plantations and dust-covered roadsides, with the occasional view of a towering volcano peering through the clouds to your left. About two hours later, **Taxisco** is the first town of any note, and the place to change buses if heading for the **Monterrico Nature Reserve** (see p. 142). Shortly afterwards, the bus arrives in **Chiquimulilla**, yet another commercial centre, and your last chance to head somewhere other than the border.

One choice is to catch a bus to the fishing village of **Las Lisas**, though there are easier beaches to reach than this one. Another possibility would be to take a bus heading north, for the town of Cuilapa. This is a back road that twists up through coffee plantations and onwards, to the dusty hills of the **Oriente**, the range of heat-cracked, sandy hills and valleys that runs almost the entire length of Guatemala's eastern border from the Pacific to the Atlantic. From there you could either make for the capital once more, or travel further into the country's eastern region.

After Chiquimulilla the Highway heads towards El Salvador. The **Salvadorean border** (open daily 6–8) is by a small settlement grandly entitled Ciudad Pedro de Alvarado, and very quiet, since almost nobody uses this route. In El Salvador, regular buses (until 6) take you onwards to Sonsonate, where you can change for San Salvador. The more usual and faster route for travelling to El Salvador is on a direct bus connecting the two capitals, via the Pan-American Highway.

Ports and Beaches

While no one has yet come to Guatemala for its beaches, there are nevertheless a few worth visiting, always bearing in mind that accommodation and facilities will normally be very basic—unless you happen to be near one of the rare hotels and want to pay a lot of money. There are two ports on the Pacific: Champerico is a forgotten place, not far from the Mexican border, while Puerto San José is the country's second largest port, and what Brighton is to Londoners, or Coney Island to New Yorkers.

The Western Pacific

In the 1930s when Aldous Huxley visited **Champerico**, it was Guatemala's third port. Yet even then he wrote about 'the unspeakable boredom of life at Champerico'. These days very little commercial shipping comes here at all—it is even duller. It would be a good place to drink oneself to death, strolling occasionally along the crumbling remains of the port, sniffing the fishy smells from the occasional small boat, wandering the beach—suitably grey—and then returning to the bar of the **Hotel Martita**.

The town is easily visited from Xela, with daily direct buses from the main terminal, or else head for Reu and change there. The journey takes about 2½ hours, and the last returning bus is at 2.30 pm, so you may want to stay overnight before heading back. If you do not like the Martita (about US$3), try the **Miramar**. Do try some of the seafood while you visit the beach, the fried fish or shrimps are often delicious.

Not far south of Champerico (in fact, you could ask one of the boatmen there to take you, a wet trip of 40 min), **Tulate** is a tiny fishing village of pole-and-thatch huts. It is perched on a sandbank, separated from the mainland by a narrow canal, and the inhabitants live either side of one sandy path leading to the ocean. The Pacific's white waves pound the sand that drops steeply to the water, and as far as the eye can see in either direction there is nothing but empty beach and distant palm trees waving in the quivering heat. Even the pigs go swimming to cool off, though they prefer the black water of the canal. Except at the weekends, there are no visitors at all, and there is absolutely nothing to do here except doze, swim, eat fried fish, and chat with the locals.

Unless you're prepared for the extremely basic accommodation on offer, you will probably not wish to stay the night. The branch road that leads off the Pacific Highway at Cuyotenango is one of the worst tarmac roads in the country, so ideally you would come this way in your own transport, and then the 60 km or so should take only $1\frac{1}{2}$ hours. There are regular buses from Mazatenango, the last one returning at around 5 pm. From Cuyotenango onwards, a drearily straight road cuts through the plantations, though the potholes and discarded sugar canes guarantee a zigzag ride that is very hot and can take up to three hours.

By far one of the easiest beaches to reach is near the village of **Sipacate**, about two hours' bus journey from Escuintla. You can be on the beach in as little as four hours from either Guatemala City or Antigua (taking the direct bus to Escuintla). Coming from Escuintla, take any bus along the Highway, and get off at Siquinalá, where buses to Sipacate leave from behind the market. The branch road is not bad at all, and the sweltering bus, packed with plantation workers and women returning from the market, takes you quite painlessly past the settlement of La Democracia (see p. 143 for archaeological remains here), the small town of La Gomera, and finally on to Sipacate. There are plenty of pick-ups travelling this road, so there is also a good chance of a fast lift for hitchhikers.

Sipacate is a forlorn place. The nearest beach is the other side of the Chiquimulilla Canal that stretches from here all the way to the Salvadorean border. Along this entire stretch, the mainland is cut off from the beaches, necessitating a short trip in a *cayuco*. If you want to eat here, rather than on the beach, your best bet for fried fish is **El Guayacán**. Otherwise follow the main street left, for a water taxi (small fee) to **Rancho Carillo**, a wooden collection of beach huts and restaurant, perched high above the waves. To stay here will set you back an outrageous US$8, for a double *cabaña* with private bathroom.

An alternative is to hitch a lift with the locals to **La Empalizada**, 5 km up the coast. There are two dirty and overpriced places to stay immediately you reach the beach, but if you ask to be dropped off at **El Coco**, a short distance further along, you find yourself with an entirely deserted beach and possibly a place to stay, depending on whether it is operational or not (secure parking available). There's even a swimming pool there, though you'll be lucky if it has water in it. The rooms are tiny concrete saunas and food, if any, is limited.

The Southern Pacific

Much more populated than the rest of the Guatemalan Pacific, the stretch between Puerto San José and the border offers its very own attractions. **Puerto San José**, the country's second port, is surprisingly small, but busy with commerce, military, and sleazy bars. A concrete maze of streets by the sea, it's certainly not beautiful in any way. It is, however, a very loud and boisterous place, and the beachside shacks and restaurants invite you to sample all the seafood delights you can stomach. At weekends and holidays the town is filled with sweaty families from the capital, and soon the beach is a mass of bodies and garbage... If the new road ever opens it should take no more than two hours to get here from the capital. The old road, however, is dreadful, and from Escuintla alone it can take $2\frac{1}{2}$ hours, bumping around potholes. Direct buses leave Guate from the main Zona 4 terminal.

Outside San José there are some exclusive holiday enclaves favoured by the Guatemalan rich, each with their fortified and guarded entrances and expensive waterside villas or hotel rooms. Here you will find such things as swimming pools, restaurants and manicured lawns—safe and clean, but also far removed from anything remotely Guatemalan. To get there you will need your own transport, or pay through the nose for a taxi. West of the town is the posh hotel **Club Palmeras de Chulamar**, and you can book rooms by calling tel 313782 in the capital. East of San José is the **Turicentro Likín** (call tel 512190 or 518490 in the capital to book), which has bungalows lined along short canals. Not much of a beach here, more a place to sunbathe by the pool or go on boat trips; restaurant and supermarket on site.

For another peaceful and clean place to laze at the beach, catch a bus to **Iztapa**, one hour from San José (direct buses from Guate also). This too was once a port, though you would never guess it. Its shipbuilding days came to an end well before Independence, and since then its sandy streets have been enlivened only by snoring drunks and panting dogs. Some of the buildings and most of the beach shacks across the canal are made of wood, giving the place a slightly romantic, wind-crooked look. As usual, the beach is impressively wide, and you can enjoy it here from the comfort of a good hotel—the **María del Mar**, with clean rooms around a swimming pool, charges $7 singles, $10 doubles during the week; and $8 singles, $12 doubles at weekends. (You can book rooms in the capital, via **ECA Tours**, 5 Avenida 13–21, Zona 9; tel 343908/343970.) Nearby, the **Hotel Brasília** charges half the price, but has no pool. A good place to eat is the **Pollo Andra**, which is also a clean and inexpensive guest house.

The coastal road is interrupted here by the mouth of the River Naranjo. You can, however, cross to the village of Pueblo Viejo by *cayuco*, and take a bus from there to Monterrico Beach and Nature Reserve. The journey along a sandy road is maddeningly slow. Coming from the capital, take a bus to Taxisco (Zona 4 terminal), and change there for the ten-minute ride to the village of La Avellana, from where water taxis take you through the mangroves and set you down by the beachside village.

Monterrico is perhaps the best-known beach on the Guatemalan Pacific, and this has a lot to do with the fact that it is the only place commercially advertised by the tourist board, because of the **nature reserve** all around. The large village is set along black sandy paths, with assorted humans and animals lazing under the shade of palm trees or porches. The beach is generously wide and stretches in either direction as far as the eye can see, with great waves crashing in on a never-ending roll.

You can stay directly on the beach here, and the best place is **Hotel Baule Beach**, although the basic rooms are overpriced at around $8 for doubles. A pleasant terrace with hammocks looks out to sea—a great place to watch the sunsets. To get there walk through the village to the beach, and then turn left. On the way you pass **Jonny's Place**, which is slightly cheaper, and worth checking out. The alternative to these two is **Las Margaritas** in the village, which offers straw mats on wooden beds, and is simply horrible. The best place to sample the local seafood is at **Divina Maestra** in the village, where the cooking lives up to the name. As usual, the main occupations here are dozing, eating and sunbathing, with the single alternative of a canoe trip around the surrounding mangrove swamps. You can hire canoes by the jetty—haggle out a price in advance.

The **Monterrico Nature Reserve** is an area of the coast that has been left more or less how it was originally, and supports an isolated ecosystem of plants and wildlife. Originally, mangroves protected the entire coast, and a swampy hinterland was covered in forest and impenetrable thickets. Only in this century has deforestation and draining changed the landscape forever. But here can you get an idea of what it was like, although you are unlikely to see anything other than birds and butterflies. The INGUAT office in the capital provides a special brochure on the reserve's flora and fauna.

Archaeological Sites

In pre-Conquest times, the Pacific Lowlands of Guatemala were colonized in part by people migrating south from Mexico. One of these groups was the **Pipile**, who probably arrived sometime during the Early Post-Classic period (AD 900–1200). Their language was close to the Aztec tongue of Nahuatl, and although they became extinct around the time of the Spanish Conquest, many names of Guatemala's towns and villages bear the mark of their linguistic influence. For example, the familiar ending -*nango* is Nahuatl for 'place of'. Most of the archaeological sites in this region have been destroyed by the relentless development of plantations. However, there are a few scattered remains hiding among the sugar-cane fields, and two locations in particular are worth seeking out.

The most interesting site for remains of Pipile sculpture is at **El Baúl**, located in a working plantation (*finca*), about 6 km outside the town of Santa Lucía Cotzumalguapa. Without your own transport the only convenient way of visiting this site is by taxi from the nearby town. The site is really only for enthusiasts, though you do have the added attraction of entering one of the country's huge *fincas*, normally closed to outsiders. Walking through you will see the machinery and migrant labourers who literally work for slave wages to create the immense wealth of the agro-export elite. El Baúl operates one of the ten largest sugar mills in the country, belonging to the powerful Herrera family, which is reputedly the second wealthiest in Guatemala.

The most significant stela found here was the 'Herrera Stela', which was discovered in 1923, and shows a plumed Maya warrior. Much disagreement rages about its age, but the Maya expert Michael Coe believes it to be the oldest dated sculpture in the Maya territory, dated AD 36. Apart from the stone carving to be seen on the *finca*'s land (ask for directions), there is also a small collection of bits and pieces held in the administrative buildings, which you can view on request.

A separate sculptural tradition in this region has strong links with the Mexican Olmec style. Unlike the ornate carvings of the Pipile, who adapted to the Maya style, the sculptural remains of these people are quite different and uniquely grotesque. They are believed to have been a subsidiary cult of the **Izapan civilization**, who were based near the Mexican town of Tapachula, by the present-day border with Guatemala. Small bulbous heads and figures stare blankly at you, and after visiting Maya sites around the country, these sculptures will seem very alien indeed. The best collection is in the small town of La Democracia, a short bus ride away from the Pacific Highway at Siquinalá. Most of the sculptures are ranged around the main square, but there is also a small **museum** (Tues–Sun, 9–noon and 2–5).

Although it is somewhat off the beaten track, you can easily stop off here on the way to the beach at Sipacate, whether in your own vehicle or on a bus, as you pass right by.

THE VERAPAZ MOUNTAINS

The Verapaz region is the heartland of Guatemala's coffee-growing industry, based around the town of Cobán, and is also one of the last areas where the quetzal's habitat of cloud forest remains to sustain it. A reserve has been set up, where you can wander about the forest and perhaps sight the bird, though the chances are slim at the best of times, which is during the April to June nesting season. A visit is still highly worthwhile, however. Once past Cobán, the roads degenerate into mud and gravel, but the scenery is superb, easily making up for the discomforts and the almost daily drizzle of rain. (You can avoid the worst of the weather by visiting from November to April.) If you have three or four days to spare, a visit to the remote pools of **Semuc Champey** will undoubtedly be one of the highlights of your journey—a truly magical place hiding in the forests east of Cobán. Alternatively, you could test your nerves on one of the country's most spectacular back roads, connecting Cobán to Huehuetenango.

History

Just one region eluded the Spaniards in the early years of conquest: the highland area covering the northeast of the country. Bordered by the Western Highlands and jungle to the north and east, and the arid Motagua valley to the south, this was the land that many Indians fled to, joining the bellicose Rabinal nation in successful defence against the invaders. Thick forests covered undulating highlands, deep river beds cut through the countryside, and crops flourished on the fertile land, enabling the Mayas to sustain themselves for many years of guerrilla warfare. They were so successful that the Spanish dubbed the region *Tierra de Guerra* (land of war), and more or less avoided it.

In the meantime, news of Alvarado's massacres had reached the Spanish Court, denunciations coming from his former leader, Hernán Cortés, as well as the first campaigner for Indian rights, Friar Bartolomé de Las Casas. Later to be known as the Apostle of the Indies, Las Casas came to Guatemala in 1533, ten years after the Conquest, and took up the Indian cause with great vigour.

His writings had such influence at the Spanish Court that he managed to gain a royal charter to attempt a peaceful Christianization of the Indians. He argued that the Indians were fellow human beings, and as such, could be reasoned with, and were capable of being converted without violence. To achieve his goal of peaceful conversion, he needed to establish two vital points: total separation of the secular Spanish from the Indians in the region he would work in; and a ban on converted Indians being forced into slavery, as was the custom.

He was granted his wishes, and the area in which he was to attempt his pacification was the notorious *Tierra de Guerra*, where the conquerors had failed. Thus, in 1536, he finally set to work. Based in present-day Antigua, his first step was to compose hymns in the Maya dialects which told the story of Christian Creation and the life of Jesus Christ. Christianized Indian merchants were then sent to the region, the following year, where they performed the novel songs before the Indian leaders they were trading with. It is said that the merchants sang eight nights in a row, their hymns becoming more popular each day, until the Indians were learning to sing them too. An emissary was sent back with the merchants, inviting one of Las Casas' friars to visit the highlands, and this was duly done.

By 1539, the friars had achieved what the conquerors had failed to do, and the region was renamed Verapaz (true peace) to honour Las Casas and his men. Or one could say that the Catholic Church successfully pacified the territory for the Spanish colonists to move in later. In the long run, the results for the Indians were not dissimilar from those elsewhere: appropriation of their land and loss of human rights. It was a tactic the Spanish and Portuguese Crowns were to use successfully for all intractable regions. Las Casas meanwhile had to flee for his life a few years later, pursued by irate conquistadors who resented their supply of Indian slaves being cut, and most of all, the idea of giving back the land they had stolen.

Baja Verapaz

Although the lower Verapaz range is situated just north of Guatemala City, it is reached by taking the Atlantic Highway east, and then heading up into the hills by the El Rancho junction. The road is excellent and bus connections between the capital and Cobán, passing through Baja Verapaz, are fast and regular.

The stretch along the Atlantic Highway takes you along the brown desert landscape of the Motagua valley. Past the El Rancho junction, a dust-covered collection of shacks and petrol stations, the bus begins the winding ascent. There is almost no colour here except for the shades of rusty brown to faded yellow, and the few thorny plants that grow are covered by layers of dust, blown up by the winds.

A crossroads marks the turning west, into the valley of Salamá, and the town of the same name. Beyond the town lies the smaller settlement of Rabinal, the first place founded by Las Casas; and beyond that, lies remote Cubulco. There is no real reason to travel this way unless you happen to be passing for the local fiestas (Salamá: 17–21 Sep; Rabinal: 25–29 Jan; Cubulco: 23 Jan). Unlike the Western Highlands, this region has a very low Indian population, and traditional clothing and colourful markets are a rare sight. On the other hand, you do have a chance to explore an area of the country where outsiders seldom stray. Ideally you would come here in your own transport, and there's a nice place to stay in Salamá, the **Hotel Tezulutlán**, which makes a good base. The Sunday market in Rabinal, the most traditional of these three settlements, is a good place to look for bargains, though the variety of textiles and embroidery is limited.

Past the Salamá crossroads, the landscape changes quite suddenly to pine forests and green pastures. Small homesteads hide in the countryside, surrounded by neat fields and grazing animals, and the scent of pines drifts into the bus. But this impression only lasts an hour or so, before you pass into the strange world of epiphytes clinging to giant trees, damp mists draped over the treetops, as the road winds into the chilly heights of a cloud forest.

The Quetzal Reserve

Three hours from the polluted capital you find yourself in the moist atmosphere of the **Biotopo del Quetzal** (daily, 8–4, free). The Cobán road leads right by the entrance; just ask to be dropped off there. A visitors' centre, with a small exhibition and a helpful guardian to answer questions, is the starting point for two paths leading through the forest. Both are very clearly marked, so there is no chance of getting lost. One route takes you on a brief 2 km tour, the other on an 8 km hike, up and down the steep mountainside.

Even the short path is a good introduction to the wonders of this special environment, and soon you find yourself padding along a soft trail, inhaling the musty smell of rotting leaves. Light is subdued by the roof of tangled leaves and branches, high above, and only the occasional clearing allows shafts of sunrays to glitter on wet foliage. Cool streams bubble down over moss-covered boulders, and if you pause in the stillness of the forest, you'll begin to discern some of the many sounds and animals that are really all around. Looking up into the vast canopy, you might be lucky enough to focus on a monkey, comfortably perched to eat some fruit. Most likely, you'll see some of the huge variety of birds that flit among the branches, the butterflies and insects of all shapes and sizes. There are other animals here too, though few of them will let you know it: there is the small green toucan, his feathers an excellent camouflage; there are mini ocelots, tapirs, and of course, snakes.

If you are up at dawn or waiting quietly at dusk, you might see the gorgeous quetzal, the tiny body of the male trailing his famous tail plumes. The small avocado fruit of the aguacatillo trees is a favourite food of the quetzal, so it is a good idea to wait near one of these trees. Your chances of seeing one are greatly reduced outside the nesting season of April to June, and even in season, the number of people around and traffic on the road may scare these lovely birds away. As Jonathan Maslow puts it, sighting a quetzal is 'one part knowledge, one part patience, and three parts willingness to get wet.'

The head and body of the quetzal is a magical array of greens, blues and turquoise, depending on how the sun lights up the feathers, while the breast is crimson red. Legend has it that when Alvarado slew Tecún Umán, a quetzal bird fell from the sky to cover the warrior's dead body. Next morning, it rose up once more, but its breast was forever stained by the Indian's blood, and so it is to this day. Guatemala's national emblem, namesake for its currency, and symbol of freedom, has always held a special place. Long before the Spanish arrived, or the independent nation made it a symbol, the bird was sacred to the Mayas. To kill it was a capital offence, and only Maya lords had the right to decorate their battle headdress with the male's arching tail feathers. Nor was the bird only for decoration: it was considered spiritual protector of Indian chiefs, accompanying them to battle, and dying with them, if they were beaten.

If confined in a cage, the quetzal dies—most apt for a symbol of freedom. Yet in spite of the fact that hunting the bird has been banned since 1895, ornithologists believe that the quetzal will probably be extinct by the year 2000. The reason is quite simply the destruction of its only habitat, the cloud forest. By 1981, the Guatemalan cloud forest had been reduced from 30,000 sq km to 2500 sq km, and land shortages and lack of alternative cooking fuel mean that squatters are still cutting down the remaining forests, even in the reserve. There are also reports of people killing the bird for food, quite apart from selling its feathers for profit. It is a sad prospect for one of the world's most exquisite birds.

GETTING THERE
From Guatemala City, there are regular Pullmans leaving every day (see p. 78), and the journey takes 3 hrs to the reserve. Ask to be dropped off, because the bus does not stop automatically. Cobán is only an hour away, so you can easily visit coming from that direction as well. Leaving the reserve by bus, you just stand by the road, and flag down the first bus heading your way.

WHERE TO STAY AND EAT
There are three choices for staying near the reserve. The most comfortable is the **Posada Montaña del Quetzal** (reservations in the capital, tel 313079/322923), which has a restaurant and swimming pool, and charges around $12 for doubles. Located 4 km from the reserve itself, this is not a good choice if without private transport. A few steps from the reserve entrance is a simple **hospedaje**, made up of two log cabins with ten beds each, communal showers and toilet. This is very basic and you will need your own sleeping bag and torch, but the location is convenient. Finally, there is a beautiful **campsite** (tents only) set in the reserve itself, behind the visitor's centre, right next to a pool fed by freezing spring water. Barbecue facilities, shower and toilets are provided.

When it comes to eating, you can either have eggs and beans at the *hospedaje*, or walk 4 km up to the Posada. So if you plan on staying more than one night, you might want to bring some food.

Alta Verapaz

Beyond the Quetzal Reserve, you are soon in coffee-growing country, with wonderfully lush valleys steaming in the sun, and farms (*fincas*) of all shapes and sizes dotting the landscape. Coffee is the mainstay of the country's economy today, and not only its number one export, but also the largest generator of employment. In spite of this, the industry is still virtually a private enterprise under the control of a small group of families, and the coffee oligarchy are a powerful force, with strong ties to the military, who protect their interests against governmental attempts at land reform. One common estimate is that 4% of coffee-growing farms produce and control 83% of Guatemala's national production. Formerly, the landowning families lived in their regional capital of Cobán, but these days the town is a rather damp and forgotten place, its high society decamped to the exclusive suburbs of Guatemala City.

History

It was only in the late 19th century, when the craze of coffee-drinking took hold in Europe, that coffee began to be cultivated in these parts; before then, the Verapaz was a relatively remote region of Indian and Church lands. But under the rule of Justo Rufino Barrios (1871–1885), who instigated the so-called Liberal Revolution, the Church was separated from the State, and most of its lands—as well as that of the Indians—was confiscated by the government and sold to foreign investors. Many of these were German immigrants, who were brought in to develop the burgeoning coffee industry, and by 1900, 95% of Guatemala's coffee farms were owned by Germans.

To provide the necessary labour force for this new industry, the president decreed that Indians should work in the plantations, as and when required by the coffee barons, and duly used the army to round them up. Made landless by the government, the Indians were now forced to work in the labour-intensive coffee plantations. From sunrise to sunset they were supervised in work teams, and at night locked up. It was an outrage that even touched the newspaper-reading Guatemalans of the time, and protests were voiced against the virtual slavery existing around the Cobán area. But the president legalized debt-peonage, and the Indians became trapped in a never-ending cycle of borrowing and debt, inherited from one generation to the next, and tying them permanently to the farm they worked on. In practice, little has changed to this day, though many of the huge plantations no longer allow permanent settlement on their lands, sending the seasonal labourers away when they are not needed. (Naturally, many of these people become squatters, having no land to work and live off, and thus deforestation continues unabated, clearly marking the quetzal and other species for extinction.)

For the Mayas, the worst of this development was not the slavery—forced labour was an integral part of the Maya empire—but the denial of their land and traditional way of life, which fundamentally attacked the whole reason and meaning for their existence. Farming the *milpa* (field) was not merely for feeding the family, but an act of worship in itself. Traditionally it was a sacred duty to grow maize, closely tied to the good will of the gods and the proper balance of the elements. It is based on the idea that the person belongs to the land, not the other way round, and it is his duty to look after it as best he can:

> To be ... exiled from the *milpa*, was to be separated from the self, to become a shiftless ghost, no longer part of the Maya weave, no longer quite human.
>
> J. E. Maslow, *Bird of Life, Bird of Death*

In the long run, most of the German immigrants fared badly also. The onset of the Second World War, and the immigrants' open support for the German side, incurred the wrath of the United States, who duly pressured the Guatemalan government into deporting the Germans and confiscating their lands. Much of this land is still in government hands today, and few Germans returned or managed to stay. But there were some who assimilated, intermarried and learnt Spanish, and were able to start again in the 1950s. This German heritage still shows in the names of some of the largest landowners such as Daetz Villela and Diesseldorf.

Cobán

A small provincial town these days, Cobán was once at the hub of the coffee-growing industry, and many of its inhabitants were wealthy landowners who gave the town an air of countrified sophistication. Now most of the grand buildings are damp and crumbling, and this is a quiet place, with little for the visitor to see or do. All around there is a rich patchwork of plantations, fields, and the odd scrap of cloud forest clinging to the hillsides, yet the white mists that sit heavily on the hilltops can create a chilly atmosphere. Here, more than anywhere else in the country, you get a sense of the permanent change that people are inflicting on the countryside. The Western Highlands suffer the same problems, yet the atmosphere is quite different. The farming terraces, pine forests, blue skies and sunshine inspire joy. By contrast, the Verapaz around Cobán can be a melancholy world of fine drizzle and milky clouds. Dead tree stumps stubbornly remind you of the displaced forest, and wooden huts topped with corrugated iron stand mud-stained by the roadside, home to the landless squatters.

The one time Cobán springs into life is during Easter Week and the National Festival of Folklore (22–28 Aug). The latter is, however, more an attempt by the tourist board to draw some action to the town than an indigenous fiesta.

WHERE TO STAY
Cobán will probably only be a stopover to somewhere else, but since most of the interesting journeys from here require an early start, you will find yourself staying at least one night. Note that during Easter Week and the National Festival of Folklore, accommodation can be scarce.

INEXPENSIVE
The top hotel in Cobán is **La Posada**, 1 Calle 4–12, tel 0511495, which is on the entrance road to town, just before the main plaza. A lovely colonial house with a restful garden, it also has an excellent restaurant. All rooms have a private bathroom.

Of the guest houses, the **Central**, 1 Calle 1–79, has modern rooms around a large courtyard, and a good restaurant. Next choice, and for the same price, would be **La Paz**, 6 Avenida 2–19, a short walk from the town's triangular plaza, next to the **Pizzeria**, which serves horrible and expensive pizzas. **Hospedaje Maya**, opposite the local cinema, is also recommended, and there are a few other places, but they are generally grubby.

EATING OUT
Apart from the restaurants attached to accommodation, there are *comedores* along the market, behind the cathedral, and also on the main road into town. Just above the bus terminal, **El Refugio** is a good place for a meal and has a bar until 11. The best coffee in Guatemala can be had at **Café Tirol**, which is diagonally across the street, from La Posada, just by the tip of the triangular plaza. You can also change dollars here if the banks are closed.

GUATEMALA

Adventurous Journeys beyond Cobán

Semuc Champey
About three hours east of Cobán, by bus, you come to the remote village of **Lanquín**, and the closest you can get to the fabulous pools of Semuc Champey. (The bus leaves at 5.30 am from outside the bank behind the cathedral, on the same street as the Pensión Central.) The road to Lanquín is rough but beautiful, passing the pretty village of San Pedro Carchá shortly after setting off. From there the stony road twists and turns along the sides of steep valleys, their slopes covered with glistening coffee bushes and the floppy leaves of banana trees. The road finally descends into the valley of Lanquín, passing a few grand *fincas* on the way.

In Lanquín you have three choices of accommodation: just by the entrance of the village is the newly opened **El Recreo**, which is attractively set on a small hillock, and is undoubtedly the best choice if you want creature comforts. In the village, the **Hospedaje Divina Providencia** is run by a very friendly man, who has been blind for many years, though he does not let that stop him tending to his coffee bushes himself. Squeaky beds go for $1 per person, and though facilities are basic, the food is good, and is your only option around here. **Tienda Mary**, on the main square, charges the same money but is not as nice.

To reach the pools, you can either get up early, and hope for a lift with a truck any time from 7 am onwards, or you can walk. (If in your own transport you should only attempt the road in a high clearance, four-wheel-drive vehicle.) If you walk it will take up to four hours along a road littered with sharp stones, winding steeply out of the valley, down into another and up again before descending to the swift waters of the River Cahabón, and your final reward. Along the way you will pass lone homesteads of Indian families, who are very reserved and often do not speak Spanish. An unusual feature is the women's habit of smoking fat cigars, and you will see them shyly turning away to light up.

It's an exhausting walk, though not difficult, and you know you are close when the suspension bridge over the River Cahabón comes into view. Just beyond it, a squashy mud path leads off to the right, taking you slipping and sliding through the undergrowth. You can hear the seven steps of pools gushing, one into another, minutes before you see them. There can be few sights lovelier in Guatemala: glass-clear, turquoise water fills a natural cascade of large pools, surrounded by massive trees covered with drooping lianas. If you had to walk twice as long, you would still think it was worth it, and a cooling swim soon refreshes tired legs. To get the best view, walk to the top pool, where there's also a clearing to camp on. Bring your own food and water, since there is nothing along the way; and if you plan to camp, be careful, since robbery does happen and it is probably better not to be alone. If you were lucky enough to get a lift in the morning, you will be fresh for the walk back, since there is almost no traffic passing towards Lanquín in the afternoon.

Only half an hour's walk from Lanquín, you can also visit a huge cave (*cueva*) here (small fee). Dark, wet, and home to thousands of bats, you cannot see very much without good lighting, and the paths are very slippery. The municipal building in the village has a switch to light up the cave (ask before setting off to have it turned on), but usually it's not working. The cave is said to go on for many miles, and locals will tell you that they've spent weeks walking into the interior and some have never returned. The walk along a

149

river is pleasant, though, and near the entrance to the cave is a good spot for a swim. Leaving Lanquín, buses set off from the main square for Cobán at 5.30, 7 am and 1 pm.

A Back Route Towards the Petén Jungle

For the hardy traveller only, there is a tough two-day route into the northern jungles, which passes quite close to Lanquín. (If coming from Lanquín, catch the 5.30 am bus and ask to be dropped off at the Pajal junction, where you can wait for the morning bus heading for the Sebol road junction and Fray Bartolomé de Las Casas.) Coming from Cobán, you need to be in the village of San Pedro Carchá early, to catch the 6am bus to Fray Bartolomé de Las Casas, a long eight hours away. Once arrived, you will have to spend the night in one of the basic *pensiones* here. Next day, look for a lift with the trucks and pick-ups that leave for the five-hour journey to jungle-bound Sayaxché, in the southern Petén.

The only possible reason for inflicting this journey on yourself is if you plan to visit the ruined Maya temples of the Petén, the most accessible of which are near Sayaxché and Flores, and you do not want to return to the capital to either fly or catch a direct bus to Flores. It is worth bearing in mind that this route is not only exhausting but potentially hazardous, since the remote northern foothills of the Verapaz are one of the last regions where guerrillas are still holding out. Occasionally they block the road and demand 'contributions' to their cause from the passengers. It is unlikely that you would be hurt, since the guerrillas do not make a habit of harming foreigners, but it would be extremely nerve-racking, at the very least.

Towards the Western Highlands: Cobán to Huehuetenango

If you enjoy spectacular scenery as well as being scared witless, then this is the trip for you: the dirt road that connects the east and west of northern Guatemala is one long rollercoaster ride, best done sitting on the roof of the bus where you get the best views. During the week it is possible to hitch a lift with large trucks that use this road. But normally you will need two days by public transport. If in your own transport, remember that petrol stations are few and far between in this region, and you will need a tough vehicle.

The journey begins in the small town of **San Cristóbal Verapaz**, reached by regular local bus from the Cobán bus terminal. An excellent place to stay here is the **Hospedaje Oly**, on the main street, which is a beautiful home turned guest house, with a very friendly owner who charges $3 for a double (coming from the other direction, this is the best place to end the journey and stay the night before heading onwards).

In the morning, you can either try your luck hitching, with the most likely destinations being Uspantán, Sacapulas, Nebaj or Huehuetenango, or you can wait for the bus to Uspantán, leaving between noon and 1. The drive will take about six hours, and the gut-churning begins when you find yourself packed into the bus and know there is no way you could get out in an emergency. Sitting on the roof rack of the bus, lodged among sacks of grain and baskets of fruit, is infinitely preferable to staying inside, not just for the space and fresh air, but your bird's-eye view. Of course, you do get the worst of the vehicle's terrifying swaying, the bus leaning just far enough for you to see the sheer drop to the river below.

The bus alternately hurtles and crawls along mountain ledges and around hairpin bends, and when you're not wondering whether to jump off immediately and walk, you can enjoy the heart-stopping vista of jagged mountain chains framing a deep river valley. The lower stretches of land are covered in the greens and golden browns of farming fields, while the river is a stunning aquamarine in places, its giant loops winding around grey rocks and boulders. Ignore the rusting wreck of a bus at the bottom of the valley.

In Uspantán, a small town, you can stay at the **Viajero**, a basic place three blocks east of the main square, or the **Golinda** *pensión*. Ask on arrival what time the buses leave for Sacapulas, where you have a choice of either staying on the bus, and ending up south in Santa Cruz del Quiché, or you can change here for buses to either Nebaj to the north-west (see p. 121), or Huehuetenango to the west (see p. 131). Again, the journey on the dirt road will be spectacular, and by the end of the day you will have a real sense of achievement: not only did you survive, but you travelled on one of Guatemala's most beautiful roads.

Heading East to Lake Izabal

Finally, there is a back road to **El Estor**, on Lake Izabal, where you can catch a ferry to Mariscos, and buses heading for the Petén jungle or the Caribbean. This is a rough option that bumps you along the Polochic valley, past coffee villages and the town of Panzós, and down to the lowlands of the lake. It is, however, off the beaten track, and the bus journey along the River Polochic is beautiful, as is the ferry trip across the great lake. The only hitch is that sometimes the ferry does not turn up for a few days, especially if the weather is bad and the water too rough.

Valenciana buses for El Estor leave the Cobán bus terminal at 5, 8, and 10 am (returning at the same times), and the journey takes around eight hours. The **Brenda Mercedez** company also runs buses on this route.

You will have to stay at least one night in El Estor, either in the lakeside **Vista del Lago**, doubles US$9 with or without private bath, or the **Hotel Villela**, behind the other one, which is simple and friendly, and charges US$5 for a double with private bath. In the unlikely event that these are full, try **Hotel Los Almendros**, and there are a few others besides that. The best places to eat in El Estor are the **Ranchón Centenario**, just past the market, and the **Bambú**, near the waterfront.

If you find yourself enchanted by the backwater atmosphere of El Estor, there is a trip you can make to a nearby canyon, a popular swimming spot with the locals. There are also some fine beaches, reached by hiring a motorized canoe, though this can be comparatively expensive (US$10). Inland, there are some traditional Kekchí villages you could visit, but you would need your own transport for that.

The ferry to **Mariscos** is supposed to leave daily at 5 am (departs at 1 pm from the other direction; journey takes 2 hrs), and there are usually buses waiting there, heading for Guatemala City. If your destination is either the Caribbean or the Petén, just get off at the junction with the Atlantic Highway, and wait for a connection. Mariscos itself is a sleepy little place, set at the foot of hills covered in tropical forest and rubber plantations, where there's nothing much to do except visit some nearby beaches. The area is still undeveloped touristically, but that is bound to change, and some wealthy Guatemalans have already built their holiday homes along the lake, west of Mariscos.

THE ORIENTE AND CARIBBEAN COAST

This was Death Valley. The earth here was finer and duller than sand... There was a dusting of it on all the cactuses, which gave them the look of stumps.

Paul Theroux, *The Old Patagonian Express*

Theroux was talking about the Motagua Valley, which leads from the capital all the way to the Atlantic. But the description fits just as well for most of Guatemala's eastern range of hills, which trace the borders with El Salvador and Honduras. Known as the *oriente*, the scorched hills and valleys rising east of the capital are cowboy country. Few Indians live in this region, and even fewer retain their traditional custom of dress. Instead there are busy market towns, full of *ladinos* going about their business, which holds little interest for the tourist. Towns like Cuilapa, Jutiapa, Jalapa, and Chiquimula are all much of a muchness. The only town that enjoys a regular stream of visitors is the pilgrimage city of Esquipulas, famous for its Black Christ, which draws the largest number of pilgrims in Central America.

If, however, you enjoy spectacular bus journeys, there is one trip in this region you could consider. It is the route from Jalapa to Chiquimula, which takes you for five long hours through the most dramatic part of the region. Broad valleys are flanked by imposing mountains, and unlike the rest of the Oriente, the landscape is green and rich in wild flowers that line the roadside. The road is not paved, which accounts for the long journey time, but if you have two days to spare, this is certainly a trip worth taking. Frequent buses leave from the capital's Zona 4 bus terminal for Jutiapa ($2\frac{1}{2}$ hrs), where there are connections for Jalapa ($1\frac{1}{2}$ hrs). The best place to stay in Jalapa is the **Hotel Casa del Viajero**, which charges US$5 for doubles with a private bath. Buses from Jalapa to Chiquimula leave the market terminal at 6, 8, 10, 11 am and 1 pm, and from Chiquimula there are constant buses back to the capital, or onwards to Honduras or the Caribbean coast.

Other than to visit Esquipulas, most visitors who pass this way are en route to Honduras, crossing the frontier either beyond that city or near Chiquimula, usually using the latter route, because it leads directly to the famous Maya city of Copán, just inside Honduran territory. Even if you do not plan to travel in Honduras, you can easily visit this special site from Guatemala City, either by organized tour or on your own. Border formalities are minimal, and even those normally requiring visas can obtain 72-hour permits to visit the ruins.

Another important Maya site is just off the Atlantic Highway, not too far from the Caribbean coast: Quiriguá, which is treasured for its stelae, rose to prominence in a very short time in the 7th century, yet only flourished for 138 years. Now it is hidden among banana plantations, and as you travel closer to the coast, so the landscape comes alive again with the green of floppy-leaved banana trees. Past the junction turning northwest, for the Petén, the landscape becomes humid and tropical, remnants of forest and spongy swamps giving way to cattle ranches. The distance to the coast is not far, but the journey is slowed down considerably by stretches where the tarmac disintegrates into dirt and gravel. Eventually you find yourself in the fetid heat of Guatemala's largest port, named Puerto Barrios after one of the country's most famous presidents. Here you can catch ferries to either Livingston in Guatemala, or Punta Gorda in Belize.

Guatemala's share of the Caribbean coast is less than 100 km long, and has few settlements apart from the large port. Livingston, however, is unique in Guatemala, since it is inhabited almost entirely by blacks, descended from African slaves and Carib Indians, who mainly arrived from the Eastern Caribbean in the 18th century. As with the Pacific, this is no place to come for spectacular beaches, but it is a very interesting place culturally, and an excellent setting-off point for journeys up the beautiful Río Dulce, and into the jungles of the Petén.

The Holy City of Esquipulas

Described as a 'religious Brighton' in Anthony Daniel's *Sweet Waist of America*, Esquipulas draws huge numbers of pilgrims from all over Latin America, but in particular from Central America, and it is true that the city lives off little else. There is a kind of religious fairground outside the great basilica, which caters for the visitors' every possible taste in trinkets, from candles and plastic flowers to straw hats; and each 15 January the place is solid with pilgrims.

The first building you set eyes on when approaching Esquipulas is the huge gleaming, white basilica. The rest of the town huddles around its elevated position, and visitors rarely bother to explore its streets. All eyes are on the church, and in particular the Black Christ behind the altar. A small side entrance by the back leads visitors single-file behind the encased wooden statue, where there is an opening so that the faithful can kiss the figure's feet, and deposit money down a conveniently placed tube. The Christ, beautifully carved out of balsam wood by the renowned colonial sculptor, Quirio Cataño, is nailed to a heavy silver cross.

Each person stays for a short time, and then gets shuffled on by the waiting line, usually retreating backwards, savouring every last minute of the pilgrimage. Around the base of the figure, you will also see endless plaques, notes and photos, testifying to the miraculous help the Black Christ has given. The figure has been here since 1595, perhaps made in dark wood to appeal better to the Indians. But its fame for miraculous healing, and the reason for its immense popularity, dates from the mid-18th century when the bishop of Guatemala, Pardo de Figueroa, recovered from a severe illness while visiting here.

Inside the church itself the cavernous dark is lit by hundreds of candles, while hanging above the main aisle are some glamorous chandeliers, which would look more at home in an exclusive restaurant than in here. Outside the church are numerous shops selling chains, votives, cards, candles, books and anything else that has even the remotest association with this place.

History

Esquipulas briefly hit the headlines in 1954, when it was invaded by a mercenary army hired by the American CIA to bring down the Guatemalan government. The cause of this intervention was ostensibly the 'communist tendencies' of the Jacobo Arbenz government. He had tried to institute land reform and come into direct conflict with the powerful United Fruit Company, who had close links with the US government.

The American company first came to Guatemala at the turn of the century, and by 1929 it had already established a monopoly control over the banana industry there. A powerful economic force, United Fruit not only owned huge parts of Guatemala's plantation country, it also owned and controlled most of the country's railway, media, telegraph and electricity installations, in fact anything that had a remote connection to the smooth operation of their business. Soon the people refered to United Fruit as *El Pulpo*, the octopus, and the company's controlling influence in Guatemalan politics was an accepted fact of life: it was a 'banana republic'.

The Arbenz government, elected in 1950, did no more than request the unused land of large estates, to be compensated by the declared tax value of that land. In the case of United Fruit, who used less than 20% of their holdings at any one time, the company was offered almost three times what they had paid for the land. Yet, like other large landowners, United Fruit objected on principle and set the propaganda machine in motion in America. Eventually, 'Operation Success' was initiated on 18 June 1954, which ended in the collapse of the Arbenz government, and the puppet government of Colonel Carlos Castillo Armas was installed.

GETTING TO ESQUIPULAS AND ONWARDS TO HONDURAS

Direct buses for Esquipulas (4–5 hrs) leave Guatemala City from near the Zona 1 bus terminal (see p. 78). There are also direct buses between here and Puerto Barrios in the mornings.

From Esquipulas, minibuses regularly shuttle between town and the border post at Agua Caliente (20 min), for crossing into Honduras. They leave from the main street, where the buses from the capital arrive and leave, daily until around 4 pm. If you need a visa, you can get it at the consulate in Guatemala City (see p. 64) or at the one in the **Hotel Payaqui**, in Esquipulas. The fee to enter Honduras is around $1. The Guatemalan exit fee hovers around $1. Moneychangers are always waiting for custom at the border, and on the Honduran side there are regular minibuses leaving for the nearest town of Nueva Ocotepeque. If you are heading for the ruins of Copán, it is better to cross at the other border, further north.

WHERE TO STAY AND EAT

There are plenty of places to stay, most of them very close to the basilica. The telephone code for Esquipulas is 0431.

MODERATE

The smartest hotel, with pool and restaurant, is the **Posada Cristo Negro**, tel 482, on the entrance road to town.

INEXPENSIVE

On the main street where the buses stop, the hotel **Payaqui**, tel 143, is simpler, but also has a pool and a reasonable restaurant. **Casa Norman** is a small place with good rooms. The hotel **Paris**, just off the main street, the other side of the church, is clean. There are many other places in the same price range as the París.

Apart from the restaurant attached to the Payaqui hotel, there are few places to recommend. The food is generally nothing special and prices are high. There are plenty of snack bars and restaurants to choose from around the main street.

Excursion to Copán in Honduras

There are plenty of agencies offering one-day tours to Copán in Honduras. However, considering it takes around 6 hours each way, it hardly seems worth doing. It is also much cheaper and quite easy to travel independently. If you're just making a side trip, allow yourself at least 3 days, so you can explore the ruins in peace on the second day.

From Guatemala City, there are direct buses to the town of Chiquimula (3–4 hrs) with the **Rutas Orientales** company, leaving daily. If you want to be sure of making the connections as far as Copán in one day, you should set off no later than 8 am. In Chiquimula, change for a bus heading for the Honduran border post of El Florido, with the **Empresa Vilma**, whose office is next to the market. Last buses in either direction leave at 4.30 pm, and the journey takes around 2 hours.

Crossing the border is usually quick, and if you're only visiting the ruins, you can get a 72-hour permit, which does not affect your Guatemalan tourist card or visa, and has no bearing on normal Honduran entry requirements for your nationality. (In other words, it is as if you never crossed the border, officials removing the permit from your passport when you return.)

If planning to continue travelling in Honduras, many nationalities, including Canadians and Americans, but not the British, need to have obtained a visa before crossing this border, obtainable at the Honduran Consulate in Guatemala City (16 Calle 8–27, Zona 10, tel 373921; Mon–Fri). You need to leave your passport at the Consulate between 10 am and noon, and collect it the next day between noon and 1.30 pm. All visas are for 30 days, renewable once only, for another 30 days at one of the many immigration offices scattered around Honduras.

The standard entry fee is about $1, payable in local currency, the lempira. The Guatemalan exit and entry fee is usually $1. There are plenty of moneychangers at the border, and once across, minibuses take you the 40-minute journey to the small town of Copán Ruinas, next to the Maya site.

Quiriguá

Past the El Rancho and Río Hondo junctions, the small turning right for Quiriguá is about 190 km from Guatemala City, along the Atlantic Highway. Virtually all traffic thunders past the turning, including the buses for Puerto Barrios, and in spite of its significance, the site is rarely visited.

Quiriguá

Located on an island of forest in a sea of banana plantations, Quiriguá was briefly a major city-state. Originally, it must have been a satellite of the great city of Copán, just 50 km away. But in 724, Quiriguá's ruler, Cauac Sky, began aggressive moves towards independence. By 738, he had succeded in taking Copán's lord prisoner, and instituted his own emblem glyph for Quiriguá, an honour only granted to Maya centres of political importance. From that date onwards, huge stelae were regularly erected, and elaborately carved with portraits of rulers, celebrating their achievements, and also important events in the Maya calendar. Nine of these great monuments remain, and they are the reason for

Quiriguá's significance today, the highly ornate and detailed sculptures being second only to Copán. The tallest of these is almost 9 m high, dwarfing its human visitors.

The Maya were obsessed with time, and their development of arithmetic and astrology was the most sophisticated of all ancient peoples. They were concerned not only with the dating of events in their own history, but most especially with locating themselves in the universal balance created by the Gods. Thus they used the calender to work out precise times in the ancient past as well, and on stelae F and D there are references to dates 90 million and 400 million years ago. Apart from the stelae, there are some monstrous carved stones, known as zoomorphs, which depict surreal creatures of the Underworld, usually entangled with one of the lords of Quiriguá. Some look like toads, others like crouched jaguars, but it is impossible to make sense of these carvings, and nobody knows what their purpose was.

The city's glory days did not endure, and the last known date carved on the site is 810. Soon afterwards, the city fell from power. Why this happened is an unsolved mystery, but the timing fits in with the general disintegration of Classic Maya civilization, which flourished from around AD 300–900. By the time the Spanish arrived, this site had been abandoned for almost a thousand years, and its remains were not significantly disturbed until United Fruit developed the land for its banana plantations.

GETTING THERE AND WHERE TO STAY

If you do not have your own transport, the most convenient way to visit is en route to Puerto Barrios or the Petén jungle, though the 4 km walk from the main road is hardly an inviting prospect if you are carrying much luggage. From the capital to Quiriguá is about 4 hours by bus, and if you're lucky, there are motorbikes and pick-ups to ferry visitors and plantation workers up and down the connecting dirt road. The site is open daily, 8–6, and there is a small fee (insect repellent is a good idea here). The nearest accommodation is the basic but clean **Hotel Royal**, in the village of Quiriguá. Doubles with private bath cost around US$8, and meals are available here.

To get to Quiriguá village, ask to be dropped off at the village of **Los Amates**, where regular buses make the short journey away from the highway. From here you can walk to the ruins by following the railway tracks to a dirt road, which heads off to the right, through the banana plantations. Pick-up trucks regularly pass by, so you could always try hitching the 3 km distance. To continue travelling to the Atlantic coast, just flag down the relevant bus on the Highway.

Puerto Barrios

In spite of the fact that the country's largest port is just next to Puerto Barrios (in Santo Tomás de Castilla) the town has a very slow, tropical atmosphere to it. Unlike Puerto San José, the Atlantic counterpart has little of the seaside garishness of streets crammed with shops and entertainment, and there is no beach here you would want to spend time on. Instead you find yourself in a pleasantly dilapidated place of tarmac and dirt roads, peeling wooden buildings, and a mixture of black and mestizo inhabitants. The Caribbean, rather than Central America, already feels close here, and Mayas stick out a mile.

Near the waterfront, warehouses and truck depots mix with dingy brothels and a few sleazy bars, but it doesn't add up to anything much, the air too hot and humid for people to get raucous. But at least there are some people on the streets at night, a welcome contrast after the silence of most Guatemalan evenings; and while there is nothing much to do except eat or drink, a night spent here on the way to Livingston or Belize is no great hardship. (Having said that, there is no need to stay here if travelling to Livingston, since there is an afternoon boat leaving daily at 5 pm.) There is a **Lloyds Bank** on 7 Calle, as well as a few others, and a **GUATEL** office on 8 Avenida. The **post office** is on the corner of 3 Avenida and 7 Calle. Note that it is very difficult to change travellers' cheques in this town.

GETTING TO PUERTO BARRIOS
From Guatemala City, the **Litegua** bus company runs an excellent service to Puerto Barrios, which takes 6 hours. At 10 am daily, there is a 'special', which only takes 5 hours, and there are a few more, later in the day. In Puerto Barrios, buses leave from 6 Avenida, at the junction of 9 and 10 Calles.

Buses also leave from the Zona 1 bus terminal, by the train station. There are some direct buses between Esquipulas and Puerto Barrios, and if you go to any of the major road junctions on the Atlantic Highway, you can always flag down a bus there.

Train buffs might want to take the railway, with connections on Tuesday, Thursday and Saturday. The train leaves at 7 am, and can take anything up to 12 hours, though it is supposed to take only 8. Remember that the journey is mostly through desert landscape, it can get very hot, and there are no services on the train. Leaving Puerto Barrios on Wednesday, Friday and Sunday, the train departs at 6 am.

ONWARDS TO BELIZE
Boats for **Punta Gorda** in Belize leave from the dock at the end of 11 Calle, on Tuesday and Friday, at 7.30 am. You must buy your ticket and complete immigration formalities the day before travelling, and both offices close at 5 pm. The ticket office is the same as for the Livingston boats, and the immigration office is two doors down on 9 Calle near the waterfront. The Guatemalan exit fee is around $1 here. The fare is just over $2, one way, and the journey takes around $2\frac{1}{2}$ hrs, not stopping in Livingston. Charters will cost at least $35 each.

Immigration procedures in Punta Gorda are quite informal: your luggage is checked on the pier. One-month permits are issued, renewable for up to 6 months. You will be asked about sufficient funds for your stay, and must have a return flight ticket to your country of residence.

WHERE TO STAY
Undoubtedly the nicest place to stay, though overpriced, is the **Hotel El Norte**, on the seafront, at the end of 7 Calle. A large wooden building, you get the best of the Caribbean atmosphere here. Doubles from $11. Closer to the ferry dock, and cheaper, is **Caribeña**, 4 Avenida, between 10 and 11 Calles. **El Dorado**, 13 Calle, between 6 and 7 Avenida, charges the same; and so does the **Europa**, 8 Avenida, between 8 and 9 Calle. If you prefer to be near the bustle and noise of the town's market, there are plenty of cheap places there, such as the **Pensión Xelajú** on 8 Avenida. Note that streets are rarely marked here, and even the locals don't seem to know which street is where, so ask for locations by their name, rather than by address.

EATING OUT

The **Hotel El Norte** has a good and expensive restaurant, and with views of the sea on two sides, you almost feel as if you are in a cruise-ship dining room. More authentic seafood cooking, at much cheaper prices, can be had in the restaurants further up 7 Calle. If you wander along the avenidas running close to the ferry dock and the ticket office, you will find some reasonable places as well. For cheap, *comedor* food, head for the centre of town and the railway tracks. **Triángulo** is one of the better places in this range. Around here and down 9 Calle you will also find bars, pool halls and the rest.

Livingston

Once you leave Puerto Barrios, you are heading for a different world, a world where history and culture are tied to the legacy of the African slave trade, a place where the predominantly black inhabitants speak a boisterous dialect of Spanish, Garifuna and English—almost impossible for any outsider to understand. Music is everywhere, but instead of marimba or salsa, you hear reggae. If you're very lucky, you might even hear some of the older people singing their sad and beautiful Garifuna songs, the African drumming and chorus singing conjuring up images of distant places and their painful past. The young people prefer West Indian music, and saunter down the muddy streets in the obligatory red, green and gold hats, dreadlocks spilling down their backs.

Livingston is a two-street place, only accessible by boat, and its mostly wooden houses cling to the muddy rise that seperates the mouth of the River Dulce from the Atlantic beach. If it was not for the steady flow of tourists, there would be very little here, and even at the best of times there is not much to do. The beach is narrow, and littered with quite a bit of rubbish, so sunbathing is not much of an option either. The reason for coming here is, in fact, simply the novelty value in the Guatemalan context, and also because it is the setting-off point for a gorgeous river trip up the Río Dulce, which can be a stepping stone to continued travel into the Petén jungle.

Christmas is one of two times when things really get going: large numbers of, mainly young, travellers come to join in the reggae 'jump-ups' in the beach discos, and listen to the spontaneous concerts of Garifuna singing outside people's homes. If you're travelling alone, then this is definitely one of the best places to be for Christmas, though you will miss the Catholic processions and Masses of the rest of the country. Another excellent time to be here is on 15 May, which is the anniversary of the Garifuna arriving in Guatemala. The first landing of Garifuna boats is re-enacted on the beach, and there is plenty of singing and partying.

History

The black settlements along the Guatemalan Bay of Amatique are a relatively recent phenomenon, part of a migration that took place in the late 18th century. The people are descendants of African slaves and Carib Indians, who originally lived on the island of St Vincent, in the Eastern Caribbean. A group of them was left stranded on the Honduran island of Roatán by the British in 1795, as punishment for staging an uprising. Happily, many survived and gradually they drifted to the mainland, settling in communities along much of Central America's Caribbean coastline, from Nicaragua to Belize. Guatemala's share of the Atlantic coast being so small, there is only one major black settlement, and there are many more in Belize and Honduras. They call themselves Garifuna, and have alway been a very independent people, keeping their history alive in a tradition of song and story-telling, and speaking their own hybrid language. Livingston is one of the most isolated communities culturally, not just because it is waterbound, but also because it is the only one of its kind in a country of *ladinos* and Indians. The Belizean and Honduran communties are much larger, and more a part of their country, though certainly distinct, even there.

Long before Livingston was founded, there was an important Maya port at the mouth of the River Dulce, refered to as Nito. An aspect of Maya culture that is rarely considered is their ocean-going trade and expert seamanship, and as many as 4000 canoes are estimated to have been operating before the Spanish Conquest. In 1502, Columbus and his crew became the first Europeans to encounter an Indian merchant canoe, and Columbus' 14-year-old son excitedly wrote that the canoe was 'as long as a galley and eight feet wide, all made of one tree.' By 1524, Nito had been captured and Spanish settlers moved here, the location of the Maya site since lost. The Spanish settlement was a failure, however, because the newcomers had no idea how to live off the surrounding jungle. Not until much later did Livingston briefly enjoy some importance as a port for the coffee trade, coming direct from the Verapaz highlands via a railway (now defunct) to Lake Izabal and then down the River Dulce.

GETTING TO LIVINGSTON

Boats for Livingston leave daily at 10 and 5 from the dock at the end of 11 Calle in Puerto Barrios, and tickets are sold a short walk away, at the end of 9 Calle, near the waterfront. To be sure of getting on the ferry, arrive an hour early, but at least half an hour before departure. If you miss the boat ($1 one-way), there are always boatmen waiting for custom, who will charge $15–25 per person. The trip normally takes one hour, but on the small *lanchas* it can take longer, and you and your luggage can get very wet.

WHERE TO STAY

EXPENSIVE

There is one 'luxury' hotel, the **Tucán Dugu**. For reservations call tel 347813 or 345242 in Guatemala City. Many of the rooms have ocean views, and there is a nice pool, with a nearby bar. The layout is bad, resulting in long walks down endless corridors and pathways, and the hotel is hardly luxurious.

INEXPENSIVE

A favourite for many is the **Casa Rosada**, a 5-minute walk from the dock, taking the first left turn, which offers thatched cabins on the waterfront. **Caribe**, on the same path, but nearer the dock, is a decent guest house. Also along here and with a good waterfront bar is the **Hotel el Viajero**, with the same prices as the Caribe.

Heading up the main street from the dock, a lovely two-storey wooden building houses the **Río Dulce**, which is a popular budget hotel because of the balcony where you can string a hammock and watch the world go by. Very good value is the **Minerva**, near the centre, on a side street (ask for directions). The second high street, turning left towards the church and cemetery, has one of Livingston's most extraordinary guest houses, the **African Place**. Built by an eccentric Spaniard with a taste for Moorish architecture, the place is a collection of white, concrete buildings, busy with turrets and bizarre decorations. It looks much better than it is—or more interesting, at least—and should be avoided if at all possible. Many are the bad experiences with the abrasive owner, and only the restaurant is worth checking. At the end of the street and down the bank, there is another guest house on the beach. This is the **Flamingo**, which is run by a German woman who has rather excessively fortified the guest house in a walled compound.

EATING OUT AND NIGHTLIFE
One of the best places for breakfast and cheap meals is **Dinis**, on the main street heading towards the cemetery. Also recommended is the **Café Margoth**. Towards the end of the other street is **Cuevas**, with excellent cooking, and nearby is the **Cafetín Lyly**, which is a good *comedor*. **El Malecón**, near the docks, is a large restaurant under a cool verandah and finally, you can eat at the **Tucán Dugu**, where prices are predictably high; only the pool and bar are worth trying really.

The most popular bar is the **Labuga**, on the street towards the cemetery, where there is often live music too. Down on the beach, there are a couple of shack bars, and beyond the **Marimba Beach Bar**, heading out of town, is the main **reggae disco**. Opposite the GUATEL office, you will also find the **Disco Raymondo**, which is a dark and sweaty place.

USEFUL INFORMATION
There is no bank in Livingston, but you can change cash at the **Koo Wong shop**, on the main street. For phone calls, there is a **GUATEL** office near the dock.

Boats for Puerto Barrios leave from the dock at 5 am and 2 pm, daily. Buy your ticket at least one hour early to be sure of getting on, which is usually a battle.

If you don't want to spend lots of money hiring someone to take you up the River Dulce, you can catch the **mail boat** on Tuesdays and Fridays, leaving around 9 am. This will take you as far as Fronteras, and the suspension bridge, where the Petén road heads north. The return journey by mail boat is on the same days. Unfortunately, the schedule changes all the time, and sometimes the boat does not turn up at all, so expect to be flexible. The other drawback of using the mail boat is that you cannot stop off along the way. But at least you will be paying only $8, which is a fraction of the usual cost.

Excursions from Livingston

Siete Altares
About an hour's walk from Livingston along the beach, there is a pretty spot for freshwater swimming during the rainy season: a waterfall here forms a number of beautiful pools in a cascade of several levels. To get there, just follow the beach past the disco, until you come to a river emptying into the sea. If you're lucky there will be someone to ferry you across, but otherwise you can wade or swim across. On the other

side the beach soon thins out, and a path leads off to the left, finally reaching the pools. The only drawback about this place is that it is notorious for robbers, and you should never walk this way on your own.

Río Dulce
By far the most popular excursion is a canoe trip up the River Dulce, and you will find plenty of boatmen offering trips down by the dock. The price for going all the way to Lake Izabal can be as high as $60 one-way, so you need to bargain hard, and preferably share the cost with others. If you're only going on a day trip as far as the nature reserve at El Golfete, the price should obviously be much less. As always, agree exactly where you want to go and how much for, before setting off.

Almost as soon as you leave Livingston behind, you enter a gorgeous jungle environment, with all kinds of tropical birds flitting across the emerald waters. The banks either side rise steeply as the river washes through a long gorge, with huge trees and a profusion of vines and plants that hang over the river's edge. If you look carefully, you will see long-legged, white herons, standing motionless as they wait for prey, and perhaps even an iguana sunning itself on a rock.

The best part of the river is this gorge that stretches a number of kilometres between the mouth and a section known as El Golfete, where the waters widen considerably to create a lake. About half way along, there is a hot spring that bubbles directly into the river, and makes for a steaming natural jacuzzi. You have to swim to it from the boat, so ask to stop here if that is what you would like to do. Further along, the area around El Golfete has been designated the **Biotopo Chocón Machacas**, which is intended to help protect the rare manatee, or sea cow, as well as the jungle flora and fauna. There is a landing jetty for boats, and trails to wander around in the forest, though you are unlikely to see any wildlife other than butterflies and birds during the daytime, and it is more fun to explore the many canals by boat. If on a day-trip from Livingston, this is as far as it is worth going.

Into the Jungle
If you plan to continue onwards to the Petén Highway for buses to the jungle or back to the capital, then you should hire a boat to take you as far as the **Castillo de San Felipe**, which is a tiny fort, built by the Spanish to protect Lake Izabal from British pirates, who regularly came to raid trading posts here. Without stopping along the way, the ride takes about 2 hours, and very close to the fort is the inexpensive **Hotel Umberto**, which also offers meals, across the mud road. The only problem with this place is that it's a long walk to the Highway if there is no one to give you a lift.

More convenient, but pretty horrible, are the *pensiones* in the village of **El Relleno**, directly by the suspension bridge. (If you do find yourself having to spend a night here, **Comedor Mary's** is the best for fried fish.) This is where all buses either for the Petén or the capital stop, as well as local buses to nearby towns, such as Morales. If your destination is anywhere along the Atlantic Highway, the fastest option from here is to take a local bus to the Ruidosa road junction, and change there. If you arrive at El Relleno and wish to travel downriver to Livingston, you can find boatmen under the bridge. They know you are more or less dependent on their service, so you will have to bargain hard.

Luxury Resorts on Lake Izabal

Hiding along the shores of the lake are a number of luxurious resort hotels, most of them only accessible by boat. The clientele are mainly rich Guatemalans and American yachting enthusiasts who come here to enjoy exclusive holidays and weekends. Fishing, water-skiing, and sailing charters around Lake Izabal, down the Río Dulce, or as far as the Belizean Cayes, can all be arranged from here, and this elite group of hotels make up the only place in Guatemala where tropical luxury is genuinely laid on, with great food, and sporting entertainment if you want it. To reach any of them, just take a water taxi from below the suspension bridge at Fronteras. This should only cost around $5, but can be as much as $20, depending on your bargaining skills.

One of the nicest places, just past the Castillo de San Felipe, is **Izabal Tropical** (no pool), which charges from $50 for doubles and $56 for triples. Another favourite is the **Catamarán**, which has the best swimming pool and tennis courts, and charges from $36 for doubles and $42 for triples. Two more resort-style places, in the same price category as the Izabal Tropical are **Turicentro Marimonte**, and **Del Río**, both with their own pools. The only place not recommended is **Mario's Marina**.

Of the various yacht **marinas** dotted around, **Susanna's Laguna** is best for meals, and **Mañana Marina** does good breakfasts and has the best bar. **Bar Hotel California** can be reached on foot from Fronteras, and is also worth checking.

THE PETÉN

From the air the Petén jungle, which makes up a third of Guatemala, looks like one green blanket, stretching endlessly into the horizon. On the ground, however, the landscape is surprisingly hilly, and the many rises were favourite places for the Mayas to build their city-states. Look at any map, and you will see it peppered with the names of ancient ruins, many still unexcavated, and many more inaccessible to the traveller without a helicopter or time for many days of jungle hiking.

Piedras Negras

The land is mostly still covered by thick ancient forest, cut by many rivers and also lakes and swamps. The wildlife is one of the most varied and profuse in Central America, which has a lot to do with the relatively recent incursion of modern man. In spite of the fact that 20% of the jungle has been destroyed in the last decade alone, the impact appears minimal, compared to neighbouring Mexico or Honduras. Here there are jaguars, magueys, snakes, tapirs, howler monkeys, anteaters, armadillos, crocodiles, tropical birds, and an infinite number of creepy-crawlies, from scorpions to bird-eating spiders—though, most likely, you will only see monkeys, birds and insects. It is always a good idea to shake out your clothes and shoes before putting them on, and insect repellent is essential.

It was in this region, the Yucatán peninsula, of which the Guatemalan Petén is a sizeable part, that Maya civilization developed into its highest form. The largest and most elaborate architecture flowered here, with huge pyramids rising above the jungle, and finely decorated plazas, ball courts, residential structures, temples, and much more. The greatest of these cities was Tikal, where successive rulers enjoyed not only political and economic power, but also fostered the arts and sciences, in particular writing and astrology. Other major sites include El Mirador, El Ceibal, Altar de Sacrificios, Yaxchilán and Piedras Negras, but there were hundreds of other settlements, usually along important trading routes or near permanent sources of drinking water.

The Maya Golden Age was during the period AD 250–900, and to many it is a mystery how they could have built cities and developed such a sophisticated society in this inhospitable region. Food supply is difficult, since agricultural farming can only be limited. Hunting and gathering in the forest can sustain a nomadic existence, but is incapable of sustaining centres like Tikal, which possibly had up to 40,000 inhabitants. The current explanation of this enigma is that the Maya were great traders, and their cities grew up in this region because of their monopoly on trade between the Mexican Gulf and the Caribbean. In their time, a lot of merchandise travelled either in ocean-going canoes, or across the Yucatán along the riverways that once existed but have long since disappeared. Thus they would have charged high taxes along their trade routes, and had the contacts to import most of their food supplies, as well as anything else they needed. Their centres of habitation were also spread out over a far greater area than previously realized, with distant satellite communities engaged in maize production solely for the central core where the elite lived.

The three most accessible archaeological ruins are Tikal, Uaxactún, and El Ceibal. The first two are virtually neighbours, and can be visited from the modern town of Flores, or you can stay the night at Tikal itself. El Ceibal needs more time and effort to reach, since you first need to take a bus to the town of Sayaxché, in the southern Petén. Travel in the entire region is by dirt roads that disintegrate into turgid soup during the rainy season from May to October, making travel virtually impossible.

Only Tikal can easily be visited at any time of year, thanks to the airport in nearby Flores, which has regular, daily flights to and from Guatemala City. Also, the road connecting Flores to Tikal is the only surfaced one in the Petén. Expect prices to be high, but do come to Tikal. You will not see another place like it and all other Guatemalan ruins pale besides this one for size, for splendour, for the jungle setting, and the magical combination of ancient architecture, mysterious rainforest and abundant wildlife.

Overland to Flores

The journey overland, from Guatemala City to the jungle capital of Flores (488 km), is famous among travellers for being one of the most harrowing experiences you could possibly inflict on yourself. What is theoretically a 14-hour bus ride takes more like 24 hours, and never less than 16. Even hardened travellers of Latin America are surprised by the seemingly endless torture of this journey, which really comes into its own after crossing the River Dulce, where the tarmac road becomes mud and the bus drivers struggle to negotiate the giant furrows in the road. Whenever it rains, great lakes form across the road, disguising its true depth until it's too late. Matters are not helped by the view out of the window, which is an endlessly monotonous stretch of forest, slashed by the red gash of what calls itself a road. None of the jungle's magic reveals itself to fuel your anticipation.

Approximately 10 to 12 hours after leaving the capital, you arrive at **Poptún**, the fastest growing town in the Petén, though you would never guess it from the miserable collection of mud-stained, concrete houses. It is, however, an excellent place to break the journey, being close to the **Finca Ixobel**, a beautiful jungle farm on the outskirts of town (3 km). It used to be run by an American couple, who lovingly built this place and offered delicious home-grown food and comfortable shelter to weary travellers. (Sadly, the husband was murdered in unclear circumstances and his wife fled the country, leaving the farm to be run by friends.) The business is still running, and there are not many other places in Guatemala where you can combine beautiful surroundings with such pleasant accommodation and delicious meals.

Many visitors turn their overnight stopover into a couple of days, since there is much more to do other than relax and eat well: there is an extensive traveller's library with plenty of books to read, there are horses to rent for jungle excursions, or you can hire a guide to take you hiking, and there are ponds for swimming. Accommodation comes in three varieties. In the main house, there are a few rooms, which are $3 for one and $6 for two, sharing the bathroom (the only snag is the lack of privacy due the absence of a ceiling covering top-floor rooms, just the roof, high above). There are outhouses, which are dormitories, and there are treehouses, both of which cost $2 per person. You can also camp on the meadows surrounding the farm. Meals are not cheap, but certainly worth it. If arriving by bus, ask to be dropped off at the entrance to the farm, which is on the main road. On leaving, you unfortunately have a 3 km walk into Poptún, though you might be able to hitch from the main road. The farm also runs a *pensión* in Poptún itself, as part of the **Restaurante Ixobel**, on the main street. Other accommodation cannot be recommended.

Heading for Flores, buses leave Poptún at 8, 10.30, 11 am, 1, 2 and 3.30 pm. In order to have any hope of a seat, you should take one of the first two buses, which actually originate in Poptún. The journey can take up to 9 hours.

Heading for Guatemala City, buses leave at 2.30, 5, 9 am and 2.30 pm, and the second bus is the only local one.

Flores

Flores comes as quite a surprise: like an overheaped plate of food, this tiny town piles onto an island on the edge of Lake Petén Itzá (which is about 32 km long and 5 km wide). Narrow streets and pastel-coloured, stone houses squeeze together around a colonial church and square at its elevated centre, where the view is refreshingly open, across rusty roofs and the glistening lake, to the jungle all around. To circle the island takes less than twenty minutes and the reason you come here is not the town or its attractive setting, but to see the glorious Maya city of Tikal, 65 km from here.

Although nothing remains to bear witness, the island was probably once the capital of the Itzá, named Tayasal. They were a people who originally came from the Mexican Yucatán, and the city of Chichén Itzá still has their name. They were extremely independent and able to resist the Spanish for over 170 years, though a steady flow of soldiers and missionaries bothered them all that time. The first to arrive here was Hernán Cortés himself, in 1524. He was on his way to a campaign in Honduras, and since the Itzá king received him willingly, he did not stop for bloodshed, and only left his lame horse. Almost one hundred years later, two Spanish priests arrived to find that a statue of the horse was being worshipped as the god of rain and storms, and had to flee for their lives after they smashed it.

Other groups of missionaries arrived with soldiers, and one such group, in 1623, was promptly defeated and sacrificed. Finally, in 1697, the Spanish attacked Tayasal via a war galley, and slaughtered every Indian they could find, while the rest swam to the mainland, never to be seen again. The Maya king was taken to the capital, and paraded in chains.

GETTING TO FLORES

By Air

Apart from the overland route, either by bus or four-wheel drive, you can fly from Guatemala City. At least four flights daily shuttle between the capital and Flores, leaving early in the morning (around 7 am) and returning in the late afternoon (around 4 pm). The flight takes about an hour, and costs around $106 return. From both ends, you can either turn up at the airport and buy direct from the airlines, or go via any travel agent. Flores is usually a stop-over for flights on their way to Belize City, so you can easily visit Tikal on your journey to or from that country.

The only honest **travel agent** for flight tickets from the Petén is in the **Hotel Petén** in Flores. The **Hotel San Juan**, on the mainland, near the causeway connecting Flores, also sells tickets and offers a free bus ride to the airport, but watch out for hidden extras, and you might be sold a seat that does not exist.

In Antigua and Guatemala City, travel agents can not only arrange flights and transport to the airport, but also 1 to 3-day **tours to Tikal**, inclusive of accommodation and guides. However, a 2-day tour can cost as much as $350 plus extras, so if you have the time and initiative you can save yourself a lot of money by travelling independently.

By Road

Other than the route already described, you can also get a bus from Sayaxché, if coming from the southern Petén, via the back road from Cobán. Buses between Flores and Sayaxché are run by the **Pinita** company, and leave at 6 am and 1, in both directions. The journey takes 4–6 hours, and most buses arrive and leave from outside the Hotel San Juan.

WHERE TO STAY AND EAT

The nicest place to stay is in Flores itself, which is generally more expensive than staying on the mainland, where modern Santa Elena and San Benito sprawl. A mud causeway connects the island, so access is easy, though very messy after rains.

In Flores

MODERATE

The best hotel on the island is the **Hotel Petén**, tel 0500–692, fax 0500662, which has a good restaurant and clean rooms with fans. Try to get a room with a lakeside view. With a pleasant waterfront terrace and bar, the **Hotel Savanna** is also a good choice. Rooms with fans and dinner included go for $20 for two, secure parking available. On the waterfront near the causeway, the **Hotel La Jungla** is a very friendly place.

INEXPENSIVE

Next door to La Jungla is the **Hotel El Itzá**, which is nothing special. Also on the lakeside, with a cosy patio for eating and drinking, is the guest house **El Tucán**, though the rooms are not that nice. Other establishments are opening fast.

Other than the hotel restaurants, there are quite a few places to eat and drink. The top restaurant is the **Palacio Maya**, with a good choice of seafood and other dishes for around $5. **La Jungla**, not to be confused with the hotel, is small and cosy, with good food at medium prices. Next door is a good *comedor*, the **S'Quina**. If you feel like trying traditional Maya cooking, such as stewed venison, armadillo, wild turkey, or fish, then head for **La Mesa de los Mayas**.

On the Mainland: Santa Elena

EXPENSIVE

Not far from the causeway to Flores, the **Hotel Del Patio Tikal** is a two-storey building set around a cool courtyard, which also shades the restaurant. Tel 501229, or fax 502-2-374313 in Guatemala City.

MODERATE

A very pleasant choice is the **Hotel Maya International**, which is a collection of wooden bungalows and a restaurant, built directly over the water, with views of Flores. Tel 501276, fax 500032.

INEXPENSIVE

The **Hotel San Juan**, tel 500041, profits from the fact that buses virtually empty passengers into its lobby, but does not in fact deserve the custom it gets. There is a restaurant attached. Two cheapies are the **Don Quijote**, which offers bare rooms and communal baths; and the **Hotel Jade**, which is better than it looks and good value for money.

Near El Remate, on the lakeshore, halfway to Tikal

LUXURY

The most exclusive hotel in the region is the new **Camino Real**, which is a sister hotel to the one in the capital, with all the same services and prices too (book via the hotel in the capital, see p. 85). Discreetly built into the jungle along the lake, this is the place to come for tropical luxury. You will need to hire a taxi from the airport or arrange to be picked up by the hotel's own vehicle.

INEXPENSIVE

On the branch road leading to the Camino Real, you will find the **campsite El Mirador del Duende**, which styles itself an 'eco-campsite', and is very basic. Either sling a hammock under cabins provided, or pitch a tent. Washing is in the lake, and the toilet is a hole in the ground. Further along the road is the **Gringo Perdido** guest house and campsite, which gets mixed reports. However, it has a restaurant, and also hires out canoes, mountain bikes and horses. **Agua y Tierra**, nearby, hires out 500cc scramblers for around $20, plus the cost of a full tank. These are excellent for making your own way to the ruins of Uaxactún, 24 km beyond Tikal.

If you do not wish to pay for an expensive taxi from the airport, you could wait for one of the minibuses heading for Tikal, on the main road. If they have space they will take you and drop you at El Remate, from where you will have to walk 3 km to reach El Gringo Perdido; or try hitchhiking from the airport.

USEFUL INFORMATION

Tour Agents
For the most impartial advice on reputable **tours, guides, boat, car or bike rental** firms, see the INGUAT representative at the airport, from Tuesdays to Sundays. Alternatively, see the staff at the Hotel Petén, or failing that, the man at the Hotel San Juan, though he is not above ripping you off. A short walk from the San Juan, there is also a tour agency, **Yaxhá Outdoor Life Tours**, which can help with adventurous trips into the jungle. But remember that the only time jungle expeditions are a realistic prospect is during the dry season, from November to April, and even then the weather might go against you.

Money Matters
There is a **bank** in Flores, and you can also change money at the Hotel San Juan; but the shop **Brenda**, opposite the Hotel Jade around the corner, gives a much better rate.

Telecommunications
There is a **GUATEL** office in Santa Elena, or you can pay a lot to use the hotel phones.

Boat Hire
Canoes for exploring Lake Petén Itzá can be rented from **El Relleno**, halfway along the causeway. A double canoe costs $2 per hour. **Boat tours** of the lake are easily arranged with the boatmen who congregate by the causeway, and a trip around the whole lake, taking in the lakeside **Petencito zoo** and a swimming stop, should not cost more than $10.

Tikal

You hear so much about the ruined city of Tikal before you get there, see images of the famous Temple of the Giant Jaguar on so many tourist posters, that you think you know what to expect. But all preconceptions are forgotten as soon as you enter the twilight jungle to walk to the Central Plaza, especially if you use one of the smaller paths, rather than the main gravel one. High above your head, the swaying branches are home to spider and howler monkeys, who occasionally like to pelt visitors with nuts, though they usually miss. Green parakeets squawk above the canopy of trees, while toucans hide from sight, only the chattering 'tock' of their giant bills hinting at their presence. Most exhilarating of all is the lucky sight of a pair of macaws, majestically spreading their red, blue and green wings, but making a very undignified racket, their screams audible far and wide across the forest.

Tikal

Before you know it, you stumble out into your first grassy clearing and come face to face with a pyramid, its damp limestone walls blackened with age and lichen. It seems oddly out of place, a monument in the middle of nowhere. But then the path leads on to the heart of Tikal and opens out onto the green carpet of the **Great Plaza**, where **Temple I** and **Temple II**, more beautifully known as Temple of the Giant Jaguar and Temple of the Masks, tower over you. Their pinnacle tops jab the pale blue sky at 58 m and 50 m respectively, and the giant stairways up their immense bulk can be a daunting prospect. But the effort of climbing Temple II is greatly rewarded by the view from its temple platform. Up here, you find yourself standing above the jungle canopy, looking out across a sea of forest as far as the eye can see, while nearby, the peaks of other pyramids rise up from the depths. One of the very best views of the Great Plaza and its famous pair, is from the **North Acropolis**, which lines one side of the square.

Incredible to imagine that the Maya had no metal tools to create these huge monuments, nor pack animals either—only generations of slave labour sweated here. For over one thousand years the ceremonial centre of Tikal was built and rebuilt to become one of the greatest Maya cities there ever was. There were settlements here as early as 600 BC, but the Golden Age of monumental building was from AD 250–900, an age referred to as the Classic Period by archaeologists. This period is sub-divided into the Early Classic (AD 250–550) and the Late Classic (AD 550–900), and what you see today is almost all from that later period, the rest buried underfoot. The great temples, for example, were built around AD 700, while the North Acropolis dates from AD 550 onwards, though the earliest constructions date from 200 BC.

An interesting feature of Maya rebuilding was that the accompanying stelae—the monumental sculptures that recorded the all-important dates of royal lineages, wars and construction dates—were ritually 'sacrificed', when a particular building had fulfilled its ordained purpose. Usually the stela carried an elaborate portrait of the ruler associated with the building in question, and the Mayas took special care to smash his face, for what reason is uncertain. The ruined or defaced sculpture would then be 'buried' under masonry near an altar, or bricked into a disused building. This is the reason why so many of the stelae at Tikal are damaged or defaced, though vandals and looters have also done much damage.

At its height, central Tikal is estimated to have had 10,000 to 40,000 permanent residents, though most recent thinking favours the lower estimate. However, if you consider that Tikal's territory actually encompassed 40 square kilometres, the subject population of Tikal's rulers may have been much greater. Central Tikal covers an area of 16 square kilometres, where over 3000 buildings of all types have been recorded so far. Added to these there are over 200 stelae and attendant altars, so the day visitor-tour cannot hope to see more than a fraction of what makes up this site. Of course the undisputed highlight of any visit is the magnificent Great Plaza, but there are two other temples worth exploring for bird's-eye views of the jungle and surrounding monuments, and those are **Temple III**, just west of the Great Plaza, and most especially **Temple IV**.

The latter is the highest structure ever built by a Native American civilization, towering a breathtaking 96 m from the ground.

Built around AD 741, this temple has not been cleared of the forest that has invaded its steps and walls, and to reach its summit, you have to clamber up ladders and over trees, unsuitable for vertigo sufferers (as are all the pyramids). A large number of toucans congregate around here, and you have a good chance of coming almost face to face with one as you climb the ladders. Another building you should be sure to visit is the Temple of the Inscriptions, some way from the centre, which is covered in mysterious hieroglyphics.

GETTING TO TIKAL
Transport to Tikal is by minibus, and most of the hotels run their own service. The journey is expensive at $6 return, and takes one hour. On entry to the National Park of Tikal, you will be charged an extra $6. In theory, this is a daily fee, but in practice, those staying overnight in Tikal itself only pay once, on entry.

A Guide to the Site

For a detailed description of the site, an excellent map, as well as historical and archaeological guidance on Tikal, you cannot do better than buy William R. Coe's handbook. *Tikal: A Handbook of the Ancient Maya Ruins* (about $10). This should be on sale at the site, but to be certain, you should buy it before arrival, and best read it before exploring the ruins too. This excellent book will tell you all you need to know in a readable style, and the map is very helpful. In Guatemala City, the book is available at the Popol Vuh Museum, and all the bookshops in Antigua sell it. You should also be able to buy it in England and the United States.

Without this handbook and its map, you will need a guide if you are not on an organized tour, not just to explain the site, but also to help you explore, since it's easy to

get lost. Official guides wait around the entrance path to the site, and especially around the Great Plaza. As elsewhere, you need to bargain out the price before setting off, and it helps if you know which parts you especially want to see.

USEFUL INFORMATION

The entrance fee to the National Park of Tikal is now $6, and the ruins themselves are open daily from 6 to 6, though you can usually stay a little longer to watch the sunset and listen to the grunting howler monkeys. There are no toilets by the ruins, only by the car park, some distance away.

There is a small **museum** near the car park (Mon–Fri, 9–5, Sat and Sun, 9–4, nominal fee), which is worth visiting to see fading black and white photographs taken by Alfred P. Maudsley in the 1880s. These will give you an excellent idea of how much work has been necessary to clear the jungle from the ruins, most of which has been done by the Tikal Project, which got under way in the 1950s. There is also a fine collection of Maya vases and pottery found at the site, as well as jade jewellery and carved bones taken from royal tombs. For the best preserved stelae, see the **Stelae Museum** next to the **visitor's centre**, where you will also find a selection of brochures and books.

Clothing for the jungle should cover your legs and arms to protect against the incessant mosquitoes and scratchy foliage, and you should certainly bring repellent. A hat and binoculars are useful, and it is best to wear comfortable, flat shoes, suitable for jungle paths and climbing the pyramids. If you plan to be here in the evenings, you will need a torch, as there is no lighting. Remember also that it can get chilly at night, and frequently rains.

WHERE TO STAY

In spite of the expense and bad value for money, you should try to spend at least one night next to the ruins, so that you can explore them in peace when most other tourists have left, and also experience them during their most magical times, at dawn and dusk. During peak seasons, such as Christmas, New Year and Easter, you can expect the hotels to be fully booked up. To reserve a room, you will have to go via a travel agent, and even then you cannot be certain that your reservation will be honoured. The only way you can be guaranteed a room is if you are flying in on an organized tour, otherwise you just have to try your luck on arrival. Prices change constantly here, so those stated can only be a general guideline.

EXPENSIVE

There is a choice of three hotels: the **Tikal Inn** is expensive and dirty, with *cabaña* style rooms around a small swimming pool. The **Jaguar Inn** offers a few simple rooms. It does have the best restaurant though. **Jungle Lodge**, nearest the ruins, offers bungalows with private baths. Limited cheaper accommodation in old buildings and dormitory rooms is also available, which is always worth asking about. This place is your best choice, even though there is sometimes no water, the service is bad, and the restaurant is totally lacking. Their minibus usually meets incoming flights, and will take you straight to Tikal, avoiding Flores.

INEXPENSIVE

There is a **campsite**, which charges $6 for you to pitch your tent or sling a hammock under leaky shelters (mosquito nets are essential). Shower and toilet facilities are available, but there is often no water.

EATING OUT
The cheapest option is to bring your own picnic and something to drink, though sodas are sold at strategic places around the ruins. The restaurant in the visitor's centre is outrageously expensive and not very good, and you are much better off at the restaurant of the Jaguar Inn. There are a number of *comedores* scattered along the entrance road to the site, but the very best is right next to the campsite and car park, a friendly place to be in the evenings too.

Uaxactún

During the dry season, buses occasionally drive the extra 24 km north, to Uaxactún, and hired jeeps can also be used. Or you could take a guide and walk to the site from Tikal, which takes about 6 hours, so you would have to camp overnight before returning—an excellent introduction to the delights and discomforts of jungle hiking. Tikal's closest neighbour, this is a small and undramatic site by comparison: the pyramids and other structures are much lower and also unrestored, though if they were cleared, it would be easy to see that this was a large Maya centre as well. There is much more of a 'lost world' feeling here, and you are unlikely to see any other tourists, since it does take time and effort to get here. The site is significant today, because of Sylvanus G. Morley's excavations and research here that have considerably advanced our understanding of Maya writing.

El Ceibal and Other Maya Sites

El Ceibal is a site that is primarily interesting for its beautiful jungle setting, on the banks of the Río de la Pasión. The stone used here was very hard, so although the temples are not impressive for size, they do retain some excellently preserved carving. El Ceibal was probably taken over by Mexican peoples in the Late Classic Period (AD 550–900), and you will notice that some of the sculptural style has a strong Mexican influence.

To reach the site, your best option is to hire a boat from the town of Sayaxché. If you can find a group of people it will be much cheaper, since the boatmen charge around $30 for the round trip. Set off early to give yourself plenty of time, as it takes 2 hours on the boat, and then 45 minutes' walking to reach the site. Bring your own food and drink, and do not forget the insect repellent.

Sayaxché

Sayaxché is a thriving jungle town on the Río de la Pasión, which is a good base for the adventurous traveller with plenty of time (and money). From here you can organize journeys of any length and distance, into the jungle, down the rivers or to visit specific sites. Of course any excursion to a Maya site involves a jungle trip, of which the one to El Ceibal is the easiest.

Although hunting has been outlawed, the fishing is still very good here, and one of the best places to do this is **Lake Petexbatún**, 48 km south of Sayaxché. There are also a couple of small Maya sites here, of which **Dos Pilas** is the only one with guards and the best place to camp. You will need to bring all necessary equipment, most of which you can hire in Sayaxché, and all food and drink. Spare a thought for the guards too, who will be much more helpful and willing to share fires and advice if you bring enough food to share with them.

You can reach Lake Petexbatún by boat (plus a 12 km walk), and you will certainly need to hire someone who can also act as guide. For the best advice about trips to and around the lake see Julián Mariona Morán, at the Hotel La Montana, in Sayaxché. Or talk to Julio Godoy at the Hotel Guayacán, who is a well-known expert on the region. One general rule about hiring a guide is that you are expected to provide his food and drink, as well as his fee. To avoid arguments, try to be as detailed as possible in the arrangements about what exactly you will do and how long it will take. The guide who asks to be paid in full before departure is a dubious prospect, and you should never pay more than half before the end of your journey. Expect a general fee of $30–40 per day.

GETTING TO SAXAYCHE

The easiest route is from Flores and **Pinita** buses leave daily at 6 and 1 from both directions. The town lies 56 km southwest of Flores, and the journey along the mud road takes 4–6 hrs, but do not even think of it during the rainy season. Boats ferry arriving passengers across the river to Sayaxché.

WHERE TO STAY

INEXPENSIVE

A long-standing favourite is the **Hotel Guayacán**, known as Hotel Godoy after its owner, which is not far from the ferry landing. Meals are also offered in the restaurant. Cheaper is the **Hotel la Montaña**, also with restaurant. Last choice should be the **Hotel Mayapan** for simple rooms. The best place to eat is the Hotel la Montaña.

Remote Maya Sites

North of Flores

Two significant sites lie in this direction: **El Mirador** and **Río Azul**. Of these, the former is the more important, and was in fact a huge city in its day, as significant as Tikal before it was eclipsed by it. To reach El Mirador, which lies just 5 km from the Mexican border, you need to hire a four-wheel-drive or hitch to Carmelita (35 km), and there enquire about a guide and mule to take you on the two-day trek to the ruins. Camping equipment, food and water must all be brought with you, and you should check with the INGUAT official in Flores whether you need permission from the authorities to travel this way. Río Azul does not merit a special expedition unless you have a specialist interest. The round trip takes up to 3 tough days by four-wheel-drive.

East of Flores

Yaxhá lies 48 km away, on the shores of Lake Yaxhá. This is believed to be a huge site, as yet unrestored, though INGUAT has plans to develop it as a new tourist attraction. One of the few things known about this site is its unusually late period of habitation, probably between the 12th century and 14th century, long after the Classic Maya civilization had collapsed. To reach the site is relatively easy, since you can catch any bus heading for the Belizean border, and ask to be dropped off at the turning for Yaxhá. From there you will have to walk up to three hours, along a clear track (turn left when the track reaches the lake). Camping equipment, food and water are all necessary, since you will have to stay the night. Alternatively, you could try reaching the site by four-wheel-drive, and by the time you get to Guatemala, there might even be tours going here, so it is worth checking with the INGUAT official.

Northwest of Sayaxché
Reaching the site of Yaxchilán is one of the most adventurous undertakings. Located on the banks of the Usumacinta river, marking the border between Guatemala and Mexico, you will have to travel over 100 km by boat, first along the Río de la Pasión, and then on the Usumacinta itself. The journey as far as the ruins will take at least two or three days one-way, and can take much longer if you decide to travel on trading boats. Commercial river traffic only goes as far as Benemérito anyway, and from there you must hire a boat. The best option is to hire a boat from Sayaxché, which will take you all the way to Yaxchilán. Either way, you will need plenty of time and money, but the site itself is beautifully located on the river bank, and certainly an interesting place to visit. If you do not wish to organize your own trip, you could always go on a tour with one of the expedition agencies working out of Guatemala City.

Onwards to Mexico

If you plan to travel into Mexico via the river town of **Benemérito**, you must get your Guatemalan exit stamp at the airport in Flores first. The Mexican immigration post is outside Benemérito, which all buses pass, leaving daily for Palenque in the early mornings. A much easier option for travelling to Mexico from the Petén is to get a direct bus from Flores to El Naranjo (Guatemalan exit stamp available here), and from there boats take you to La Palma in Mexico.

Onwards to Belize

There are daily buses leaving Flores for the border town, **Melchor de Mencos**, leaving at 5, 7, 10, 11 am, and 3pm. The mud road is really awful, and the journey of about 80 km can take quite a few hours. On the Belizean side, the small town of Benque Viejo is a few kilometres from the border, and is best passed by as soon as possible. Buses for Belize City leave the border regularly, and all pass through San Ignacio, which is the first town from the border where you will find pleasant accommodation (see p. 212, Belize Chapter).

Part V
BELIZE

Fewer than 200,000 people live in this tiny country; the majority are black or creole, their language a lilting English and their preferred music Caribbean reggae. Even the Indians speak English to a West Indian tune, and Spanish is only the second language, in spite of a sizeable number of mestizos.

Most of the population lives on the coast, leaving the interior of swampy plains, rainforest and jungle covering the mountains almost uninhabited. As a result, the species of wildlife and tropical flora are some of the richest and most diverse in all of Central America. The endangered jaguar and the scarlet macaw are just two of many rare animals that thrive in Belize and, in this part of the world, only Costa Rica can rival the variety of birds. There are even areas that have never been explored by outsiders—thick tropical forests hiding innumerable Maya ruins in their twilight world.

About 300 km long, the country looks like a large bite out of Guatemala, by which it is traditionally claimed, and whose maps pointedly include Belize in its national territory. However, the wild Maya Mountains stand as a bulwark against Guatemala's pretensions and make up almost the entire western border of a country that is never more than 109 km wide. Mexico and Guatemala mark the northern and southern borders respectively, while the east consists of a 288 km Caribbean coastline with hundreds of islands scattered along its entirety—outcrops of the largest barrier reef in the northern hemisphere.

The islands, or cayes, as they are known, provide the main focus for travellers to Belize. Life here is even more laid back than on the mainland, and refreshing sea breezes make dozing in a hammock or sunbathing highly pleasurable. In the surrounding sea a magical world lies just off the beaches, and the diving and snorkelling are excellent. The

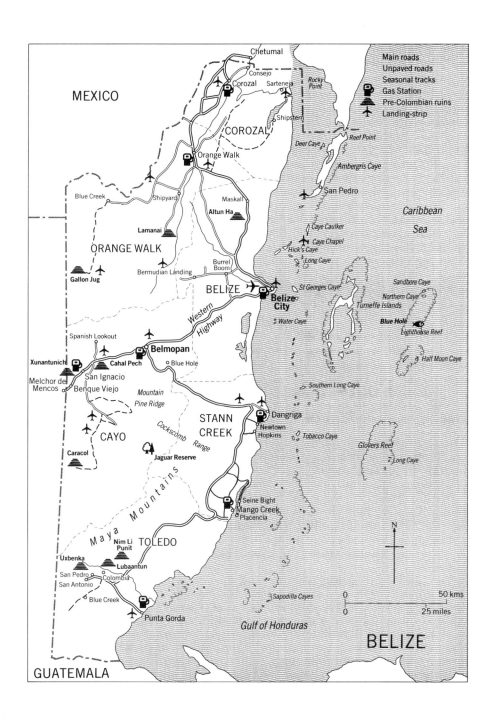

most developed resort island is Ambergris Caye, but there are plenty of hideaway places too, both exclusive and cheap, so it is easy to escape the crowds.

A favourite saying among travellers is that 'the best thing about Belize is underwater', but this is simply not true. The tropical forests of the interior are equally exciting, especially if you travel along any of the rivers, where you will most likely see giant iguanas sunning themselves on the shore, brilliant kingfishers and gorgeous butterflies, sleeping bats, and lizards that can walk on water.

The great variety of wildlife, both in the sea and on land, as well as the friendly people, make Belize a very enjoyable country to visit. To the south, the remote districts of Toledo and Stann Creek combine some of the best features: tropical forests and rich wildlife; Maya villages and ancient ruins in the highlands; and some of the finest mainland beaches. More accessible, the western Cayo district hides jungle lodges along the Rivers Mopan and Macal, while also being home to the Mountain Pine Ridge, a region of pine forests, meadows and waterfalls, ideal for hiking and camping. Northern Belize is mostly flat and the least interesting for the visitor, though there are some significant Maya ruins in the region. But if it is sun, sea and surf you want, you can hardly beat the Belizean cayes.

It is not just the country's natural heritage that is exceptional—Belize is also distinguished by a government founded on parliamentary democracy, with a very good record on peace and human rights. The economy is reasonably stable too, tourism providing a major boost to income from agriculture and fishing.

Post-Independence History

Buccaneers and Pirates

The history of Belize, formerly British Honduras, is unique among the Central American countries. It was ignored by Spanish conquistadors, who only passed by on their way from Mexico to Panama, and the coast was left to be settled by British seafarers, the first of whom were shipwrecked on the treacherous Barrier Reef in 1638.

In the early days, the region was known as the Honduran Bay Settlement, and only consisted of a tiny patch around Belize City and St George's Caye, which was an ideal base for maritime bandits. The Barrier Reef provided protection from heavy Spanish galleons, who were unable to pass through the shallow waters, yet the pirates could still swoop on the seasonal migration of colonial ships weighed down by gold and other treasures.

The British government, eager to crack the Spanish monopoly on trade in the Americas and West Indies, actively encouraged piracy at that time. Some were even commissioned by the British government, such as the buccaneers and privateers. One of the most famous buccaneers was Sir Henry Morgan, whose most spectacular feat was capturing Panama in 1670, and holding it to ransom for 780 pieces of eight. His reward was to be named lieutenant governor of Jamaica. Privateers, unlike Sir Henry who was a soldier of fortune loyal to his regent, were simply hired to rob trading vessels of competing nations such as Spain, and their reward was to keep whatever bounty they found. Finally, at the bottom of the criminal scale were the pirates, who served no one but themselves and robbed any boat they could. Among the many legendary figures is Edward 'Blackbeard' Teach, who apparently was so fearsome that Spanish ships would give up their cargo without so much as a fight.

Creole Society

From the early pirate camps developed a society that was not characterized by a blending of Spanish and Indian blood, but of mainly British and African, with a limited amount of Indian. It was a society that eventually developed its own governmental institutions, far removed from the 'strongman politics' that grew up elsewhere in Central America. No plantation elite developed here, with a country enslaved to bananas, coffee or sugar, rather a society that lived from logging and the sea. The Baymen, as they were called, constructed an early form of democratic rule, where they elected governing magistrates at public meetings. For over 200 years the Honduran Bay Settlement survived even though it was entirely surrounded by hostile Spanish forces, and did not become a British Colony until 1862. Not only does the racial and political heritage differ from that in the rest of Central America—the social and economic history does too.

Slavery was officially abolished in 1838, and multiculturalism flourished throughout the 19th century, though certainly not without tension. Not all blacks who came to the Honduran Bay Settlement were slaves in the first place. For example, 500 black members of the 5th West India Regiment arrived in 1817, after their regiment was disbanded and they were given the option of land grants here. Most became free woodcutters in the emergent logwood and mahogany trade. Other blacks arrived as free survivors from shipwrecked slaving vessels or were simply given their freedom by captains who had fallen out with their contractors.

The racial melting pot was not just one of white and black, however. At least 8000 mestizo and Indian refugees remained after the end of the War of the Races in the Yucatán, in 1874, while almost twenty years earlier, 1000 East Indian Sepoys arrived after being deported by the British. The Sepoys had been responsible for a bloody uprising against British rule in India, killing many colonials in New Delhi and elsewhere. Once the British had granted the territory Colony status, they also began an immigration incentive programme for Chinese farm workers. By that time the logging trade was already going into decline, and new labour was needed to develop agriculture. Unfortunately, less than half of the 474 Chinese arrivals in 1865 remained three years later; they had either died from tropical diseases or returned to their own country. A small number of Lebanese mercantile families also settled in British Honduras, as did German-speaking Protestant Mennonites, emigrating from Canada and Mexico.

A Controversial Territory

At first Belize consisted solely of Belize City and St George's Caye, but soon the settlement spread. One reason for the expansion was that the logging trade required large tracts of forest to search for mahogany. The Spanish were always keen to assert that the British settlers had no territorial rights, and could not found permanent towns and villages. However, the 1783 Treaty of Versailles established the first outline for the

Baymen's territory. According to that agreement, the northern border was the River Hondo, the southern one the Belize River, and the western border Petén Itzá. But only three years later Belizean loggers were operating as far south as the Sibun River, and the country's present-day outline was established from this time onwards, even if the Spanish and British authorities both tried to deny it.

The 1783 Treaty had been signed by the Spanish on condition that the British government did not establish a colonial government in the region, and also gave up its claim to the Mosquito Coast. But the Baymen, with their tradition of self-rule, were never easily persuaded to curtail their operations according to British foreign policy, and thus this early territorial agreement was soon ignored. It was a thorn in the Spanish colonial side, and forces from the Mexican Yucatán repeatedly threatened the Baymen.

Finally, in 1798, a huge Spanish fleet of 32 ships, 500 seamen and 2000 soldiers set sail to rout Belize City once and for all. But as luck would have it, three ships of the West India Regiment came to the aid of the ragged flotilla of Baymen boats, in addition to 171 slaves who agreed to fight in return for their freedom, and their combined forces actually succeeded in repelling the enemy fleet. It was the last time the Spanish tried to remove the settlers by force, and the Battle of St George's Caye is still celebrated as a national holiday in modern Belize.

Once Mexico and the Central American region had gained independence from Spain, in 1821, the United Provinces of Central America were founded, from which British Honduras remained apart. However, in 1839, the union disintegrated, Guatemala claimed it had inherited sovereign rights over Belize from Spain, thus initiating a conflict that is still simmering at present. The British, in turn, declared the territory to be under the law of England and instituted a governor general to rule the country. As far as the Baymen were concerned, it was a necessary evil, but British rule always sat uneasily with a society that was founded on personal freedom and home rule.

The conflict between Britain and Guatemala continued until the Treaty of 1859, when Guatemala officially recognized British sovereignty over British Honduras—now known as Belize. The agreement was signed on condition that the British would build a road connecting the Petén with the Caribbean coast of Belize, but this part of the bargain was never kept, and thus successive Guatemalan governments have declared the 1859 and later 1863 Treaties invalid. To this day Guatemala claims the entire territory of Belize, occasionally hotting up the argument with some military threats, and this is the principal reason why the British armed forces remain in independent Belize, and why the country did not gain full independence until 1981. A new treaty of recognition was signed in 1991, but it is unlikely to hold since many Guatemalans oppose it and the next president could revoke it.

Independence and Democracy

British Honduras officially became known as Belize in June 1973, and instituted its own Belizean dollar in 1974, but did not become a fully independent member of the Commonwealth of Nations until 21 September 1981, with George Cadle Price elected as the first prime minister. He is the leader of the People's United Party (PUP), founded in 1950, and has been the country's premier on many occasions, most recently elected in 1989, when his party narrowly won the last elections with a majority of just two seats. Elections must be held at least every five years, and there is universal suffrage for all over the age of 18.

The system of government in Belize is a parliamentary democracy based on the British model, and the prime minister rules the country with an elected cabinet of ministers and ministers of state. The Queen is still the titular head of state, but she is represented by a governor general who is always a Belizean and takes his cue for appointing members to the cabinet from the Belizean prime minister.

General Information

Ze-haad pikini go da maakit two time'
Children who don't listen go to market twice: listen to advice.

Creole proverb

Getting to Belize

By Air
International airlines with regular connections from North America to Belize are American Airlines (tel 800 624 6262), Belize Trans Air (tel 305 261 3069), Continental (tel 800 0856), Taca (tel 800 535 8780), and Tan-Sahsa (tel 800 327 1225). The most frequent flights are from Miami, but there are also daily direct flights from Houston and Los Angeles, and regular flights from New Orleans.

There are no direct flights from Europe. The best option is to fly to Miami on British Airways, Continental, KLM, Eastern or Virgin Atlantic (cheapest), and then on to Belize. The cheapest option of all is to fly to Cancún in Mexico, via the US, and then catch a bus southwards to Belize. There are also flights between Cancún and Belize run by Tropic Air. Prices are much the same as to neighbouring Guatemala, so you should expect to pay around US$350 roundtrip from Miami, and around £600 from Europe. On leaving Belize, you will be charged BZ$20 departure tax, unless you have been in the country for less than 24 hours. There are also frequent direct services to Belize from all the Central American countries, except Nicaragua. The one international airport, **Philip Goldson Airport**, is 16 km outside Belize City.

Without prior notice, you can only arrive by **private aircraft** at the international airport. If you are coming from Cuba or Guatemala, the latest requirements can be obtained from the airport officials. Belizean airspace is open during daylight hours, and pilots must file a flight plan. Landing fees are around BZ$9.75 for a 6000 lb aircraft, and BZ$1.60 for every additional 100 lb.

By Boat
Ships occasionally sail to Belize from New Orleans and Florida ports, but flying will be easier to arrange and cheaper. The only scheduled ferry service arriving in Belize is the

ferry between Puerto Barrios in Guatemala (see p. 157) and Punta Gorda in southern Belize. The ferry leaves on Tuesdays and Fridays, in either direction, and the journey takes about 2½ hours. For up-to-date information in Punta Gorda itself, contact **Indita Maya**, tel (07) 2065.

Arriving by **private yacht**, you are expected to report to the police or immigration officials immediately. You do not require any special permits, but you will have to present the vessel's official document; clearance from the last port of call; four copies of the crew and passenger manifesto; and four copies of stores used or a list of cargo on board. If there is no cargo, then you just need an imballast manifesto.

By Train
There is no railway in Belize, and none leading to its borders.

By Bus
There are cheap long-distance buses from the United States, through Mexico, to Belize. This is, however, a very long and arduous trip. From Texas the journey takes up to 6 days; from California, more like 2 weeks.

From Mexico, there is a frequent, daily service of direct buses between Chetumal and Belize City, run by the **Batty** and **Venus** bus companies. The first bus leaves Chetumal at 4 am, last one at 6 pm. The journey takes about 4 hours.

Arriving overland from Guatemala, there is one road connection from Flores, in the Petén jungle, crossing into Belize at Benque Viejo (see p. 173). The **Novelo** bus company runs daily direct buses from the border to Belize City, between 4 and 11 am, and a **Batty** bus leaves at 1 pm. The journey takes 3 hours from the border. Arriving at any other time, just take a taxi from the border to Benque Viejo, 2 kilometres away. From here there are buses leaving for nearby San Ignacio, where there are regular buses to the capital, until around 6, though services are always limited on Sundays. San Ignacio is the best place to stay the night, if you don't wish to travel further.

By Car
Arriving by car, you will need your driver's licence and registration document, and third party liability insurance is mandatory. You can buy it at the border. You will also be asked to show sufficient funds for your stay. In theory you are supposed to have US$50 per day; in practice US$1000 per month should be acceptable. Drivers without an International Driver's Licence will have to apply for a temporary Belizean driver's permit from the Chief Licensing Officer, in Belize City, valid for 90 days. On leaving the country you will be charged a BZ$5 exit fee for the car.

Embassies and Consulates
As these offices are not directly responsible for tourism, you can expect very limited information on anything other than official entry requirements and investment opportunities.

In the UK: Belize High Commission, 19a Cavendish Square, London W1M 9AD, tel (071) 499 9728, fax (071) 491 4139.

In the US: Belize Embassy, 3400 International Drive, NW, Suite 25, Washington, DC 20008, tel (202) 363 4505, fax (202) 362 7468. Belize Mission to the United Nations, 820 Second Avenue, New York, NY 10017, tel (212) 599 0233.
In Canada: Belize High Commission, 112 Kent Street, Suite 2005, Place de Ville, Tower B, Ottowa, Ontario K1P 5P2, tel (613) 232 7389.

Tourist Offices

In the UK: There is only limited information available from the High Commission, and you can probably find out more by going to your local travel agent. Your best option could well be to phone or fax the Belize Tourist Board in Belize (tel 02 77213, fax 02 77490) requesting the latest brochures.
In the US and Canada: There are a very large number of tour operators specializing in Belize in the United States, and some in Canada. A full list is available from the Belizean Tourist Board, in their brochure entitled *Belize: The Adventure Coast.* **Belize Tourist Board**, 415 Seventh Avenue, New York, NY 10001, tel (212) 268 8798, fax (212) 695 3018. You can call toll-free from continental US and Canada on 800–624–0686.

Maps

Detailed maps of Belize are difficult to get hold of, and the tourist map sold by the Tourist Board is the best you will get in the country itself. Only the main roads and highways are marked, but there are street maps of most of the major towns. Petrol stations are only indicated in the towns.

A trip to your local map shop is highly recommended, as they may have more detailed maps. In England, the best place to go is **Stanfords International Map Centre**, 12–14 Long Acre, London WC2P 9LP, tel (071) 837 1321. Also worth trying in England is the Overseas Surveys Directorate, which has published maps of Belize to a scale of 1:250 000 and 1:50 000.

Passports and Visas

All visitors need a valid passport to enter the country, and are given permission to stay for one month, with extensions possible for up to six months in total. Extensions are available from the **Immigration Office**, 115 Barrack Road, Belize City, tel (02) 77237 (open Mon–Thurs 8.30–11.30 and 1–4, closing at 3.30 on Fri). Or you could try any police station. You will also be asked to show sufficient funds for your stay and, unless arriving in private transport, an onward flight ticket. As a general rule, $50 per day is considered sufficient funds by the officials. If you have less, you can always bluff, and hope they do not ask you to prove it, which they often do not. Alternatively, showing a credit card would help.

Nationals from the United States, Great Britain and Commonwealth countries do not need visas. Nor do people from Belgium, Denmark, France, Finland, Greece, Iceland, Italy, Liechtenstein, Luxembourg, Mexico, Netherlands, Norway, Panama, Spain, Sweden, Switzerland, Tunisia, Turkey or Uruguay. If you do need a visa, you must apply for it before arrival in Belize.

GUATEMALA AND BELIZE

Customs

You cannot bring any fruit or vegetables into Belize, but otherwise there are no unusual restrictions. Electrical goods may incur duties, refundable on leaving the country. Leaving the country by air, there is an exit fee of BZ$20. Leaving by land, the exit fee is BZ$2. If arriving by air, you must have a return ticket in order to enter the country. You may be asked where you intend to stay and what you intend to do. However, if you have no fixed plans this will not cause any problems.

On Arrival

Fishaman neva say e fish 'tink.
Self-criticism is rare.
Creole proverb

Tourist Offices

There are many tour operators offering everything from sightseeing tours to sailing charters, and a full list is available from the Belize Tourist Board. The office sells maps of the country, and also a few special interest books. Free brochures are available on everything from nature reserves and Maya sites to the country's government structure. The staff can help with hotel and tour reservations. The office is open Mon–Thurs, 8–noon and 1–5; Fri till 4.30.

Belize Tourist Board, 53 Regent Street, P.O. Box 325, Belize City, tel (02) 77213/73255, fax (02) 77490.

Getting Around Belize

Hurry, hurry, get deh tomorrow; tek time, get deh today.

By Air

There are local airports in almost all of the country's main towns and some cayes (reef islands), and getting around by air is easy, if not cheap. There are three airlines providing internal flights: **Maya Airways**, tel (02) 77125/72312, has the most flights; **Island Air**, tel (02) 31140; and **Tropic Air**, tel (02) 45671. Tickets can be booked at any travel agent. There are airports in Belize City (both the international and municipal airport are used for domestic flights), Corozal, Caye Chapel, Dangriga, Big Creek (for Placencia), Punta Gorda and Ambergris Caye.

Flights to and from the municipal airport in Belize City are always cheaper than to the international one. Sample return airfares from the Belize City municipal airport are: Ambergris Caye, BZ$70; Corozal, BZ$75; Caye Chapel, BZ$54; Dangriga, BZ$81; Big Creek, BZ$141; Punta Gorda, BZ$188. Flights connecting Ambergris Caye with Caye Chapel are around BZ$30 one-way, though at the time of writing, the only resort on Caye Chapel was closed for refurbishment. Children under 12 only get a 30% discount on their tickets.

There are also many airstrips by smaller and remote settlements, and it is easy to charter small aircraft. Ask about reputable companies at the Tourist Board in Belize City, or go direct to either of the airports.

By Train
There is no railway in Belize.

By Bus
Getting around Belize by bus is easy. There are regular daily services (greatly reduced on Sundays) to all corners of the country, and fares are cheap. As elsewhere in Central America, the buses tend to be old American school buses, rather uncomfortable for tall people. The main highways are all paved, except the Southern Highway beyond Dangriga, which makes travel in southern Belize slow. Apart from local buses operating out of the major towns, four companies have carved out their specific regions, all with their main terminals in Belize City: **Batty Bus Line** serves western Belize and northern Belize; **Venus Bus Line** also runs a service to the north; **Novelo Bus Service** runs west to the Guatemalan border; and **Z-Line Buses** serve southern Belize.

By Car
Having your own transport in Belize is very worthwhile, since the roads are generally excellent, and even in the more rustic south, the dirt roads are well maintained. It will make it much easier to visit places away from the main highway. Local buses do serve outlying areas, but not very often, and not usually when it will suit you. None of the Maya sites are served by commercial buses, but most have roads leading to them. (See above for entry requirements for bringing your own car.)

The only region where a high-clearance vehicle, and possibly four-wheel-drive, is recommended, is in southern Belize. However, the dirt road leading to the remote Maya site of Caracol also requires a tough, four-wheel-drive vehicle, and even then, you can only use it during the dry season from November to May. You also need permission to enter the Mountain Pine Ridge area from the local Forestry Commission.

Traffic drives on the right, but there is one important rule to remember: when you want to turn left, both traffic behind you and oncoming vehicles have right of way, and the custom is to move to the side of the road, allowing traffic in both directions to pass before turning left. There is only one traffic light in the entire country, on a bridge in San Ignacio, and residents are petitioning to have it removed. There are few petrol stations outside the main towns, so always keep an eye on the tank.

In southern Belize, road signs are almost non-existent and it is easy to get lost. Dirt roads can go on for a very long time before they end at a logging camp, so a road map and regular enquiries from the locals are essential. As a Belizean explained it: 'We know where we're going, so what do we need road signs for?' An entertaining book, published locally, is Emory King's *Driver's Guide to Beautiful Belize*, on sale in bookshops and from the Tourist Board in Belize City.

Car Hire
The best place to hire a vehicle is in Belize City, but there are other towns with local rental agencies too. You will have to reckon on around $90 a day for a jeep with unlimited mileage, so renting is not cheap. If you rent by the week, you get a better deal. The following agencies are officially recommended:

IN BELIZE CITY
Avis, Radisson Fort George Hotel Plaza, Belize City, tel (02) 78637; **Budget,** 771 Bella Vista, Belize City, tel (02) 32435, fax (02) 30237; **Crystal Auto Rental,** Northern Road, Belize City, tel (02) 31600, fax (02) 31900; **Elijah Sutherland,** 127 Neal Penn Road, Belize City, tel (02) 73582; **Gilly's Car Rental,** 31 Regent Street, Belize City, tel (02) 77613/77630; **Lewis Auto Rental,** 23 Cemetery Road, Belize City, tel (02) 74461; **National Car Rental** at Philip Goldson International Airport, tel (02) 31586; **Pancho's,** 5747 Lizarraga Avenue, Belize City, tel (02) 45554; **Smith's and Sons Auto Rental,** 125 Cemetery Road, Belize City, tel (02) 73779.

IN PUNTA GORDA
Alistair King, Texaco Service Station, Punta Gorda, tel (07) 2126.

By Bicycle
Belize is easy to explore on two wheels, since the roads are the best in Central America. Only in the south, where clouds of dust rise from the dirt road every time a vehicle thunders by is cycling less pleasant, and you will certainly need a sturdy mountain bike. Remember, however, that Belize is very hot and humid. Especially inland, away from the coastal breeze, cycling along shadeless roads can be utter torment. The only place where you will find spares is in Belize City. Not all Belizean buses have roof racks, but if they do, you should have no trouble transporting your bike.

Embassies and Consulates

Even though Belmopan is the capital, many offices prefer to stay in Belize City, which has always been the commercial and cultural heart of the country.
UK: High Commission, 34/36 Halfmoon Avenue, Belmopan, tel (08) 22146/22147.
EC: Commission of European Communities, 1 Eyre Street, Belize City, tel (02) 72785.
Costa Rica: Consulate, 8–18th Street, Belize City, tel (02) 44796.
El Salvador: Consul General, 120 New Road, Belize City, tel (02) 44318.
Honduras: Consulate, 91 North Front Street, Belize City, tel (02) 45889.
Mexico: Embassy, 20 Park Street, Belize City, tel (02) 30193/30194.
Panamá: Embassy, 79 Unity Boulevard, Belmopan, tel (08) 22714; Consulate, 5481 Princess Margaret Drive, Belize City, tel (02) 44940.
US: Embassy (Consular section), 29 Gabourel Lane, Hutson Street, Belize City, tel (02) 77161/73886.

Local Agencies
Belize Department of Archaeology, Belmopan, tel (08) 22106. It is housed in the National Assembly complex.

Money Matters
The Belizean currency is the Belize dollar, whose value is fixed at BZ$2 to US$1. US dollar travellers' cheques or cash are the best currency to bring with you, though sterling

can also be changed. Barclays Bank is represented in Belize City and Belmopan, and you can use your normal chequebook to buy Belize dollars there. Branches of the Belize Bank are in all the major towns, and their business hours, along with other banks, are Mon–Thurs 8–1, Fri 8–1 and 3–6.

Wiring money from abroad is best done to Barclays Bank in Belize City, or by using the American Express office. As always, having to wire money can be a tedious and time-consuming business in Central America, and should be avoided if possible. Credit cards are widely accepted, and certainly necessary when hiring a vehicle. American Express and Visa are the best known here, but others should also be acceptable.

Post Offices

There are post offices in the main towns only, and the rates are fixed at BZ$0.60 for letters to the US, and BZ$0.75 for letters to Europe, taking roughly a week to ten days in both cases. Their business hours are Mon–Fri, 8–noon and 1–5. If you want to send a parcel, you will have to use a cardboard box and take it open to the parcel office in Church Street, Belize City, where it will be checked by customs before you can close it with string.

Receiving post is straightforward: just have it mailed to **Poste Restante**, The Main Post Office, Belize City, Belize. Letters will be kept for up to three months before being sent back. Remember to take your passport for identification. Alternatively, holders of American Express cards or travellers' cheques could use their office as a postal address: **American Express**, Belize Global Travel, 41 Albert Street, Belize City, Belize.

Telecommunications

Phoning to and from Belize is easy and international calls from here are the cheapest in Central America. Public payphones are very rare, and your best option is to use the phones in hotels and restaurants, which usually charge a flat fee. For example, a local call of three minutes officially costs no more than BZ$0.25; long-distance calls within Belize cost around BZ$0.60 for three minutes. International calls cost around BZ$10 for three minutes to North America, and BZ$20 to Europe.

Belize Telecommunications (BTL) has offices in all the major towns, normally in the same building as the post office. In Belize City, their office is at 1 Church Street, open daily, 8 am–9 pm. If you wish to make an international call, you will be asked for a BZ$30 deposit. Direct dialling is possible, and collect calls can be made to the United States, Great Britain, Australia and France. To make a collect call, dial the operator in the country you are calling.

Telephone codes around Belize are: Belize City: 02; Belmopan: 08; Benque Viejo: 093; Caye Caulker: 02; Corozal: 04; Dangriga: 05; Orange Walk: 03; Punta Gorda: 07; San Ignacio: 092; San Pedro/Ambergris Caye: 026.

The **emergency number** for the police, fire department or ambulance is 90.

Police and Military

Belize is the happy exception to the Central American rule: its defence forces are not known for human rights abuses or a high level of corruption. Politically motivated killings or disappearances are unknown here, though Central American refugees and non-English-speaking Belizeans have occasionally suffered abuse from the authorities. Belize even has its own Human Rights Commission, founded in 1987, which has been responsible for such projects as incorporating human rights into police training courses.

Small rudda control big ship.
Size isn't everything.

Creole proverb

The country's civilian police force is made up of just 500 people, and called the Belize Police Force (BPF). The Belize Defence Forces (BDF) were founded in 1980, a year before independence, its army not much larger than the police force. The BDF is trained and, to a large extent, financed by Britain, the United States and Canada. British military officers command them; however, the Belizean government has a programme for replacing the foreign commanding officers.

There are also still about 2000 British soldiers stationed in Belize, traditionally to protect the country from Guatemala's claim on its territory. However, Guatemala formally recognized Belize in 1991, and the British have at last agreed to honour their promise of building a road from Guatemala City to Belize City (basically the Petén road, via Flores and Benque Viejo), which they made in 1859. Thus one of the region's most futile disputes should be over, and possibly the British troops will eventually withdraw altogether. On the other hand, if you read the Guatemalan press you will see that recognition of Belize may only be temporary.

Medical Matters

Chemists stock most drugs and toiletries you might need, including contraceptives, suntan lotion and mosquito repellent. Outside Belize City, you are unlikely to find tampons, but sanitary towels are always available. See your embassy or consulate for a list of recommended doctors. If you require outpatient attention at a hospital, it's free. The **Belize City Hospital** is on Eve Street. If in the south or west of the country, you could always try the British military bases for medical help, which they often provide for the locals. There are camps outside Punta Gorda and San Ignacio.

Public Holidays and Opening Hours

New Year's Day
9 March—Baron Bliss Day
Good Friday
Easter Saturday
Easter Sunday
Easter Monday
1 May—Labour Day
24 May—Commonwealth Day
10 September—St George's Caye Day
21 September—Independence Day
12 October—Columbus Day
13 October—Pan-American Day

19 November—Garifuna Settlement Day
25 December—Christmas Day
26 December—Boxing Day

There are very few museums in Belize, so always check information for an individual institution in the relevant town. Normal business hours are Monday–Friday, 8–5. Commerce and industry hours are Monday–Friday, 8–noon and 1–5. Very few businesses are open on Sundays. Most nature reserves and archaeological sites are open to the public daily, from 8–5, though regulations vary, since you can camp in some reserves, and some Maya sites just have a local guard, but no official hours. Details are given in the guide text.

Festivals

Belize is not blessed with many festivals, but its Caribbean culture ensures there is no lack of entertainment, with parties and discos almost every weekend. Reggae music predominates, but Latin American music is also popular.

The main national celebrations are Independence Day (21 September), Columbus Day (12 October) and Garifuna Settlement Day (19 November). The latter is one of the most interesting times to be in Belize because there is a good chance of seeing some traditional Garifuna dancing if you head for Dangriga or any of the Garifuna villages further south. The Garifuna are descendants of African slaves and Carib Indians, and their festivals are rich with African songs and drum rhythms, the dancing a mesmerizing mixture of African and Caribbean.

Markets

Interesting markets are not a feature of Belize, though you may enjoy a stroll around the fish and vegetable market in Belize City, newly housed in the extension of North Front Street, past the post office. You will find all sorts of tropical food here and the vendors are always willing to explain their uses. On the other hand you may be horrified by the writhing sea animals, and the stench can be overwhelming. Trading is finished by noon, so you need to get there early.

Shopping

> *Gati gati no wanti, an wanti wanti no gati.*
> If you've got it, you don't want it, and if you want it, you can't have it.
>
> *Creole proverb*

Belize is not the place for handicrafts, though plenty of trinkets are made of sea creatures, shells, wood, and coconuts. As you browse through jewellery made of tortoiseshell or black coral, it is worth remembering that the former comes from an endangered species, and the latter is banned from export. It is also illegal to import black coral into the United States.

The quality of weaving and embroidery is very primitive compared to Guatemalan standards. The few remaining Maya settlements in southern Belize have entirely lost their artisan knowledge, and are only now trying to relearn it, in order to benefit from tourism. But what you find will be expensive—and Belizean Mayas do not seem to appreciate the art of bargaining either. The best buys are probably the wood carvings.

The Media

Belize has a large number of publications for such a small country. There are five weekly newspapers, but their reporting is dominated by school functions and personality profiles, with little useful political coverage. *The Reporter* is a business paper, with a heavy bias towards the conservative United Democratic Party (UDP), presently the country's main opposition. *Amandala*, although basically a sports paper, has the most varied political coverage. *The Beacon* is another mouthpiece for the UDP, and so is the *People's Pulse*. The *Belize Times* serves the interests of the reigning People's United Party (PUP), which is also conservative, though its origins lie in the social democratic tradition.

The left-wing periodical *Spearhead*, published by the research foundation SPEAR, concentrates on long-term issues concerning community development, education and social welfare. *Belize Studies* is published three times a year, and is a forum for Belizean and international research on the country. *Belize Currents*, published by Emory King in Belize City features local creative writing. Finally, an excellent source of tourist information and local issues is the monthly *Belize Review*, subtitled 'News, Views and Ecotourism'. Unfortunately, it only seems to be available in Belize City; you can buy it direct from their offices at 7 Church Street, Belize City.

There are two national radio stations: Belize Radio One broadcasts in English and Spanish; and Radio Krem is a newly established station, under the same ownership as the Amandala paper. National television programming is still in the early stages, and most of what you see are pirated programmes from the United States. A local company, Great Belize Productions, is trying to redress the balance with documentaries and features on local life and culture.

The only towns with cinemas are Belize City, San Ignacio, and Orange Walk, predictably dominated by the latest US releases.

Where to Stay

Belize has an enormous variety of tropical luxury hotels, though service standards are occasionally lax. To meet tourists' highest expectations, the **Belize Tourism Industry Association** is trying to establish training courses for hotel and catering staff, but this programme is in its infancy.

There are hotels and guest houses to suit all pockets, though it has to be said that Belize is expensive compared to the rest of Central America. The cheapest price range for one person, per night, is BZ$15–BZ$25, which can be a shock for travellers coming from neighbouring Guatemala. Moderately priced hotels charge anything from BZ$50 to BZ$100, and expensive resort hotels begin at BZ$100. International reservation procedures are observed by Belizean hotels.

Added to these prices is a 5% government hotel tax, and some places charge up to 15% service tax on top of that. Always make sure you know whether the price quoted includes these two taxes or not, as many places do not openly display their charges.

There are no youth hostels in Belize, and camping is forbidden in almost all parts of the country. Two exceptions to this rule are the Cockscomb Basin Wildlife Reserve and Mountain Pine Ridge, though both are difficult to reach without your own transport, and there is no food available in either place. Both sites are administered by the Audubon Society in Belize City, which can provide up-to-date information and help for organizing visits.

Commercial renting of holiday homes is common in all the touristic areas, especially on the cayes. Contact the Belize Tourist Board, 53 Regent Street, Belize City, tel (02) 77213 for information on long-term lets. Outside the main tourist season, from May to November, you should have no trouble finding a self-catering apartment or beach house, even if you haven't booked in advance.

Eating Out

In spite of Belize's Caribbean character, the food is not as good or as exotic as you might expect. Burgers and chips predominate, with Chinese food a close second. Even these are not normally very exciting, and meals are expensive for what you get. Between March and July lobster is not officially available, to protect them during their breeding season, though unscrupulous restaurants and tour operators often ignore this ban. Unfortunately you will also find turtle steaks on some menus, even though the animal is a threatened species. There is plenty of legal seafood, however, and it is best eaten on the cayes, where dishes include shark, snapper, wahoo, conch and shrimps.

Creole cooking rarely finds its way onto any restaurant menu, though one item you sometimes see is *fried jacks*. This delicious alternative to toast consists of hot slices of deep-fried dough smeared with jam. Another local dish is rice and beans, normally served with stewed meat of some kind, or fried fish. If you happen to be in southern or western Belize during Easter, you may be lucky enough to find delicious iguana, which tastes a bit like tender chicken, and is eaten especially at that time.

Drink

There is just one kind of beer available in the entire country, and that is the nationally brewed **Belikin** beer, a very mediocre variety. Only the top hotels will serve imported beers, and those will usually be American and overpriced. The best local alcohol is the rum.

Fizzy drinks and canned fruit juices are standard, though you can usually find delicious, freshly made juices as well. One of the most refreshing is made from watermelon, but many other tropical fruits are used. The strangest drink is sickly sweet seaweed, mixed with milk and cinnamon, which is certainly an acquired taste but worth trying at least once. Drinking water from the taps is not recommended, although it is claimed that the water in Belize City is safe.

Itineraries

Most visitors head straight for the reef islands (cayes), but the country has plenty to offer besides its spectacular reef.

The Cayes and the Barrier Reef

The Belizean Barrier Reef is unquestionably the country's star attraction. Situated very close to the mainland (from 1 km to 25 km away), the reef is a great underwater wall, whose unique underwater formations include the **Great Blue Hole**, which is an eerie sinkhole descending into the seabed. The main dive resort is **San Pedro**, on Ambergris Caye. There are also remote, offshore resort hotels such as on **Caye Chapel, Glovers Reef and Turneffe Islands**. For a less commercial location than San Pedro, and a relaxed atmosphere, head for **Caye Caulker**.

The West: Cayo District

Cayo District is the most accessible area for hiking and jungle excursions, the heart of which is the friendly town of **San Ignacio**, quickly reached in 3 hours from Belize City. Based here, or in one of the jungle lodges nearby, you can explore some of the best the country's tropical interior has to offer. An excellent way to spot animals is to take a canoe trip along the **Rivers Mopan or Macal**, where you will also have the best chance of seeing the astonishing variety of birds that live here.

Apart from the rainforest, there is also the **Mountain Pine Ridge**, with an almost alpine atmosphere. Camping is permitted and, properly equipped and provisioned, this is a rewarding hiking area. Many of the jungle lodges also offer tours on horseback to this area.

There are a number of Maya ruins to visit, and most spectacular of all is the huge ceremonial centre of **Caracol**, hidden deep in the jungle near the Guatemalan border.

The South: Toledo and Stann Creek Districts

The southernmost region of Toledo District is home to the majority of the country's Maya Indian communities, and a programme is being developed which will allow visitors to stay in some of their villages. Expect to find very simple accommodation and facilities: sometimes just a hammock in the thatched home of an Indian family. In some villages a special guest house has been built by the community, and each guest is fed by a different family each mealtime. Visits can be arranged in **Punta Gorda**.

Stann Creek District, with the town of Dangriga as its regional centre, is home to the **Cockscomb Basin Wildlife Reserve**, the only jaguar reserve in the world and an ancient tropical forest that even has areas never yet explored. Hidden deep in the reserve is also the country's highest mountain, the Victoria Peak, rising 1120 m from sea level. The other attraction of Stann Creek is the string of Garifuna villages lining the coastline. Heading south from Dangriga, villages such as Hopkins, Seine Bight, and Placencia are traditional fishing communities of people who still cherish their unique heritage as descendants of slaves and Carib Indians. The beaches are endless stretches of white sand. The best place to stay is **Placencia**.

The North: Orange Walk and Corozal Districts

The Belizean north reveals its few attractions only grudgingly. For the most part inaccessible, unless you're travelling by chartered aircraft or four-wheel-drive, you need plenty of time and money to visit most of the Maya sites or nature reserves located here. The prize destination is the luxury resort at **Gallon Jug**, where wealthy birdwatchers stay in lodges built on the main plaza of a Maya site—great if you can afford it. Or there are the ruins of **Lamanai** and **Altun Ha**, both significant Maya sites, best reached with an organized tour.

The **Baboon Sanctuary** at Bermudian Landing is one of the few places of interest accessible by public transport (from Belize City). Butterfly buffs will certainly want to visit the **Shipstern Nature Reserve and Butterfly Breeding Centre**, in the far north of the country, a few kilometres from Sarteneja.

Belize City

Belize City is no longer the dangerous place travellers warn each other about. In fact, its dilapidated wooden buildings and putrid canals have something magnetic about them, and a handful of colonial buildings add a dash of faded glamour. Built on reclaimed swamp, many houses stand raised off the ground on short wooden posts, allowing just enough space for chickens to scratch the dirt. Their back doors look onto the canals that are more like ditches, while the main streets are lined by modern concrete architecture, billboards and neon signs jostling for position over unhurried pedestrians. There is just one large waterway, Haulover Creek, and a humpy swing bridge is at the hub of people and traffic, soon a familiar marker for all visitors. Most boat traffic to and from the sea passes by the bridge, and local captains are always tempting passers-by to hop on and visit the coastal cayes, just a short distance from the city.

It takes no more than half an hour to walk from end to end of the city centre, and its cracked pavements and dirt roads, its ancient beggars and wanna-be studs—seedy details in themselves—are somehow not sleazy at all. The city is too small to be intimidating, and street crime is not a major problem, though unlit side streets should be avoided at night. Generally the city is relaxed, and women alone need take no more than the obvious precautions: such as not wearing jewellery, walking briskly and never making eye contact.

The atmosphere is more reminiscent of a Caribbean town than a major city. Uniquely in Central America too, the voices around you speak the languid English of creoles, and the hustlers somehow seem less frightening because of it. Certainly drugs are offered to tourists on the streets, and crack is a serious problem, but if you ignore the pushers you will not generally be pursued.

History

A quarter of the country's population live here, and the city has been the political, cultural and economic centre of Belize for over three centuries. The fact that it is no

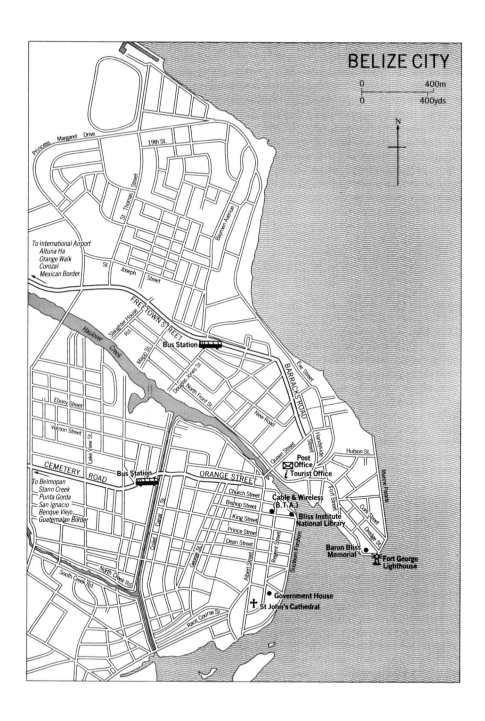

longer the official capital has done nothing to lessen its leading role, which is underlined by the reluctance of foreign embassies to move out to Belmopan, the country's capital for over thirty years now. The first people to settle here permanently were British pirates and loggers: the pirates hiding amongst the many islands of the Barrier Reef, the loggers basing themselves at Belize Point, on the mainland. The loggers called themselves Baymen, since they had operations stretching along the whole Bay of Honduras, searching out mahogany trees for Europe's gentry, and it was from their camps that Belize City grew.

The settlers used broken bottles and wood chips to fill the swampy land, and by the late 18th century, the city was a thriving frontier town: a rough place, where the families of the Baymen awaited their periodic return from the bush. The tough and dangerous work of logging was done by African slaves, and by the end of the 18th century, 75% of the country's population was made up by them, hence the predominantly black and creole population of Belize today, whose ancestors were emancipated from slavery in 1834.

The city's most glorious moment came in 1798, when the Baymen, helped by their slaves and the British navy, resoundingly defeated the Spanish naval assault that was to have established the Spanish Crown's claim to the region. The famous Battle of St George's Caye was fought in the waters off Belize City, and centered around the island which has given the battle its name. In spite of this, it took the British another 73 years to make their territorial claim official, and the country did not become a Crown Colony until 1871. It was known as British Honduras and Belize City was the capital. The city lost its political status in 1961 after Hurricane Hattie pushed a huge tidal wave through the city, destroying most of its wooden buildings and claiming many lives, and it was decided to move the capital 50 miles inland. The new capital, Belmopan, was carved out of the bush. However, all but the civil servants working in the new government offices have chosen to stay in Belize City so in practice it is still the capital of the country.

GETTING TO BELIZE CITY

By Air

Philip Goldson Airport, 16 km outside Belize City is the country's only international airport. A bus shuttle to the city leaves from outside the airport at 6, 8, 10.30 am, noon, 2.30, 4 and 6 pm everyday. Coming from Belize City, there are numerous pick-up points: Pound Yard Bridge, the corner of Cemetery Road and Central American Boulevard, the corner of Central American Boulevard and Vernon Street, and the bus stop by Palotti High School. Departure times from the first stop are at 5.30, 7.15, 8.30, 11.15 am, 1.45, 3.30 and 5.30 pm. You will need the **exact fare**, which is BZ$2, one-way. For more information on the international airport shuttle, tel 73977/77811, in Belize City. If you hire a taxi, expect to pay no more than BZ$30, and always agree on a price before departure.

There are daily flights from the following Central American cities: San Pedro Sula, Tegucigalpa, San Salvador, San José and Panamá, Flores, Guatemala City; and Cancún in Mexico.

The **Municipal Airport** lies a few kilometres north of Belize City. Taxis should cost about BZ$5, or you can walk (20 mins). Domestic flights from here include Corozal, Punta Gorda, San Pedro, Caye Chapel and Dangriga.

If you don't wish to go to the main representatives of the airlines, you can always buy tickets via any of the travel agents along Regent or Albert Street.

Aerovías, Mopan Hotel, 55 Regent Street, tel 77351.
Belize TransAir, Albert Street, just past King Street, heading south.
Continental, Albert Street, by the Hindu temple, south of Dean Street.
Eastern, 26 Queen Street, tel 78646.
Maya Airways, 6 Fort Street, tel 77215.
Taca, 41 Albert Street, tel 77185/77363
Tan-Sahsa, Valencia Building, on the corner of Queen Street and New Road, tel 77080.
Tropic Air have their office at the municipal airport, tel 45671.

By Boat
There are regular boats between Belize City and the cayes (see Cayes section p. 201 for details).

By Train
There is no railway in Belize.

By Bus
There are four main bus companies connecting Belize City with the rest of the country. They all have their main terminals here.

Batty Bus Line covers western and northern Belize, and has its terminal at 54 East Collet Canal, tel 72025/77146. For Belize City to Chetumal, stopping in Orange Walk and Corozal on the way, buses leave at 4, 5, 6, 6.15, 7, 8, 9, 10 and 11 am. The Northern Highway is the country's best road, and the journey only takes 3 hrs to Mexico, $2\frac{1}{2}$ hrs to Corozal. Services to San Ignacio, via the capital, Belmopan, leave daily at 6.30, 8, 9 and 10 am. On Sundays all buses leave half an hour later. **Venus Bus Line** also runs a service to the north, and its terminal is on Magazine Road, tel 73354/77390. Buses to the Mexican border and all towns along the way leave every hour between 4 and 10 am and in the afternoons from noon to 7.

Novelo Bus Service goes to the Guatemalan border, passing Belmopan and San Ignacio. The terminal is at 19 West Collet Canal, tel 77372. Buses leave from noon to 7 pm.

Z-Line Buses run to southern Belize, calling at Belmopan, Dangriga, Big Creek and Punta Gorda. Their buses leave from the same terminal as Venus buses. Buses for Dangriga leave at 10 am, 3, and 4 pm. On Sundays buses leave at 2 and 3 pm. A direct bus for Punta Gorda leaves at 10.30 am, leaving 30 mins earlier on Sundays. It is worth getting the direct bus, unless you want to break the journey in Dangriga, as the journey takes up to 10 hrs, due to the unpaved road south of Dangriga.

GETTING AROUND BELIZE CITY
You can easily walk around the centre and find everything you will want to see. You only need transport to get to the international and municipal airports, and the bus terminals.

Taxis are plentiful on the main streets. Official taxis have green numberplates, and a journey within the city should cost no more than BZ$4. There are no meters, so always agree on a price before departure.

TOURIST INFORMATION
The **Belize Tourist Board** is at 53 Regent Street, P.O. Box 325, Belize City, (tel (02) 77213/73255, fax (02) 77490; Mon–Fri, 8–noon and 1–5.) The office is on the first floor. The staff are very helpful and there are a great variety of free brochures on everything from car rentals to tours. A few interesting books and some maps are also available here.

ORIENTATION
Belize City is such a small place that the main thoroughfares are never far away, and even if you lose your bearings, the noise from the commercial streets or sight of the sea will guide you back on course.

WHAT TO SEE
As you walk along the seafront, with the waves lapping at the crumbling sidewalk, you sense how easily houses can be washed away—something that has happened on a number of occasions, most notably during Hurricane Hattie. As a result the central city is a mix of old and new, with wooden colonial houses, raised slightly off the ground, breaking up the streetlines of modern concrete homes. There are no grand palm-fringed boulevards here. Instead you have a handful of main streets that cut through a tangle of quiet back streets, and after a day of wandering around, the city quickly becomes familiar.

The heart of the city is divided into a northside and a southside by Haulover Creek, with the **Swing Bridge** the main crossing point. The southern part of town is the oldest sector, with just two main streets: **Regent Street** and **Albert Street**. Both streets are lined by shops and offices and, before you know it, you find yourself at the far end, where **Government House** and **St John's Cathedral** mark the beginning of a rather grand residential quarter, where many gardens are met directly by the sea. Government House is a fine colonial wooden building, painted white and set in an attractive tropical garden. The cathedral is a small redbrick church, built in 1812, and looks rather provincial by comparison. It is the oldest Anglican church in Central America, and the kings of the Mosquito Coast were once crowned here by the British. The Mosquito Indians formed an alliance with them between 1815 and 1845, in the hope of avoiding Spanish colonial rule in their territory, which stretched along the Caribbean coast from Honduras to Nicaragua. Thus their 'kingdom' was under British protection and the Spanish risked the ire of the British Navy if they tried to encroach.

Near the Swing Bridge are the main BTL office, as well as the **Bliss Institute** (Mon–Fri, 8.30–noon and 2–8, Sat 8.30–noon), on the Southern Foreshore, which is the city's main cultural centre and library. Occasionally there are exhibitions here of local art or national features, such as the flora and fauna or the latest Maya finds, and it is always worth having a look.

On the north side of town, **Queen Street** makes up the main thoroughfare, also lined by shops and bars, with the **main post office** at the intersection with North Front Street and the Swing Bridge. Around the eastern tip are a number of beautiful colonial houses, as well as the market, where each morning traders sell the morning catch. A fine example of colonial architecture is at no. 4, Fort Street, which is now a popular hotel and bar/restaurant. Another attractive building houses the US embassy, on Hutson Street. If you follow Fort Street to the end, you come out onto the seashore, where the **Fort George Lighthouse** stands above the **Baron Bliss tomb**. An eccentric Englishman, with a Portuguese title, he loved the deep-sea fishing here so much that he bequeathed his fortune to the local authorities. He died on 9 March 1926, and that day is now a public holiday, celebrated as Baron Bliss Day. Following Marine Parade along the seashore, you soon reach the ugly glass box of the Fort George Hotel, which is rapidly losing its position as the city's top hotel to the nearby Villa Hotel.

WHERE TO STAY

Belize City is not a cheap place to stay in comparison with other Central American cities. Most of the up-market hotels are in the northside of the city, while moderate and inexpensive hotels are located in the southside. The telephone and fax code for Belize City is 02. The international code for Belize is 501. All hotels are subject to a 5% government tax.

Northside

LUXURY

The top-priced hotel in the centre is the **Fort George Hotel**, 2 Marine Parade, tel 77400/45600, fax 43820. All services, such as restaurant, valet service and swimming pool are provided. Across the street is the **Villa Hotel**, 13 Cork Street, tel 45751/45755, fax 30276, which is much nicer because of the smaller scale and more personal atmosphere, and is better value for money. It also has a pool and restaurant. All rooms have air-conditioning and TV. Both these hotels add a 15% tax to bills.

EXPENSIVE

Hotel Chateau Caribbean, at 6 Marine Parade, tel 30800, fax 30900, is housed in a wooden colonial building, looking out to sea, and the restaurant is excellent. Also in an attractive colonial mansion is the **Fort Street Guest House**, 4 Fort Street, tel 45638, fax 78808. There are just six rooms, all with fans, and communal bathroom. Apart from the bar/restaurant, there is also a spacious lounge and a small library.

Newly opened, but more than walking distance from the centre, is the **Ramada Royal Reef**. Part of the American chain, the hotel is on the seafront, at Newtown Barracks, tel 31591, fax 31649. Out of town altogether, and only suitable if you have your own transport, is the brand new **Belize Biltmore Plaza**, 3 miles up the Northern Highway, tel 32302. Check with the tourist office or contact direct for the prices of these new hotels.

MODERATE

Popular with Americans is **Mom's Triangle Inn**, 11 Handyside Street, tel 45073, fax 31975. Air-conditioning is available for a daily supplement of US$10, and secure parking is also available. (As always in Central America, it is best not to leave your vehicle unattended in cities.) Downstairs is a mediocre restaurant serving bland fast food, whose main advantage is its useful travellers' notice board.

INEXPENSIVE

One of the friendliest budget hotels in the city is **North Front Street Guest House**, 124 North Front Street, tel 77595, which is safe and conveniently located for catching boats to Caye Caulker. Cheapest of the lot, but still clean, safe, and friendly, is **Marin's Travel Lodge**, 6 Craig Street, tel 45166.

Southside

EXPENSIVE

Centrally located and very pleasant is the **Bellevue Hotel**, 5 Southern Foreshore, tel 77051/77052, fax 73253. All rooms have air-conditioning and TV, and there's also a popular bar/restaurant. The hotel also maintains an extension on nearby St George's Caye, where wooden cottages offer guests a choice of self-catering beach holidays, or all the facilities of a hotel. At the far end of Regent Street, the **Mopan Hotel**, 55 Regent Street, tel 77351/77356, has the advantage of a quiet location, but is otherwise a grubby place, that has seen better days; overpriced for what you get. Nearby, the **Glenn Thorn Manor**, 27 Barrack Road, tel 44212, is a friendly and extraordinary place, squeezed into a colonial house, with every room a different colour, from pink to green. Fridge and kitchen are available to long-term guests. Somewhat claustrophobic, but conveniently located, is **El Centro**, 4 Bishop Street, tel 72413, fax 74553. An immaculate hotel, but rather overpriced, is the **Orchidia Guest House and Café**, 56 Regent Street, tel 74266, fax 77600. Prices include a continental breakfast.

MODERATE

Friendly and good value is the **Sea Side Guest House**, 3 Prince Street, tel 78339. Just around the corner from the Bellevue Hotel, this place is close to the waterside and the hub of Regent Street.

EATING OUT

The most generally available, cheap food, is usually Chinese, and there are plenty of places to choose from, especially around Queen Street. Otherwise, you will find delicious meals in some of the hotel restaurants, notably at the **Chateau Caribbean**, which serves the most authentic Chinese food, and the **Villa Hotel**, which offers Lebanese dishes. Note that many restaurants close on Sundays.

Northside

A good place for breakfast, and meeting other travellers, is at **Mom's Triangle Inn**, 11 Handyside Street. Pricey, but in beautiful surroundings of polished mahogany, the restaurant at **Four Fort Street Guest House** makes delicious fruit drinks and tropical cocktails, and their Sunday brunches are renowned. The **Nile** restaurant, at 49 Eve Street, is a simple place serving Middle Eastern food. On the corner of Queen Street and Handyside Street, the **Shangri-La** serves a mixture of Chinese and international dishes. For an up-market international menu head for **The Grill**, on Barracks Road, near the Ramada Hotel, where you can expect to pay around US$30 for a meal for two.

Southside

The best creole meals are to be had at **Macy's**, 18 Bishop Street. Also good, and cheaper, is **Caribbean**, at 36 Regent Street. **G.G.'s Patio**, 2 King Street, has a pleasant little courtyard, but its menu is dominated by mediocre hamburgers. Also on King Street, **Mexican Corner** has cheap and good Mexican food; and **Pizza House** offers filling meals for big appetites. The restaurant at the **Orchidia Guest House** (see above) is pricey, but the menu is varied and tasty.

ENTERTAINMENT AND NIGHTLIFE
Belize City has the busiest nightlife in the country, which is not to say there is that much choice. Most places do not get going before 11 pm, and stay open till the early hours of the morning. You should note that drugs are a serious problem (crack, cocaine, grass), and you will most likely be offered them. Penalties are heavy and usually involve a prison sentence.

The best bars are generally in the larger hotels, though these are not very exciting places, the clientele tending to be middle-aged businessmen. A popular, rowdy bar is the **Hard Rock Café**, on the corner of Queen Street and Handyside Street. Another drinking spot favoured by travellers and locals is the **Marlin Restaurant and Bar**, at 11 Regent Street.

Big Apple, 67 North Front Street, is a dark and sweaty disco with a young crowd. The **Hard Rock Café** is best for music on Thursday nights, and occasionally has live bands. **Legends**, 30 Queen Street, is best on Saturday nights. **Lindbergh's Landing**, 162a Newtown Barracks (near the Ramada Hotel), is where young professionals go for a romantic dinner and dance, from 8 onwards, where the atmosphere is respectable and no one gets too loud. **Miami Nites I**, on the corner of Cemetery Road and American Boulevard, and **Miami Nites II**, on Orange Street, near the Batty bus terminal, are nothing flash, but wildly Belizean: vibrant atmosphere and energetic dancing till you drop.

There are two cinemas in the city, the Majestic on Queen Street and the Palace on Albert Street, usually showing imported American films.

SHOPPING
Cottage Industries, 26 Albert Street, and Di Creole, 7 Graboural Lane, both have a good selection of Belizean handicrafts. The best buy is probably wood carvings out of *zericote* wood. It is sometimes better, and always cheaper, to buy these from the street hawkers—best of all is to buy them direct from the woodcarver, if you can track one down.

USEFUL INFORMATION
Emergencies
Police: The main police station is on Queen Street, near the Swing Bridge, tel 77210.
Medical: The Belize City Hospital, Eve Street, tel 77251. Also check with your embassy or consulate for recommended doctors.

Belize Audubon Society:
29 Regent Street, P.O. Box 1001, Belize City, tel (02) 77369.

Tour Agencies
A full list of Belizean tour agencies (including diving), as well as ones operating from the US and Canada, is available from the Tourist Board.

Money Matters
The most efficient place for exchanging money is Belize Bank, on the small park south of the Swing Bridge. Barclays Bank and Bank of Novia Scotia are both on Albert Street. It is possible to change up to US$100 travellers' cheques directly into US dollars, but you must prove that you are about to leave the country with an airline ticket. The major banks will also change money. Street vendors are not recommended since sharp practice is very common and you do not get a better deal than with the banks.

The **American Express** office is at Belize Global Travel, 41 Albert Street, tel 77363/77185. Open Mon–Fri, 8–noon and 1–4.30; Sat, 8–noon.

Books
The largest bookshop is the Belize Bookshop, opposite the Mopan Hotel, and there's also a newsagent that sells foreign papers on North Front Street, by the Swing Bridge. The major hotels should also sell *Time* and *Newsweek*. If you can't find the useful what's-on magazine *Belize Review*, you can buy it at their office at 7 Church Street.

Post Offices
The main post office is on the corner of Queen Street, just north of the Swing Bridge. The *poste restante* is on the ground floor. The parcel office is on Church Street.

Telecommunications
Belize Telecommunications Ltd. (BTL) is on Church Street, open daily, 8 am–9 pm. Fax services are also offered by the large stationers on Queen Street.

Boats to the Cayes
Catch boats to Caye Caulker from the Shell Station on North Front Street, right by the Swing Bridge. They leave daily between 7.30 and 10 am. For Ambergris Caye head for the Bellevue Hotel pier, at 5 Southern Foreshore, where a boat leaves at 4 pm, Mon–Fri, and at 1 pm on Saturdays.

Day Trips from Belize City
Two places best visited from the city are the Belize Zoo, 48 km along the Western Highway, and the Community Baboon Sanctuary, 40 km northwest of Belize City. An important Maya site, unfortunately not accessible by public transport, is Altun Ha, 50 km north of the city. If you would like a taster of what the cayes are like, there is a string of tiny islands, with St George's Caye in the north and English Caye in the south, easily visited from the city in a day.

The Belize Zoo
The New Belize Zoo (BZ$10) is a pioneering place that has endeavoured to show captive animals in as natural a way as possible. Large areas of bush, forest and riversides have been fenced in to house a great variety of indigenous species of the cat family, including jaguars, puma, ocelot and maguey. Tropical birds, such as toucans, vultures, and parrots are to be found, as well as crocodiles, and forest animals such as tapirs.

Nature trails take you around all the sights, giving you a good chance to spot wild animals in a controlled environment.

Across the road, a **Tropical Education Centre** opened in 1990, located on the former property of an American, Dora Weyer, who lived in Belize for thirty years, working in support of the country's natural environment. 140 acres of wilderness, with educational trails, a visitor's centre (including a dormitory) with a small library, and lecture rooms for slide shows, are all part of the services offered here. Any bus heading for Belmopan passes the entrance to the zoo, but you must ask to be dropped off there.

The Community Baboon Sanctuary

The **Community Baboon Sanctuary** is equally pioneering, since it is one of the first conservation projects in Belize that runs with the cooperation of the local population. The sanctuary covers an area of 18 square miles on the properties of over 60 different owners. The local farmers living here have agreed to protect significant areas of forest on their land in order to sustain the troop of black howler monkeys (known locally as baboons) who live here. Administered by the Belize Audubon Society, you can find a useful booklet on the sanctuary at their offices (29 Regent Street, Belize City, tel (02) 77369). A system of trails leads visitors through the area, and there is also a visitor's centre and museum in the village of Bermudian Landing. Guides must be hired for walks along the reserve trails.

Accommodation is available in the homes of local people; see the reserve manager, Fallet Young, or contact the Audubon Society (at the above address). Alternatively, you are allowed to camp here, but remember to bring your own food and drink. To reach Bermudian Landing, follow the Northern Highway as far as the Burrel Boom turn-off, from where it is only a short drive. (You could catch any bus heading north as far as the turn-off, and then try to hitch, but there is little traffic passing this way.) Alternatively check with the tourist office for direct buses from Belize City to the village of Bermudian Landing.

Altun Ha

Altun Ha (8–5, small fee), meaning Water of the Rock, is a small but attractive site. Close to the sea, it was an important trading post during the Classic Period (AD 250–900), and merchants came by sea and land from distant parts of the Maya empire. Extensive archaeological excavations have produced some of the country's most exciting finds, such as the beautifully carved head of the Maya Sun God, Kinisch Ahau. This is one of the largest Maya jade carvings ever found, weighing almost ten pounds and nearly six inches high. It is now kept in a bank vault in Belize City.

To get there, the easiest option is to either go on a tour, or drive your own vehicle. Many of the larger hotels organize tours, or you could enquire at the tourist board. Accommodation nearby is either very simple, with locals in Maskall village, or very luxurious, at **Maruba Resort**, tel (03) 22199, near Maskall village. (You could also get any bus heading north, as far as Sand Hill, and then try to hitch. Traffic is scarce, however, and this is a very uncertain option.)

Nearby Cayes

Only 14 km northeast from the city, **St George's Caye** is the site of the famous battle and was the country's first official capital from 1650 to 1784. Even though virtually nothing remains to bear witness to the historic battle, it is a popular weekend picnic spot, and home to two resort hotels: **St George's Lodge**, tel (02) 44190, fax (02) 30461; and the newly opened annexe of the Bellevue Hotel.

English Caye, and neighbouring **Goff's Caye**, are about 16 km southeast of Belize City, and lie along the main entrance lane for ships coming in from the Caribbean. The sandy beaches here make these two a favourite weekend spot, and this is the most likely time you will find day charters leaving from the city's piers. For an organized day trip, enquire at the larger hotels.

THE CAYES

Snorkelling or diving, all you can hear is your own breathing, all you can feel is the water washing over your body, but what you see is electrifying: monstrous coral that look like brains; orange branches that can cut like a knife; countless tentacles sway in the currents; while all around flit a kaleidoscope of fish, so close you think you could reach out and touch them. Shoals of tiny fluorescent neon tetras open up to let you pass, while barracuda just stare indifferently and orange starfish ignore you altogether, slowly wending their way across the seabed. Few other natural environments will allow you to feel so close to its inhabitants.

296 km long, the Belize Barrier Reef is a giant wall of limestone and coral that has taken millennia to form, harbouring some of the most extraordinary plants and animals on the planet. The hundreds of islands (cayes) and atolls are just the crest of this underwater wonderland, and make for excellent bases from which to explore. Traditionally inhabited by fishermen, the atmosphere on the islands is relaxed, and even the most commercial places are tempered by Caribbean ease. The best time to be here is from April to June, when the sea tends to be calm. The hurricane season is from June to November, and although Belize is rarely hit, this is the time when rough weather might be a problem.

Taking a boat trip, you often find yourself being followed by dolphins dancing in the waves and, if you are really lucky, you might even see a giant turtle. Out on the reef, you can reasonably expect to see conch and starfishes, as well as countless tropical fish, such as barracuda, jacks, parrotfish, angelfish, and grunts, while the deeper waters are favoured by the harmless nurse sharks—to name but a fraction. Naturally, the fishing is excellent, and the most common catches include grouper, snapper and jewfish. To find out more about the sea creatures here, see *A Guide to Corals and Fishes of Florida, The Bahamas, and Caribbean* (Seahawk Press), by I. and J. Greenberg.

The most developed diving resort is San Pedro, on Ambergris Caye, with a full range of hotel accommodation, from budget to luxury, and offering any kind of watersport you could wish for. Neighbouring Caye Caulker has no airport, and is a much less commercial place, favoured by young and budget travellers. The other main groups of islands, such as Turneffe Islands (protective mangroves here make for great fish variety),

Lighthouse Reef and Glover Reef (interesting for underwater limestone formations, especially the Great Blue Hole), all have their own character, and you can visit them, either on a day charter, or by staying in the up-market resorts that hide there. Diving and fishing tours are offered by most of the hotels, ranging from day trips, to 'live-aboard' excursions lasting as long as you wish. Diving certification courses are available in San Pedro and Caye Caulker, as well as at the top resort hotels.

Diving Equipment

Almost all equipment can be hired locally, though the experienced diver should note that firms often only provide cylinder and air without a back-pack or harness. They do provide weightbelt and weights. The best kind of clothing for diving in these parts is a lightweight, lycra body suit, and if snorkelling, you might want to bring surf shoes to protect against cuts from coral.

Safety Precautions and Diving Code

It is unsafe to fly directly after a dive, because the change in pressure can induce the 'bends'. As a general rule, you should not fly for a period of 24 hrs after a dive that required a decompression stop, and not for 12 hrs after a dive that did not. When snorkelling, it is worth wearing shorts and a T-shirt, because you can get very badly sunburnt without feeling it while in the water.

There are no official rules for divers, but there is a voluntary code, which is designed to protect the reef. Please avoid:

1. Walking on or damaging the coral.
2. Collecting shells or coral.
3. Using spearguns or supporting speargun-fishing operations.
4. Diving near working fishermen.
5. Hand-feeding fish.
6. Allowing anchors to drag over the coral.

Ambergris Caye

Ambergris is the largest of the reef islands. Located 58 km north of Belize City, and a spectacular short plane ride away, it is the country's most visited attraction. San Pedro, the only town on any of the cayes, caters to the tourist who wants to be entertained and most of its 2000 residents are involved in some aspect of the travel trade, with the result that the place is somewhat touristy—trinket and beachwear shops crowding into every space available. San Pedro was originally a tiny fishing community of wooden houses and, in spite of the dizzy speed of development, there is still a very intimate feeling to the place. It has to be admitted that San Pedro's charm is limited but if you are here to explore the reef, you will find the widest range of opportunities, and a very helpful tourist centre.

Restaurants and bars are expensive, and unfortunately the prices are not often matched by the service. However, the hotels do their best to offer every kind of diversion a tropical holiday can provide, from beach games, to sailing, windsurfing, diving, snorkelling and deep-sea fishing. There is never a shortage of things to do and open-air bars provide the main focus for socializing in the evenings.

One of the country's best-known reserves is just off the island: the **Hol Chan Marine Reserve** is an area of particularly beautiful corals, as well as plenty of fish, easily explored by snorkelling. Unfortunately, the daily groups of tourists that are brought here have taken their toll, and it is ironically one of the most damaged areas of the entire reef. Great stumps of dead, white coral testify to thoughtless visitors, who touched the coral and thereby helped to destroy it.

GETTING TO AMBERGRIS CAYE

By Air
The fastest way to reach the island is to fly from the international or municipal airports in Belize City. If coming from Mexico, you can also fly directly from Corozal, in northern Belize. Flights are daily and frequent, so you should have no trouble making a connection without prior bookings. You can walk to most hotels in less than ten minutes from the airport. The more distant and exclusive resort hotels will come and pick you up on arrival.

By Boat
From Belize City there is a regular ferry service leaving from the pier in front of the Bellevue Hotel, 5 Southern Foreshore. It departs Mon–Fri at 4 pm; Sat at 1 pm; and no service on Sun. The fare is around US$10.

From Caye Caulker, you can always find someone to take you to San Pedro if you ask around near the main pier. The fare should not be more than US$8 per person.

Boats to Caye Caulker and Belize City leave from the Texaco pier in San Pedro, Mon–Fri at 7 am and 2 pm, Sat at 8 am and 2 pm. Alternatively, hire someone to take you, but this will prove expensive.

TOURIST INFORMATION
The most efficient and friendly place to get advice on anything from travel arrangements, hotels or diving excursions, is the **San Pedro Tourist Centre**, tel and fax 2434. This is a privately-run office, mainly catering to wholesalers from the US, but the staff are also the best source of information for the general tourist. The telephone code for San Pedro is 26.

WHERE TO STAY
Being the country's top tourist resort, prices tend to increase regularly and vary according to season. Always ask for the latest price list, not forgetting three crucial questions: Which currency is being quoted? Are prices per person or not? Are the two taxes included? Unlike the rest of the country, prices often relate to each individual, which can come as a nasty surprise to couples. The following is just a selection of the best choices, and there are many more places to stay. Prices have been listed in detail to indicate that they do not fall into the categories normally used in the book and are often substantially higher. If you cannot get hold of a particular hotel, you can always book via the San Pedro Tourist Office, tel and fax (26) 2434.

In San Pedro

Around the southern end of San Pedro, there are quite a few very pleasant hotels. Virtually next to the airport is the **Sunbreeze Beach Hotel**, P.O. Box 14, tel 2191, fax 2346. Motel-type accommodation, with air-conditioning, is offered around a small garden and private beach. Singles US$80–US$90, doubles US$90–US$105, triples US$120–125, plus 15% tax. About five minutes walk from the town, the **La Joya Caribe Hotel**, tel 2050, fax 2316, is moderately priced, and of a good but unpretentious standard. The beach is lovely and lined by palm trees, and the restaurant is recommended whether you stay here or not. Beach *cabañas* are US$65 for single or double occupancy, US$72 with air-conditioning. The **Royal Palm Inn**, P.O. Box 18, tel 2148, fax 2329, is a small hotel on the beach, rather crowded by other buildings. There's a choice of rooms or private apartments: rooms are US$55 singles, US$70 doubles, US$80 triples. Apartments are US$90, US$110, US$120 respectively, and meals are extra. The **Victoria House**, P.O. Box 22, tel 2067, fax 2429, is a luxurious place, expensive but good, and you have a choice of beach *cabaña*, suite, or rooms around a lovely private beach, within walking distance of San Pedro. All prices are per person plus 15% tax: rooms are US$85 singles, US$50 doubles, US$37 triples. Beach *cabañas* are US$110 single, US$65 double, US$37 triple. The suite is US$110.

Closest to 'downtown' San Pedro, the top hotel is **Ramon's Village Resort**, tel 2071/2213, fax 2214, which has a collection of beach *cabañas* that look rustic on the outside, but inside are first-class, with fans or air-conditioning. There is a private beach, as well as a pool, bar and restaurant. Prices are US$110–US$225 per person, depending on the standard required.

At the northern end of town, there is the **Paradise Resort Hotel**, tel 2083, which also has *cabañas* around a private beach, plus restaurant and bar, and prices are in the medium range. **Rock's Inn**, tel 2326, fax 2358, is a short walk along the beach from San Pedro. A small, comfortable and expensive hotel, that also offers apartments, it suffers from being squashed between other buildings, and its beach is nothing special.

There are some **less expensive** hotels in San Pedro: just around the corner from the beachfront, the **San Pedrano**, tel 2054/2093, is excellent value for money and friendly too. Singles US$20–US$25, doubles US$25–US$30, triples US$30–US$37. Self-catering apartments are also available at US$375–US$425 per week. **Martha's Hotel**, tel 2053, fax 2589, is the best of the budget hotels, and offers private bathrooms with all rooms. Singles are US$15–US$25, doubles US$27.50–US$35, and triples US$37.50–US$46. **Rubie's Hotel**, tel 2063, is right on the beach, nearest the airport. There is only one shower for all rooms, but the place is friendly and has a pleasant beachfront; US$12.50 per person. The **Barrier Reef Hotel**, tel 2075, has a very popular bar and expensive restaurant. All rooms have private baths, fans or air-conditioning. Singles are US$30–US$48, doubles US$30–US$65, triples US$75. The **Coral Beach Hotel**, tel 2013, offers simple rooms with private bath, fan or air-conditioning, but is too expensive for what you get. Singles are US$55, doubles US$90, plus 15% tax. Right on the beach, and operated by the same people who run the ferry to Belize City, the **Conch Shell Hotel** is by the Texaco pier. It is overpriced at singles US$20–US$50, doubles US$30–US$50.

North of San Pedro: Accessible by Boat Only

If you want to be exclusive, then the following options may be for you. Farthest away of all (10 mins by boat), is **Journey's End Caribbean Club**, tel 2173, fax 2028. Described by the manager as 'Club Med without the hassle', this is a self-contained resort hotel, which unfortunately has no proper beach. Guests have free use of surfers and Hobie Cats, and there is a dive shop on site. The pool is the most elegant on the island, and sports a great poolside bar, the stools actually in the water. Accommodation ranges from *cabañas*, to poolside rooms, to mangrove-lagoon-facing rooms. TVs in all but the *cabañas*. Singles US$137–US$152, doubles US$184–US$199, triples US$231–US$246. Air-conditioning is US$15 extra per day.

The nearest neighbour is **The Belizean**, tel 2138, fax 2635, which offers 21 rooms in individual stone cottages with beautiful interiors of polished tropical woods and also a stunning luxury suite complete with sunken bathtub. Of all the hotels along here, this is the most luxurious and quiet, with an attractive beach, as well as a pool. The only drawback is that there are no watersport facilities, which the hotel arranges via the commercial operators in San Pedro. Singles US$135–US$185, doubles US$170–US$220, triples US$195–US$255, suite US$300–US$375, plus 15% tax. All rooms have air-conditioning, TV, video, fridge and phone. Meals are extra.

A short walk further south, **Captain Morgan's Retreat**, tel 2567, fax 2616, has rustic *cabañas* with fans only, on a private beach. There is a restaurant, and all watersports can be arranged. Singles are US$125, doubles US$100, plus 15% tax.

Finally, **El Pescador**, tel and fax 2398, is a family-run hotel in a traditional, wooden colonial building. Right on the beach, the rooms are nothing fancy, but all have private bathrooms, and a restaurant provides the meals. The hotel caters almost exclusively to deep-sea-fishing enthusiasts, though others are always welcome. Singles are US$100, doubles US$160, plus 20% tax, all meals included.

WHERE TO EAT AND DRINK

Apart from the numerous hotel restaurants, **Elvie's Kitchen** is one of the most popular eating places, and **Fido's**, on the beach, is the best place for breakfast, as well as other meals such as burgers or pizza. Wherever you go, however, you will find meals very expensive.

There are three bars worth looking out for. The first is the **Sandals Bar**, at the end of the main street. Best at night is the **Tackle Box**, on the main beach, though they tend to charge an entrance fee after a certain hour. There is a water enclosure, where three giant turtles, three sharks, and various other creatures are crammed into a depressingly small area. This spectacle is a popular tourist attraction—if you feel strongly enough about the cruelty of keeping creatures in such conditions, why not write a letter of protest to The Director of Tourism, Belize Tourist Bureau, 53 Regent Street, PO Box 325, Belize City.

The bar at **Fido's** is also a popular hangout. The main disco in town is the waterfront **Big Daddy's**, which raves to the sound of reggae each night.

SPORTS AND ACTIVITIES

Dive shops and charter boats: There are a great number of these in San Pedro, and you can find out about many more by contacting the tourist office. In Belize City, you could also visit **Personalised Services**, Musa Building, 91 North Front Street, tel

77593/77594, fax 75200. This office will have all the latest information on live-aboard yachts and tours. They can also plan and arrange any trip, as well as provide any service to do with the sea. Most of the hotels can make arrangements for you too.

Bottom Time Dive Shop, tel 2348, rents out all types of diving equipment, and offers tours and courses. **Manta IV**, tel 2371, is a very popular motor yacht for live-aboard diving tours and day trips. **Out Island Divers**, tel 2151, is a specialist operator for dive tours to the atolls, especially the Great Blue Hole. For example, they offer a day trip to Lighthouse Reef, flying you out from San Pedro, so you get the most time diving. **San Pedro Water Sports**, tel 2013, runs the 50-ft *Offshore Express* motor yacht, for live-aboard diving tours. **The Dive Shop**, tel 2437, in the Holiday Hotel, rents out diving equipment and offers tours and courses.

Courses to become a certified scuba diver cost in the region of US$300. Half-day introductory courses, which involve an actual dive, only cost US$50. Much cheaper and just as rewarding is snorkelling, and snorkel equipment can be hired for around US$5.

USEFUL INFORMATION
For **exchange** there are two banks in San Pedro, and you can generally also change cash or travellers' cheques in shops and hotels. The **post office** is in the same building as the Atlantic Bank.

The Island Photos shop are specialists in underwater photography and hire out equipment at good rates.

Caye Caulker

Caye Caulker lies just south of Ambergris, 35 km from Belize City, and is a fraction of the size. Many of the roughly 1000 inhabitants still retain their traditional industry, which is lobster fishing, and tourism remains firmly in second place. The island is therefore much more relaxed and less touristy, and has long been favoured by young budget travellers, who come here to hang out with the locals, preferably in the **Pirates Bar,** which is one of the best nightspots in the whole country. There is no airstrip, though there are continuous arguments about finishing the half-built construction site, and facilities are not geared to the big-spending visitor. What you will find here is a tiny community of wooden houses on stilts, two sandy streets with hardly any vehicles, beaches, and friendly places to stay. Most accommodation is rustic, but there are a few medium-range hotels as well. Note that from December to February the sandflies can drive you crazy here, coming out whenever the breeze dies down. Insect repellent helps, but they are persistent critters. Mosquitoes are always around, as elsewhere on the cayes.

GETTING TO CAYE CAULKER
Getting here is easy: from Belize City there are daily morning boats leaving from Haulover Creek by the Shell station. From Ambergris there is the ferry from the Texaco pier, and if you ask around by the Tackle Box bar, you will always find someone to take you. Alternatively, if arriving by air at Belize City, you could fly on to Caye Chapel, and phone Caye Caulker from there for someone to pick you up by boat.

TOURIST INFORMATION

There is no official tourist information on the island, though the **Aberdeen Restaurant** is a good place to find out about snorkelling and diving trips, contact individuals, or rent equipment.

WHERE TO STAY

The more up-market places tend to be at the southern end of the village, located on the beach, while the inexpensive hotels are at the northern end, near the main pier. None of the accommodation prices rise above the moderate category used throughout this guide. If staying long-term, you can always find houses or apartments to rent, such as **M. & N. Apartments**, tel (022) 2111, located behind the grubby Hotel Martinez.

The **Anchorage**, a short walk beyond the southern edge of the village, on a lovely beach, is the nicest place to stay in your own *cabaña*. **Shirley's Guest House**, tel (022) 2145, furthest away from the village, is also good, very clean and quiet. **Tom's Hotel**, tel (022) 2102, closest to the village and also on the beach, has moderately priced huts with private bathrooms, and the rooms are good value too.

The **Tropical Paradise Hotel**, tel (022) 2124, is at the southern end of the village, and offers simple *cabañas* and there's a restaurant attached. **Vega's Far Inn**, tel (022) 2142, is just past the police station, in the middle of the village, facing the beach. All rooms share the bathroom. A private hut with bathroom is also available and you may also be allowed to camp on the hotel property.

At the northern end of the village, the **Reef Hotel**, tel (022) 2196, and **Rainbow Hotel**, (022) 2123, are both popular—all rooms with private bath. A favourite budget hotel is the **Rivas Guest House**, above the Aberdeen Restaurant, tel (022) 2127. The **Split Beach Resort** has pleasant beach huts facing the sea and mangroves. It is named after the split where Hurricane Hattie cut the island in two pieces.

EATING OUT

A popular place for travellers is the **Aberdeen Restaurant**, which offers local and Chinese meals, and there are a couple of private houses near here, offering breakfast in the morning or snacks. Just walk by and see what's on offer. Most of the restaurants are at the other end of the village, though, along the main street leading to the Tropical Paradise Hotel. New places are opening all the time, and you are bound to find something to your taste.

Apart from the nightly scene at the **Pirates Bar**, the favourite bar to spend time is the **Reef Bar**, by the main pier. Drugs and theft are sometimes a problem on Caye Caulker, so be careful. Belize City is not far away and there are crack addicts here too.

SPORTS AND ACTIVITIES

Snorkelling day trips to the reef cost around US$12.50, which includes the Hol Chan Marine Reserve and a stop in San Pedro. If just going to the reef off Caye Caulker, you can expect to pay around US$8, plus US$2.50 for renting gear. For scuba diving trips and equipment rental, contact **Belize Diving Services**, tel 2143, near the football pitch.

Charlie at the Aberdeen Restaurant is trustworthy and a good sailor, though he normally uses a motorized skiff for snorkel trips. The Rastafarian Zarmusa is also highly recommended, and sails people to all parts of the Barrier Reef. His sailing practices are unorthodox, but you will certainly have lots of fun if your nerves can take it. Amado Perez, and his sailboat *Miss Conduct*, offers both day trips and sailing tours in a more conventional style. Tours cost around US$50 per person, per day, and include three meals daily, and all equipment, which is excellent value. His father, Ernan Perez, also offers charter services and does regular runs to Belize City, on his speedboat *Chispa*.

Other Cayes

All except Caye Chapel are accessible by charter boat only, and but for the few resort hotels, are generally uninhabited. There are only seven atoll reefs in the entire Caribbean, and three are in Belizean waters. For the diver or fisherman, these far-flung specks in the Caribbean Sea are the highlight of any tour. Turneffe Islands, Lighthouse Reef and Glover's Reef are atolls, peeking out from two great underwater ridges. At the centre of each you find an aquamarine lagoon, with calm water over pristine sand, while all around the seaward rim you find innumerable ledges and great walls encrusted with coral and teeming with marine life.

Live-aboard dive tours are the best way to reach these places, and although expensive, prices are still cheaper than elsewhere in the Caribbean, and the diving is often more exciting. Contact **Personalised Services** (see p. 205 for address) for a rundown on all the latest options.

Caye Chapel

This tiny, privately-owned island, just south of Caye Caulker is given over to luxury tourism, with a resort hotel and all the trappings you would expect (**Pyramid Island Resort**, tel (02) 44409, fax (02) 32405). The bar is a popular weekend destination. Get there either by plane or charter boat from Caye Caulker or Belize City. If you plan to stay here, check first with the Tourist Board, as the hotel's future is uncertain.

Turneffe Islands

About 40 km east of Belize City, this is the largest of the atolls, comprising over 200 little cayes covered in mangroves that form a great oblong shape, 48 km long. The eastern shore has a great vertical reef descending into the sea with giant horizontal ridges that make for fascinating diving. The only resort hotel is **Turneffe Island Lodge**, P.O. Box 480, Belize City, fax (03) 0276. A budget option is the **Turneffe Flats**, which you can contact via 56 Eve Street, Belize City, tel (02) 45634.

Lighthouse Reef

About 113 km east of Belize City, this is the most distant atoll, situated on a separate ridge, with six cayes surrounding a shallow lagoon. Sandbore Caye, at the northern end, has a lighthouse and is home to a keeper and his family, while Half Moon Caye, to the south, has another lighthouse and is home to the **Half Moon Caye Natural Monument**. Made up by the entire caye of just 45 acres, it was established in 1982, and is administered by the Audubon Society. Two separate ecosystems, of dense vegetation and open palm tree clusters, provide a home to countless bird species, among them the red-footed booby and great frigatebird with a seven-foot wing span. Lizards are also found here, with odd names like 'bamboo chicken' and 'wish willy'. And if you're lucky, you might see the magnificent loggerhead and hawksbill turtles, both endangered species. Visitors must register with the lighthouse keeper, who is a mine of information and sells maps of the area. Camping is permitted, but you must bring all your own food and water, and pets are not allowed.

For divers, **The Great Blue Hole**, just off Half Moon Caye, is a 'once in a lifetime' treat. Located at the heart of Lighthouse Reef, this is a huge circular hole about 305 m wide and 145 m deep and was formed millions of years ago, when an earthquake caused the roof of an underground cave to collapse. Stalactites give vivid evidence of the catastrophe: those formed before the earthquake hang at a slight angle, while the ones formed afterwards hang straight down. The 'Half Moon Wall' is also one of the most spectacular diving sites to be found, with lots of fish and a patchwork of corals of all shapes and sizes.

There is now a resort hotel nearby, the **Lighthouse Reef Resort**, on Northern Two Caye, P.O. Box 26, Belize City. You can book via the Tourist Board or Personalised Services.

Glover's Reef

Southeast of Belize City, this atoll is nearer Dangriga, in southern Belize, and the least visited of the lot. This is not a reflection on the diving opportunities, however, and about 64 km of reef await to be explored. Snorkelling as well as diving is excellent, and some say you find the greatest variety of marine life here. Most exciting of all, you may see the harmless Great Whale Sharks, especially between April and June, and you will definitely see dolphins, who play around here all the year round.

Two medium-priced resort hotels are located on the atoll, both on South Water Caye. The cheaper is **Blue Marlin Lodge**, P.O. Box 21, Dangriga, tel (05) 22243, fax (05) 22296. **Leslie Cottages**, tel (05) 22004, offers just two rooms in pleasant cottages.

Bluefield Range

A string of tiny inlands running parallel to the mainland, between Belize City and Dangriga, this is a remote area, where fishermen are better catered for than divers. There is just one place to stay, and that is on a working fishing camp called **Ricardo's Beach Huts**, contactable via 59 North Front Street, P.O. Box 55, Belize City, tel (02) 44970; VHF Channel 68.

Tobacco Reef

Located just off the mainland by Dangriga, two of the cayes—Tobacco Caye and Water Caye—are sparsely populated and offer one of the cheapest offshore diving and snorkelling bases. Both are easy to reach from Dangriga, and you can find out about lifts with local fishermen just by asking around. You should not have to pay more than US$12.50 for the journey, whereas chartering a boat to take you will cost nearer US$100. A good place to make enquiries is at the **Hub Guest House**, by the central bus stop in Dangriga. Simple lodgings on the cayes cost around US$15–US$25 per person.

Commercial accommodation is all on Tobacco Caye. **Fairweather & Friends** offers simple lodgings, and you can contact them via P.O. Box 240, Belize City. **Island Camps** is a campsite only, and you can contact them via 51 Regent Street, Belize City, tel (02) 72109. Finally, **Reef End Lodge** can be contacted via P.O. Box 10, Dangriga.

THE WEST: CAYO DISTRICT

The western Cayo District is a place where black orchids (just one of 250 species) sprout from tropical pines, and waterfalls, pools and streams provide delicious swimming after a long day's hiking or horse-riding. Here the lowland savannah west of Belize City gradually gives way to a hilly landscape covered by humid forests which hide a number of Maya ceremonial centres. Many of these sites are small and easily reached, but there are also the magnificent remains of **Caracol**, deep in the Mountain Pine Ridge, which are possibly more important than the famous ruins of Tikal in nearby Guatemala. The forest has hardly been cleared by the archaeologists, and huge buttress roots support towering trees festooned with epiphytes, parasitic plants that cling to their branches.

The slightly higher altitude of the region, rising to 1120 m, makes the country's heat more bearable, yet even here the temperatures can be limb-deadeningly hot. In **San Ignacio**, the district's friendly heart, the streets are often empty during mid-afternoons while the locals take their long siestas. It has a larger Spanish-speaking mestizo population than the rest of Belize, many of them originally refugees from Guatemala, but others descendants of the original loggers who used to search out valuable mahogany for export to Europe and North America. The atmosphere in San Ignacio is relaxed, yet the evening nightlife can be as lively as in Belize City or the most popular cayes. Quite a few English and Americans have made their home here, not to mention the British army base close by, so there are more bars and nightclubs than you would expect. By contrast, the country's official capital, Belmopan, has no nightlife at all and very little happening in the day.

Cayo is also the perfect place to escape into nature, staying at one of the many jungle lodges that hide in the forest along the Rivers Mopan and Macal. No other part of the country will give you such a good chance to glimpse the huge variety of Belizean birds, such as kiskadees, blue-crowned motmots, or vermilion flycatchers. If you're lucky, you might even see a jaguar, tapir or howler monkey drinking from the rivers at dawn and dusk. Certainly the sounds of the forest will become familiar, the lone 'tock' of the toucan easy to distinguish.

Belmopan

The bus left the paved road and followed a gravel track to a parking area beside a tree... 'You looking at it', the bus driver said when I asked where the town centre might be.

R. Wright, *Time Among the Maya*

Situated 80 km west of Belize City, Belmopan is a kind of Brasília gone wrong: government buildings and a few hotels stand in what looks like an overgrown building site, and the visitor imagines there must be some mistake. This can't be a capital city, and to all intents and purposes it isn't, because nobody wants to live here, and almost nobody works here, except the civil servants, who have no choice, many commuting from Belize City.

Few tourists visit unless they have official business at the two embassies (see p. 184 for addresses). Anyone who does go to Belmopan may like to visit the archaeological vault in the Department of Archaeology on the Government Plaza. Guided tours are given on Mondays, Wednesdays, and Fridays, and you should make an appointment two days prior to arrival, by phoning (08) 22106. There are plenty of precious pottery objects and artefacts of obsidian and jade, and recent excavations in Caracol have unearthed a wealth of new treasures, including a priceless jade mask, that would make an impressive display in a proper museum. As it is, many objects are locked away for safekeeping.

There is one time in the year when it is worth making a visit to Belmopan, and that is for the country's largest fair, the **National Agricultural Show Weekend**, held every April. This is an interesting event, not just for the party atmosphere, but also for seeing the range of agricultural stands, including beautiful horses, and exhibitions from many aspects of Belizean life and culture. If you haven't tasted creole cooking yet, you will find stands selling traditional fried chicken, as well as seaweed milk or plantain dishes. At night, the country's favourite bands come to play here, and large crowds dance the night away in huge tents. If you go—be careful. Theft and rape are common at this time, and it is not a good idea to go alone in the evenings.

GETTING TO BELMOPAN
The journey takes about an hour from Belize City, taking any bus heading west, including buses for Dangriga, which all go via the capital. From Belmopan to San Ignacio takes another 45 mins, to the border a further 20 mins. Heading south, to Dangriga, takes around two hours along the Hummingbird Highway, as the dirt road is prosaicly named. Wherever you are coming from or heading to, you will end up at the main bus terminal, which is the busiest spot in town.

WHERE TO STAY
Staying in Belmopan is expensive and not recommended. However, there are three places if you have no choice: **Circle A Lodge**, 35–37 Halfmoon Avenue, tel (08) 22296, is the cheapest; the **Bull Frog Inn**, 25 Halfmoon Avenue, tel (08) 22111, fax (08) 23155, is slightly more expensive; and finally, the **Belmopan Convention Hotel**, 2 Bliss Parade, tel (08) 22130, fax (08) 23066, is the top address.

The nicest place to stay near Belmopan, is the American-run **Banana Bank Ranch**, tel (08) 23180, fax (08) 22366. Here you can rent out horses, eat good food, and make trips on the Belize river, which runs past the ranch. Phone them for exact directions if coming in your own vehicle, or take a taxi from Belmopan.

San Ignacio

San Ignacio—always called Cayo—is a small town, 37 km west of Belmopan, and just under 15 km from the Guatemalan border. On first glance it is not very attractive, with a ragged collection of wooden buildings and rusty corrugated roofs mixing with rain-washed concrete buildings. But the people are friendly, and its location at the confluence of the Mopan and Macal rivers makes it an excellent base for exploring inland Belize. You could easily spend a week here, discovering something new each day.

GETTING TO SAN IGNACIO

Getting to San Ignacio is an easy journey from Belize City with the regular **Batty** or **Novelo** buses that ply this route daily. Coming from Dangriga, you need to change buses in Belmopan.

TOURIST INFORMATION

There is no official tourist office in San Ignacio, but Bob Jones, who runs **Eva's Bar and Restaurant** on Burns Avenue, is an excellent source of information, and holds brochures and price lists for most of the surrounding lodges, as well as official taxi fares. Whether you want to book a tour or need a doctor, he can point you in the right direction.

WHERE TO STAY

There are plenty of places to stay, in town or in one of the lodges in the surrounding countryside.

In San Ignacio

EXPENSIVE

The top hotel in town, which is nothing special, is the **San Ignacio Hotel**, P.O. Box 33, tel (092) 2034/2125/2220, fax 2134. The location, perched on the steep hill above the town centre, makes for great views, and the pool is a popular place for evening drinks.

MODERATE

A bit further up the road is the **Piache Hotel**, tel (092) 2032, which has a very attractive garden and equally good hilltop views. Rooms are simple and have private baths.

INEXPENSIVE

In the town centre hotels are very affordable and the **Central Hotel**, 24 Burns Avenue, tel (092) 2253, is the best value. Rooms are clean, all have fans, and there are two bathrooms. The **Jaguar Hotel**, opposite, is horrible, though the restaurant is worth trying. Much better is the **Venus Hotel**, 29 Burns Avenue, tel (092) 2186, which has clean, simple rooms with fans. The **Hi-Et Hotel**, 12 West Street, is a pleasant family house, offering rooms with shared bathroom. Last choice is the **Hotel Belmoral**, 17 Burns Avenue, tel (092) 2024, which is loud and grubby.

Campsites around San Ignacio
If you follow the dirt road past the bus depot, you shortly see a sign to the **Cosmos Campsite**. About a 20-minute walk from town, this is a pleasant site on the banks of the River Mopan, where you can pitch your own tent or rent one for the night. Showers, toilets and cooking facilities are available, or you can eat vegetarian meals in the main thatched house. US$2.50 to stay the night, another US$2.50 to rent a tent. Halfway between town and the Cosmos Campsite is **Midas Campsite**, which has thatched huts by the river (nice beach), and also provides bathroom facilities, though no meals. If in your own transport, you might prefer the remoter **Black Rock Campsite**, which is on the River Macal, reached by the same mud track that turns off the main road for DuPlooy's (see below).

Jungle lodges near San Ignacio
All of these are relatively expensive, and few can be reached by public transport, which makes them great hideaways, but not necessarily convenient without your own vehicle. (If you decide to take a taxi, remember to check the official rate at Eva's Restaurant first.) However, most lodges will send someone to pick you up if you make it as far as San Ignacio, and all arrange tours and excursions (expensive) to the surrounding countryside and Maya ruins. If you book in advance, Chaa Creek and DuPlooy's might even be persuaded to pick you up from the airport, in Belize City.

LUXURY
Chaa Creek Cottages, P.O. Box 53, San Ignacio, Belize, tel (092) 2037, fax 2501, is the most exclusive lodge, with 16 rooms in beautiful stone cottages overlooking the River Macal. A short distance upriver is **DuPlooy's**, tel (092) 2188, fax 2057, which is less exclusive, but extremely beautiful, with a very friendly, family-run atmosphere. The best feature is the bar, which is on a high platform, with great views of the surrounding jungle and river below. Full board is in the luxury category but bed and breakfast is cheaper. Children under 6 years are charged at around 15% the adult fee. A 15% tax is added.

EXPENSIVE
Nabitunich Lodge, San Lorenzo Farm, tel (093) 2309, is halfway between San Ignacio and the Maya ruins of Xunantunich. In fact, on a clear day you can see the tip of the main pyramid rising above the jungle. This is one of the easiest lodges to reach by public transport, close to the Mopan river, just off the main road to Benque Viejo. Excellent value for money, even though 18% tax is added. **El Indio Perdido**, Callar Creek, tel (092) 2460, is 2 kms off the main road, just before you reach Nabitunich Lodge. The location, right on the Mopan river, is lovely, but without your own transport you are marooned here, and taxis cost around US$30 from San Ignacio. Check at Eva's Bar whether the place is open, as it is rather erratic.
   Windy Hill Cottages, tel and fax (092) 2017, on the main road to Benque Viejo, about 2 kms outside town, has the advantage of a pool and easy access, but is neither near the river nor in the forest. 15% tax added. **Maya Mountain Lodge**, Cristo Rey Road, P.O. Box 46, San Ignacio, tel (092) 2164, fax 2029, close to town, promises more than it

comes up with and charges an outrageous 20% tax on all bills. **Las Casitas**, 22 Surrey Street, San Ignacio, tel (092) 2475, is just outside town, on the Macal river, and cannot be recommended.

MODERATE
Finally, a popular lodge, close to the ruins of Xunantunich, is **Rancho Los Amigos**. To get there take any bus heading for Benque Viejo, and get off at the village of San José Succotz.

EATING OUT AND NIGHTLIFE
One of the most popular meeting places in town is **Eva's Restaurant**, run by Bob Jones, an Englishman who decided to stay on after serving here in the British Army. Meals, including breakfast, are simple and filling, and prices are reasonable. Across the street is the **Jaguar**, which is occasionally good. Also on Burns Avenue is **Serendib**, which serves good curries and creole dishes, worth the slightly higher prices. The restaurant of the **San Ignacio Hotel** is highly recommended, and not as expensive as you might expect. Make sure you try the fruit juices here. There are also a few ice-cream parlours and snack shacks, which you will easily find around the centre of town.

Other than Eva's, which closes early, there are three bars/nightclubs. The **Blue Angel**, in the centre of town, is always packed at weekends, and is the most popular place. Up on the hill, the **Cahal Pech**, is a large thatched venue, which regularly has live music. This is a good place for dancing as it is open to the night breeze. On Sundays, when things are pretty dead around here, the most lively place is the **Central American Art Centre**, opposite the bus depot. There is nothing noticeably arty here, but there is usually a local band playing.

SPORTS AND ACTIVITIES
Bicycle rental: mountain bikes are available outside Eva's. However the quality is bad, and the bikes are useless for excursions outside town. Check to see if things have improved.

Float Belize, tel (092) 2188, also contactable via Eva's Bar, rents out canoes and also offers tours on the rivers. An exciting option would be spending a few days heading downstream on the River Mopan, which becomes the River Belize, teeming with wildlife, including crocodiles. To reach Belize City takes about a week, camping on the riverbank at night.

Mountain Equestrian Trails, mile 8, Mountain Pine Ridge Road, Central Farm, fax (092) 2060, attn: Jim and Marguerite Bevis, is worth visiting if in your own transport. This is an excellent base for horse-riding tours to Caracol and the surrounding reserve. Expensive at US$45 per person for half a day; a full day costs US$65.

Tours to Caracol, the only way to get there, are reliably run by Philip Burns, tel (092) 2076 or ask Bob Jones, who uses four-wheel-drives. He also does day trips to Tikal in Guatemala, or anywhere else you care to visit. Fees for Caracol are around US$50 per person, which is expensive but definitely worth it.

Camping in Mountain Pine Ridge: The only place you can legally camp in the Mountain Pine Ridge is at the entrance or the forestry station of St Augustine. Ask at

Eva's Bar about how to get there and applying for permission to enter the reserve. You will have to bring all your own food and drink, as there is none on sale at St Augustine. Hikers will find this the best base for exploring the reserve, though good maps (and possibly a compass) are essential, since you are very much on your own here. The most detailed maps are available at Edward Stanfords Ltd, in London, or directly from the Survey Department at the Ministry of Natural Resources, in Belmopan, which is also much cheaper. The most useful sheets are numbers 24, 28 and 29.

USEFUL INFORMATION
There is a **bank** and **BTL** office (Mon–Fri, 8–noon and 1–4; Sat, 8–noon) on Burns Avenue, and the **post office** is above the police station, by the suspension bridge.
   Car rental is from **Godsman Ellis**, Buena Vista Road, tel (092) 2109, and **Three Flags Auto Rental**, in Santa Elena, tel (092) 72060.

Around San Ignacio

Branch Mouth

This is the point where the River Macal joins the Mopan, eventually to become the River Belize. It is a delightful, quiet spot, 30-minutes' walk outside San Ignacio. At weekends, it is popular for picnics and swimming. To get there, just walk along the dirt road that also passes the Cosmos Campsite. Diagonally across the river, you can see the thatched roof of **Las Casitas** (see above).

Cahal Pech

Its name meaning 'the place of ticks', this was an important site as early as 200 BC. Archaeologists believe it was the exclusive home of Maya nobles in the later, Classic period. Excavation work has only been carried out in recent years, but already many artefacts have been found here. The most intriguing of all is a large stone bench that still retains much of its original red colouring, as well as ancient graffiti. Perhaps it was a sleeping platform, but specialists are undecided.
   Situated on the hillside above San Ignacio, you can walk here in 20 minutes. Follow the road straight up to the thatched Cahal Pech bar, next to the radio station. Opposite the bar, turn left, and then first right, along a dirt road leading into the forest, where the site hides.

Xunantunich (daily, 8–5, small fee)

Pronounced 'shoo-nan-too-nitch', this is a small Classic Maya site, with one of Belize's largest ancient pyramids, **El Castillo**, affording great views across the jungle canopy. About 40 m high, it was believed to be the highest building in Belize until the temples of Caracol were discovered. Only two plazas remain clearly visible, dotted by a few stelae, and the remaining buildings are badly eroded, the surrounding jungle creeping ever closer. However, the location and the path leading to the site are very beautiful, and even when jungle mists obscure the view, the atmosphere is quite magical.

To get there, take any bus heading for Benque Viejo, and ask to be dropped off at the ferry, by the Maya village of Succotz. Here a hand-drawn ferry (free) takes vehicles and pedestrians over the Mopan river, from where a steep track leads 1 km through the forest and up to the ruins. Unfortunately, this track is notorious for robbers, so it's best not to go alone. Also, make sure you don't miss the last ferry crossing back at about 5.

Caracol

The journey to Caracol can only be attempted during the dry season, from January to May. It is a long trip and you should take along a packed picnic and water. Setting off early, the four-wheel-drive takes you east, towards Belmopan, and then turns south, onto a dirt road leading to the Mountain Pine Ridge Reserve. Soon you're winding through the hills, until you reach Augustine, a small collection of wooden buildings among the trees, where the families of the foresters live. The pine forest could almost be in North America, but look closely, and you will see orchids growing from niches in the trees. Once past the reserve entrance, the road takes you through forests festooned with bromeliads, getting ever thicker and moister, until you find yourself surrounded by tall rainforest, hung with creeping vines and sprouting palms. The shadowy light filters through the canopy above, and the mud road is increasingly difficult.

Approaching the great city itself—which is estimated to cover a total area of 80 square kilometres, including its satellite communities—the jungle becomes especially beautiful, with huge buttress roots folding around giant trees. At the entrance, you pass **Canaa Temple** (Temple of the Sky), its huge limestone staircase gleaming white once more. This pyramid now holds claim to being the highest building in Belize, rising 42 m above the forest floor.

An archaeological team from Florida University works here every dry season, and members voluntarily take time out to show visitors around (a donation to the University

Jade object shaped like an ear flare (Pomona, Belize)

project is appreciated). Caracol was only rediscovered in 1936, when chicle (gum) gatherers stumbled upon the site, and archaeological work is still in the very early stages; the Caracol Project was begun in 1985. Being shown around the temple structures, stelae, ball courts, tombs and living quarters by dedicated and enthusiastic professionals is a highly educative experience.

It is believed that at the height of its era as many as 300,000 people lived in the city and its surrounding territory—which is more than the entire population of Belize today— though others argue for lower estimates of around 180,000 people. What is known for sure is that the site was occupied from Pre-Classic to Classic times, and in AD 563 its rulers defeated nearby Tikal, rising to great power and influence, which is reflected in increased building after this period. Magnificent tombs have been uncovered here, and as recently as 1991, the second largest jade mask found in Belize was retrieved from one of the temples. Eventually, Caracol may well emerge as the most important Maya city in the Guatemala and Belize region, overshadowing Tikal as the major tourist attraction, just as it once defeated its neighbour in war.

About 13 km south of Caracol, an outstanding natural phenomenon is the **Chiquibul Cave System**, which is the longest in Central America, and has the largest cave room in the Western Hemisphere. Unfortunately, however, these caves are inaccessible to all but the expert caver and guide.

On the return journey, the driver should be willing to stop for a swim at the **Río On**. This is a gorgeous place for a cool swim, where the river flows over limestone rocks to form a succession of pools, their waters fragrant with the scent of pine. If you head for the top pool, you will also find a natural jacuzzi, where boulders squeeze the water into a churning tub, just big enough for four people.

If you don't have the time or money to visit Caracol, you can still visit the reserve, by taking a shorter **Mountain Pine Ridge Tour**, which will take in the **1000 ft Falls** and the **Río On** pools, and possibly the **Río Frío Cave**. This costs around US$17.50 each, for a group of five people, and Bob Jones can help you arrange it.

Macal River Trip

This is an excellent excursion by canoe, taking in a few swimming stops, as well as an optional visit to the **Panti Medicine Trail** (US$5), next to Chaa Creek Cottages, where you stop for lunch. Along the way you'll see a tremendous variety of birds, such as egrets, pygmy kingfishers, toucans, cormorants, herons, kiskadees, kite hawks and vultures. Most startling are the huge iguanas sunning themselves on rocks or branches, their prehistoric-looking spikes giving them a terrifying appearance. Specimens of 4 ft and over are quite common. You will also pass a colony of tiny fruit bats, sleeping upside down on the roof of a limestone ridge, overhanging the water.

The Panti Medicine Trail, named after a local Maya healer, is an interesting opportunity to learn about the forest's medicinal qualities, and a marked trail tells you about which plants take care of what, ranging from contraception, headaches and upset stomachs, to malaria or headlice.

The best person to take you on this trip is the Rastafarian Tony, who charges US$12.50 per person, and does most of the work paddling you in his canoe, though it helps if you offer to paddle too. He's immensely knowledgeable about the river's wildlife, and you won't see half the birds and animals without his expert eyes and ears to point them out. Contact him via Eva's restaurant.

Onwards from San Ignacio

The last town before the Guatemalan border is Benque Viejo. There is nothing to see here, and if coming from Guatemala, you should try to make it as far as San Ignacio. The only place remotely worth visiting is the local art centre, where you can buy hand-painted T-shirts. If you do get stuck here, the best place to stay is the inexpensive **Hotel Maya**, 11 George Street, tel (093) 2116. Buses connect Benque Viejo with San Ignacio regularly, but you can always find a taxi too.

If heading for Guatemala, your best bet is to catch a bus that leaves San Ignacio and goes all the way to the border, a few kilometres beyond Benque Viejo. The border operates between 6 am and midnight, and if you intend to catch a bus to Flores from the border town of Melchor de Mencos, you are strongly advised to get here early in the day. If there are no buses leaving when you arrive in Guatemala, there are always minivans and taxis awaiting charters, but the prices will be outrageous, and it would be worth staying the night, and waiting for the next bus.

THE SOUTH: STANN CREEK AND TOLEDO DISTRICT

If western Belize is interesting for its tropical landscape and wildlife, then southern Belize is interesting for its diversity of people and cultures. As you head south on the unpaved Hummingbird Highway, you cross over the furthest outcrops of the western highlands before heading out into the open plains. Here you are surrounded by huge citrus plantations and row upon row of orange trees stretch into the distance. From here onwards the traveller follows a route between the contours of the western Maya Mountains and the coast.

Almost no one lives beside the Southern Highway and so there is a tantalizing sense of emptiness. You wonder if there are any people here at all. Yet the intensely farmed countryside tells you villages cannot be far, and small tracks lead off towards the jungle-covered mountains or the sea, inviting you to break your journey and discover what might be at the end of the road. Independent transport is essential if you want to make these kind of detours, since no public buses leave the highway. If you can overcome this inconvenience, you will find few tourists and a pleasing sense of discovering rarely visited places.

The first town on the coastal plain is Dangriga, 'capital' of the Garifuna people and the country's second largest town. Descendants of African slaves and Carib Indians, the Garifuna are part of the same group that inhabit many settlements along the Gulf of Honduras, in Belize, Guatemala, Honduras and Nicaragua. To the outsider they look indistinguishable from other Belizeans. Their culture and original language, however, are quite different and, particularly in the small fishing villages further south, the people are as likely to use a traditional healer as a modern doctor.

Beyond Dangriga, the pace of life really slows down. Tracks lead off the dirt highway to coastal Garifuna settlements such as the traditional fishing village of Hopkins. Further south, you will find the most beautiful mainland beaches on the thin peninsula that culminates in the lovely village of **Placencia**, which is rapidly becoming a popular holiday resort. Here you can walk for ages and ages along white sand lapped gently by the sea, and the chances are you will meet nobody along the way. Shrubs and the occasional cluster of palm trees line the shore, and there are plenty of places to play out your Robinson Crusoe fantasies.

South of Dangriga, you find yourself in the country's remote Toledo District, where Mopan and Kekchi Mayas live in traditional villages embraced by the thick forests near the Guatemalan border. Their homes are made to the ancient designs of their forebears: square or oblong wood constructions, sometimes raised slightly off the ground, and covered by a thatched roof made of palm leaves. The strong Maya heritage of the region can also be seen at three small but interesting sites: **Lubaantun, Nim Li Punit** and **Uxbenka**.

Out on the coast, the small town of **Punta Gorda** is the main centre of population, where Garifuna mix with Creoles, while surrounding areas are settled by East Indians, descendants of American Confederates, German Mennonites, and other foreigners. In fact, walking down the street in Punta Gorda, you are as likely to meet a Rastafarian sauntering to his reggae music as a dungaree-clad Mennonite, an East Indian worker or a Kekchi Indian farmer.

Although the south has this varied cultural mix, it is sparsely populated and substantial areas are still untouched by human hand. This is especially true of the Maya Mountains which trace the border with Guatemala and, with a bit of initiative, you can find yourself deep in the ancient forests that cover the region. An ideal introduction to this kind of environment is in the **Cockscomb Range**, where you will find the world's only jaguar reserve and the country's highest mountain, Victoria Peak. Solitary mahogany and ceiba trees tower above the jungle canopy, while marked trails take you through the hidden world below.

Dangriga

If you could head straight along the coast, the distance from Belize City to seaside Dangriga would only be around 58 km. In fact, if you have the time, you might consider hiring a boat, which would take you through two interesting inland lagoons, before cruising out to sea and into Dangriga harbour. Taking this route, you might even spy the rare sea cow (manatee), which hides around Gales Point, and is said to have inspired the myth of mermaids. There is a small luxury hotel here for those who want the best chance to see this legendary animal.

By road, the 168 km journey from Belize City takes three hours, first taking you west to Belmopan, before heading southeast to Dangriga, which is a town of fewer than 9000 residents. On the way, you pass one of the country's national parks: **The Blue Hole National Park** (daily, 8–4) where you can swim either in the River Sibun or the Blue Hole itself. This is a karst sinkhole, filled with water from the river to form a perfect swimming pool. If you are feeling energetic, you could also hike to **St Herman's Cave** from here. Unfortunately, this park has a bad reputation for mugging and rape, so it is best not to go alone, and you should also remember to lock your car.

In spite of the fact that Dangriga is the administrative centre of Stann Creek district, the atmosphere is provincial; the mostly wooden houses sit in a haze of dusty heat, the inhabitants moving slowly under the shade of huge umbrellas. The town was almost completely destroyed by Hurricane Hattie, and the place still has a somewhat ragged appearance, even after thirty years. From here you can take a boat to nearby Tobacco Reef or Hopkins village, along the coast. The only time when the town springs to life is during Garifuna Settlement Day on 19 November. At this time you will find plenty of street parties and dancing, singing and heavy drinking. Highlight of the festivities is the re-enactment of the Garifuna settlers arriving by boat from Honduras in 1823. However, many Garifuna had already come to Belize prior to this date, brought in as free labourers for the logging trade.

In fact, the Garifuna heritage has much more to do with freedom than slavery, although their roots lie with Nigerian slaves who were shipwrecked in the early 17th century on the Caribbean island of St Vincent. It was there that their ancestors mixed with the surviving Carib Indians and became known as the Black Caribs, evolving their own unique language which still survives today. Their descendants were never again enslaved, and even though the British tried to subdue them, they were not entirely successful. Eventually they did manage to beat the Black Caribs militarily, in 1796, and decided to get rid of them once and for all by leaving them on the Honduran island of Roatán. From there the Garifuna, as they called themselves, migrated to the Honduran mainland, working as labourers and even soldiers for the Spanish.

For the casual observer it is almost impossible to distinguish the Garifuna from other Belizean blacks, since their dress and appearance is the same, and they only speak their language among themselves. Many of the younger generation do not speak their traditional language at all, and in many ways, the Garifuna culture in Belize is something that is being revived for tourism, unlike in Honduras, where their numbers are far greater and communities are self-contained and close-knit, outsiders rarely settling among them.

GETTING TO AND FROM DANGRIGA

If at all possible, it is highly recommended that you have your own transport for southern Belize, since there are few buses, and journeys are long because of the unpaved roads. (Car rental is available in Punta Gorda.) There is almost no public transport to the coastal villages or inland regions, and you will find it very difficult to visit any of the Maya ruins or other interesting places. You could always try hitchhiking, but there are very few vehicles on the country roads, and a better, if more expensive, option would be to go on one of the organized tours that leave from Dangriga, Placencia or Punta Gorda.

By Air

Since the bus journey is only 3 hours long it hardly seems worth flying. However, there are daily flights from Belize City to Dangriga, which is a stopover on the way to Mango Creek (Independence) and Punta Gorda. If you wish to book flight tickets from Dangriga, you can do it at the Pelican Beach Resort hotel.

By Sea
Coming from Belize City, you could hire someone to take you south, which will be very expensive but a novel way to travel. Get advice from the tourist office before striking a deal with the local boatmen, and remember never to pay the full fee before the journey is completed.

By Bus
There are regular daily buses run by **Z-Line**, between Belize City and Dangriga (3 hrs). Coming from San Ignacio, you need to change buses in Belmopan, where all buses from Belize City pass by. Coming from the south, there are direct buses from Punta Gorda, also run by **Z-Line**. The bus depot is by the bridge over the North Stann Creek, in front of the **Hub Guest House**. The ticket office is opposite, in the Tropic Zone Club on St Vincent Street, and if you want to be sure of getting on the bus, you should buy your ticket in advance.

There is also a direct bus connecting Placencia with Dangriga, on Mondays, Wednesdays, Fridays and Saturdays. The bus leaves Dangriga at 2.30, and the journey can take up to 3 hrs. Coming from Placencia, the bus goes on the same days, but leaves at 5 am.

TOURIST INFORMATION
The local tourist information office is located in **B. J.'s Gift Shop**, tel (05) 22266, on the corner of Commercial Street and Lemon Street. This is an interesting little place to visit, which sells tourist maps and booklets, as well as various locally made handicrafts such as drums.

WHERE TO STAY
If you choose to travel from Belize City via the lagoons, you will pass by the luxury hotel **Manatee Lodge**, Gales Point Caye, P.O. Box 170, Belmopan, tel (08) 23321, fax (08) 23334; alternatively, the hotel will arrange transport for you if you book accommodation in advance.

EXPENSIVE
The **Pelican Beach Resort**, P.O. Box 14, Dangriga, tel (05) 22044, fax (05) 22570, is the top hotel, which isn't saying much. Located on the seafront, on the northern edge of town, the colonial-style house is clean and very quiet. They offer boat charters for up to 8 people costing around US$135 per day; van rentals for 4 people are US$135, for 5–10 people US$150. The hotel also rents out holiday cottages on Southwater Caye. At the lower end of this price category, the **Bonefish Hotel**, 15 Mahogany Road, tel (05) 22165/22447, is a friendly, small hotel with excellent meals in the restaurant. All rooms have private bathrooms and TV. Tours also arranged.

MODERATE
Soffie's Hotel, 970 Chatuye Street, tel (05) 22789, is a friendly and clean place, with meals available, just south of the Creek mouth. Facing the sea, across the road, is the **Río Mar Inn**, 977 Southern Foreshore, tel (05) 22201, also with restaurant.

INEXPENSIVE
Right by the bus stop is the basic **Hub Guest House**, 573a South Riverside, P.O. Box 56, tel (05) 22397. The outdoor restaurant is a good place for a snack or breakfast. All rooms should have fans. **Cameleon Hotel** and **Tropical Hotel** are cheap and bang in the middle of town, on Commercial Street, but not recommended for single women.

South of Dangriga
The new **Sittee River Lodge**, 19 High Sand, Sittee River Village, tel (05) 22006, located 35 km south of Dangriga, is ideal for nature and fishing enthusiasts and the price category is moderate. Equipment for fishing, camping and snorkelling is available on site, and there are also tours you can join, if you would prefer. All rooms with bath, or you can camp, for which daily rates are US$5, US$15 if hiring camping equipment.

EATING OUT
The best meals are to be had at the **Bonefish Hotel**, or the **Pelican Beach Resort**, though the latter is about 10 minutes' walk from the town centre, and more expensive. In the centre, most people prefer the filling meals offered by **Burger King**, on Commercial Street, whose name has nothing to do with the restaurant chain. The snacks at the **Hub Guest House** are worth trying, and there are a few indifferent Chinese restaurants too.

ENTERTAINMENT AND NIGHTLIFE
The entertainment options are rather limited, apart from getting wrecked in the local pool bars—take a walk along St Vincent and Commercial Streets, and you will easily find these places.

USEFUL INFORMATION

Money Matters
There is a Barclays Bank and Novia Scotia Bank (Mon–Fri, 8.30–noon; Fridays 3–6 as well) on Commercial Street, north of the river.

Tour Agents
Rosado's Tours, 35 Lemon Street, tel (05) 22119, is the place to go for car and van tours, as well as boat charters to the cayes for snorkelling and fishing. An all-day fishing trip costs around US$50 per person for a group of four. **Lester Eiley**, 25 Oak Street, tel (05) 22113, works as a tour guide, and offers boat charters.

Post office
This is at Caney Street, south of the river.

Taxis
Tino's Taxi Service, 127 Commerce Street, tel (05) 22438.

Art Centre
Dangriga Art Centre, 174 St Vincent Street, is recommended for local handicrafts and Belizean music.

Around Dangriga

To reach Tobacco Caye, either contact your hotel before arrival, so they can pick you up, or ask around for lifts with local fishermen. The tourist office or guest houses in Dangriga should be able to help. The same goes for boat lifts for the short journey to Hopkins village, south along the coast. Whichever way you arrive in Hopkins, you will find a photogenic fishing village of thatched houses on the beach, and you can even stay the night, in the **Sandy Beach Lodge**, tel (05) 22023, which offers local-style accommodation and interesting home cooking.

Placencia

Placencia is the kind of place you come to see for a few days, and end up staying a few months. This is the real thing: white sandy beaches, palm trees fringing the shoreline, and windswept houses on stilts hiding in the shade. The village is small and the people say 'hello' to each other when passing. 'All right', they say, with a creole lilt, and you feel like you've landed in Caribbean heaven. Great mounds of conch shells pile up by the village path like rubbish, their pinkness gleaming in the sun. In fact, there is such an abundance of these lovely shells that they are just tossed away or used for building fill.

San Pedro, on Ambergris Caye, must have once been like this, and the people of Placencia village are very aware of how much they have to lose. Originally a fishing village, many inhabitants still make a good living this way, and are loath to sell themselves or their land to tourism. One can only hope that they keep that attitude. You will not, therefore, find a resort with people eager to fulfil your every wish, but you will find a beautiful place, friendly locals, and accommodation ranging from luxurious hideaway to simple rooms.

GETTING TO PLACENCIA

By Air
Flights to Independence, which is in fact the same place as Mango Creek, can stop off here, coming either from Punta Gorda or northern towns. If there are no boatmen at the airstrip, you can phone the post office in Placencia, tel (06) 2946, and a boat will come and collect you. The fare should not be more than BZ$30 (US$15). If you have booked accommodation in advance, your hotel will send someone to pick you up.

By Bus
From Belize City, you need to take a bus to Dangriga, and change there for a direct bus to Placencia (75 km), which leaves at 2.30, Mondays, Wednesdays, Fridays and Saturdays. Coming from northern or western Belize, you can change buses for Dangriga in Belmopan. The bus departs from Placencia at 6 am, on the same days.

Coming from Punta Gorda, in the south, you can take any bus heading north, and get off at Mango Creek. Here you should walk to the waterside, and ask around for a boatman to take you to Placencia. The journey takes about 25 mins, and you should not have to pay more than BZ$30 (US$15), whether there is one passenger or three.

TOURIST INFORMATION

There is no official tourist office, but then there are few things you will need to know. The handful of resort hotels offer their guests every kind of land or sea tour, while other visitors will always find a group to join if they make themselves known to Janice, who runs the **post office**. Located in a wooden shack, just past the village pier, she can coordinate snorkelling trips or visits inland. The village **telephone** is here as well, and the code for Placencia is 06.

WHERE TO STAY

Up-market Beach Hotels

As in San Pedro on Ambergris Caye, accommodation prices outstrip the usual categories used in the guide, especially at the top end of the market. Prices have therefore been listed as a general guideline.

Furthest away from the village (30 mins walk) is **Rum Point Inn**, tel and fax (06) 22017. It is also the most expensive. There are five concrete *cabañas* that look like they have just landed from outer space, while the main house is a more traditional wooden structure, with a good bar and library. Singles are US$140, doubles US$165, plus US$50 for an extra person, all meals included. A short walk further south (15 mins walk from the village) is **Kitty's Place**, P.O. Box 528, Belize City, tel and fax (06) 22027, which is a delightful small hotel, with a choice of rooms, either in the main house, in beach *cabañas*, or two-room apartments. The bar and restaurant are a great place to socialize, and there is a good library too. This is also the only place with a **Dive Shop** with a diving instructor, and **bicycle rental**. (Diving certification courses cost around US$325.) The cheapest rooms are around US$25 singles, US$35 doubles, sharing the bathroom; while the two-person apartment is around US$75. 15% tax is added to bills.

The **Turtle Inn**, tel (06) 22069, is a beautiful spot, with six thatched cottages looking out to sea. Total capacity is twenty people, so this is the place if you want peace and quiet; and personal service from the friendly proprietors is assured. Meals are served family-style at one table. There is a bar and lending library. Prices include all meals: singles US$72, doubles US$123, plus US$35 for an extra person. A fully equipped beach house for two people is US$400 per week. Finally there is the **Cove Resort**, just outside the village, which has six rundown beach *cabañas* that sleep up to three people each. It is outrageously overpriced at US$75 per person, all meals included.

In the Village

EXPENSIVE

Beautiful beach *cabañas* are for rent via **Jene's Restaurant**, which go for around US$50 per person, per day. Janice, from the post office, also rents out beach *cabañas*, with great views of the lagoon, at the same price. **Sonny's Resort**, tel (06) 23103, in the middle of the village, has a mediocre restaurant and unhelpful staff.

MODERATE

The best hotel in Placencia is the **Sea Spray Hotel**, tel (06) 23148, which is a pleasant wooden building, raised slightly off the beach. Rooms are clean and simple, and there's a small bar on the beach.

Next to the best bar, at the southern end of the village, is the **Paradise Vacation Hotel**, tel and fax (06) 23179, which is plain and friendly.

INEXPENSIVE
Ran's Travel Lodge, tel (06) 22027, is a good budget choice. There are also plenty of families renting out rooms, and one of the best is **Conrad and Lydia's Rooms**. Conrad can also take you on boat trips. There are five basic rooms, sharing the bathroom.

EATING OUT
The best restaurant in the village is **Jene's**, which offers delicious meals and good drinks. Right on the beach, the **Kingfisher** (6–midnight only) offers tasty seafood at reasonable prices, while the **Tentacles Bar/Restaurant** is good but pricey, more popular for drinking than eating. The **Stone Crab** is also excellent and good value for money, while **Sonny's** is not. Home cooking is offered by **Jaimie's** and **B.J.'s**.

ENTERTAINMENT AND NIGHTLIFE
While all the restaurants in the village double up as drinking spots, some of the nicest places to drink are the beachside bars of the hotels outside the village. The **Turtle Inn** bar is recommended, and **Kitty's Place** is very popular. The only disco is the **Cozy Corner Disco**, which is right on the beach, in the village, blasting reggae music out to sea.

SPORTS AND ACTIVITIES
You will see many signs for tours and charters around the village so you have plenty of choices. A snorkelling trip to the reef generally costs US$15 per person, gear included, for a group of six. Sailing charters are around US$35 per person, for a group of four.

USEFUL INFORMATION
The nearest **bank** is in Mango Creek, and only open on Friday mornings, 9–noon. No need to worry, however, since most hotels and shops in Placencia should change travellers' cheques or cash.
Flight tickets can be booked at **Sonny's** restaurant, who can arrange transportation to the airstrip as well. Mango Creek also has the nearest **immigration office**, at the police station, where you can get extensions for your visitor's permit, or an exit stamp.
If you're self-catering, the **market store** is at the entrance to the village, on the dirt road, and the only place to buy groceries.

Around Placencia

Cockscomb Basin Jaguar Reserve
An interesting inland excursion is to visit the **Cockscomb Basin Jaguar Reserve**. It can be reached by a one-hour bus journey from Placencia, to the village of Maya Centre, on the way to Dangriga. By the time you read this, there should also be a shuttle bus from Maya Centre to take you into the reserve—otherwise you have a hot 8 km walk ahead of

you, which takes 2 hours (remember that you have to be back at Maya Centre by 3, if you want to catch the bus back to Placencia). Tours to the reserve are also offered (US$25 per person), which is an expensive option, but perhaps more convenient.

Covering an area of 100,000 acres, the reserve is a wonderful place for hiking, and although you are unlikely to catch sight of the elusive jaguars and other cats, you will certainly see many bird species, even the endangered scarlet macaw. Beautiful trails, none longer than 3 km, have been cut into the forest, and there is a clear river to cool off in afterwards. A visitor's centre with a small exhibition can provide further information, and if you contact the Audubon Society (address on p. 198) in advance, you can also arrange to stay at the campsite or cabins here. There are no provisions available, so you should bring all your own food and drink. If you plan to hike as far as Victoria Peak, you must obtain a permit before arrival from the Audubon Society. Remember also that you will need a good map for this tough hike, and it would probably be a good idea to hire a guide to come with you, since this is a remote and uninhabited region.

Punta Gorda

Punta Gorda, or P.G., as it is generally known, is a quiet little town at the end of the Southern Highway, with just over 3000 inhabitants. A handful of roads, lined by dilapidated buildings, give the place a pleasant atmosphere of a forgotten film set, and nothing happens very quickly here. Most days the heat is freshened by a sea breeze, but to be in a room without a fan is almost unbearable. Being so far from the rest of Belize, P.G. never gets many visitors, and those that do pass this way are usually on their way somewhere else, only stepping off the ferry from Guatemala and onto a bus heading north. It is nevertheless a useful base from which to see interesting destinations inland, most of them relating to the Maya heritage, past and present.

In an effort to vitalize the tourist trade, and more importantly, help the Maya (and Garifuna) population share in the profits, a highly innovative programme is being developed, which should be fully operational by 1992. The **Toledo Eco-Tourism Association** plans to help six villages in the region, one of which is Garifuna, build guest houses, so that tourists can get the best out of visiting their traditional communities. The idea is that guests will sleep in the village guest house, but eat each meal with a different family, thus getting an excellent opportunity to meet the local inhabitants and learn about their culture. Local guides will also be provided to take a maximum of four people at a time along trails in the surrounding jungle. Profits from this project will go into a central fund, helping to improve the living standards and opportunities of the communities. To find out more, contact Chet Schmidt at **Nature's Way Guest House**, 65 Front Street, tel (07) 2119.

In the meantime, there is also a private project being run by Alfredo Villoria, called the **Indigenous Experience**. It is an unfortunate aspect of increased tourism opportunities that two competing operations are under way. This threatens to split local communities since they cannot belong to both. The idea behind this programme is to bring foreigners and Mayas together, but the project is potentially damaging. The Indian households who have been chosen as suitable hosts are paid directly by the guests, thus giving them a lucrative income over others in the village, which will undoubtedly lead to bitter friction and undermine traditional communal systems. Not only that, but chosen families do not necessarily have the resources to host foreigners, whose expectations of bathroom facilities may not match the hole in the ground they are bound to find. Nor does a family always have space for an extra person, resulting in a member of the family having to give up their sleeping place for the guest. This is wrong, and also potentially embarassing for the visitor, who would not wish to impose to such an extent. To find out more, you can contact Alfredo Villoria, who will put you in touch with a host family on payment of a registration fee, either at his **visitor's centre** at the Punta Gorda dock (daily except Thursday and Sunday, 8–noon); or via P.O. Box 73, Punta Gorda.

Whichever programme you choose to use, the experience of staying in a Mopan or Kekchi Maya village is a memorable one. An extraordinary aspect of meeting these people is that they speak English—if you have just arrived from Guatemala, you will find it very odd to hear soft, Belizean creole coming from an Indian mouth. In fact, a 'traditional' Maya community in Belize is very different from its Guatemalan equivalent. Here, many of the communities developed from refugees fleeing from persecution or slavery in Guatemala, and although their traditional architecture and cooking remains, their language and dress have often been lost. Only in recent years has there been any effort to regain old traditions. The children go to English-speaking schools, and many never learn their Maya language. Equally, the famous Maya weaving and embroidery is not to be found here. Instead, the most rewarding thing about visiting these villages is meeting modern, Belizean Mayas, who have a unique knowledge of the surrounding forest flora and fauna, which they are happy to share with you.

GETTING TO AND FROM PUNTA GORDA

By Air
There are six daily flights from Belize City, which stop at all main towns along the southern coast.

By Bus
Since Punta Gorda is the end of the line for the Southern Highway, you really cannot miss the place. It is 171 km from Dangriga, a hot and dusty journey along unpaved roads which takes 6 hours. Coming from Belize City, you can travel by comfortable Pullman bus with the **James Bus Line**, leaving Mondays, Wednesdays, Fridays and Saturdays, at 9 am. In the other direction, buses leave at 6 am on Sundays and Thursdays, and 1 pm on Tuesdays and Fridays. Phone (07) 2056 for information and booking tickets.

By Sea: to and from Guatemala
For information on the ferry service from Puerto Barrios, Guatemala see p. 157. Leaving Belize, the ferry goes on Tuesdays and Fridays, between 2 and 3, but supposedly at 2.30. Try to buy your ticket (US$5.50) as early as possible on the day, or you have little chance of getting on the boat. The ticket office is at 24 Middle Street. Remember to take your passport for buying the ticket, and get your exit stamp at the police station (on Front Street) before you leave. The journey to Puerto Barrios takes around $2\frac{1}{2}$ hrs.

TOURIST INFORMATION

There is a small information booth at the town dock, run by the friendly Alfredo Villoria, who can advise you on tours or regional buses, and also keeps a selection of brochures. Another excellent source of information and organizer of all kinds of tours is Chet Schmidt, at **Nature's Way Guest House**, 65 Front Street, which also happens to be the nicest place to stay. Get there by walking south along Main Street, until you come to a small sign pointing left for the guest house.

WHERE TO STAY

MODERATE

Nature's Way Guest House, 65 Front Street, tel (07) 2119, is a beautiful house, cooled by sea breezes, with meals cooked to order. All rooms share the bathroom. At the other end of town, the new **Charleston Inn**, on the corner of Main Street and North Street, has clean rooms, with fan and private bathroom. Close by, **Mahung's Hotel**, tel (07) 2044, offers good rooms around the back of the hotel only. **St Charles Inn**, 23 King Street, tel (07) 2149, is very respectable, but rather expensive for the town. The **Lux Drive Inn**, 43 Front Street, and the **Mira Mar**, 95 Front Street, are overpriced and unpleasant.

The only up-market hotel is the **Safe Haven Lodge**, 2 Prince Street, tel and fax (07) 2113.

EATING OUT

The best place for creole cooking is **Lucille's**, on Main Street. Get there early, since you usually have to wait a long time, which goes for all the eating houses in town. Another good creole restaurant is **Scheibers**, on Front Street, and surprisingly, so is the **Airport Café** (Mon–Sat, 8–6).
Bobby's Restaurant Bar, on Main Street, is best for soups, and if you feel like a Chinese meal, head for the **Kowloon** restaurant.

USEFUL INFORMATION

The **airport** is right in the town, so everything is within a short walking distance. **Pennel & Son**, 50 Main Street, is an agent for Tropic Air and Maya Airways. The **bus terminal** is located opposite the army barracks in the southern part of town, on West Street. Local buses leave from the municipal park, at the junction of Main Street and Queen Street. **Cars** can be rented from Texaco service station, tel (07) 2126.

There are a couple of **tour agencies**: **Briceno Taxi and Tour Services**, 6 Cemetery Lane and, for tours and boat charters, **Julio and Placida Requena**, 12 Front Street, tel (07) 2070.

The **Belize Bank** is located on Main Street, near the municipal park.

Around Punta Gorda

Maya Ruins and Villages

Nearest to Punta Gorda is the Kekchi village of **San Pedro Columbia**, which you can reach by local bus, either direct to the village or by taking a bus to San Antonio and getting off at the appropriate junction. The second option involves a 3-km walk. Located about 20 km northwest of Punta Gorda, the village is on a clearing in the forest, close to the emerald waters of the broad River Columbia. Houses are a variation on the pole and thatch design, and the people live from slash and burn agriculture, only venturing to town on market days.

The surrounding landscape, in the foothills of the Maya Mountains, is very attractive, and a walk of around 45 minutes will take you to the most important ruins in the region: **Lubaantun**. Two major pyramids remain, their most significant feature that they were built without the use of mortar. Unfortunately, an English adventurer used dynamite to explore them early this century, so they look like a giant has given them a good kick, causing them to cave in and tilt at odd angles. Stones litter the site, and looting has done its worst here. The site's name, meaning 'Place of Fallen Stones' is sadly apt. However, the location is beautiful, and certainly worth making an effort to see.

An unresolved controversy originated here: the mysterious **Crystal Skull** was discovered by the North American F. A. Mitchell Hedges, in 1926. He found the skull—which is perfectly shaped, yet has no trace of tool marks on it—on his daughter's birthday. Some believe it was a hoax for her benefit—his daughter, however, insists otherwise, and still owns the skull today.

San Antonio village, about 5 km west of San Pedro Columbia, has a direct bus service from P.G., and also has a hotel, which makes a good base from which to visit the **Uxbenka** ruins. Inhabited by Mopan Maya, this is a modern village, with a stone church built by resident American missionaries. The community has strong ties to its traditions, however, and the best time to see this is on 5 August, on San Luis Rey Day. The Maya ruins are about 5 km away, just off the dirt track leading to Santa Cruz village. Situated on a small hilltop, the site was not officially discovered until 1984, and what you find is a small, unexcavated ceremonial centre, with good views over the surrounding jungle.

About 1 km further along the road, a small track leads off to the left to **New Falls**, which is an excellent place for a swim and picnic. The river broadens out into a wide pool under some waterfalls, embraced by thick jungle on both sides (if you reach St Elena village, you have gone too far).

The only place to stay in San Antonio is the basic **Bol's Hilltop Hotel**. Meals must be ordered in advance, and this is the only place to serve food in the village. If you would like to hire a guide for exploring the region, you could not do better than Matilde Kaal, who, in spite of his name, is male, and extremely knowledgeable and friendly. You will find his home by asking around in the nearby settlement of Crique Lagarto.

The Maya site of **Nim Li Punit** is not conveniently accessible by public transport, but if you have your own, the place is worth visiting for the terrific views across the coastal plain and nearby highlands. Its name means 'Big Hat', and it was only discovered in 1976, hiding on a small hilltop above some Indian homesteads. The best preserved details are the stelae, of which no fewer than 25 have been found, indicating that this was an important ceremonial centre. The site is near Indian Creek settlement, off the Southern Highway, 40 km north of P.G.

Blue Creek

At the junction for San Pedro Columbia, where **Roy's Coolspot** offers snacks and cold drinks, there is a turning for Blue Creek, which is a beautiful place for swimming, huge trees shading the deep green water (unfortunately, you need your own transport to get here). Heading up the right-hand side of the river on foot, you soon come to a lovely natural pool, perfect for tranquil swimming without any currents.

Dem Dats Doin

Finally, for anyone interested in integrated farm systems, a visit to Dem Dats Doin is a must. Run by a Hawaiian couple, Alfredo and Yvonne Villoria, their farm is a delightful place, full of innovative and simple technology that anyone could use to create a self-sufficient, tropical farm. There are also a huge number of fruit trees grown, and a tour (US$5) around the farm is not only educative, but beautiful as well. To get there, follow the road to San Pedro Columbia, and turn right where a wrecked car is parked, with the farm's name painted on its side. There is also one room available for overnight stays, moderately priced. To book the room or a tour, contact Alfredo at his information booth in P.G., or via P.O. Box 73, Punta Gorda, Toledo District, Belize.

NORTHERN BELIZE

Much of northern Belize is flat and swampy, dotted by lagoons and marshes that make an ideal habitat for aquatic birds, but not for spectacular views (unless you're a birdwatcher, of course). The coastal lagoons stretch endlessly and are for the most part uninhabited—fishermen are the only regular visitors. The exception to this is near the Mexican border, where the town of Corozal nestles in a bay surrounded by small ancient and modern settlements. Only the western reaches of Orange Walk differ from the general description. Here the landscape becomes hilly and is covered by thick tropical forests which are some of the least accessible and least explored in the country. Exploring the region without your own transport is difficult, though if you have the time and money there are some worthwhile sites, such as the ancient ruins of Lamanai, and the Shipstern and Crooked Tree reserves.

Historically, northern Belize has often been a refuge for people fleeing from violence elsewhere. Some of the earliest refugees were the Santa Cruz Maya of the Mexican Yucatán who came to Belize in 1901. They were a group of Mayas who had allied themselves with the British after defeat in the Caste Wars of 1847, during which the Spanish had violently put down an Indian uprising. After their defeat, the Santa Cruz Maya were among a larger group, who formed separate and independent Maya states in the Mexican region of Quintana Roo. However, the Mexican authorities could not allow independent Indian states in their country, and so they mounted another attack in 1901, which resulted in final and bloody victory. Thus the Santa Cruz Maya fled to the lands of their former allies, to what was then British Honduras, and their descendants remain until this day.

Other groups that have come to the region include German Mennonite communities, who settled in Shipyard and Blue Creek; and Nicaraguan and Salvadorean refugees, squatting in various remote parts, including around the Maya site of Lamanai. The Spanish language predominates here, unlike in the rest of the country, and the closer you get to the Mexican border, the more likely you are to meet people who speak no English at all, being mestizos not creoles.

The paved Northern Highway cuts straight through the region, and travel from Belize City to Mexican Chetumal is just a matter of four hours. The only significant town on the way is Orange Walk, which was once at the centre of a lucrative sugar-cane industry, but has now become severely impoverished. In response, farmers have turned to marijuana cultivation, and Belize has become a signigicant drug exporter, as well as a stopover for cocaine aircraft on the way to North America.

Along the Northern Highway

Crooked Tree Wildlife Sanctuary

Located about 53 km northwest of Belize City, this reserve is the first point of interest beyond the close environs of the city. Established in 1984 and administered by the Audubon Society, the sanctuary's landscape is predominantly wetlands, which are the ideal home for all kinds of resident and migratory birds. In particular during the dry season, the place is a safe haven for thousands of birds, including many types of heron, two species of duck, egrets, kingfishers, ospreys, hawks, and many, many more, the largest of which is the Jaribu stork. The best time to see birds here is from November to May, and a visitor's centre in the village of Crooked Tree offers further information.

Orange Walk

86 km north of Belize City, the town of Orange Walk is a scruffy place that holds no attraction for the tourist in itself, but is a starting point for visits to the Maya site of **Lamanai**. Originally a timber camp, the town became an important centre for sugar-cane and citrus production. It is now a depressed area, where a significant proportion of local agriculture is now the illicit cultivation of marijuana, popularly known as 'Belize Breeze'. A rough town, Orange Walk was also the scene of gory battles in the 19th century, when the local Indian population regularly attacked settlers. The last battle was in 1872, and the ruins of Fort Cairns and Mundy are a legacy of the time when Orange Walk was frequently besieged and needed military protection.

WHERE TO STAY
Jane's Guest Houses in Bakers Street and Market Lane are recommended for budget travellers; **Baron's Hotel** tel (03) 22518, is more expensive.

Lamanai

The ruins of Lamanai (8–5, small fee) are located about 20 km southwest of Orange Walk, on the shores of the New River Lagoon. An important site, it is estimated that in the 6th century, it was home to around 20,000 people. The earliest inhabitants came here in 1500 BC and this site has one of the longest records of occupation, long before it became a Maya ceremonial centre. The earliest stone architecture appeared in the 9th century BC, and the largest Pre-Classic structure in the Maya territory is to be found here, a pyramid rising 33 m above the surrounding savannah, whose earliest building phase dates back to 100 BC. The site's name is the original Maya one, and means 'Submerged Crocodile', and images of crocodiles appear frequently amongst the carvings found here.

Maya descendants were living here as late as the 16th century and the Spanish duly built a mission church to Christianize them. The results were poor, however, and the Indians burnt the place down in 1640. In the 19th century the British built a sugar mill nearby but this failed too, when the manager died of a fever and the ruins have been left in peace, the surrounding area sparsely populated, until this day. As you wander around this unspoilt site you will find abundant wildlife, especially birds and butterflies.

GETTING TO LAMANAI
To reach Lamanai, your best bet is to go on a tour from Orange Walk (Mr Godoy, tel (03) 22969) or Belize City (such as Gilly's Inland Tours, tel (02) 77630). Otherwise you must make your way to the villages of Guinea Grass or Shipyard (closer), from where you can hire a boatman to take you south along the New River. There are no facilities there, though the resident archaeology camp has a small museum showing artefacts found here.

Río Bravo Conservation Area

The north's most exotic resort hotel is the **Chan Chich Lodge**, built in the middle of a Maya plaza in a remote jungle bordering Guatemala (contact via 1 King Street, Belize City, tel (02) 75634, or P.O. Box 37, Belize City). This is a private reserve, administered by the Programme for Belize, and the lodge is a superb place to discover the colourful flora and fauna of tropical forests while enjoying the comforts of rustic luxury. To get there you have to charter a plane to Gallon Jug airstrip, or during the dry season, tough vehicles can get there via Orange Walk, San Felipe and Blue Creek.

Shipstern Reserve

This reserve is in a remote region northeast of Orange Walk, near the village of Sarteneja, about an hour's drive from the town along a dirt road. There is an efficient visitor's centre where you can arrange for a guided tour around the reserve which covers 31 square miles and a variety of habitats, ranging from the shallow Shipstern Lagoon to savannah and forests. One of the most interesting trails is the 'Chiclero Botanical Trail', where you can learn about the uses for many of the trees. Almost all the species of animal found in Belize are found in this region, including the jaguar. Over 60 kinds of reptiles and amphibians have been recorded, and a staggering 220 species of birds. A special attraction is also the nearby **Butterfly Breeding Centre**. Visit on a sunny day, and you will have the best chance to see some of the 200 species of butterflies.

Corozal

Of all the northern settlements, this is the most pleasant to visit, facing out to the turquoise seas of Corozal Bay, 134 km north of Belize City and 14 km from the Mexican border. Corozal was badly damaged by Hurricane Janet in 1955, however, and so it does have a somewhat empty feeling to it. Like Orange Walk, the town has suffered from the decline of the sugar industry, and employment is scarce. Bored youths hang around street corners and there isn't very much to do for the visitor either. It is a good spot to break the journey to or from Mexico. There are also flights to Ambergris Caye from here.

GETTING TO COROZAL

By Air
Corozal's landing strip is set amongst fields but a cab or two are always ready to meet arrivals. For flight tickets from Corozal contact **Menzies Travel**, Ranchito village, tel (04) 22725, and they will send someone to pick you up free of charge.

By Bus
Batty buses stop at 4 Park Street North, and Venus buses stop at 7th Avenue. You should have no problem travelling to and from Corozal by public transport, as all buses between Belize City and Chetumal stop here.

WHERE TO STAY

EXPENSIVE

The top place to stay is the attractive **Tony's Inn**, at South End, tel (04) 22829, fax (04) 22829, which is right by the sea. Rooms have either a fan or air-conditioning and TV.

Outside Corozal, near the village of Consejo, you will find the reasonably up-market **Adventure Inn**, P.O. Box 35, Corozal Town, tel (04) 22187, fax (04) 22243. Overlooking the bay the hotel is made up of a main lodge and 14 cabins, and all watersports, especially fishing, are catered for.

MODERATE

Hotel Maya, South End, tel (04) 22082, is clean and simple. Rooms with fan and private bath are available.

INEXPENSIVE

Capri, on the corner of 14th Avenue and 4th Avenue is loud and grubby, and the best budget choice is **Nestor's Hotel**, 123 5th Avenue, tel (04) 22354, which also has a restaurant.

LANGUAGE

Excepting Belize, where the majority speak English, the most widely used language in Central America is Spanish, followed closely by the many Maya Indian languages spoken predominantly in Guatemala. There are at least ten major language groups for the Maya people and among those the variety of dialects is staggering. Even communication from one region to the next can be impossible, and foreigners cannot hope to learn about the indigenous linguistic complexities on a short visit. Suffice it to say that most Maya can speak Spanish, and only in very remote areas will you find villagers unable to use it.

Few people have a working knowledge of English or other European languages, and your visit will be immeasurably improved if you can at least communicate in basic Spanish. There are plenty of language schools in Central America, most notably in Antigua, Guatemala, and many travellers find that even one or two weeks of tuition makes all the difference. The courses are also much cheaper here than in the West, and tuition is generally one-to-one, making your advance very rapid. One week of daily four-hour sessions can cost you as little as US$45 or around US$100, depending on which language school you choose (see p. 103 for Antigua's practical information).

Formal Greetings
Buenos días	Good morning
Buenas tardes	Good afternoon
Buenas noches	Good evening
Buenos días, don (doña)...	Good morning Mr (Mrs)...
¡Señor!	Sir/Madam (applied to both)
¿Como está (usted)?	How are you?
Adiós	Goodbye

Informal Greetings
Hola!	Hello!
¿Qué tal?	How's it going?
Adiós	Hello (in passing)
Hasta pronto	See you soon
Que te vaya bien	Stay well
Dios te cuida	May God keep you

Travel
Disculpe	Excuse me/sorry
Lo siento	Sorry
¿Habla inglés?	Do you speak English?
Dónde está...	Where is?
Terminal de buses	Bus station

LANGUAGE

Camioneta — Bus
Estación de tren — Train station
Aeropuerto — Airport
Parada — Bus stop
Barco — Boat
Puerto — Port
Aduana — Customs
Cuánto cuesta... — How much?
¿A qué hora sale el bus? — What time does the bus depart?
¿Cuándo sale el próximo? — When does the next one leave?
¿De dónde? — From where?
¿Cuánto es el pasaje? — How much is the bus fare?
El boleto — Ticket
Ida y vuelta — Return ticket
Solo ida — Just one way
¿Hasta dónde? — Where to?
Hasta Antigua — To Antigua
Asiento — Seat
Lleno — Full
Atrás hay lugares — There are seats at the back
¡Buen viaje! — Have a good trip!
Quiero un taxi — I'm looking for (want) a taxi

Directions and Locations
Izquierda — Left
Derecha — Right
Adelante — Forward
Atrás — Backward
Arriba — Up
Abajo — Down
Dos cuadras de aquí — Two blocks from here
Lejos — Far/distant
Cerca — Near/close
Recto — Straight (ahead)
Norte — North
Sur — South
Oeste — West
Este — East
Entrada — Entrance
Salida — Exit
Esquina — Corner (exterior)
Rincón — Corner (interior)

Accommodation
Hotel/Posada — Hotel
Hospedaje/Pensión — Guest house

¿Hay cuartos?	Do you have rooms?
Para una persona	For one person
Para dos (tres) personas	For two (three) people
¿Cuánto son or A cómo son?	How much are they?
¿Hay con baño privado?	Are there rooms with private bath?
¿Hay unos con cama matrimonial?	Do you have ones with double beds?
Con dos camas	With two beds
¿Hay cuartos más barato?	Do you have cheaper rooms?
Hay agua caliente?	Do you have hot water?
Funcionar	to work/function/to be in working order
Está bien	That is good (I accept)
¿A qué hora hay desayuno?	What time is breakfast?
¿Hay comida?	Do you have meals/Is there food?
¿Qué hay para comer?	What do you have to eat?
¿Tiene (usted) un candado?	Do you have a padlock (for the room)?
¿Tiene (usted) candelas?	Do you have candles?
Tiene (usted) un ventilador?	Do you have a ventilator?
Quiero salir muy temprano	I wish to leave very early
Jabón	Soap
Toalla	Towel
Papel Higiénico	Toilet paper

Driving

Carro	Car
Moto	Motorbike
Bicicleta	Bicycle
Alquilar	to rent
Gasolinera	Petrol station
Gasolina	Petrol
Garaje	Garage
Carretera	Road
Camino	Path/road
Permiso (Carnet) de conducir	Driving licence
Conductor (Piloto)	Driver
Peligro	Danger

Shopping, Service, Sightseeing

Guía	Guide
Abierto	Open
Cerrado	Closed
¿A qué hora abre el museo?	What time does the museum open?
¿A qué hora cierra el museo?	What time does the museum close?
El dinero	Money
Pisto	Money/income (slang)
La tienda	Shop
La golosina/pulpería/sastrería	Shop (Honduras)

El mercado — Market
Barato/Caro — Cheap/Expensive
Cuánto vale eso? — How much is that?
Está demasiado caro — It's too expensive
Hay rebaja? — Is there a discount?
No se puede — It's not possible
No hay — There isn't any
El correo — Post office
El banco — Bank
La oficina de turismo — Tourist office
Agencia de viaje — Travel agent
La farmacia — Chemist
Artesanía — Crafts
La Policía — Police force
Comisaría — Police station
La playa — Beach
El mar — Sea
La iglesia — Church

Maya Clothes and Market Goods

Indígena — Indian/Indigenous person
Traje — Traditional costume
Artesanía/Típica — Crafts
Huipil — Blouse/Top
Corte — Skirt/Wrap
Faja — Belt/Sash
Cinta/Bola/Tzute — Headdress
Cubrecama — Bedspread/Cover
Alfombra — Carpet/Rug
Mantel — Tablecloth
Servilleta — Napkin
Cinturón — Belt
Sombrero — Hat
Joyas — Jewellery
Pulsera — Bracelet
Collar — Necklace
Anillo — Ring
Plata — Silver
Oro — Gold
Máscara — Mask
Carraca — Rattle
Escultura — Carving

Useful Words and Phrases

¡Cuidado! — Careful
¿Puedes ayudarme? — Can you help?

Por favor	Please
Gracias	Thank you
Lo siento/disculpe	Sorry
De nada	It's a pleasure
¿Cómo te llamas?	What's your name?
Mucho gusto conocerte	It's a pleasure meeting you
Con mucho gusto	With pleasure
Sí/No	Yes/No
Quizás	Maybe
¿Por qué?	Why?
No sé	I don't know
No entiendo	I don't understand
Déjame en paz	Leave me alone
Habla despacio	Speak slowly
¿Qué es esto?	What is that?
¿Para qué es esto?	What is that for?
Servicio/Baño	Toilet/Bathroom
Aquí	Here
Allá	There
Que	What
Quien	Who
Como	How
Cuando	When
Bueno	Good
Malo	Bad
Tengo hambre	I'm hungry
Tengo sed	I'm thirsty
Estoy cansado (masc.), *cansada* (fem.)	I'm tired
¿Tiene fuego?	Have you got a light?
No fumo	I don't smoke
Tomar	to drink (slang)
Estoy casado/a	I'm married
Marido	Husband
Esposa	Wife
Niño/a	Child
Novio/a	Boyfriend/Girlfriend
Prometido/a	Engaged
Embarazada	Pregnant
Divorciado/a	Divorced

Time

¿Qué hora es?	What time is it?
Tiempo	Time
Hace tiempo	A long time ago
Ahora	Now
Después/Más tarde	Later

LANGUAGE

Temprano	Early
Hoy	Today
Ayer	Yesterday
Mañana	Tomorrow
Mañana	Morning
Tarde	Afternoon (late)
Noche	Evening
Mediodía	Midday
Año	Year
Mes	Month
Semana	Week
Día	Day

Days

Lunes	Monday
Martes	Tuesday
Miércoles	Wednesday
Jueves	Thursday
Viernes	Friday
Sábado	Saturday
Domingo	Sunday
Feria	Bank holiday
Vacaciónes	Holidays

Numbers

Uno/a	One
Dos	Two
Tres	Three
Cuatro	Four
Cinco	Five
Seis	Six
Siete	Seven
Ocho	Eight
Nueve	Nine
Diez	Ten
Once	Eleven
Doce	Twelve
Trece	Thirteen
Catorce	Fourteen
Quince	Fifteen
Dieciséis	Sixteen
Diecisiete	Seventeen
Dieciocho	Eighteen
Diecinueve	Nineteen
Veinte	Twenty
Veintiuno	Twenty-one

Treinta	Thirty
Cuarenta	Forty
Cincuenta	Fifty
Sesenta	Sixty
Setenta	Seventy
Ochenta	Eighty
Noventa	Ninety
Cien	One hundred
Ciento uno	One hundred and one
Quinientos	Five hundred
Mil	One thousand

Restaurants and Food

Restaurante	Restaurant
Comedor	Eating place
Comida corriente	Meal of the day
Desayuno	Breakfast
Almuerzo	Lunch
Cena	Dinner
Pan	Bread
Mantequilla	Butter
Queso	Cheese
Jalea	Jam
Miel	Honey
Azúcar	Sugar
Pan tostado	Toast
Huevos (fritos/revueltos)	Eggs (fried/scrambled)
Huevos a la mexicana	with tomato, onion and hot sauce
Huevos rancheros	with hot sauce
Hervir	Boil
Mosh	Porridge
Pastel	Pastry/cake
Mesa	Table
Silla	Chair
Cuchillo	Knife
Tenedor	Fork
Cuchara	Spoon
Sopa	Soup
Condimento	Salt and pepper
Salsa picante	Hot sauce
Mostaza	Mustard
Cenicero	Ashtray
Cuenta	Bill
Anafre	Beanpaste snack (Honduras)
Pinchos	Meat kebabs
Chile relleno	Stuffed pepper

Chuchitos — Stuffed maize dumplings
Enchilada — Crisp tortillas with salad/meat topping
Quesadilla — Flour tortilla stuffed with cheese
Taco — Stuffed tortilla
Tamale — Maize pudding wrapped in palm leaf

Drinks
Bebidas — Drinks
Agua — Water or fizzy drink
Jugo — Fruit juice
Licuado (leche/agua) — Milkshake (with milk or water)
Cerveza — Beer
Vino — Wine
Café negro — Black coffee
Café con leche — White coffee
Té (con limón) — Tea (with lemon)

Meats
Carne — Meat
Lomito — Meat (usually beef)
Carne de res — Beef
Bistec — Steak
Marano (Cerdo) — Pork
Chorizo — Sausage
Tocino — Bacon
Jamón — Ham
Chuleta — Chop
Guisado — Stew
Milanesa — Breaded meat
Cordero — Lamb
Ternera — Veal
Venado — Venison
Pollo — Chicken
Gallina — Hen
Pato — Duck
Pavo — Turkey
Conejo — Rabbit
Tepezcuintle — A jungle rodent (good)
Hígado — Liver
Asado — Roasted
Al horno — Baked
A la parrilla — Grilled

Fish and Shellfish
Pescado entero — Whole fish

Pescado frito   Fried fish
Tiburón   Shark
Bacalao   Cod
Trucha   Trout
Atún   Tuna
Ceviche   Raw fish salad
Mariscos   Shellfish
Camarones   Shrimp
Langosta   Lobster
Calamares   Squid
Cangrejo   Crab

Vegetables
Verduras   Vegetables
Ajo   Garlic
Cebolla   Onion
Papas   Potatoes
Arroz   Rice
Maíz   Maize/Corn
Frijoles   Beans
Tomate   Tomato
Hongos   Mushrooms
Aguacate   Avocado
Col   Cabbage
Coliflor   Cauliflower
Lechuga   Lettuce
Pepino   Cucumber
Zanahoria   Carrot

Fruit
Coco   Coconut
Plátano   Banana
Papaya   Pawpaw
Melón   Honeymelon
Sandía   Watermelon
Durazno (Melocotón)   Peach
Piña   Pineapple
Pitaya   Guatemalan fruit (purple inside)
Fresas   Strawberries
Guayaba   Guava
Limón   Lemon
Naranja   Orange
Manzana   Apple
Toronja   Grapefruit
Uvas   Grapes

COUNTRY INDEX

The following seven **Country Indexes** contain references to place names, and all practical information that is relevant to the country in question.

On page 248 the **General Index** contains non-specific references to subjects and activities, major players and events—such as tobacco, bird-watching, the Maya, Christopher Columbus and the Spanish Conquest.

Note: Page references in **bold** type indicate maps; those in *italics* indicate illustrations.

Belize 174–233, **175**
accommodation 188–9
Altun Ha ruins 191, 199, 200
Ambergris Caye 176, 182, 202–6
  accommodation & restaurants 203–5
  San Pedro 201–2, 204–5
  travel 203, 233
army 186

Barrier Reef 176, 191, 193, 201–3
beaches 190, 201, 219, 223
Belize City 191–9, **192**
  accommodation 196–7
  Bliss Institute 195
  entertainment & nightlife 198
  Fort George Lighthouse 196
  Government House 195
  history 176–8, 191–3
  restaurants 197–8
  St John's Cathedral 195
  shopping 198
  travel 193–5
Belmopan 193, 194, 210, 211–12
  accommodation 211–12
  travel 211, 221
Benque Viejo 173, 180, 218
birdwatching 190, 231
Blue Creek 230
Blue Hole National Park 219–20
Bluefield Range 209
Branch Mouth 215
and Britain 177–9, 186, 195, 210

Cahal Pech ruins 215
camping 189, 190, 200, 207, 209, 213, 214
car hire 183–4, 215, 228
Caracol ruins 3, 30, 190, 210, 216–17
  travel 183, 214
caves 217
Caye Caulker 191, 201–2, 203, 206–8
  accommodation & restaurants 207
  sports 207–8
Caye Chapel 182, 191, 193, 208
cayes 174–6, 191, 199, 201–10

Cayo District 176, 190, 210–18
Chetumal 194
Chiquibul Cave System 217
cinema 188, 198
climate 201, 210
Cockscomb Range 219
Cockscomb Basin Jaguar Reserve 3, 24, 189, 190, 225–6
Community Baboon Sanctuary 191, 200
consulate 180–1, 184
Corozal 193–4, 203, 230, 233
creole society 177, 189
crime 211, 216
Crooked Tree Sanctuary 231
customs 157, 182

Dangriga 187, 190, 218, 219–22
  accommodation & restaurants 221–2
  travel 193, 194, 210, 220–1, 223
Dem Dats Doin 230
diving 3, 174, 191, 201–2, 205–6, 207–10

eating out 189, *see also* restaurants
ecotourism 24, 226–7
embassies 180–1, 184, 196
English Caye 201

festivals 3, 187
flora and fauna 23, 174–6, *174*, 199–201, 209, 210, 217, 219, 230–2
food, *see* restaurants

Gallon Jug 190, 232
geography 174
Glover Reef 191, 202, 209
Goff's Caye 201
and Guatemala 174, 178, 186
guides 200, 226, 229

Half Moon Caye Natural Monument 209
hiking 190, 215, 220, 226
history 32, 176–9, 230

243

Belize *(continued)*

Hol Chan Marine Reserve 203
Hopkins 190, 219, 220, 223
independence 178–9
itineraries 190–1
jungle 190
Lamanai ruins 190, 231–2
Lighthouse Reef 202, 208–9
Lubaantun site 219, 229

Macal River 190, 217–18
Mango Creek 220, 223, 225
maps 181, 215, 226
markets 187
Maya Centre village 225–6
Maya Mountains 219, 229
media 188
medical concerns 186, 198
Melchor de Menchos 173, 218
money matters 184–5, 199, 222, 225, 228
Mountain Pine Ridge 176, 183, 189, 190, 214–15, 217

National Parks 24
Nim Li Punit site 219, 229

opening hours 187
Orange Walk 194, 230, 231
orientation 195

Panti Medicine Trail 217
Placencia 190, 219, 223–5
  accommodation & restaurants 224
  entertainment & nightlife 225
police 186, 198
public holidays 186–7
Punta Gorda 60, 219, 226–8
  accommodation & restaurants 228
  travel 157, 180, 190, 193, 220, 221, 223, 227, 242

rainforest 25, 176, 210, 216
restaurants 189, *see also under individual destinations*
Rio Bravo Conservation Area 25, 232
Rio On 217

St George's Caye 176, 177, 193, 201
San Antonio 229
San Ignacio 210, 212–15
  accommodation 212–14
  restaurants & nightlife 214
  sports & activities 214–15
  travel 173, 180, 190, 194, 212
San Pedro Columbia 193, 228–9
Seine Bight 190

Shipstern Nature Reserve & Butterfly Breeding Centre 191, 232
shopping 187–8
Stann Creek District 176, 190, 218–26
swimming 217, 219, 229, 230

Tobacco Reef 209–10, 220, 223
Toledo District 176, 190, 219, 226–30
tourist offices 181, 182, 195, 203, 207, 212, 221, 227
tour operators 198, 222, 228
travel 173, 179–80, 182–4
traveller's cheques 184, 199, 206
Tropical Education Centre 200
Turneffe Islands 191, 201–2, 208

Uxbenka site 219, 229

Victoria Peak 190, 219, 226
visas 386

watersports 202–3, 205–6, 225

Xunantunich ruins, El Castillo 215–16

Zoo 199–200

Guatemala 50–173, 52–3

Acatenango volcano 104, 106
accommodation 71–2
Acul village 121
Agua Caliente border post 59, 154, 270
Agua volcano 88, 105–6
Aguacatán 68, 132
Almolonga 68, 125, 128
Alotenango 93
Alta Verapaz 146–8
Altar de Sacrificios ruins 29, 163
Amatitlán, fiesta 68
Antigua 3, 73, 90–103, **91**
  accommodation 71, 99–100
  Ayuntamiento 94
  Casa Kojom 97
  Casa Popenoe 95
  cathedral 93–4
  Cerro de la Cruz 96
  Concepción Convent 95
  El Calvario church 97
  entertainment & nightlife 101–2
  Escuela de Cristo church 98
  fiesta 3, 8, 67, 68, 69, 70, 96, 97–9
  history 31–2, 45, 76, 90–2
  La Merced church 96, 98
  La Recolección church 96
  markets 70, 96, 102

Guatemala *(continued)*

museums 94
Palace of the Captains General 94
Pedro de Betancourt tomb 95
Plaza Mayor 93–4
restaurants & cafés 100–1
San Francisco church 95, 98
San José el Viejo church 97
San Pedro church & hospital 94
Santa Catalina Convent 95
Santa Clara church 94
Santa Teresa Convent 96
tourist information 94
travel 78, 92–3, 118
archaeological sites 142–3
army 45, 55–8, 65–6
Atitlán volcano 113

Baja Verapaz 144–6
bananas 44, 56, 137, 153–4
Bananera 45
beaches 74, 109, 136, 139–42, 151, 158
Benemérito 173
Biotopo Chocón Machacas Nature Reserve 161
birdwatching 114–15, 143, 145–6, 174

camping 72, 146, 164, 166–7, 170–1
Cantel, fiesta 69
car hire 63, 103
Castillo de San Felipe 161
caves 149–50
Champerico 139
Chiantla 133
Chichicastenango 74, 115, 116–19
    accommodation & restaurants 71, 119
    El Calvario church 117
    fiesta 3, 39, 67, 69–70, 116, 117–18
    markets 3, 70
    Santo Tomás church 116–17
    shrine of Pascual Abaj 117
    travel 118–19
Chimaltenango, travel 92, 106, 108
Chiquimula 78
Chiquimulilla 139
cinema 71, 87, 100, 123, 127
Ciudad Vieja 104
climate 137
Coatepeque 62, 125, 138
Cobán 74, 148
    accommodation & restaurants 148
    fiesta 68, 148
    travel 78, 122, 132, 146, 151
coffee 46, 55, 73, 137, 143, 146–7
consulate 60, 64, 127, 138, 154, 155
crime 66, 82, 149, 161
Cubulco, fiesta 68, 144

Cuchumatanes Mountains 50, 74, 131, 133–6
customs 61, 157
Cuyotenango 137, 140

death squads 46, 47, 57
Dos Pilas 172
Duenas 93

eating out, *see* restaurants
El Baúl site 142
El Ceibal ruins 26, 163, 171
El Coco 140
El Estor 151
El Golfete Nature Reserve 161
El Mirador ruins 172
El Relleno 71, 74, 161, 167
El Salvadorean border 139
embassies 60, 64
Escuintla 62, 92, 137, 139
Esquipulas 68, 78, 152, 153–4

festivals 67–70
flora and fauna 114–15, 142, 143, 145–6, 161, 162
food, *see* restaurants
Flores 51, 62, 74, 163, 164–7
    accommodation & restaurants 165–7
    travel 59, 78, 150, 164, 165, 218
Fray Bartolomé de Las Casas 150
Fuego volcano 104, 106
Fuentes Georginas springs 3, 128

geography 50–1, 89
Guatemala City 22, 74–88, **75**
    accommodation 71, 84–5
    Aurora Park 83–4
    cathedral 81
    entertainment & nightlife 87
    fiesta 69
    history 32, 76
    Iglesia Yurrita 82
    Jardín Botánico y Museo de Historia Natural 82
    La Merced church 80
    markets 70, 81, 82, 87
    Mercado Central 81, 87
    money matters 64, 87–8
    Museo de Arte e Industria 81
    Museo de Historia Natural 79, 84
    Museo Ixchel 83
    Museo Nacional de Arte Moderno 79, 83–4
    Museo Nacional de Historia 81
    National Museum of Archaeology and Ethnology 37, 79, 83
    Palacio Nacional 81
    Parque Central 79, 80–1
    Parque Concordia 79, 81
    Popol Vuh archaeological museum 3, 37, 82, 169
    restaurants 76, 83, 85–7

Guatemala *(continued)*

San Francisco church 80
Santa Clara church 80
Santuario Expiatorio church 80
Teatro Nacional 79, 81
tourist information 12, 80, 82
travel 76–80, 383, 450
guides 104, 113, 127, 169–70, 172

hiking 121, 126, 131, 164
history 32–3, 45, 46–7, 54–8, 120, 143–4, 147–8, 153–4, 158–9
Huehuetenango 73, 74, 131–3
  fiesta 69
  travel 78, 122, 131–2, 151

itineraries 73–4
Ixil Triangle 115–16, 120–1
Iximché 30, 106
Iztapa, beach & fiesta 69, 141

Jalapa 152
Jocotenango 93
Joyabaj, fiesta 69

Kaminal Juyu, Maya site 29, 84

La Democracia ruins 140, 143
La Empalizada 140
Lake Amatitlán 77, 88
Lake Atitlán 3, 23, 73, 107–9, **107**, *109*, 122
Lake Chicabel 128–9
Lake Izabal 74, 151, 161, 162
Lake Petén Itzá 164, 166–7
Lake Petexbatún 172
language schools 90, 93, 103, 127
Lanquín 69, 149, 150
Las Lisas 139
Livingston 51, 74, 153, 158–60
  accommodation & restaurants 71, 159–60
  fiesta 70, 158
  history 158–9
  travel 159
Los Aposentos lake 104

maps 61–2, 63, 103, 127
Mariscos 151
markets 51, 69, 70, 129–30
Mazatenango 62, 125, 130, 138, 140
medical concerns 66, 87, 102
Mixco Viejo 88–9
Momostenango 39, 68, 70, 125, 130
money matters 87–8, 102, 113, 127
Monterrico, beach 141–2
Monterrico Nature Reserve 24, 137, 139, 141–2

Nahualá, fiesta 69, 122
National Parks 24, 108

Nebaj 116, 121–2
  fiesta 69
  markets 70, 121
  travel 118, 122, 132, 151

orientation 61, 80
the Oriente 139, 151

Pacaya volcano 3, 16, 22, 88, 103, 105–6
Panajachel 65, 68, 69, 70, 107–8, 109–13
  accommodation & restaurants 71, 72, 110–12
  entertainment & nightlife 112
  markets 70, 110
  sports 112
  tourist information 110, 113
  travel 78, 110, 118
Parque de las Naciones Unidas 88
Parque Minerva 84
Parque Nacional Atitlán 114–15
Pastores 93
Petén jungle 3, 9, 51, 62, 150, 162–73
police 63, 65, 87
politics 42–3, 47, 50, 54–8
Poptún 164
public holidays 66–7
Puerto Barrios 59, 62, 152, 156–8
  fiesta 68
  travel 77, 78, 157, 159, 180, 227
Puerto San José 62, 137, 140–1
Quetzal Reserve (Biotopo del Quetzal) 74, 78, 145–6
Quezaltenango 73, 123–8, **124**
  accommodation & restaurants 71, 123, 126
  entertainment 123, 127
  fiesta 69
  San Nicolás church 123
  tourist information 126
  travel 78, 119, 125, 138

Quiriguá ruins 29, 35, 83, 152, 155–6

Rabinal, fiesta 68, 144
rainforest 145–6, 148
restaurants 72–3, *see also under individual destinations*
Retalhuleu 62, 125, 138
Río Azul ruins 172
Río Dulce 24, 74, 157, 161

Sacapulas 132
Salamá, fiesta 144
San Andrés Itzapa, Maximón cult 39–40, 69, 93, 104–5
San Antonio Aguas Calientes 93, 104
San Antonio Palopó 68, 115
San Cristóbal de Totonicapán, church 129
San Cristóbal Verapaz 150
San Felipe 130

Guatemala *(continued)*

San Francisco el Alto 69, 125, 129
San Juan Atitán 135–6
San Juan del Obispo 93, 104
San Lorenzo el Tajar 104
San Lucas Sacatepéquez 93–4
San Lucas Tolimán 108, 109, 110, 111
San Luís de las Carretas 93
San Martín Sacatepéquez 128
San Mateo Ixtatán 133
San Pablo la Laguna, fiesta 68
San Pedro Carchá 149, 150
  fiesta 68
San Pedro La Laguna 108, 109, 110, 112, 115
  fiesta 68
San Pedro las Huertas 93
San Pedro volcano 113, 115
Santa Catarina Palopó 69, 111, 115
Santa Cruz del Quiché 74, 115, 118, 119–20, 122
Santa Cruz la Laguna 108, 109, 110
  fiesta 68
Santa Elena 165, 166, 167
Santa Lucía Cotzumalguapa 137, 138, 142
Santa Lucía Milpas Altas 93
Santa María de Jesús 93, 104, 105
  fiesta 67
Santa María Visitación, fiesta 68
Santa María volcano 126, 127
Santiago Atitlán 107, 108, 109, 110, 112, 113, 114–15
  fiesta 39, 68, 114
Santiago Sacatepéquez, fiesta 67, 69
Sayaxché 150, 163, 165, 171–2, 173
Semuc Champey 74, 143, 149–50
shopping 70–1, 81, 87
Siete Altares 160–1
Sipacate beach 138, 140, 143
Sololá 69, 109, 110
Soloma 132, 133–4

Sumpango 93
swimming 140, 146, 151, 160

Tacana 3
Taxisco 137, 139, 141
Tikal 3, 29, 30, 36, 51, 74, 83, 162–3, 165, 167–71
  accommodation & restaurants 72, 170–1
  Great Plaza 168
  museum 170
  Temple of the Inscriptions 169
  Temple IV 168, 169
  travel 169
Todos Santos 73, 131, 134–6
  accommodation & restaurants 135
  fiesta 3, 8, 67, 69, 134–5
  markets 70, 134
  travel 134, 135
Tojcunanchén ruins 135
Tolimán volcano 113
Totonicapán 69, 125, 129
tour operators 87, 102, 165, 167
travel 51, 59–60, 62–3, *see also under individual destinations*
traveller's cheques 61, 64, 157
Tulate 138, 140

Uaxactún ruins 30, 163, 171
Uspantán 122, 132, 150, 151
Utatlán, ruins 30, 47, 83, 120

Verapaz Mountains 51, 74, 143–51
visas 60–1, 154, 155
volcanoes 50–1, 103–4, 105–6, 113, 127–8

watersports 111, 112, 162
Western Highlands 89–136

Yaxchilán ruins 38, 173
Yaxhá ruins 172–3

Zaculeu ruins 131
Zunil 69, 125, 128

GENERAL INDEX

Note: Page references in **bold** type indicate maps; those in *italics* indicate illustrations.

accommodation 18–19, prices 19, *see also under individual destinations*
air travel 10–11, 13, *see also* travel *under individual destinations*
Alvarado, Pedro de 31
   Guatemala 46, 89, 90, 94, 106, 113, 120, 143
archaeology 20, 87, 142–3, *see also* Maya, ruins
architecture 3, 73, 94, 195–6
Arias, Oscar 382
art galleries 113
artesania 20
   Belize 187–8, 198, 222
   Guatemala 3, 20, 69–70, 81, 96, 102, 104, 109
Asturias, Miguel Angel 42, 55

baggage checklist 10
banana republics 32, 44–5, 153–4
banks 12–13, *see also* money matters *in this index and under individual destinations*)
bargaining 20, 70, 188
beaches
   Belize 190, 201, 219, 223
   Guatemala 74, 109, 136, 139–42, 151, 158
beggars 17, 80, 191, 258
Belize 174–233, **175**
bicycles
   hire 103, 113, 214
   travel 14, 63, 184
birdwatching 3, 21, 23
   Belize 190, 231
   Guatemala 114–15, 143, 145–6, 174
Bonampak ruins 43
books 3, 88, 97, 102, 131, 169
bookshops 62, 82, 199, 261, 281, 387
bribes 63, 66
British Honduras, *see* Belize
buses
   international xiv, 12, 14
   see also travel *under individual destinations*

camping 18, 25
   Belize 189, 190, 200, 207, 209, 213, 214
   Guatemala 72, 146, 164, 166–7, 170–1
car hire
   Belize 183–4, 215, 228
   Guatemala 63, 103

car travel 11, 14, *see also* travel *under individual destinations*
cinema, *see under individual destinations*
climate 7, 8, 27, *see also under individual destinations*
clothing 10, 16, 170, 202
coffee 3, 46
   Guatemala 55, 73, 137, 143, 146–7
Columbus, Christopher 31, 159, 291
comedores 19, 72, 81
conquistadors 31–2, 40, 46–7
consulates, *see under individual destinations*
Cortés, Alfonso 42
cotton 22, 362
credit cards 15, 61, 65, 181, 185
crime 15–16, 46 *see also under individual destinations*
cuisine 19–20, 72–3, 85–6, 166, 189
currencies, local 15, 64
customs formalities 12, *see also under individual destinations*

Darío, Rubén 41–2
death squads 46, 47
disabled travellers 14–15
diving 21, 23
   Belize 174, 191, 201–2, 205–6, 207–10
dress 16
drinks 20, 73, 189
drugs 17, 46, 191, 198, 231

earthquakes 8, 47, 54, 57, 76, 92
eating out 19–20, *see also* restaurants
ecotourism 24–25
   specialist operators 25
electricity 18
embassies *see under individual destinations*
exchange rates 64, 88

fiesta 3, 8
Figueres, José 44
fishing 21, 201, 222
flora and fauna 20, 22, 23, *see also under individual countries*
food, *see* restaurants

Garifuna people
   Belize 187, 190, 218–19, 220
   Guatemala 158–9

248

GENERAL INDEX

generals 45–6, 47
geography 7–8, 26–27, 50–1, 84, 174
Guatemala 50–173, 52–3
guest houses 18, 71, 109
guides, *see under individual destinations*

health concerns 9, 10, 19, 66, 137
hiking 9, 10, 18
  Belize 190, 215, 220, 226
  Guatemala 121, 126, 131, 164
history, before independence 26–33, *see also under individual destinations*
hitch-hiking
  Belize 220
  Guatemala 132, 135, 140, 149, 150, 156
horse-riding 214

Independence 32–3, 41, 49, 340
insurance, travel 9, 11, 60, 180

jungles 3, 22, 23, 26–27, 74, 161, 162–73, 289–90

ladino culture
  Guatemala 51, 54–5, 67, 68, 115, 131, 134, 136, 138, 152
Las Casas, Bartolomé de 40, 143–4
literature 40–43

mail, *see* post offices
Mam Indians 30, 89, 128, 131, 134, 135
maps 13, *see also under individual destinations*
marimba 44, 97
markets 3, 19, 20, *see also under individual destinations*
Maximón cult 39–40, 69, 93, 104–5, 114, 122
Maya 28, 29–30, 32, 51, 54–5, 58, 143–4
  Ball Game 36
  calendars 30, 38–9, 130, 156
  culture 34–40, 58, 67, 116, 130, 162–3
  languages 89, 128
  ruins 20
    Belize, Altun Ha: 190, 200; Caracol: 210, 215–17, 229, 231–2
    Guatemala: 84; Mixco Viejo: 88, 131, 142; Quiriguá: 155–6; 162–3; Tikal: 167–71, 171–3
  script 37–8, 273
mestizos 32, 51, 54, 210, 231, 234
Mexico
  La Mesilla border post 78, 125, 131, 132
  Talismán border post 125, 138
  Tecún Umán border post 62, 77, 79, 138
  travel via 10–11, 59, 173, 179–80, 203
Miskito Indians 32

modernismo 41–2
money matters 15–16, *see also under individual destinations*
Morgan, Sir Henry 176
museums 3, *see also under individual destinations*
music 43–4, 97, 158, 187

Nahuatl language 142, 321
National Parks 24
newspapers 18, 71, 88, 188, 199

Olmec people 28, 34, 38, 142–3
opening hours, *see under individual countries*
ornithology 21

Palo de Mayo 44
passports 9
photography 17, 117, 206
Pipile people 142
pirates 176–7, 193
Pocomam Indians 89
police 14, 15–16, *see also under individual destinations*
post offices 18
potholing 21
prehistory 27–28
public holidays 66–7, *see also under individual destinations*

Quiché Indians 30, 89, 117, 120

rail travel
  international 11–12, 14, 59, 137
  see also under individual destinations
rainforest 22, 145–6
Ramírez, Sergio 43
Reagan, Ronald 47–8
restaurants and cafés 19–20, *see also under individual destinations*
river rafting 22
rum 3, 20, 73, 189

sea travel 10–12, 59, 157, 179–80, 221, 227
Selva, Salomón 42
sexual attitudes 16–17
shopping 20, 70–1
slavery 31, 54, 144, 147, 193
Spain
  conquest 31–2, 40–1, 45–6, 143–4, 164–5, 334
  independence from 32–3, 41–2, 48–9, 235–6
Spanish language 27, 89, 174
sports 20–22, 162, 203
sugar 22, 142
swimming
  Belize 217, 219, 229, 230
  Guatemala 140, 146, 151, 160

taxis, *see* travel *under individual destinations*
telecommunications 19
television, *see* media *under individual destinations*
tipica music 44, 463
tipping 17, 309
Torrijos, Omar 47
tour operators 12, 22
  Belize 198, 222, 228
  Guatemala 87, 102, 165, 167
tourist cards 12, 60–1, 131, 138
tourist offices 13, 60, 61, 80, 181, 182
travel
  internal 12–15
  international 10–12
  see also travel *under individual destinations*

travel agents, *see* tour operators
traveller's cheques 10, 15
  Belize 184, 199, 206
  Guatemala 61, 64, 157
US dollar 15, 64, 184, 199
USA
  in Guatemala 32–3, 45, 47, 54–6, 153–4
  investment 56
  travel from 11–12, 179–80

vaccinations 9
visas 9 *see also under individual destinations*
volcanoes 3, 8, 22

women travellers 16–17, 191